Defeat at Gallipoli

Also by Nigel Steel

THE BATTLEFIELDS OF GALLIPOLI

Nigel Steel and Peter Hart

Defeat
at Gallipoli

MACMILLAN

LONDON

First published 1994 by Macmillan London

a division of Pan Macmillan Publishers Limited
Cavaye Place London SW10 9PG
and Basingstoke

Associated companies throughout the world

ISBN 0 333 55314 4

135798642

A CIP catalogue record for this book is available from
the British Library

Typeset by CentraCet Limited, Cambridge
Printed and bound in Great Britain by
Mackays of Chatham plc, Kent

To
Captain Eric Wheeler Bush DSO** DSC RN
Lieutenant Colonel Malcolm Hancock MC
and
Joe Murray

Contents

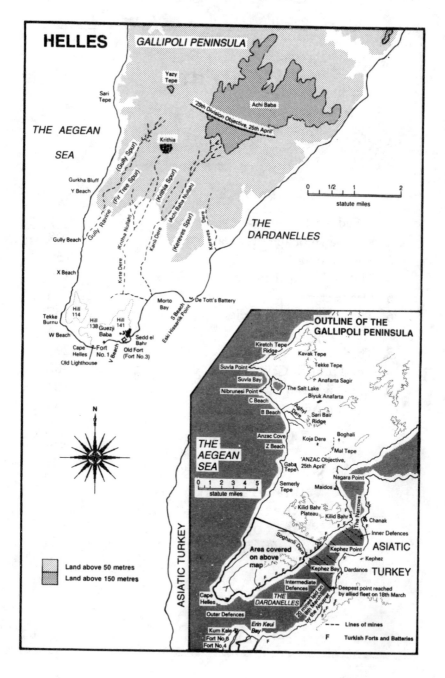

HELLES

GALLIPOLI PENINSULA

Yazy Tepe

Sari Tepe

Achi Baba

"29th Division Objective, 25th April"

THE AEGEAN

SEA

Krithia

Gurkha Bluff

Y Beach

(Gully Spur)

(Fir Tree Spur)

(Krithia Spur)

(Achi Baba Nullah)

(Kereves Spur)

Gully Ravine

Gully Beach

Kirte Dere (Krithia Nullah)

Kanli Dere

Achi Baba Nullah

Kereves Dere

Dere

THE
DARDANELLES

X Beach

statute miles

0   1/2   1   2

De Tott's Battery

Morto Bay

S Beach

Eski Hissarlik Point

Tekke Burnu

Hill 114

Hill 138 Guezji Baba

Hill 141

W Beach

Cape Helles

Fort No.1

V Beach

Sedd el Bahr

Old Fort (Fort No.3)

Old Lighthouse

N

**OUTLINE OF THE
GALLIPOLI PENINSULA**

Kiretch Tepe Ridge

Kavak Tepe

Tekke Tepe

Suvla Point

Anafarta Sagir

Suvla Bay

The Salt Lake

Biyuk Anafarta

Nibrunesi Point

C Beach

Aghyl Dere

Sari Bair Ridge

B Beach

Anzac Cove

Boghali

**THE
AEGEAN
SEA**

Z Beach

Koja Dere

Mal Tepe

'ANZAC Objective, 25th April'

statute miles

0   1   2   3   4   5

Gaba Tepe

Nagara Point

Semerly Tepe

Maidos

Kilid Bahr Plateau

Kilid Bahr

The Narrows

Chanak

Inner Defences

ASIATIC TURKEY

Soghanli Dere

Kephez Point

ASIATIC

Area covered on above map

Kephez

Kephez Bay

Dardanos

TURKEY

Intermediate Defences

Deepest point reached by allied fleet on 18th March

Cape Helles

THE DARDANELLES

Outer Defences

Erin Keui Bay

20 mines laid on 8th March by the Nusret

Kum Kale

Fort No.6

Fort No.4

Lines of mines

F   Turkish Forts and Batteries

Land above 50 metres

Land above 150 metres

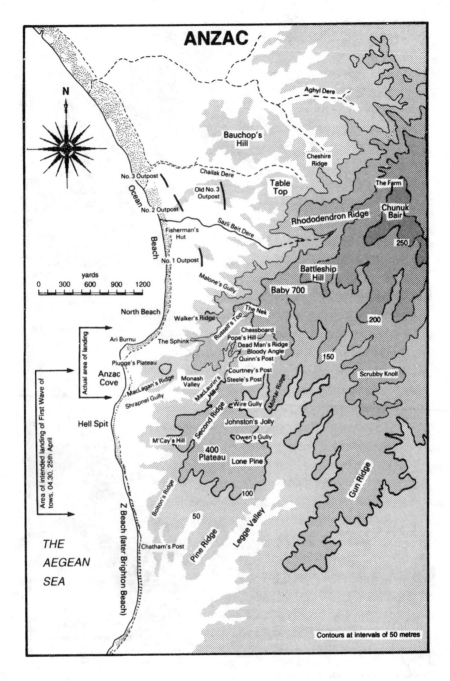

ANZAC

Aghyl Dere

Bauchop's Hill

Cheshire Ridge

Chailak Dere

No. 3 Outpost

Table Top

The Farm

Old No. 3 Outpost

No. 2 Outpost

Ocean

Sazli Beit Dere

Rhododendron Ridge

Chunuk Bair

Fisherman's Hut

Beach

No. 1 Outpost

250

Malone's Gully

Battleship Hill

yards

0   300   600   900   1200

Baby 700

200

North Beach

Walker's Ridge

The Nek

Ari Burnu

Actual area of landing

The Sphinx

Russell's Top

Chessboard

Pope's Hill

Dead Man's Ridge

Bloody Angle

Quinn's Post

150

Scrubby Knoll

Plugge's Plateau

Anzac Cove

MacLagan's Ridge

Monash Valley

Courtney's Post

Steele's Post

MacLaurin's Hill

Shrapnel Gully

Second Ridge

Wire Gully

Mortar Ridge

Hell Spit

Johnston's Jolly

M'Cay's Hill

Owen's Gully

Area of intended landing of First Wave of tows, 04.30, 25th April

400 Plateau

Lone Pine

Gun Ridge

Bolton's Ridge

100

50

Z Beach (later Brighton Beach)

Chatham's Post

Pine Ridge

Legge Valley

THE
AEGEAN
SEA

Contours at intervals of 50 metres

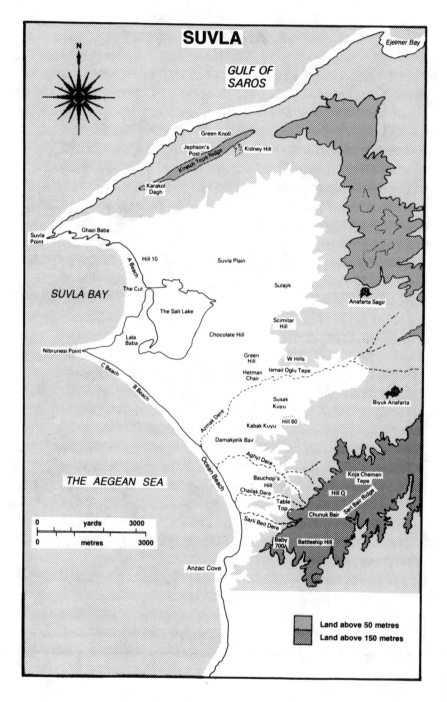

SUVLA

Illustrations

With the exception of numbers 28 and 30, all photographs have been taken from the Department of Photographs, Imperial War Museum, and the authors would like to thank the Keeper of that Department and the Museum's Trustees for their permission to reproduce them; IWM negative numbers are given in brackets after the brief captions in the following list. The authors would also like to thank Rona Buchanan for allowing them to copy the 1914 picture of Harry Baker, and Joe Murray for the use of his 1915 picture from *Gallipoli – As I Saw It*.

1. General Sir Ian Hamilton and Vice Admiral John de Robeck (Q13503)
2. Winston Churchill (Q42037)
3. Lieutenant General Sir William Birdwood and Field Marshal Lord Kitchener (Q13589)
4. Lieutenant General Sir Aylmer Hunter Weston (Q13307)
5. Lighters round the *River Clyde* on 25 April 1915 (Q50473)
6. Lancashire Fusiliers waiting to land at the start of May (Q13219)
7. The *River Clyde* from the *Queen Elizabeth* on 25 April (HU57757)
8. Hunter Weston, Hamilton and Major General Walter Braith-waite on 30 April (HU57800)
9. V Beach, Sedd el Bahr and the Old Fort on 30 April (HU57802)
10. The ruins of Sedd el Bahr on 2 May (HU57795)
11. The Hood Battalion, RND, at the White House on 6 May (Q61127)
12. The 1/1st East Lancashire Field Ambulance on 4 June (Q13258)

Preface

By the end of August 1915 the fighting at Gallipoli had left at least one British soldier, Private Ernest Lye, severely disillusioned. In the vanguard of the battle he had seen neither romance nor glory. Instead the squalor and degradation of the battlefield, the intense disappointment and loss of hope he had experienced now appeared like a nightmare that he would remember as long as he lived. It is the intensity of this experience that *Defeat at Gallipoli* explores in detail by concentrating on the perspective of the ordinary British soldier, in the belief that this is of outstanding importance. More so than the politicians, generals and admirals whose strategic decisions may have lost the campaign, it was the ordinary men and their officers, in the miserable trenches and the bowels of the warships, who knew best what the Gallipoli campaign really entailed, and it is their experiences, recorded in letters, diaries and interviews, that are here used to tell the full history of the sordid and bitter events that occurred.

Although the Allied soldiers and sailors were ultimately defeated by the Turks, they retained their dignity and deserve our respect. Much of the written material included here was never intended for the public eye, and consequently the descriptions of combat have a raw intensity absent from texts honed for publication. The oral sources also cover topics central to the Gallipoli experience but not usually written down in diaries or letters home, revealing for the first time the horror of conditions there. A unique view is also given of the great and the good as their contemporaries saw them, often in incongruous circumstances.

One of the overwhelming interests of a campaign such as Gallipoli is the opportunity that it offers for speculation on what *could* have happened. Any study continually leads towards the seductive charm of 'what if', 'maybe' and 'might'. For example, what if the 29th Division and the 1st Australian Division had landed not respectively at Helles and Gaba Tepe, but the other way round? Maybe, in that instance, the strengths that they revealed on 25 April – such as the professional discipline of the British regulars and the spontaneous initiative of the Australians – could have been put to better use. The British might have retained their cohesion in the confusion of the gullies and hills between Gaba Tepe and Chunuk Bair, and the Australians might have moved with bravado and confidence from the flanks at S and Y Beaches to encircle the Turks defending Sedd el Bahr. But events did *not* happen in this way and the pursuit of these retrospective daydreams is ultimately of little value, even if intellectually interesting. Concerned with what did happen and how it felt to take part, *Defeat at Gallipoli* has deliberately tried to avoid this kind of speculation.

To a large extent the book is based on the extensive archive holdings of the Imperial War Museum in London, and the nature of the Museum's collections means that it concentrates in greatest detail on the experience of the British soldiers at Gallipoli. Many previous books have dealt in similar detail with events at Anzac, which have become almost legendary with the passage of time. *Defeat at Gallipoli* hopes to redress this imbalance, without in any way disparaging the efforts of the Anzacs, through its recognition of the pre-eminent role of the British forces and the fact that, although the Anzacs suffered severe casualties and terrible privations, the ordinary British soldiers suffered in far greater numbers from the mistakes of the High Command in London.

Quotations from written sources, taken mostly from the Museum's Department of Documents, are given literally in all instances. To ease the flow of the narrative, punctuation and spelling in quotations has been standardized without specific reference, but otherwise any additions to or omissions from the original texts are indicated by conventional symbols. The extracts from oral interviews have been drawn from the Museum's Department of Sound Records. Oral quotations are more difficult to edit but changes in the actual words spoken in interviews have been avoided, although the order of material may have been slightly changed and deletions made to ensure a quotation is fully understandable. A three-dot ellipsis has been used to convey the naturally dramatic flow of speech where appropriate.

In the middle of May 1915 the War Office decided to number the divisions of the Territorial Force in line with the divisions of the New Army, and the East Lancashire Division was retitled the 42nd Division and the Lowland Division the 52nd Division. To avoid subsequent confusion, although not technically correct, both divisions are referred to throughout the book as the 42nd and 52nd Divisions. The country which today is known as Turkey was in 1914 the Anatolian region of the much larger Ottoman Empire, which reached from Constantinople to Basra and from the borders of Egypt to those of Russia and Persia. The Ottoman Empire's citizens, and so also its soldiers, included ethnic Turks, Arabs, Greeks, Armenians, Kurds and many other smaller groups. To talk of Turkey and the Turks instead of the Ottoman Empire and the Ottomans is therefore anachronistic. A similar anachronism applies to the capital city of the Ottoman Empire, which remained known to the Christian nations of northern Europe as Constantinople until after the First World War, despite the fact that it had been known to the Ottomans as Istamboul since their capture of it in 1453. However, for simplicity these long-standing anachronisms have been followed once again and the names Constantinople, Turkey and the Turks used throughout the book.

Many people have generously assisted in the research for *Defeat at Gallipoli* and their assistance is here gratefully acknowledged. Foremost we would like to thank the Keepers of the two Museum Departments whose collections have formed the basis of so much of the book, Roderick Suddaby and Margaret Brooks. Elsewhere in the Museum we have also received a great deal of guidance and advice from other colleagues and in no particular order we would specifically like to mention: Simon Robbins, Mike Hibberd, Paul Cornish, Bryn Hammond, Chris McCarthy, Janice Phillips, David Shaw, Wendy Lutterloch, Lyn Smith and our honorary colleague Malcolm Brown. Outside the Museum we would like to thank those people who own copyright in the documents quoted in the book and those veterans who allowed their recollections to be recorded on tape; both the written and oral sources used are listed by name in the Bibliography. The three veterans to whom the book is dedicated, Captain Eric Wheeler Bush DSO** DSC RN, Lieutenant Colonel Malcolm Hancock MC and Joe Murray, must be mentioned above all others. Without their combined but independent efforts the Museum's Gallipoli holdings would be much less rich and comprehensive than they are. We hope that all of them would have approved of the way in which the fruits of their efforts have been used here. We would also like to thank the Trustees and staff of the other archives where we have carried out research for allowing us access to their collections, namely: the Liddell Hart Centre for Military Archives at King's College, London, the National Army Museum, the National Maritime Museum and the Public Record Office. Steve Snelling, whose book on Gallipoli VCs is eagerly awaited, has been more than generous with his help, and the patience and persistence of Peter Robinson and Roland Philipps have also been of great help since the inception of the book. Finally on a more personal note we would like to thank Ruth and Leslie Hart, Kathleen and Robin Steel, and Joan Ryan and Marion Musselwhite who have now lived with Gallipoli for too long.

1

A Bad Start

'Something must happen soon. The situation seems absurd – 2 huge armies sitting & watching each other like this,'[1] concluded one junior British officer in France at the beginning of December 1914. The opening phase of the First World War had not developed according to plan. The grand strategic movements prepared over the previous decades by the French and German General Staffs had failed to produce the rapid, decisive victory that both had expected. Following the eruption of hostilities at the start of August, for almost three-and-a-half months a frantic, fast-moving battle had flowed like molten lava across northern France and western Belgium, and along its trail, from the English Channel to the borders of neutral Switzerland, two lines of opposing trenches had evolved. The ensuing stalemate showed that the war would be neither short nor mobile, a fact that the politicians soon realized once the armies had dug in.

In Great Britain for the first time alternative strategies began to be considered. The battles and plans which had consumed the British Expeditionary Force (BEF) were not of the traditional British style. As a result of an historical antipathy to large standing armies, the natural defence of the English Channel and the international power of the Royal Navy, the British Army had always been small, professional and largely geared to defending the British Empire. Imperial service, particularly in India, bred soldiers more used to confronting small-scale conflicts in isolated parts of distant countries than preparing to fight grand strategic battles on their own borders. Only in the years immediately prior to 1914 had political associations with Russia and France slowly drawn the British Army into the grand strategic confrontations of the continent.

1

After the outbreak of war, the traditional strength of the British forces appeared to be most clearly appreciated by the First Lord of the Admiralty, Winston Churchill. Since August he had been concerned with the possible use of Britain's amphibious power. On 31 August he had discussed with the Secretary of State for War, Field Marshal Lord Kitchener, the idea of an attack against Turkey which had arisen from the offer of the Greek Prime Minister, Eleutherios Venizelos, on 19 August to place the full military resources of Greece at the disposal of the Triple Entente of Russia, France and Britain. This had been followed ten days later by news from Athens that the Russians had formally inquired of the Greeks whether they would be prepared to land an army on the Gallipoli Peninsula in support of an attack on the Dardanelles, the strategically important channel forty-one miles long which separated the peninsula from the Asiatic mainland and linked the Aegean to the southwestern seaboard of the Sea of Marmara. On the opposite northeastern side of the Marmara lay the Turkish capital, Constantinople, through which a second channel, the Bosphorous, linked up with the Black Sea and the southern provinces of Russia. The Russians had long coveted the Turkish territories in Europe, and Constantinople in particular. But the Greeks, too, had ambitions to absorb them and it was an unexpected development for Russia to invite Greece to assist in their capture.

At that time Turkey still proclaimed an outward neutrality and great care was needed by the Allied nations in pursuing these ideas not to push Turkey into joining the two Central Powers, Germany and Austria–Hungary. Following the *coup d'état* launched by the Young Turks in July 1908, political power in Turkey had been in the hands of the Committee of Union and Progress (CUP), and in particular two of its principal leaders, Talaat Bey, the Minister of the Interior, and Enver Pasha, the Minister of War. After the coup many of the Young Turks hoped for the growth of strong links between Turkey and Britain, a long-standing Turkish ally. But British attitudes cooled when the early promises of constitutional reform failed to materialize. In contrast Germany saw in Turkey a useful ally in its ambitions to expand towards the east and developed a strong hold upon the leadership of the Young Turks, especially upon Enver, who at one stage had been Turkish Military Attaché in Berlin. However, British and German influence over the Turkish armed forces was cleverly balanced. A British Naval Mission led by Rear Admiral Arthur Limpus was appointed in 1912 and a German Military Mission led by General Otto Liman von Sanders the following year. On 2 August 1914 a secret treaty, known only to Talaat, Enver and Mehmed Said Halim Pasha, the Grand Vizier and Minister for Foreign Affairs, was signed between Turkey and Germany, offering the Turks German protection against any threat from Russia.

Although many other prominent members of the CUP hoped to maintain the neutrality of Turkey, the Germans were determined to draw it into the war on the side of the Central Powers. Their cause was helped on 3 August by the British appropriation of two Turkish battleships, the *Sultan Osman I* and the *Rechadieh*, then being built in Britain. This act caused outrage within Turkey for much of the cost of the ships of several million pounds had been raised by public subscription. No attempt was made by the British government to mitigate the seizure and it was left to the German government to compensate the Turkish people instead. Two German cruisers, the *Goeben* and the *Breslau*, were immediately ordered from the Mediterranean to Constantinople.

After an adventurous voyage, during which the ships outmanoeuvred the British First Cruiser Squadron, the ships arrived at the entrance to the Dardanelles on 10 August. As Turkey was still neutral, the German ships needed the permission of the Turkish government to pass through to the Marmara. But the granting of permission would contravene the terms of the international treaties which safeguarded the Dardanelles and compromise Turkish neutrality. Presented with this dilemma Enver, under German military pressure, decided that afternoon not only that the *Goeben* and the *Breslau* could pass through, but also that the British ships in pursuit would not be allowed to follow. British protests were met by the explanation that Turkey had bought the German ships to replace the *Sultan Osman I* and the *Rechadieh*. Less than a week later, on 15 August, control of the Turkish Navy was removed from the British Naval Mission and assumed instead by Rear Admiral Wilhelm Souchon, who had arrived in the *Goeben*. Germany's hold over Turkey was now complete.

Despite the delicacy of the situation, in London it was felt that general plans could still be drawn up in response to the Greek and Russian proposals without undue provocation. Churchill therefore followed up the discussion by writing next day to the Chief of the Imperial General Staff, Lieutenant General Sir James Wolfe Murray, about the possibility of two officers each from the War Office and the Admiralty working out a plan to seize the Gallipoli Peninsula using an adequately sized Greek army, with the aim of admitting a fleet of British ships to the Marmara. The idea of an attack on the Gallipoli Peninsula and the Dardanelles was far from new and had been considered many times before. During the Napoleonic Wars in 1807, as part of an attempt to provide assistance to Russia, Admiral Sir John Duckworth had successfully forced his way through the Dardanelles into the Marmara. But his ships had become becalmed before they could threaten Constantinople. As the Turks declined to surrender without being threatened, Duckworth was forced to return humiliated through the Dardanelles to the Mediterranean. More recently Admiral of the Fleet Lord Fisher, who was recalled from retirement to become First Sea Lord again in October 1914, had studied the question of forcing the Dardanelles both when he had been Commander-in-Chief, Mediterranean at the turn of the century and shortly after his first appointment as First Sea Lord in 1904. He had concluded that even in co-operation with the army such a venture would be 'mightily hazardous'.[2]

The most detailed examination had been made at the end of 1906 in a report by the General Staff at the War Office on behalf of the Committee of Imperial Defence, which before the war had advised the Cabinet on matters of defence policy. As part of an examination of the alternatives for attacking Turkey, careful consideration had been given to all aspects of an attack on the Dardanelles, including an attempt by naval vessels alone, an unsupported surprise attack by a military force and a combined assault by the navy and the army. Once again it was concluded that any attack would be fraught with difficulties, and the report ended with the statement that 'the General Staff, in view of the risks involved, are not prepared to recommend its being attempted'.[3]

On 3 September 1914, the Director of Military Operations, Major General Charles Callwell, who had been involved in preparing the report in 1906, responded cautiously to Churchill's approach. Estimating the Turkish garrison of the peninsula to be about 27,000, he felt that an attacking force would need to be at least 60,000 strong and that even then an attack would be extremely difficult. However, although he drew Kitchener's attention to the report of 1906, he did not actually reject the idea of an attack and, despite his deliberate attempts to appear unenthusiastic, this was taken as tacit approval, of the principle at least.

The following day the British government informed the Greeks that, should Turkey join the Central Powers, Greece would be a welcome ally and that they would be willing to undertake a joint attack to seize the Gallipoli Peninsula based on a plan drawn up by the Greeks in 1911–12. Working on the basis that the Dardanelles could not be seized until the minefields laid to protect it had been swept and this could not be done until the forts which protected the mines had been captured, the Greek plan was very thorough and involved large numbers of troops. Sixty thousand men were to be landed south of Gaba Tepe, a promontory on the Aegean coast, to capture the villages of Maidos and Kilid Bahr on the edge of the Dardanelles, before moving south to take the village of Sedd el Bahr, on the southern tip of the peninsula. A smaller landing of two battalions would also be carried out at Kum Kale, a village opposite Sedd el Bahr on the Asiatic coast. These landings around the Dardanelles would be followed at a later stage by the capture of the neck of the peninsula at Bulair, situated at its extreme northern end, using a further 30,000 men and possibly also landings at other points of strategic importance further afield.

Greek willingness to participate in such an attack was dependent on the assurance that Bulgaria would not attack them while they were involved in it, and the only way to assure them of this was to persuade the Bulgarians to take part as well. To achieve this would have required a diplomatic feat of considerable skill. But continued Turkish neutrality meant that the need to begin this very difficult task did not arise and instead, as the weeks of September rolled by, Venizelos's hold on his pro-German King weakened and Greek enthusiasm ebbed away.

At the Dardanelles, British ships had begun a blockade of the entrance after the government in London refused to recognize the legality of the nominal Turkish purchase of the *Goeben* and the *Breslau*, and on 9 September Limpus and the British Naval Mission finally withdrew from Constantinople. But, in order to avoid inflaming the situation by taking advantage of his privileged knowledge, Limpus was sent to assume command of the Dockyard at Malta instead of the blockading squadron. On 27 September, after the British squadron refused to allow a Turkish torpedo boat to leave the Dardanelles, the Turks declared it closed and completed the minefield begun on 3 August.

Despite the fact that a Turkish declaration of war on the side of the Central Powers now appeared to be likely, this final, irrevocable act was delayed for a further month, as the Turkish Army completed its mobilization. But eventually the Germans decided that Turkish prevarication must end and on 27 October Souchon led the Turkish fleet into the Black Sea. Two days later it sank two Russian ships and bombarded the cities of Odessa and Sevastopol. The moment had now arrived. On 31 October, Turkey declared war against the Entente and this act was reciprocated by Britain on 5 November. Between these dates, against Limpus's advice, Churchill ordered the blockading squadron to bombard the entrance to the Dardanelles. On 3 November this was done with some success at both Sedd el Bahr and Kum Kale. The Germans had been conscious of the need to increase the strength of the Dardanelles defences since the arrival of the British squadron and had already begun to make significant improvements. Yet it was not until after the bombardment that the urgency to do so was also recognized by the Turks, and from that moment on the overall strength of the defences inexorably increased.

At the beginning of November in London the newly constituted War Council took over responsibility for the detailed conduct of the British war effort from the complete Cabinet, its principal members being the Prime Minister, H. H. Asquith, Churchill and Kitchener. On 25 November the War Council met for the first time to discuss the possible options open to Britain. Eventually the meeting considered the best way to protect the Suez Canal and the British presence in Egypt from a Turkish attack across Sinai.

Churchill initially suggested an attack on the Gallipoli Peninsula, but the idea was rejected as unfeasible. He then proposed that Gallipoli could be used as a feint to cut communications between Turkey and Syria and Palestine. This was more favourably considered, but, as the threat to Egypt was still only latent, no immediate action was felt to be necessary. Finally, in case they might prove useful, he asked that transports should be collected in the Mediterranean to be available for immediate use if needed. But this too was rejected because of the already high demand on Britain's limited numbers of merchant ships. Churchill's malleable persistence shows how strongly the idea of an attack on the Dardanelles had already taken hold of his imagination.

Over the weeks of December the feasibility of an operation at the Dardanelles was significantly reduced by improvements to the defences. But this fact was unknown in London and by the end of the month Churchill's suggestions had begun to appear more desirable. In considering the best way in which to use the first of the New Army troops who had volunteered for military service after the outbreak of war, two new initiatives were put forward. The first, known as the 'Boxing Day Memorandum', was written by the Secretary of the War Council, Lieutenant Colonel Maurice Hankey, and contained three of the four objectives that eventually made the Gallipoli campaign strategically attractive. Hankey proposed an attack on Turkey – the Dardanelles were not specifically mentioned – with the overall aim of threatening Constantinople. Primarily, he believed, this would terminate the active role of the Turkish Army, as communication between it and the only munitions factories in the Ottoman Empire would be cut by seizing the city, making it difficult for the Turkish forces to continue to operate.

Constantinople itself was also very vulnerable to attack from the sea. Foreign embassies, government buildings, railway stations and factories could all be bombarded by an approaching fleet. The effect of such material damage on the morale of its population would almost certainly be profound and might even prompt the overthrow of the Young Turks. If this occurred, the other Balkan states would then look to the Entente for leadership, and Austria–Hungary, the Germans' main ally, would become vulnerable to the united threat of these countries, diverting German attention away from the campaigns in both East and West. Finally, the reopening of the Dardanelles would allow the Russians to export grain from the isolated Black Sea, free from frozen waters that blocked the Baltic during the winter and from the threat of the German submarines that operated there during the summer. The West would get the grain and in return the Russians would get money to support their war effort.

The second initiative was outlined on 1 January 1915 by the Chancellor of the Exchequer, David Lloyd George, who believed that the Western Front should become a purely defensive theatre, garrisoned by the French. The British Army could then be removed for an offensive role elsewhere. He too saw the weak spot of the Central Powers as Austria–Hungary, but dispensed with the idea of Turkey altogether, except for a severance of its communications with Egypt to protect the Suez Canal, and based his scheme on a thrusting attack through the Balkans from the Greek port of Salonika.

On 2 January, events began to move away from this possibility when the fourth strategic aim of the campaign arose. The government received a telegram from the British Ambassador in Petrograd which explained that the Russian position in the Caucasus was desperate following a strong Turkish advance; in order to relieve the pressure it asked that a move be made against the Turks elsewhere to divert their attention. Kitchener and Churchill both agreed that something must be done to help the weakest member of the Entente and, although no British troops were available to launch a military attack, it was felt that the Royal Navy could still produce an economical demonstration in the eastern Mediterranean to prevent fresh Turkish troops being moved to the Caucasus. That evening Kitchener conveyed this decision to Petrograd. At the same time he made it clear to Churchill that he had in mind only a minor operation, heavily reliant on fear and bluff and that 'the only place that a demonstration might have some effect in stopping reinforcements going east would be the Dardanelles'.[4] In the Caucasus the Russians had already started to defeat the Turkish attack, launched on 27 December under the personal command of Enver. Help in fact was no longer needed; but this dramatic reversal of fortune was not known in Petrograd, and in London a chain of events had been set in motion which would lead to a protracted campaign against Turkey.

The initial reaction of Fisher to these developments was enthusiastic and in a letter to Churchill on 3 January he outlined a detailed plan of combined operations based on Hankey's Memorandum. He saw a number of essential elements, each as important as the other and all of which must be adhered to and carried out quickly. All the Indian and 75,000 regular British troops currently in France were to be replaced by British Territorials. Under the pretence of going to Egypt, the troops from France would land near the Dardanelles at Besika Bay, eight miles to the south of Kum Kale. At the same time the Greeks were to land on the Gallipoli Peninsula, the Bulgarians to march on Adrianople and the Rumanians, Russians and Serbs to attack Austria–Hungary. While these battles were taking place on land a squadron of outdated British battleships of the pre-dreadnought *Majestic* and *Canopus* class were to force the Dardanelles. Fisher's suggestion was absurdly ambitious. Kitchener was adamant that there could be no removal of troops either from Egypt or from the Western Front and there was also strong resistance to the latter in France. Greece would not move without Bulgaria; Bulgaria would do nothing until it was clear who was going to win, and the chances of combining the other Balkan countries in a joint attack were remote.

Only Churchill, who was under pressure from Asquith to do something significant with the Royal Navy, saw in Fisher's plan a gleam of hope. Previously, he had only seriously thought about the possibility of a combined naval and military operation; but, ignoring the other elements of Fisher's plan, he now saw in its final proposal to use pre-dreadnought battleships to force the Dardanelles an opportunity to satisfy both Asquith's demands and the Russian plea for assistance. On the same day he telegraphed to Vice Admiral Sackville Carden, who was in command of the ships blockading the Dardanelles, which had been designated the Eastern Mediterranean Squadron (EMS), the question: 'Do you consider the forcing of the Straits by ships alone a practicable operation? . . . Importance of result would justify severe loss.'[5] Two days later Carden replied: 'I do not consider Dardanelles can be rushed. They might be forced by extended operations with large number of ships.'⁶

After mentioning Carden's reply to a meeting of the War Council on 5 January and encountering no adverse reaction to its suggestion, Churchill asked Carden for elaboration on 6 January. Five days later, on 11 January, he received the details of a plan involving a series of methodical steps to advance the EMS from the Mediterranean into the Marmara. Carden also stressed the importance of aerial reconnaissance, the heavy expenditure of ammunition that it would entail, the difficulty of estimating the exact time that the operations would take because of the capricious nature of the weather in the Aegean and the need for an increase in the strength of his squadron. Despite these caveats, Churchill was satisfied. The plan differed in one important respect from his earlier conception. Initially he had been thinking in terms of a powerful rush through the Dardanelles along the lines of the attack made by Duckworth. But Carden now proposed instead a gradual reduction of the defences and a slow progression under cover of the direct and indirect fire of the heavy-calibre naval guns. Unfortunately this change of emphasis incorporated two unrecognized flaws. First, it concentrated on the forts and their fixed gun positions; but, since the naval bombardment of 3 November, the emphasis of the Dardanelles defences had been switched from these permanent fixtures to a network of minefields closely covered by mobile field howitzers. Second, it overvalued the effect of the ships' gunfire against targets on shore.

Carden's plan was presented to the War Council on 13 January and after only a brief discussion it was accepted. Despite the recognized need for troops to garrison both the Dardanelles and Constantinople if it fell, it was agreed that the British fleet could be withdrawn at any stage prior to that without loss of prestige under the pretext of only ever having intended to undertake a series of limited operations. This would protect Britain against repercussions in the Middle East and India and any attempt to exploit it to subvert the Empire's large Muslim population.

On 15 January Carden was instructed to begin preparations in earnest. He was also promised the reinforcements which he had requested, and in addition, at Fisher's suggestion, the most modern battleship in the Royal Navy, HMS *Queen Elizabeth*, equipped with huge 15-inch guns was to be sent out to complete her final sea trials and gunnery calibration as part of the operation. Churchill informed both the French and the Russians of the British intentions. The French immediately agreed to send ships and in due course the Russians also sent the cruiser *Askold*. There remained only the need for the final approval of the War Council before operations could begin; this was given at a suitably melodramatic meeting on 28 January.

By then Fisher had begun to express his growing concerns both about the wisdom of an operation to be carried out by ships alone without military support and about the potential effect of any casualties on the Grand Fleet, in terms of both ships and their crews. On 25 January he submitted a memorandum outlining his objections to Asquith, who mistakenly believed that they arose not from an assessment of the merits of the Dardanelles operation, but from his preference for an alternative operation in the Baltic. Failing to realize that Fisher's objections were much deeper than this, Asquith felt that, once Fisher had acknowledged that an operation in the Baltic was not presently viable, his support for the Dardanelles would remain unchanged. Three days later, immediately before the meeting, Asquith met both Fisher and Churchill and the two politicians believed that a working agreement had been reached. However, when Fisher realized at the meeting that a final decision was about to be taken he decided to resign. While the bemused politicians concluded their discussion, Kitchener pointed out to Fisher that he was the only member of the Council to disagree with the plan and, after he had been persuaded not to resign, a tentative agreement was reached. The final decision was postponed until a second, early-evening meeting, by which time both Kitchener and Churchill had spoken to Fisher and told him that it would be better if he supported the plan for the sake of unity. This he did.

An operation to force the Dardanelles using ships alone, because soldiers could not be spared, was finally agreed. Churchill alone was enthusiastic. In bringing about the War Council's decision his energy and determination had been paramount. Less concerned with the technical difficulties of the operation than his professional advisers, he increasingly overlooked their objections. Other members of the War Council remained diffident and had agreed to the operation only because it involved such a limited part of Britain's remaining resources. Their agreement had been characterized by caution and a deliberate avoidance of committing Britain to a protracted campaign outside the Western Front. The operation was a compromise between doing nothing and a whole-hearted commitment and represented an ill-considered snatch at a cheap option.

On 5 February Carden was sent his formal orders and told to begin operations, if possible, ten days later. This communication was noticeably more cautious, particularly in respect of the *Queen Elizabeth*, than earlier signals and stated that 'it is not expected or desired that the operations should be hurried to the extent of taking large risks and courting heavy losses'.[7] Four days later, after learning that it was now likely that Bulgaria would join the Central Powers, the War Council discussed the possibility of sending support to Serbia if this occurred. Over the past weeks, intervention via Salonika had emerged as the most promising way of doing this and on 9 February Kitchener offered to send the 29th Division, the last division of British regular troops, to Salonika for this purpose. The proposal came to nothing, but, at precisely the moment when a naval operation was about to begin at the Dardanelles without military support, Kitchener's offer revealed that there were troops available for operations outside the Western Front.

On 6 February Churchill ordered two battalions of Royal Marine Light Infantry (RMLI) from the Royal Naval Division (RND) to be sent out to the eastern Mediterranean to help with the naval operations, and on 15 February an Admiralty memorandum, analysing the exact strength of the Dardanelles defences, again stressed the vital importance of having troops available to secure the land and fortresses as the navy destroyed them. The subject was discussed at an impromptu meeting of the War Council on the following day. In an important conclusion the meeting decided to send the 29th Division to the Aegean island of Lemnos, so that it would be available to support the naval operations if necessary, but only by providing troops to garrison any positions on land taken by the navy or to act as small-scale landing parties. The 29th Division was not to be an invading force.

On 18 February the remaining battalions of the RND, which had been able to resume their training after the unsuccessful attempt to defend the city of Antwerp in October 1914, were ordered to follow the two battalions of Marines which had recently left Britain. The French government also decided to send a specially formed division of mixed troops from French depots in France and North Africa under the title of the Corps Expéditionnaire d'Orient (CEO), commanded by General Albert d'Amade. The destination of all these troops was the large natural harbour of Mudros on the island of Lemnos. On 16 February Rear Admiral Rosslyn Wemyss was appointed Senior Naval Officer and Governor of Mudros; he arrived there with his staff nine days later to begin preparations to turn the harbour into a base for the rapidly expanding campaign. Although all these moves took place less than three weeks after the decision to begin naval operations, they had not yet begun and it would still have been possible to suspend them until the military force arrived. But the idea was not mentioned.

By the end of February the defences of the Dardanelles consisted of three distinct zones. The Outer Defences at the entrance, where the Dardanelles met the Aegean, were formed by two permanent forts on each of the European and Asiatic coasts. Between the entrance and Kephez Point were the Intermediate Defences incorporating the first five of ten lines of mines. Complementing further permanent gun positions, the approach to the minefield was protected along both coasts by batteries of mobile howitzers and field guns intended to prevent the sweeping of the mines by small, unarmoured vessels. To safeguard the mines at night powerful searchlights had been installed and among the plentiful cover of the shorelines dummy batteries which fired black smoke had been constructed. Beyond Kephez Point ran the Narrows and the Inner Defences, which consisted of eleven forts each equipped with several heavy guns, together with more mobile field guns and the remaining five lines of mines. Above the Narrows the Dardanelles were relatively unprotected.

Phase 1 of Carden's plan, which entailed the reduction of the Outer Defences, finally began on 19 February, coincidentally the anniversary of Duckworth's attempt in 1807. Initially it was to be carried out by the ships from long range using their heavy, primary armament. Then, once the guns in the forts had been silenced, the ships were to move in to close range and continue the bombardment with their lighter, secondary armament before levelling a final onslaught to overwhelm what remained of the guns on land. The rate of fire was to be carefully controlled, both to conserve ammunition for the subsequent phases of the attack and to minimize wear on the ships' guns.

The attack began shortly before 10.00 and the first ship to open fire, at a range of 12,000 yards, was the battleship HMS *Cornwallis*, as her gunnery officer, Lieutenant Harry Minchin RN, proudly explained in a letter to his grandfather:

> I gave the order to fire the first gun of the whole proceedings & scored a jolly good hit first go. The rate of fire was very slow, about one round every minute, as we were outside their range. This lasted for the forenoon. In the afternoon us & the *Vengeance* got closer, at about 8,000 yards to 5,000 yards & the *Vengeance* was then under quite a heavy fire. So we rushed in to support her & fairly blazed at the fort, every gun in the ship going off together & doing two rounds a minute at least from every gun. We blew No. 1 fort to a perfect inferno, rocks & smoke, flame, dust & splinters all in the air together. We then got under fire from another fort, so we switched onto her then & never in my life have I had such a ripping time. We weren't hit, although we had a few close shaves. I think our rate of fire must have put them off their stroke. 3,000 lbs of shell a minute bursting all round one must be a bit disconcerting, you know.[8] (Lieutenant Harry Minchin RN)

Early signs of success from the long-range bombardment were soon shown to be deceptive. When the ships closed in, the Turkish gunners revealed that they were simply waiting for their targets to approach and fire began as soon as they did. Before nightfall it was clear that the actual achievements of the first day had been limited. The hope that the weight of the ships' gunfire would devastate the targets on land proved to be forlorn. The flat trajectory of the naval shells meant that they were relatively ineffective. Shrapnel might have proved more effective against the crews of the Turkish guns. But stocks were limited and the gunnery officers of the ships were inexperienced in using it. The expectations of the Royal Navy, which for many years had focused on a fleet action between the Grand Fleet and the German High Seas Fleet, placed little emphasis on shrapnel.

Carden had intended to resume the attack on the following day, but bad weather developed overnight and operations on 20 February had to be suspended for three nights. This delay allowed the Turks valuable time to recover from the first attack and repair the limited damage that it had caused. It was not until 25 February that the opening phase of the operation could finally be completed. By the end of that day the four modern guns of the outer forts had been successfully silenced, the forts themselves abandoned and the entrance swept of mines. The next phase of the plan, involving the reduction of the Intermediate Defences, began immediately on 26 February as the fire of the ships turned to the Turkish positions between the entrance and Kephez Point.

Reports issued in London of the beginning of the naval operations had an immediate impact on international opinion. The resumption of Russian grain exports was imminently expected and the capricious nations of the Balkans believed for the first time in the possibility of a Turkish defeat. Once again Venizelos proposed that Greek troops should be landed on the Gallipoli Peninsula. But his proposal was quickly countered both by the Greek General Staff and by the Russians, who, in contrast to the previous summer, now viewed Greek participation in any attack as totally unacceptable. The possibility of the British ships forcing their way through the Dardanelles also threw Constantinople into a state of consternation, and preliminary preparations were made to move the Turkish government into Anatolia. But exactly how effective the British ships would have been in precipitating a Turkish surrender had they appeared off Constantinople, even at this early stage, has always remained a matter of speculation, as has the question of whether the ships would have been ordered to open fire on the city if this had proved necessary. In London, the intense international interest in the operations soon made it clear that it would now be extremely difficult to withdraw from them in the event of a setback, as had been agreed by the War Council. The attempt to avoid a major commitment to a new campaign appeared to have failed. But the question of whether the limited resources that had been allocated to the operations would be sufficient to bring them to a successful conclusion was not addressed.

In London on the opening day of the naval operations Kitchener reneged on his decision to send the 29th Division to Lemnos and announced to the War Council that it could not after all be spared from the Western Front. However, he proposed to send instead the Australian and New Zealand troops which had been collected in Egypt since December to complete their training prior to moving to France. Despite Churchill's protests, Kitchener insisted this was the best that could be done and on 20 February he ordered Lieutenant General Sir John Maxwell, who commanded the troops in Egypt, to embark as many of the Australians and New Zealanders as possible in the transports then in Egypt and send them to Mudros. The remainder would follow in transports that were to be sent out from Britain immediately. By 23 February Maxwell had collected sufficient transports for one brigade, and the 3rd Australian Brigade was detailed to leave for the Aegean.

In command of the Australian and New Zealand troops was Lieutenant General Sir William Birdwood, an Indian Army officer who stood slightly outside the mainstream of the British Army establishment. For many years he had been closely associated with Kitchener, who knew his character well, and Birdwood's energetic, self-confident personality was ideally suited to commanding the Antipodean troops. Kitchener ordered Birdwood to precede his men to the Aegean to assess the situation from a military point of view. Kitchener's perception of the soldiers merely as a garrison force had not changed and he did not expect a military landing to be necessary. However, he asked Birdwood for his private opinion of the likely success of the naval operations and whether he felt troops would in the end need to be landed to take the forts in reverse.

After arriving in the Aegean on 1 March and consulting with Carden on the following day, on 4 March Birdwood sent two telegrams to London. If troops did become involved, he concluded, it would be impossible to limit them to the minor role Kitchener had in mind. Large numbers would be needed from the start and both he and Carden agreed that the best plan would be to make a diversionary landing at Bulair and land the main force at the extreme southern end of the peninsula around Cape Helles. The Asiatic coast looked more difficult for military operations and it was hoped that the guns positioned there could be dominated by troops from the European shore. After receiving an assurance from Churchill that Carden's squadron would be through to the Marmara soon after 16 March, Kitchener advised Birdwood to be cautious and reminded him that he was not to get involved in large-scale landings without further orders from London. In a third telegram on the following day Birdwood answered Kitchener's private question. In his opinion the navy could not successfully force the Dardanelles on their own.

The progress of the ships against the Intermediate Defences was proving to be slow. As they moved forward they found that the fire of the mobile guns, carefully hidden on the shore, was more of a hindrance than the permanent works and, despite regular attempts to locate them, this fire persisted. On 5 March a new approach was adopted. The *Queen Elizabeth* took up a station off Gaba Tepe and shelled the forts around Chanak across the peninsula. Her huge 15-inch shells bursting on the forts out of the blue appeared to cause significant damage and on the next day the operation was repeated. But when on 8 March she entered the Dardanelles to try firing directly at the forts, they opened fire on her as if nothing had happened. The previous days' bombardments had apparently had no effect.

Beginning on 26 February, demolition parties had been successfully landed near the Outer Defences to complete the destruction of the guns at Kum Kale and Sedd el Bahr. A second landing was made at Sedd el Bahr on the following day. But bad weather prevented a second landing at Kum Kale until 1 March, at which point it was discovered that in Fort No. 6 seven out of the nine guns had not in fact been damaged by the naval bombardment and only one had been put out of commission. The largest landings were made on 4 March by the Plymouth Battalion, RMLI, led by its commanding officer, Lieutenant Colonel Godfrey Matthews. At Kum Kale the landing began at around 09.00, but soon got into trouble. Attempts to move south met strong Turkish opposition and eventually the landing had to be abandoned. At Sedd el Bahr it was equally unsuccessful. In all, the battalion suffered twenty-three killed, twenty-five wounded and four missing[9] and achieved nothing. No further landings were made before 25 April. It was an inauspicious start to military involvement and the defending Turkish troops gained a considerable boost to their morale.

The mine-sweeping operations had also been encountering greater difficulties than expected. The failure of the ships to silence the mobile guns meant that the sweeping, which was being carried out by trawlers with civilian crews instead of naval mine-sweepers, which had not been sent out from Britain, was continuously hampered by unchecked fire from the shore. The trawlers were also able to make little headway against the current which flowed down the Dardanelles; in order to sweep through the fields they were forced to position themselves above the field and then sweep back through it using the strength of the current to aid them. Attempts to use destroyers for mine-sweeping failed. The sweeping of the minefields at the head of the Intermediate Defences by day was abandoned soon after the beginning of March, but was maintained by night. On the night of 11/12 March, Able Seaman P. Rooke formed part of a picket-boat crew sent from the battleship HMS *Canopus* to escort the trawlers.

> It was a very dirty night. Never shall I forget that night as long as I live. We were close to the shore and I think that they fired everything at us, from an 11″ gun to a pistol, and the screaming of the shells was enough to drive you off your head. But our Officer was very cool. He gave orders for mine-sweepers to retire. We destroyed several lines of mines after being in the minefield for about 4 hours. We returned to the ships at 8 am the following morning after being in the boat for 14 hours without anything to eat or drink, cold and wet through. I was very bad after it, as it had shaken my nerves very much. We were all recommended to the Admiralty and they acknowledged it, but have heard nothing more about it since. We were lucky to get away with our lives.[10]
> (Able Seaman P. Rooke)

On 12 March, in the hope of speeding up the sweeping, Carden decided to bolster the crews of the trawlers with naval personnel.

But these men were still unable to overcome the trawlers' fundamental lack of power. At the Admiralty Churchill was beginning to grow impatient. On 13 March he sent a personal and secret signal to Carden complaining that he did 'not understand why minesweeping should be interfered with by firing which causes no casualties. Two or three hundred casualties would be moderate price to pay for sweeping as far as Narrows. . . . This work has to be done whatever the loss of life and small craft and the sooner it is done the better.'[11]

At a meeting of the War Council three days earlier Kitchener had announced that he had changed his mind again and decided after all to order the embarkation of the 29th Division. On its arrival the military force in the eastern Mediterranean would now comprise five divisions, although not all of them were complete. Birdwood had naturally assumed that when military operations began he would command them. But, as a result of d'Amade's appointment to command the CEO, moves had been afoot in London for some days to appoint a British general senior to d'Amade as Commander-in-Chief and on 11 March Kitchener informed the War Office that he had decided on General Sir Ian Hamilton, at that time in command of Central Force in Great Britain. This decision, naturally, was a great disappointment to Birdwood. Hamilton was called in to see Kitchener on the following day and abruptly told of his new appointment. He and as many of his General Staff as were ready would leave London within twenty-four hours in a special train and embark at Marseilles in the light cruiser HMS *Phaeton*, which would take them to the eastern Mediterranean as quickly as possible.

It was all done with great rapidity. Since Kitchener had first revealed a month earlier that the 29th Division was available to support the Serbs via Salonika, the involvement of a significant military force at the Dardanelles had been brought about under the momentum of outside events. Its evolution had been *ad hoc* and unplanned. Although the navy had made a firm commitment to force the Dardanelles, the army was sceptical about its ability to succeed. Yet there had been no discussion at the War Office of the implications of a naval failure and no staff appreciation had been drawn up to consider exactly what the military force would do if the naval force proved to be inadequate. This lack of preparation did not augur well for success. Perhaps sensing this, on his departure from London Hamilton was overcome by a superstitious depression. As his train pulled out of Charing Cross on 13 March, he turned to Captain Cecil Aspinall, one of the staff officers in the Operations Branch of his General Staff, and said: 'This is going to be an unlucky show. I kissed my wife through her veil.'[12]

Hamilton and his staff arrived at the island of Tenedos, where the EMS was based, on the evening of 17 March. The journey from London, faultlessly organized by Churchill, had swept them in an almost dreamlike state across the breadth of Europe. Its speed engendered a sense of invigoration and adventure throughout the General Staff which compounded the suddenness of their appointment. On the outbreak of the war Hamilton had seen more action and held a wider variety of appointments than perhaps any other general in the British Army. Since first entering the 2nd Gordon Highlanders in November 1873, he had progressed steadily through the hierarchy of the army via a mixture of field and staff appointments. He had fought at different levels in several small campaigns in Afghanistan and North-West India and taken part in the Gordon Relief Expedition. He had been severely wounded during the First Boer War at Majuba Hill in February 1881 and, for his actions there, recommended for the VC, a recommendation rejected on the grounds that he was too young. During the Second Boer War, after distinguishing himself as an infantry brigade commander at Elandslaagte in October 1899 and earning a second recommendation for the VC, which was this time rejected on the grounds of his being too senior, he had held a number of conspicuous posts which culminated in Chief of Staff to Kitchener, who was then Commander-in-Chief in South Africa. Over the next decade he had advanced through a succession of senior appointments in a brilliant career. The opportunity of leading the MEF to Constantinople now appeared to be its pinnacle. Unlike many of his contemporaries in the army, Hamilton was also known as a refined and cultured social figure. He knew many literary and artistic figures and had himself written both poetry and a novel.

His relationship with Kitchener was unusual and had a significant effect on his command of the campaign. Many of Hamilton's letters to Kitchener revealed an almost reverential attitude and on leaving Britain he took the unfortunate decision not to write to any correspondents – particularly Churchill, with whom he had also been friends since South Africa – who might be able to undermine Kitchener's position. Frequently Hamilton dealt with Kitchener as if he was his direct military commander, which of course he was not. Kitchener was Secretary of State for War, and no longer his Commander-in-Chief. But Hamilton's respect and deference appeared to prevent him from making this distinction.

Throughout his discussions with the War Council Kitchener had perceived the MEF as a garrison, or at the most a decisive landing party; it was not intended to lead the assault on the Dardanelles. The instructions he issued to Hamilton made it clear that this role had not altered. The MEF was a limited military force, the most that could be spared in the face of other pressing demands. Hamilton was told plainly that the 29th Division was only a temporary loan from the Western Front and, whereas all the divisions going out to France with the BEF in 1914 had taken with them a 10 per cent reinforcement draft to make good the first battle casualties and keep the divisions up to strength, a similar draft was not to be sent with the 29th Division, despite the much greater distance that it would be fighting away from Britain.

Under pressure from Churchill to speed up the naval attack, on 13 March Carden's second-in-command, Rear Admiral John De Robeck, chaired a meeting of the senior officers of the EMS to discuss the idea of a rush through the Dardanelles, which Carden had specifically rejected in his first reply to Churchill at the beginning of January. One of those who attended, Commander Worsley Gibson RN, the gunnery officer in the battleship HMS *Albion*, included a detailed record of the meeting in his diary.

> Everyone, or nearly so I believe, knew really that it would be madness to try & rush them. The Narrows are sure to be mined. It has been proved that bombardment silences forts but does little material damage to guns & only silences because gunners take cover. Personally I feel sure that it is pressure from our cursed politicians on the VA [Vice Admiral] which is making him even

21

consider such a thing. A large army 60 or 70 thousand is collecting for [the] purpose of co-operation, the only way to tackle this job, & why not wait for them? Apart from the certain loss of men & ships of a rushing attempt now, the moral effect on navy would not be good if we failed, as I think very likely, & the effect on the enemy would be tremendous. I hope it is not tried & I somehow think it won't.[13] (Commander Worsley Gibson RN)

On the following day a second meeting was called to consider a scheme not for a rush through the Narrows but for a concentrated attack on its defences and the guns and forts which protected the minefield at the head of the Intermediate Defences. The aim was to establish control over the defences and allow an effective sweep of the minefield to be made. Carden forwarded an outline of the proposed plan to the Admiralty; in his signal agreeing to it Churchill toned down his earlier impatience, warning Carden that he should not risk losing the successes he had gained by attempting to rush the Narrows too fast. On 16 March the strain of the past weeks finally overwhelmed Carden and he was placed on the sick list, being replaced in command by De Robeck.

The attack was put into practice on 18 March, the day after Hamilton's arrival. The fleet was divided into three lines of attack, 'A', 'B' and 'C'. Line 'A', made up of the more modern ships, was to proceed first into Erin Keui Bay and open fire at a range of 14,000 yards on the forts positioned around Kilid Bahr and Chanak. As soon as this had started to take effect, the French battleships making up Line 'B' were to pass through Line 'A' and engage the same targets until they had closed to a range of only 8,000 yards. The flanks of both of these lines were to be covered by two detached ships. The remaining British ships of Line 'C' were to act as reliefs, to replace Line 'B' and the flank guards. Minesweeping was to begin two hours after the start to clear a passage through which the fleet could advance beyond Kephez Point and from there further reduce the forts of the Narrows. Pressure was to be maintained on the forts during the night, although the majority of the fleet was to withdraw temporarily, and on the following day the forts were to be finally smashed at close range.

The ships would then begin their preparations for an entry into the Sea of Marmara.

By the morning of 18 March the Dardanelles were reported clear of mines to within 8,000 yards of the Narrows forts, which meant that the area in which the fleet would have to manoeuvre was presumed safe. Unfortunately this was not the case. Ten days earlier, on 8 March, the Turkish minelayer *Nousret* had successfully laid a line of twenty mines parallel to the shore of Erin Keui Bay after observing the British battleships manoeuvring there on the previous day. This single line of mines was to prove fatal to the Allied plan.

At 10.30, Line 'A' entered the Dardanelles and advanced to their firing positions, coming under irritating but relatively ineffectual shelling from the Turkish howitzers and field artillery, before beginning their attack on the target forts at about 11.30. The ships fired well and it appeared that the bombardment was having a material effect; the guns in the forts for the most part remained quiet. In view of this apparent success, at 12.06, De Robeck ordered Line 'B' to pass through Line 'A'. But, as the French ships began to move forward, more and more of the concealed Turkish batteries and intermediate forts started to attack the British ships in Line 'A', particularly those closest to the Asiatic shore. The Narrows forts, apparently relatively undamaged by the efforts of Line 'A', also joined in the fray. When the French ships reached a range of 10,000 yards a tremendous duel began between the battleships and the forts. At 13.45, De Robeck judged that the Turks' fire was slackening and ordered the mine-sweepers to begin clearing the channel beyond Kephez Point. The British relief ships were also ordered up to replace the French in Line 'B', who were inevitably beginning to suffer damage.

Shortly after this the first real disaster occurred. From the *Queen Elizabeth* Lieutenant Douglas Claris RN noted that 'the French ships, still firing, started retiring. At 2pm a small cloud of yellowish smoke, which turned black afterwards, came out of the starboard quarter of the *Bouvet*.'[14] The *Bouvet* had discovered the line of mines that the sweepers had missed.

I noticed the *Bouvet* was heeling to starboard & said so to McB.
& even as I spoke she was listing more & more & it was evident

23

she was badly wounded. She was steaming quite fast & went over & over until she was on her beam ends & her masts went into the water, a lot of smoke & steam rolled out but no explosions took place & she turned bottom up for a few seconds.[15] (Commander Worsley Gibson RN)

The sheer speed of the sinking shocked the helpless observers.

She heeled over very rapidly and in what seemed about 30 seconds she went down by the stern. Only 21 lives were saved out of about 700, in spite of the fact that each ship had a picket boat and destroyer attending on them looking out for mines, and all these darted at once to the place where the *Bouvet* went down. . . . Forts opened a tremendous fire on destroyers and picket boats during the rescue work, but none of them was hit.[16] (Lieutenant Douglas Claris RN)

Despite this shattering spectacle the British relief ships continued their advance. The effect of the naval fire on the forts was becoming increasingly difficult to determine, as the forts began to stop and then recommence firing at intervals. But the fleet worked steadily to maintain the bombardment. The firing of the guns was a noisy and complicated business and one Royal Marine gunner, Private William Jones of the battleship HMS *Prince George*, recalled that the inside of a gun turret was not a pleasant place to be:

I was a member of one of the 6″ guns on the lower deck. There were eight of the crew and two by the ammunition hoist. We were in that casemate eleven hours. It was about fourteen feet wide and twelve feet deep. Inside it was very hot. Some of us were very scantily dressed. I was wearing a bathing costume and a pair of heavy boots in case a projectile dropped on your toe. Well you can just imagine being in a very hot atmosphere like that. The old fellow, a corporal in the marines with a very heavy moustache, poor old chap! We gave him the lightest job that was there, but out he went – he was right out. We went round to see him and the gunlayer sergeant said: 'Leave the old "B" alone', and we carried on. Then the old fellow came a kind of around. It was no good trying to get him outside – we were forbidden to open the casemate door. There was cocoa – it was cold – and there was

24

biscuits. No bread. Biscuits and some corned dog, otherwise known as corned beef! We were all packed in there in the morning and we were not allowed outside. There was an officer outside with a revolver, walking up and down. We were forbidden to go outside whatever. What we wanted to do we had to do in the casemate, whatever it might be. When we loaded the gun it was quite a big job because the shell was about 112 pounds. You open up the breech of the gun, pulling the breech back. Up comes a No. 4. He gets a shell on top of the shell guide, gets a rammer and rams home. A No. 6 comes along with a cylinder and enters the tube, pushes it right home. A No. 2 closes the breech. 'READY'. Immediately you stand clear from the gun and it's fired by the No. 1, the gunlayer. Then open the breech again. Get the extractor on your arm, that fits around the back of the cartridge, and you fling it aside, and I can assure you it's red hot. Then the whole procedure is gone through again.[17] (Private William Jones)

In front of Line 'A' the mine-sweeping trawlers had begun to sweep for mines. Three mines, probably from the line of twenty laid on 8 March, were exploded in an area thought to have been cleared. But no details of this were forwarded to De Robeck until the following day and within a short time the severity of the Turkish fire forced the trawlers to retreat with their task uncompleted. Had De Robeck been informed on 18 March of the possible presence of mines in the area where his fleet was manoeuvring many lives might have been saved.

At 16.11, the battle-cruiser HMS *Inflexible*, on the right of Line 'A', ran into a mine on her starboard bow which her captain reported as causing severe damage:

The electric light failed and most of the emergency oil lamps were extinguished. Men stationed in 'A' magazine and shell room were thrown off their feet. The fore turret was felt to lift bodily. All communications failed and orders to the engine room had to be conveyed by messenger. . . . Speed of the ship was increased to twelve knots and the trim corrected by flooding the provision room, but the ship remained down by the bow six feet. Casualties amounted to three officers and thirty men killed, and thirteen wounded.[18] (Captain Richard Phillimore RN)

Three minutes later, at 16.14, the battleship HMS *Irresistible* also struck a mine. From the *Albion* her plight was painfully obvious. 'The batteries got the range of her & began to drop shell all around her & occasionally hit her. It was simply damnable to see her drifting helplessly along there with her crew quietly standing about or throwing planks & anything that would float overboard.'[19] The destroyer HMS *Wear* transferred most of the crew to the *Queen Elizabeth*, while the *Irresistible*'s captain and a few selected volunteers remained aboard to prepare the ship for towing.

Reports were sent to De Robeck that the damage had been done by a mine. But trusting earlier reports that the area had been swept, he concluded that it was probably a floating mine launched by the Turks higher up the Dardanelles. Feeling that no further progress could be made until an effective defence against this new threat had been devised, he ordered the advanced British ships to withdraw and sent back his Chief of Staff, Commodore Roger Keyes, in the *Wear* to direct Captain Arthur Hayes-Sadler RN, of the battleship HMS *Ocean*, to take the *Irresistible* in tow if necessary.

By the time the *Wear* reached the *Irresistible* at 17.20 she was under heavy fire and had drifted close to the Asiatic shore. In answer to Keyes's entreaties, Hayes-Sadler declined to intervene and instead, once Keyes had set off in disgust to report to De Robeck, he withdrew the *Ocean* under heavy fire. Almost inevitably, at 18.05 she also struck a mine and moments later was hit by a heavy shell. Her situation seemed hopeless; at least so it appeared to Hayes-Sadler, who was not, it seems, overly optimistic about the possibilities of salvaging crippled pre-dreadnoughts. The nearby destroyers were immediately ordered to rescue survivors and their promptness meant that the *Ocean*'s crew were safely taken off before she was abandoned at 19.30.

Keyes was confident that both the *Irresistible* and the *Ocean* could still be saved and obtained De Robeck's permission to re-enter the Dardanelles to search for the abandoned hulks. By the time he arrived in Erin Keui Bay both ships had already disappeared. But his experience during the search convinced him that, despite the losses and difficulties which had characterized the day, it had been a success and the Turks were 'a beaten foe. I thought he was beaten at 2pm, I knew he was beaten at 4 pm – and at midnight

I knew with still greater certainty that he was absolutely beaten; and it only remained for us to organize a proper sweeping force and devise some means of dealing with drifting mines to reap the fruits of our efforts.'[20] This was not the impression gained by other experienced naval commanders in the area; but Keyes firmly believed it, agitating for a resumption of the naval offensive throughout the campaign and maintaining his belief for the rest of his life.

Of the other damaged ships, as a result of Phillimore's skilful seamanship, the *Inflexible* was saved and eventually run aground at Tenedos. The French battleship *Gaulois* was also beached on one of the smaller islands near by after being badly hit and taking in water. The reality of 18 March was that it had been a failure for the Allied fleet. Of the sixteen capital ships engaged, three had been sunk and three more put out of action for a prolonged period. Yet almost nothing had really been achieved. Although the forts had been heavily damaged they had the great advantage of not having to stay afloat. Repairs could, and would, be made, but the *Bouvet, Irresistible* and *Ocean* were irrecoverable. The sinking of the *Bouvet* had highlighted the speed with which these 'expendable' old predreadnoughts could sink, leaving no opportunity to rescue their crews. The attempt to speed up the rate of progress through the Dardanelles had been counter-productive. The fleet had in practice been set back and the minefields – the true defenders of the Straits – remained intact. In what was to prove one of the most concentrated naval actions of the war, the Royal Navy had been defeated.

> This is just what one might expect, & what we really did more or less. Every book on war ever written always states the fact that politicians interfering with Commanders in the field always lead to disaster but still they think they are born strategists & know alls & do it again & again.[21] (Commander Worsley Gibson RN)

2

The Dawn
of a Perfect Day

After seeing the peninsula for the first time on 18 March and entering the Dardanelles in the middle of the naval battle, Sir Ian Hamilton and his staff realized immediately that military intervention would be needed before the operations could be successfully concluded. On 19 March Hamilton explained to Kitchener that the army's part would now have to 'be more than mere landings of parties to destroy Forts, it must be a deliberate and progressive military operation carried out at full strength so as to open a passage for the Navy'.[1] Kitchener replied in apparent agreement, adding 'that if large military operations on the Gallipoli Peninsula are necessary to clear the way, they must be undertaken, and must be carried through'.[2] He had not previously stated this view quite so unequivocally and might not have intended it to give definite approval to a full-scale military landing. But Hamilton believed that this had now been given. Kitchener was naturally disappointed by Hamilton's conclusion. Earlier in the day he had attended a meeting of the War Council at which a report by Vice Admiral De Robeck on the previous day's attack had suggested that he still had every intention of resuming it in due course, and in response the War Council had agreed to send out a squadron of four more old British battleships under the command of Rear Admiral Cecil Thursby to replace his losses, together with a French battleship to replace the *Bouvet*.

De Robeck initially suspended operations on 19 March because of uncertainty over the cause of the sinkings, being reluctant to resume them until these had been fully explained. But on 20 March the return of bad weather finally put an end to any prospect of an immediate resumption. It is doubtful whether De Robeck would have done this anyway. Despite his resolute report to the War

Council, in person on 19 March Rear Admiral Wemyss 'found him naturally enough somewhat depressed at the turn of events. He spoke of disaster, a term I begged him not to use.'[3] Both men agreed that no further naval progress in clearing the minefield could now be made until the shoreline had been seized. This had been the view of many senior naval officers since before 18 March and the events of that day confirmed their belief that a full-scale landing would have to be undertaken. Nevertheless they did not dispute that a renewed naval attempt should eventually be made.

With these views fresh in their minds, on 22 March Hamilton and De Robeck attended a meeting on board the *Queen Elizabeth*, the ultimate consequence of which was the landing on 25 April. A degree of confusion surrounds the meeting over which party finally changed the operation from a naval to a military one, from the Dardanelles to Gallipoli. De Robeck suggested to Churchill shortly afterwards that it was only after hearing Hamilton's views that this decision was reached. But Hamilton recalled a meeting in which the navy relinquished the initiative and made it plain that they wanted the army to land. Despite this apparent disagreement, the outcome of the meeting was the same. An opposed landing would now have to be made and discussion turned to the details of how to carry it out. This conclusion was forwarded to London and on 27 March Churchill was reluctantly forced to agree to a combined operation.

Yet the MEF was in no position to begin operations straight-away and the earliest date it would be ready was likely to be the middle of April. Although its nominal strength was five divisions, the overall number of front-line troops totalled only around 75,000. In his instructions Kitchener also made it absolutely clear that no operations were to start until the whole force had been collected in one place. However, the 29th Division and all but one brigade of the Australians and New Zealanders had not yet arrived in the Aegean. Neither the RND nor the CEO, which were already in place, had been embarked in their transports in the expectation of landing directly on a hostile shore and before this could be done both divisions would have to be completely reorganized, something that could not be done at Mudros. Lieutenant General Maxwell offered to make Egypt available as a base for the reorganization, an offer that was taken up on 25 March, and the RND, CEO and 29th Division were all directed there for this purpose. The leading transports of the 29th Division had just entered the Aegean and after receiving this order on 27 March had to reverse their course away from the Dardanelles. The only positive aspect of the reorganization was that it allowed Hamilton and his General Staff time to draw up a detailed plan.

The most important advantage needed by a force landing from open boats on a defended shoreline is surprise. But doubts about British intentions at the Dardanelles had completely disappeared by the end of March. Only a limited degree of tactical surprise remained in the selection of the landing places; the Turks might realize that a landing was imminent but they did not know where it was going to take place. If this part of the plan could be kept secret then it was hoped that the Turks would weaken their defences by attempting to cover all eventualities. There were two determining factors in the selection of the landing sites. First, as the main purpose of the landing was to allow the mine-sweeping to be completed and the Inner Defences at the Narrows to be reduced at decisive range, it had to be of immediate and direct assistance to these naval operations. This pointed to an operation close to the Dardanelles entrance, probably on the European coast, where the country was less difficult than along the parallel stretch of the Asiatic shore; in his instructions Kitchener had also 'strongly deprecated'[4] any occupation of the Asiatic coast. Second, it had to remain within the capabilities of both the soldiers who were to land and the sailors who were to land them, the speed and diversity of the landing being strictly bound by the number of boats available to carry it out.

After rejecting a landing on the Bulair Isthmus, which, although superficially attractive through its difficult terrain and vulnerability to counter-attack from two directions, was in fact fraught with difficulties, the General Staff concluded that the landing should take place on the southwestern half of the peninsula with the overall aim of capturing the Kilid Bahr Plateau, a strongly fortified arc of high ground which surrounded Maidos and Kilid Bahr. From this position the MEF would be able to dominate both the shoreline immediately beneath it and the Asiatic coast across the Dardanelles, allowing the naval attack to be resumed as part of a combined operation.

The possible sites were reduced to four: at or around Suvla Bay, a wide inlet on the northern corner of the Aegean coastline; immediately to the north of Gaba Tepe; immediately to the south of this point; or at the southern tip of the peninsula around Cape Helles and Sedd el Bahr. Of these options, despite its attractive openness and easily accessible beaches, Suvla was felt to be too far from the Narrows and the Kilid Bahr Plateau and its capture would do little to forward the progress of the fleet. To the south of Gaba Tepe there were several clear landing beaches. But all had been heavily fortified and any landing there would be difficult to execute and would also produce a line that would be vulnerable to attack from all sides except the rear. The most favourable option was Helles, where, although the difficulties of landing would be no less, the enclosure of the tip by the sea would allow the fleet to provide greater support to the troops as they advanced inland. If a landing there could be linked to a subsidiary landing north of Gaba Tepe, along the more difficult and therefore less fortified southern slopes of the Sari Bair Ridge, both sides of the Kilid Bahr Plateau would be threatened, together with Turkish communications along the Dardanelles. The simultaneous execution of two landings would also increase the degree of local surprise and disguise which of the two was in fact the main thrust.

On 23 March the General Staff presented a basic outline of this scheme to Hamilton, who approved it immediately. The main landing at Helles was to be carried out by the 29th Division supported by the French, and the landing at Gaba Tepe was to be made by the Australians and New Zealanders. A feint landing to distract Turkish attention would also be made at Bulair by those troops who were unable to land in the first instance at the real sites due to the limited number of boats, principally the RND. The following day Hamilton and his General Staff left for Egypt. On 27 March General Headquarters (GHQ) was established in Alexandria and immediately set to work on the details of the plan. When Hamilton had left London a fortnight earlier, only the General Staff had been ready to accompany him with the two other administrative branches of GHQ not even having been appointed, and for the remainder of March their absence proved a significant hindrance to the co-ordinated drawing up of plans. As many of the precise details involved questions of naval resources, the separation of GHQ from the headquarters of the EMS also proved frustrating.

Although trenchant questions had been asked in London on 16 March by Lieutenant Colonel Hankey in a memorandum to the Prime Minister about the way in which the military operation had evolved and the extent of the preparations that had been made for it, this led to no serious appraisal of whether the strength of the MEF was sufficient for its expanded role. It had been formed to support and complement the naval attack, not to lead it, and even for its original task it had been the smallest force that Kitchener could assemble to satisfy the competing demands for troops at the Dardanelles and in France. Now that a full-scale landing was to be made this number of men was clearly inadequate. In addition the MEF was lacking a great deal of specialist equipment and stores. Its ammunition stocks, having been allocated primarily for a garrison role, were low with only 500 rounds available per rifle in the 29th Division and 430 in the RND. The 18-pounder field guns of the 29th Division had only 623 rounds per gun, all of which was shrapnel and of little help to the infantry if it became held up by fortified Turkish positions. Once ashore there was also considerable anxiety about the availability of water. The difficulty of transporting the limited supplies of both water and ammunition on land was eased by the attachment to the force of an Indian Mule Corps and the Zion Mule Corps, formed from expatriate Russian Jews living in the Levant. But naturally these troops would be among the last to land and until then the soldiers themselves would have to carry all supplies.

Despite the lack of preparation for the more difficult task that was now to be undertaken, the War Office remained complacent. No suggestion was made that these deficiencies should be made good either immediately or even once military operations had begun. Hamilton's relationship with Kitchener prevented him from sending a firm demand that this should be done. Instead, having taken on the job he felt obliged to see it through without asking for an increase in his strength. Once in Egypt he became aware of the large number of troops stationed there to defend the country and he did at least allow himself one small request, to which he received no immediate reply, for a brigade of Indian infantry, particularly Gurkhas, who he felt would be ideally suited to the rugged landscape of the peninsula.

Shortly afterwards, Kitchener decided to increase the overall strength of the Egyptian garrison and on 6 April told Maxwell that he 'should supply any troops in Egypt that can be spared, or even selected officers or men that Sir Ian Hamilton may want, for Gallipoli. . . . This telegram should be communicated by you to Sir Ian Hamilton.'[5] The precise level of assistance was left to Maxwell's discretion. With the questions of the security of Egypt and the Suez Canal still uppermost in his mind, he was naturally reluctant to relinquish anything and, despite Kitchener's clear instruction to do so, he did not forward a copy of the telegram to Hamilton, who remained ignorant of its contents.

From the day after his arrival in Egypt Hamilton began regular inspections of the troops stationed there and for the first time was able to assess for himself the men who formed the MEF. His first visit on 28 March was to see the 42nd Division, a British territorial division largely recruited from the heavily populated conurbations of East Lancashire, which, although not actually part of his command, did eventually join it. Following Kitchener's request in August 1914 for territorial volunteers to serve outside Britain, approximately 90 per cent of the 42nd Division had done so and the division was selected as the first to be sent overseas to join the Egyptian garrison. They departed from Southampton on 10 September, sailing at midnight. Part of one of the Manchester Regiment's battalions embarked in the SS *Aragon* together with the 2nd County of London Yeomanry; and one of the troopers in the latter, clearly a man of social pretensions, found the Lancastrians utterly objectionable. 'We watched our new companions coming aboard in their thousands: the rawest of the raw Lancashire Laddies and bakers' boys, mill hands, butchers' lads and all the roughest. . . . Bit by bit the ship began to smell like a third class smoker in a closed shed – or even worse. . . . By this time we had come to detest our travelling companions. They misused everything from the washing places to the decks. They clog dance on all occasions and look dirty and untidy and have bad manners.'[6] Some did have finer feelings which the disgusted trooper was unable to see. 2nd Lieutenant George Horridge, a young officer in the 1/5th Lancashire Fusiliers, saw a different side to his own men.

At night the fellows used to have a sing song, and I always remember one thing we sang:

> Homeland, Homeland,
>   When shall I see you again?
> Land of my birth,
>   Dearest land on earth,
> Homeland, Homeland,
>   When shall I see you again?
> It may be for years or it may be for ever,
>   Dear Homeland. . . .[7]

On 25 September the division arrived in Egypt, where they found a range of dangers awaiting them. Although doubtless warned by their mothers, many unwary young soldiers seeing the temptation grabbed it and suffered. The first lesson according to Private Robert Spencer was the peril of drink. 'Some of these men who were used to having beer were craving for it by the time we got to Alexandria. There a lot of these Gyppos, Egyptians, were offering these bottles supposed to be whisky, but they were more methylated spirits. Some of the men got hold of them and I think there were one or two killed through drinking this so called whisky.'[8] The second was the sins of the flesh. 'There was always these here loose women men were after and then they had to suffer for it after. Many a time, lads that you knew, you'd say, "Where is so and so?" "Oh, he's up at Citadel" – a lot of that was turned into a VD hospital.'[9]

In Egypt the Lancastrians, such as Private George Peake of the 1/8th Lancashire Fusiliers, also encountered strange people from faraway lands. 'I thought the Australians were the biggest set of men I'd seen in my life. I don't think I hardly saw one that was under six feet, all big stout fellows. It's alright seeing them but one little bullet will put them down, them big fellows made a big target!'[10] Mostly their time was taken up with training and by the spring of 1915 six months of this had become monotonous. The inspection by Hamilton, together with the rumours about the Dardanelles and the sudden appearance in Egypt of new troops, caused many to hope that they too would be taken away from Egypt to somewhere more interesting.

On the day after his inspection of the 42nd Division Hamilton visited both the 1st Australian Division, commanded by Major General William Bridges, and the New Zealand and Australian (NZ&A) Division, commanded by Major General Sir Alexander Godley. As it had been in Britain, the outbreak of war in both Australia and New Zealand had been greeted by many young men with an enthusiasm coloured by a deep strain of national pride. There was a new awareness of nationality in both countries and the war seemed to offer an opportunity for them to take an active part in international events under their own identity for the first time. Individual desire to take part in the war was also widespread, often making competition for places in the army intense. For many, such as Rupert Westmacott, who succeeded in joining a battalion of the New Zealand Expeditionary Force, a degree of initiative was needed even to enlist:

> We went up to the drill hall in a large crowd. They were calling out the names of people they had in their territorial list. As each name was called out the man shouted: 'Yes Sir,' and marched in. I thought I'd never get in but then a name was called out, nobody answered and I shouted out: 'Yes Sir,' and I marched in. When they sorted the people I was left and they said: 'Who are you?' I said my name. 'But your name wasn't called out.' I said: 'I thought it was.' 'Anyway, we're not taking any more. The only people we want is cooks.' So I said: 'You've got the very man!' He said: 'Where have you cooked? In a survey camp?' Well I'd never heard of a cook in a survey camp, but I said: 'Yes, in a survey camp.' So they enlisted me as a cook. I joined the 3rd Auckland Regiment. We only had open fires and cooked entirely in dixies – nothing but porridge and stews. I came across another fellow cooking and found he was the son of the Chief Justice. I said: 'How the hell did you get the job as cook?', and he said: 'Influence, old boy, influence!'[11] (Private Rupert Westmacott)

35

Towards the end of September 1914 the first New Zealanders were ready to leave to join up with the Australians. But a lack of adequate naval protection against the German Pacific Squadron delayed their start and it was not until 16 October that they set sail. Twelve days later the New Zealand transports arrived at King George Sound near Albany in Western Australia. After uniting with the transports of the Australian Imperial Force, the convoy set sail again on 1 November and arrived at Aden on 25 November. Shortly after leaving there a telegram from London ordered the troops to disembark in Egypt to continue their training, rather than proceed to Britain, where facilities for the first Canadian troops had already proved inadequate. The telegram also announced that, under the command of Lieutenant General Birdwood, they were formally to be designated the Australian and New Zealand Army Corps, which in due course inevitably became known by the acronym ANZAC and the troops as Anzacs.

On 2 April Hamilton saw part of the RND, as well as some of the Indian troops who were near by. The RND was a strange hybrid unit, a basically military force under the control of the Admiralty. The first part of it to be formed in August 1914 was the Royal Marine Brigade, which initially consisted of three battalions of RMLI and one battalion of Royal Marine Artillery. The latter was replaced at the beginning of September by a fourth battalion of RMLI. At the same time two naval brigades were formed from officers of the Royal Naval Volunteer Reserve, stokers from the Royal Fleet Reserve and selected ratings from the Royal Naval Reserve, none of whom were at that point required for service at sea. To these were added the surplus requirements of several northern regiments and men recruited directly for the new formations. Basic training was carried out at a divisional depot which opened at Crystal Palace in September. Before any real semblance of military organization had been established, particularly in the 1st and 2nd Naval Brigades, all three brigades were sent to Antwerp, where they did as well as might be expected. Although battle casualties were not high, unfortunately a large part of the division, including many of the Hawke, Collingwood and Benbow Battalions, were captured by the Germans or interned in Holland,

and on the division's return these three battalions had to be reformed.

From these unusual beginnings and the varied mixture of its personnel the RND naturally developed a unique character which served it well at Gallipoli and during its later service on the Western Front. As a new and unconventional unit, the division attracted a high proportion of striking personalities. Many of its officers were renowned society and literary luminaries. Most famous of all was the distinguished and colourful group which collected in the Hood Battalion towards the end of 1914 including the Prime Minister's son Arthur ('Oc') Asquith, the poet Rupert Brooke, the talented musician Denis Browne, an energetic American Johnny Dodge, a fearless New Zealander Bernard Freyberg (later Lieutenant General Lord Freyberg VC), another musician, this time an Australian, F. S. 'Cleg' Kelly, and the scholar-turned-banker Patrick Shaw-Stewart. But the Hood Battalion was not alone. Douglas Jerrold, later an established author and publisher, found the officers in the reconstituted Hawke Battalion as diverse and original as those in the Hood, including Vere Harmsworth, the son of Lord North-cliffe, and A. P. Herbert, a humorist and columnist in *Punch* who later became the last independent MP for Oxford University and author of the powerful novel about Gallipoli, *The Secret Battle*.

A diversity of equal measure was found among the rank and file, where life proved to be a great melting pot in which the innocent, such as Private Harry Baker of the Chatham Battalion RMLI, met the very knowing:

> Bob Waldren was a huge miner and he used to go out and get solidly tight. I was in the second bed in the barrack room and when Bob came in drunk or semi-drunk he always insisted in kissing me goodnight. He said I looked like his son. I probably did but he used to say: 'Goodnight Baker boy, I love you.' Of course I had to put up with him. I didn't mind.[12] (Private Harry Baker)

When these men met their officers, as A. P. Herbert discovered with his platoon, even the most basic form of communication was sometimes difficult. 'They were all Tynesiders, and most of them were miners. At first I understood little of what they said, and they did not understand much of me: and there were two good fellows, from some Durham valley, whom *nobody* understood. They might have been foreigners.'[13]

With the exception of the three reconstituted battalions, the infantry of the RND began to move to a new camp at Blandford at the end of 1914 and had all concentrated there by 28 January 1915, the day on which the attempt to force the Dardanelles using ships alone was finally sanctioned. The orders for two battalions of Royal Marines to begin preparations to go out to the eastern Mediterranean were issued on the following day and the Plymouth and Chatham Battalions were selected. Within days, general rumours began to circulate of the possibility of operations at the Dardanelles and Ordinary Seaman Joe Murray even received a letter from his parents addressed, '"Hood Battalion, 2nd Naval Brigade, care of Constantinople Expeditionary Force" . . . but it was supposed to be secret!'[14] Given this serious breach of security, it was ironic that when the Hood Battalion did leave on 28 February its departure was made with belated secrecy.

> We had lots of friends in Blandford. But instead of going to Blandford Station, we were marched across the Downs. . . . We missed all our people. All our friends who were waiting at Blandford to see the lads off. We didn't see anybody. You see it was a secret army – but we knew where we were going![15]
> (Ordinary Seaman Joe Murray)

After embarkation the division's transports proved to be very crowded and the strangeness of being on board ship also created problems. But these discomforts were leavened by the naturally high spirits of both the officers and the men. For the officers, classically educated and highly literate, their wit often focused on the romantic and historical associations of their journey, while for the other ranks the humour was usually more closely related to their immediate environment, and some of the older men were clearly glad of the opportunity to bring out their equally old jokes for a fresh audience. 'One of our fellows – Collier – he was an ex-merchant seaman, and he'd get in the hammock with his feet sticking out and he'd shout: "Land Ahoy." It was his dirty great feet he was looking at!'[16]

By the beginning of April the French Division under General d'Amade had also arrived in Egypt from Mudros and three days after visiting the RND Hamilton attended a colourful parade of the CEO. Finally, on 6 April, he saw the 29th Division and after his inspection concluded that 'if we don't win, I won't be able to put it on the men'.[17] The 29th Division was regarded by Hamilton as a '*division de luxe*'[18] and his '*pièce de résistance*'.[19] It was the last of three divisions formed in Britain from regular army battalions which had been serving overseas on the outbreak of war, and despite also including a number of territorial units it retained its regular character, forming a sharp contrast with the RND. This character was based upon a fierce regimental loyalty and a strongly developed sense of competition and rivalry. The commonest vehicle used to encourage this was sport and in the division's battalions there were a number of distinguished sportsmen who had won championships in India, particularly at the Delhi Durbar military tournament in 1911.

The division was formed in the West Midlands in January 1915 and after being overseas for many years the regulars were determined to make the most of the opportunities which their clearly brief spell in Britain offered. Both officers and men sought out their favourite recreations. Many of the officers went shooting or hunting and the ordinary soldiers also took up the hunt. But their quarry lay closer to home, the local girls. Captain Aubrey Williams, the Adjutant of the 2nd South Wales Borderers (SWB), noticed that 'a number of Coventry girls found their husbands from members of the Regiment'.[20] Lieutenant Douglas Talbot, a subaltern in the 1st Lancashire Fusiliers, looked a few months further into the future. 'Our men are having the time of their lives in the billets; the whole place swarms with very pretty hat factory girls, not bad looking either. I should think that in 9 months time there should be the makings of a new army in Nuneaton alone.'[21] Such a prospect filled the chaplains of the division with alarm, and on 31 January the Reverend Oswin Creighton, chaplain to the 86th Brigade, warned the 2nd Royal Fusiliers of the dangers:

I said that the women and girls were having a very difficult time during the war. They had never had military in the place before, and were naturally very excited, and thought a lot of the soldiers who had just come from India and were going so soon to the front. I asked the men to do all they could to help the girls, so that the memory they left behind them should always be of the good they had during their stay.[22] (Reverend Oswin Creighton)

Once again the soldiers saw things in a different light. Private Robert Bird, who was a wartime volunteer serving in the 147th Brigade, Royal Field Artillery (RFA), noticed something about the regular soldiers in his unit which might have made the chaplains more concerned for the physical, rather than the moral, health of the girls:

Nearly all them men who came from India had gonorrhea and things like that. Nearly all of them suffered with it or were in trouble, some worse than others. I always steered clear of them. Coming from India that's how they used to go on I believe. We had short arm inspections periodically to see that they weren't a menace to us in any way.[23] (Private Robert Bird)

On 12 March Major General Aylmer Hunter Weston was appointed to command the division. As a brigade commander during the autumn of 1914 Hunter Weston had already shown that he was energetic and personally brave; little daunted by unpromising situations, he attacked them with verve and determination. For a new division about to set off on an unexpected campaign he seemed to be an ideal choice. Beginning three days later the last of the pre-war regular British Army began to make their way to Avonmout o begin their journey to the eastern Mediterranean. Unfortunately, like the RND, the 29th Division did not embark in the expectation of an immediate landing. Inexplicably, units were separated and men detached from their equipment, making the facilities of Egypt just as necessary for them as for the rest of the force.

Once the MEF had arrived in Egypt, the individual units were then reorganized and allocated to transports. The process of re-embarkation began on 4 April and for the next fortnight a steady succession of transports left Egypt for the Aegean. It also became important for GHQ to return to Mudros to finalize arrangements with De Robeck's staff, and on 8 April they also set sail once again. Having arrived from Britain only on 1 April, the Adjutant General's and Quartermaster General's Branches remained behind in Egypt. On the day before he prepared to leave, Hamilton, who had received no response to his request for the Indian brigade, reminded Maxwell about it and received a reply as he was sailing out of Alexandria harbour. Maxwell promised he would do his best but hoped he might receive some naval seaplanes in return.

GHQ arrived back at Mudros on 10 April and almost immediately Hamilton and his senior commanders went on board the *Queen Elizabeth* for a conference with De Robeck. The plan that had been drawn up over the past weeks was formally adopted and it was agreed that three seaplanes would be sent to Egypt to smooth the way for the addition of the Indian brigade. Over the next two days the joint naval and military staffs discussed the precise details of the landing and on 13 April GHQ issued its first specific orders. The initial objective for the 29th Division was the ridge of high ground running through the hill of Achi Baba, six miles inland from Cape Helles, and for ANZAC a similar ridge of ground running through the hill of Mal Tepe, about five miles to the east of the beach on which they were to land to the north of Gaba Tepe.

Four important amendments to the original plan, which were eventually incorporated into the overall scheme, originated in the discussions between 10 and 12 April. First, in order to speed up the landing of the first wave of troops, it was decided to land the covering forces not from their transports but from warships, into which they would be transferred on the eve of the landing. Second, Commander Edward Unwin RN further suggested that the number of men landed at Helles in the first wave could be doubled by running aground a specially adapted ship filled with soldiers who would then disembark quickly from its holds on to the beach. The idea was adopted as part of the landing on the beach to the west of Sedd el Bahr and, under Unwin's command, a collier named the *River Clyde* was selected for the task. It was also proposed that a similar ship should be employed at Gaba Tepe. But as the plan there was based on a wide landing along a single beach the idea was not seen to offer any great advantage and what little it did appeared to be outweighed by the risk of the ship being sunk by gunfire from Gaba Tepe. The *River Clyde* was to be run aground on the beach and driven by her momentum as far inland as possible. But to bridge any remaining gap a steam hopper and three lighters were also to be towed alongside her. The troops were to disembark through four large doors, cut into both sides of the ship, on to a gangway which ran to the bows. As many soldiers subsequently observed, it was a modern Trojan horse.

Thirdly, instead of keeping the French Division standing idle while the 29th Division landed, one infantry regiment and an artillery battery were to be landed near Kum Kale to prevent the Turkish guns there from firing into the backs of the British at Sedd el Bahr and further to confuse the Turks by making a third landing. However, the landing was only to be temporary and once the British were firmly established inland from Sedd el Bahr the French troops were to be re-embarked and landed at Helles as originally planned. While the landing was in progress the remaining French transports were to appear off the coast of Besika Bay opposite Tenedos and carry out a feint landing there, similar to that which was to be made at Bulair by the RND. With the fire across the Dardanelles silenced by the Kum Kale landing it was also felt that a landing could now be made just inside the entrance of the Dardanelles in Morto Bay and three of the SWB's four companies were detailed to land there in the far northeastern corner near Eski Hissarlik Point.

The final addition was a proposal put forward by Hamilton himself for an additional landing along the Aegean coast at Helles which would be carried out under his personal command. His intention was to land a small force at a difficult, and therefore unexpected, site between the Turks' main defences at Cape Helles and their reserve positions behind the village of Krithia, which lay four miles inland from there on the lower slopes of Achi Baba, in order to threaten communications between these two points and harass their retreat in the face of the main British landing. A landing site was chosen along the coast to the west of Krithia, where there was a slight break in the steep cliffs caused by two nullahs, or dry water courses, running down the face of the cliffs to sea level which would hopefully be climbable. The Plymouth Battalion was selected on the grounds of its experience on 4 March and attached to the 29th Division to make the initial landing supported by the 1st King's Own Scottish Borderers (KOSB); this order was subsequently reversed, the KOSB landing first with the Plymouths in support. As the size of the force, later further increased by the addition of the SWB's fourth company, was considerably larger than the one first envisaged by Hamilton it was removed from his direct command and placed instead under the orders of the 29th Division. Landings were now to be carried out on five beaches at Helles, positioned round the tip of the peninsula from Morto Bay to a point due west of Krithia, and they were lettered respectively S, V, W, X and Y. At Gaba Tepe one broad beach was to be used and, in line with the beaches at Helles, this was lettered Z.

During GHQ's absence in Egypt the naval arrangements for supporting the landing had also been drawn up. Since 18 March the four battleships brought out from Britain by Thursby had joined the EMS, together with two cruisers which had been based since February on the Suez Canal, bringing its principal strength to eighteen battleships, twelve cruisers and twenty-nine destroyers. For the landings the fleet was divided into seven squadrons. The strongest and most important of these were to support the two main landings, with the 1st Squadron under the command of Wemyss responsible for the landing at Helles and the 2nd Squadron under Thursby the landing at Gaba Tepe. Within these squadrons the ships were further divided into two groups. Covering ships were to provide overall covering fire for the landings, both beforehand and as the troops established themselves on shore, while attendant ships were to land the covering forces and then provide logistical support for the landings until the whole force was ashore. Once the first troops had landed, the attendant ships would also be available to supplement the fire of the covering ships. Plans were also drawn up for a renewed naval attack on the Inner Defences of the Dardanelles once the MEF had driven the Turks back to the Kilid Bahr Plateau. With this eventuality in mind, during the first weeks in April the mine-sweeping operations were maintained and warships made regular patrols along the coast and into the Dardanelles to harass the Turkish defences.

The reorganized transports started to arrive back in the Aegean towards the end of the first week of April. On 11 April, after learning about the possibility of a further French division being added to the strength of the MEF, Hamilton informed Kitchener that only the 29th Division and the two divisions of ANZAC would be able to be accommodated at Mudros and the RND and the 1st French Division would have to go instead to Trebuki Bay, another natural harbour on the island of Skyros, eighty miles to the southwest of Lemnos. One of the 29th Division's last transports to leave Egypt was the SS *Manitou*. At 10.00 on 16 April she was approached and ordered to stop by a Turkish torpedo boat which had left the port of Smyrna and evaded the British blockade. The captain of the torpedo boat told the captain of the *Manitou* that he had three minutes to abandon ship before he torpedoed her. 'One wag shouted out: "Make it ten, Governor," to which the reply was shouted back: "All right, make it ten."'[24] All the boats were lowered and the order given to clear the ship. Despite the lack of immediate threat the troops on board began to panic. Many were not wearing lifebelts and further problems occurred once the crew started to lower the lifeboats.

> In their anxiety they didn't do it properly. We got them hung out. We got half way down the side of the ship and it dumped us all out, the whole damn lot, and the boat turned turtle. Blokes started chucking hatch covers over the side and they killed two or three of our men. The lifebelt saved me, I swallowed pints of sea water, pints. . . . I just paddled about and in no time I was picked up.[25] (Private Robert Bird)

After closing on the transport and waiting for the allotted time the captain of the torpedo boat fired three torpedoes, all of which missed. The 'officer was so excited he had got such a target that he got too close to us. You see when you fire a torpedo they drop and come up again – these all went under the boat.'[26] A wireless distress call had been sent out immediately by the *Manitou* and once the third torpedo had been fired two British destroyers appeared in the distance steaming towards the scene at full speed, forcing the torpedo boat to flee. Eventually it ran aground on the island of

Chios. It had been a tragic incident, with '51 deaths from exposure and drowning'.[27]

Once at Mudros the senior officers of the 29th Division and ANZAC embarked on regular inspections of the coastline and from their observations it became clear that over the past weeks the Turks had been busy developing their defences. On 24 March Enver Pasha had appointed General Liman von Sanders, who held the temporary Turkish rank of Marshal, to the command of the newly formed Fifth Army, responsible for the defence of the Dardanelles and the surrounding region. The appointment of Liman von Sanders on this day gave him exactly the same length of time to prepare the peninsula's defences as Hamilton had to prepare his invasion. Liman von Sanders arrived at the town of Gallipoli, a short distance to the south of Bulair on the edge of the Sea of Marmara, on 26 March and immediately began a reorganization. At that time his force was roughly equal to the MEF, but, unlike Hamilton, over the ensuing weeks he received a steady influx of reinforcements so that by the start of May the size of the Turkish force had significantly increased. On his arrival the troops defending the peninsula were scattered thinly around the coastline. His first decision was to concentrate them into three zones and improve communications between each of these so that troops could move more easily between them. Of the divisions at his disposal he placed two in the northernmost zone, with one beyond Bulair on the European mainland and another around Bulair itself, and, from the beginning of April, two more on the Asiatic shore between Kum Kale and Besika Bay in the southernmost zone. The remaining central zone, which spanned the whole of the southwestern half of the peninsula, he decided to hold with only the 9th Division, concentrating the final 19th Division in reserve at Boghali to the north of Maidos.

The 9th Division's zone was further subdivided into a northern sector running from Aghyl Dere to a point called Semerly Tepe, just over a mile to the south of Gaba Tepe, and a southern sector reaching from Semerly Tepe to Cape Helles. Of the division's three regiments, each of which contained three battalions, the 27th Regiment was set to defend the northern sector, the 26th Regiment the southern sector and the 25th Regiment was placed in divisional reserve at Serafim Farm on the edge of the Kilid Bahr Plateau. Liman von Sanders's arrival and his emphasis on mobility reinvigorated the Turkish defences and, despite persistent harassment by the British fleet, the Turks used every night to build stronger and deeper positions facing the possible landing sites. The results of these nocturnal labours were visible every morning in new banks of barbed wire and freshly dug trenches. With each new day the difficulty of the task confronting the MEF increased, along with the apparent impregnability of the peninsula.

Yet the sight of the burgeoning defences did little to diminish the confidence of the General Staff in the ultimate success of the landing. The failure of Hamilton and the key members of his staff who planned the landing to recognize the likely tenacity of the Turkish defence of the peninsula stands as one of the sharpest indictments of the conduct of the campaign. The roots of this failure lay in their military background with its belief in the ability of a well-trained, modern army to overwhelm superior numbers of inferior native troops almost by will power and innate racial superiority. When combined with the abysmal Turkish military record both in the years immediately preceding the war and in the months since its outbreak this attitude appears to have convinced them that the Turks would be easily driven back from the defences of the beaches. But a hint of the true state of the Turks' abilities was given less than a week before the landing in a telegram from Kitchener which reported the 'good discipline and determination of the Turkish troops'[28] in recent fighting in Mesopotamia.

The troops were to be landed from tows of rowing boats pulled by either a steam pinnace or picket boat and at both Mudros and Trebuki, whenever possible, the British troops practised disembarking into their tows and landing from them on the shore. At first the novelty of these rehearsals and the welcome exercise that they offered after the containment of the transports kept spirits high. But the capricious weather regularly disrupted them and created long periods of boredom. As the days passed an initial sense of fun gradually changed to one of frustration, and an air of depression spread among many members of the force, including Creighton. 'My present feeling is that the whole thing has been bungled. The

Navy should never have started the bombardment without the Army. Now there has been no bombardment for some weeks. Meanwhile the Turks, under German direction, have perfected their defences.'[29]

The strain also took its toll among some of the commanding officers of the 29th Division. On 18 April Brigadier General Steuart Hare, in command of the 86th Brigade, noted that Lieutenant Colonel Henry Newenham of the Royal Fusiliers had 'been seedy for a day or two with a slight heart attack, brought on I believe by doing physical drill before breakfast with the rest of his officers'.[30] On the following day he recorded that Lieutenant Colonel Harold Ormond of the Lancashire Fusiliers was 'going off his head or having a nervous breakdown'[31] and on 20 April he took Ormond to see Hunter Weston, 'reporting that I do not consider him in a fit state to command. After about an hour's talk G.O.C. succeeded in persuading him to ask to be sent home sick. It will be the making of the battalion.'[32] It was a sad end to a lifetime's career on the eve of leading his regiment into battle.

On 19 April all the senior naval and military commanders, of the British, French and Anzac forces, convened once again in the *Queen Elizabeth* and completed the outstanding details of the landing. No decision had yet been reached about whether it should begin before first light under cover of darkness or after dawn in full daylight preceded by a concentrated naval bombardment to compensate for the loss of surprise. Hamilton and Birdwood both preferred a landing in the dark. But Hunter Weston disagreed and was afraid that a night operation might become confused. In this he was partly supported by De Robeck, who felt that it would be more difficult for the navy to carry out the landing in the dark and almost impossible at Helles, which involved landing troops on a number of small beaches spread around a rocky shoreline swept by the strong current of the Dardanelles. A compromise was reached. At Gaba Tepe, along the straight, sandy shore, the covering force would land before first light. But at Helles the landing would not begin until after dawn and be preceded by a thirty-minute bombardment. The one exception to this would be the landing at Y Beach, which would begin shortly before the bombardment.

The other important decision reached by the conference was

the date on which the operation was to begin. Thursby and the 2nd Squadron were ready to begin at Gaba Tepe immediately. But, largely due to a shortage of boats, Wemyss and the 1st Squadron would not be ready for another four days. Consequently St George's Day, 23 April, was chosen and, as it would take two days to prepare the ships and distribute the troops among them, the preliminary stages were ordered to begin on 21 April. Following the agreement of these details GHQ issued a revised order for the landing which also incorporated all the changes that had been made since 13 April.

On 20 April, although the weather was fine, a strong wind developed and by the following morning, when the timetable for the preparations was set to commence, it had worsened into rain and gale-force winds. As it was impossible to carry out the landing under these conditions, the timetable was delayed for twenty-four hours. On 22 April a second twenty-four-hour delay was necessary and it was not until 23 April, the day on which it had first been intended to land, that the wind finally dropped and the ships began to disperse to their destinations for the landing.

The first to leave was the *River Clyde*, which set off at 13.00 for the north side of Tenedos, where, on the following day, the transports holding the Helles covering force were due to rendez-vous with their attendant ships to transfer their troops. Later in the afternoon the first three transports of the 29th Division also began to make their way through the crowded harbour towards the open sea and just before dark the warships of the 1st Squadron, including the three attendant ships, the cruiser HMS *Euryalus*, the battleships HMS *Implacable* and the *Cornwallis*, followed suit. Some of the transports had been painted with names and slogans, such as 'Turkish Delight' and 'To Constantinople and the Harems', and, as they passed through the harbour, bands played popular tunes including 'Tipperary' and the 'British Grenadiers'. As the ships moved towards the harbour's entrance, cheering broke out from those who remained behind, causing ripples of energy to rebound across the water, and the scene became highly emotional. But on the transports Captain Guy Geddes, an officer in the 1st Royal Munster Fusiliers, felt that the mood remained sombre: 'What struck me most forcibly was the demeanour of our own men, from whom, not a sound, and this from the light hearted, devil may care men from the South of Ireland. Even they were filled with a sense of something impending which was quite beyond their ken.'[33]

The following day the exodus continued. Starting soon after dawn, at regular intervals the transports holding the main body of the 1st Australian Division moved to the northern coast of Lemnos, where they were to remain until early evening before taking up their position in support of the Gaba Tepe covering force. Around midday the reorganization of the latter began. Destroyers approached the 3rd Australian Brigade's transports and transferred the 500 men from each of the three battalions who were to land in the first wave of tows to the attendant battleships which were to carry them to the landing, embarking the men of the 9th Battalion in HMS *Queen*, the 10th Battalion in HMS *Prince of Wales* and the 11th Battalion in HMS *London*. In due course, the 2nd Squadron, including these ships, also began to leave the harbour, headed by the *Queen Elizabeth*, into which Hamilton and selected members of his staff had embarked. Behind them came the four transports holding the remainder of the 3rd Brigade. The destination of all these ships was the northern coast of Imbros, where they were to rendezvous to transfer the remainder of the covering force into seven destroyers, which were to follow up the first wave of tows.

Once the last of the 1st Australian Division's transports had left, the main body of the 29th Division also started to leave for the outer anchorage at Helles three miles off the coast. While they were leaving, the KOSB and one company of SWB were transferred to the two cruisers, HMS *Amethyst* and HMS *Sapphire*, from which they were to land at Y Beach. Unlike the other troops at Helles, they were to proceed to their landing direct from Mudros together with the Plymouth Battalion's transport and rendezvous with the Y Beach covering ship, the battleship HMS *Goliath*, four miles due west of the beach. After their departure only the NZ&A Division, not due to leave until after midnight, remained together with the last remnants of the 29th Division, including the infantry battalions' transports and the chaplains, who were to leave only after the landings had started and did not expect to go ashore until the division had advanced a considerable distance inland. Among these last troops was Creighton, and the inspiring sight of the exodus over the past two days had restored his faith in the campaign: 'I feel a little more hopeful now. Everything possible seems to have been done, and the victory surely will be ours if it is for the good of the world that it should be.'[34]

The Helles covering force and the 1st Squadron spent 24 April in the harbour at Tenedos preparing for their landing. It had been intended to start the reorganization of the troops there as soon as the ships arrived from Mudros. But a strong wind delayed the process until late afternoon. Once the weather had calmed, the various battalions were transferred from their transports to the attendant ships, the *River Clyde* and the fleet sweeper which was to land the 1st Royal Dublin Fusiliers at V Beach. Once the transfer was complete the boats for the tows were collected alongside each of the ships and shortly after 21.30 the ships started to leave Tenedos for Cape Helles. Conditions on the warships were crowded, but congenial. The soldiers were well fed and looked after by the sailors in their various messes and the officers were offered the same hospitality in the wardroom. In the *Euryalus* Fleet Surgeon Thomas Jeans RN felt that the Lancashire Fusiliers were deservedly well treated:

> If their officers did not have the best dinner they had had since leaving England it was not our fault, and the crew did their best to entertain the men on the lower-deck. The younger officers gathered round the ward-room piano and started a sing-song. They begged for just one more song at eleven o'clock and sang 'John Peel', many of them singing for the last time; and then we made them as comfortable as possible for the night, while the whole expedition steamed slowly across to the mouth of the Dardanelles.[35] (Fleet Surgeon Thomas Jeans RN)

At Imbros, between 23.00 and midnight, the remaining Australian soldiers of the 3rd Brigade transferred to the destroyers, from which they were due to land in the second wave of the covering force. On the transports leaving Mudros conditions had been relaxed and Corporal Thomas Louch of the 11th Battalion told his mother that it was 'splendid to see how quietly everyone is taking things. In a few hours we shall be right in the thick of things, yet everybody is cheerful – some playing cards, others singing ragtime, a few like myself writing – you would think there was no war within miles. When we get to the Golden Horn you can expect to get a letter; but now there seems little to say.'[36] Once in the destroyers, conditions were less comfortable and one of the 11th Battalion's officers, Captain Dixon Hearder, in HMS *Chelmer* remembered being 'packed all ranks on the decks, like sardines, it was impossible to shift the position of your legs without affecting two or three other men. The sailors were A 1, and twice passed round hot coffee and hot chocolate, every man of course carried his own mess tin and helped himself.'[37] The transports holding the main body of the 1st Australian Division left the northern shore of Lemnos after dark and steamed into position behind the covering force. On the *Derfflinger*, a German prize ship that was being used as a transport, the 3rd Battalion was addressed by its commanding officer. To Private Henry Blaskett his words were anything but rousing: 'The colonel told us that we were going into action and that our job was to support the 3rd Brigade who would be ahead of us and who would make the initial landing. He said: "God Bless you all, boys. There won't be many of you alive by this time tomorrow night," which didn't cheer us up very much.'[38]

Shortly after midnight the ships of the 2nd Squadron hove to, but did not anchor, about five miles off Gaba Tepe. It was a very bright, moonlit sky and the outline of the coast was clearly visible. The squadron's boats were lowered and taken to the attendant ships. Twelve tows were to be formed, each one composed of a steam boat and three pulling boats, numbered according to their position in the line with No. 1 Tow on the southern flank and No. 12 on the northern. Four tows were drawn up alongside each attendant ship and a soldier of 'C' Company of the 11th Battalion, unfortunately anonymous, described the scene in the *London* as they embarked:

> At 12.30 A.M. we were awakened from our last peaceful slumber and ordered to fall in on the quarter deck, where in marked squares our platoons fell in in perfect order and silence. Then we filed down, two and three abreast, the long wooden ladders into the cutters lying alongside, manned by three blue jackets to each cutter. This was carried out in wonderful precision and silence,

each warship unloading its two companies of men at the same time.[39] (Anonymous Soldier of 'C' Company)

Private Walter Stagles, embarking from the same ship, remembered that 'as we went over the side each man was given a tot of rum'.[40]

At Helles when the 1st Squadron began to approach its rendezvous three miles off the coast at around 03.00, the soldiers were roused and provided with breakfast. While they ate, the tows were brought alongside and shortly after 04.00 the soldiers began to embark. Captain Richard Willis of the Lancashire Fusiliers felt that 'it was a tight fit to get the men in, cumbered as they were with eighty pounds weight of kit each. But it was done without a sound.'[41] Once full, the boats formed up into line and slowly started to head in towards the shore. The concentrated weight in each small boat of around seven sailors and twenty-eight to thirty soldiers each carrying an average of over 80lb made them extremely unstable. 'The sea was like glass, but as the piquet boats drew off to get in formation, our boats heeled over dangerously, and one of the men remarked to the cox, "I 'listed to get killed, not to get drowned." I expect he got what he 'listed for, poor chap!'[42] By this time it was well after first light and from the *River Clyde* the outline of the coast was just discernible two miles away. Geddes noticed that it was 'a beautiful morning'.[43] In fact, he felt, 'the day was as perfect as a day could be'.[44]

3

The Landing

The ANZAC covering force, the 3rd Australian Brigade under Colonel Ewen Sinclair-MacLagan, was to land to the north of Gaba Tepe before dawn in two waves and, maintaining as wide a front as possible, advance rapidly inland as far as Gun Ridge, with its left flank reaching north to beyond Battleship Hill. The 11th Battalion was to land on the left, the 10th Battalion in the centre and the 9th Battalion on the right, with the 12th Battalion in reserve. Although the military orders stated only that the landing would be 'between Gaba Tepe and Fisherman's Hut',[1] the naval orders were more specific. The boats landing from the *Queen* on the southernmost flank were 'to land on the beach about 1 mile North of Kaba Tepe', those from the *Prince of Wales* 'four cables North of "Queen"' and those from the *London* 'four cables North of "Prince of Wales"'.[2] The twelve individual tows, taking their station from No. 1 Tow on the southern flank, were to be distanced 'approximately 150 yards'[3] apart, creating a total frontage of 1,650 yards.

The transfer of the first wave of the 3rd Brigade into its tows was complete by 02.35. But the ships could not begin their approach of the coast until the bright, clear moon, which still lit up the sky, had set. Originally, when Lieutenant General Birdwood had proposed landing under cover of darkness, it had been hoped that the moon would set earlier and, had the landing taken place on 23 April as initially intended, by 02.30 it would already have done so. But on the morning of 25 April moonset was not until 02.57, leaving barely an hour of complete darkness before first light around 04.00. The moon finally disappeared at around 03.00 and almost immediately the line of battleships, trailing the strings of boats, proceeded at 5 knots towards the land. As they did so the last of the steamboats moved alongside to pick up their tows. When

Midshipman J. Savill Metcalf RNR approached the *Queen* to pick up No. 2 Tow he found No. 1 Tow still in position and, after being told to lie off and wait, was not called back until 03.20:

> It was very dark by this time. My sternsheetmen secured the towing rope of the pulling boats to our towing slip, and I eased the boats away from the *Queen*'s side. *Queen* was moving slowly eastwards all this time, and my engines were going slow ahead to keep abreast of her. I took station, with the troop-filled boats in tow, about fifty yards south of *Queen*'s bridge, and could just see No. 1 Tow about fifty yards south of me, on the beam.[4] (Midshipman J. Savill Metcalf RNR)

Soon after this the battleships stopped their engines but did not anchor. After drifting forward for ten minutes under the momentum they had built up, at 03.30, when around two and a half miles from the coast, orders were shouted by megaphone from the ships for the tows to go ahead. The landing had begun.

Straightaway it started to go awry. Although the opaqueness of the night prevented the Turks from observing the ships off the coastline, it also made it impossible for the tows to distance themselves 150 yards apart; if they had done this, they would immediately have lost sight of one another. Instead they took up stations only 50 yards apart and were able to maintain this distance only by following the phosphorescent bow waves made by the steam boats at the head of each tow. From an expected length of over 1600 yards, the line of tows was reduced to less than 600 yards, instantly throwing out the calculations on which the landing had been based.

Shortly after this, an event of even greater significance occurred which resulted in the tows landing a considerable distance further to the north than specified in the naval orders. Forced together in a greatly reduced and much confused line, all the boats eventually landed around the point of Ari Burnu, with none beaching south of Hell Spit. The subsequent official explanation,[5] was that the current off the beach drew the whole line to the north as it headed in along its correct eastward course. Yet this explanation remains unconvincing. It is difficult to understand why the still conditions which prevailed should have produced a current off Gaba Tepe of greater strength than the normal north-north-westerly flow of 4 knots[6] which would have been insufficient to move the tows the distance it suggests. The first plausible explanation, which did not emerge for sixty years,[7] showed that the northward movement of the tows in fact resulted from the misplaced initiative of one particular midshipman and his failure to obey without question given orders, a combination of human failings that appears much more convincing than the intervention of an uncharted current.

As a result of his observations of Gaba Tepe from the foretop of the battleship HMS *Triumph*, Metcalf later explained that he deliberately moved No. 2 Tow, and consequently the course of the whole line, to the north to avoid the devastating enfilade fire from Gaba Tepe which he believed would engulf the southern flank as it drew level with the promontory. While reading Metcalf's account, it is worth remembering that, unlike many of the other midshipmen commanding tows in the line who until the outbreak of war had been schoolboys in their first year at the Royal Naval College, Dartmouth learning the exact discipline of naval officers, Metcalf was a member of the Royal Naval Reserve and a career Merchant Navy officer aged nineteen who had been at sea since 1910. The initiative and confidence he displayed in his actions are perhaps a little more understandable in this light.

About 3.40 a.m. the order was called from *Queen*'s bridge 'Go ahead picket boat.' I warned my engineroom 'Stand by for full speed,' and watched No. 1 Tow for the first sign of her increase in speed but could not see any. An angry hail came from *Queen*'s bridge, 'Will you go ahead, picket boat.' Realizing that it was imperative, and I might be accused of cowardice if I did not comply, I rang full speed ahead on the engine room bell, and away we went. A few minutes later I looked astern and could just see No. 1 Tow off my starboard quarter. I was too occupied looking ahead to look astern again, as it was very dark and I had no idea how far we were from rocks or sand. About a quarter of an hour later I realized we were heading very close to the north side of Gaba Tepe which, because of its height, is very conspicuous. Knowing that there were Turkish troops there, and we would get an enfilading fire all along the starboard side as well as from ahead, I was confident that we must be heading for a wrong place. There was no one to consult and I felt the lives of the men I was towing were my responsibility. Without any delay I altered course two points to port to get away from Gaba Tepe. After a quarter of an hour, finding that the tows to port of me had conformed, I again altered course a point and a half to port.[8] (Midshipman J. Savill Metcalf RNR)

Metcalf's first change of course of two points, equivalent to 22.5 degrees,[9] was made when the tows were still a considerable distance from the beach, just as the first signs of light were becoming apparent above the land. It was noted without comment in the journals of at least two other midshipmen in the line. Yet there was no reason why the change of course would have appeared unusual, as the orders issued to the midshipmen specifically stated that 'the flotilla must be prepared to alter course up to four points to port or starboard'.[10]

Metcalf's movement isolated No. 1 Tow on the southern flank which should have been acting as guide to the whole line. The Guide Officer in No. 1 Tow was Lieutenant Commander John Waterlow RN, who since the middle of March had been engaged with the mine-sweeping operations inside the Dardanelles and was entirely unfamiliar with the coastline around Gaba Tepe. The account of the landing which he recorded in his diary corroborated that given by Metcalf:

All the other 11 steamboats were to keep station on me, and we started off about 2 points on the starboard bow of 'Queen', trying to make Gaba Tepe. It was now so dark we could see but little, but . . . it did seem as if a prominent headland, such as I had been given to understand Gaba Tepe was, loomed ahead of us, so we went gaily on. As we approached the shore it became clear that there was a very prominent headland to the northward of us and we began to vacillate – our faith in our course was more shaken by the fact that all other boats were steering more to the northward. At last I altered course to the northward also and steered for the high land we could clearly see. We had to assume that the 'Queen' was in her correct billet, and working on that assumption this prominent headland *could not be* Gaba Tepe. So my uncertainty increased – but still the boats steered to the northward. At last I altered course and went down the line astern trying to draw them to the southward with me. This failed, and I was now convinced that my prominent headland was not Gaba Tepe. It was too high, and also on its summit there was not visible the ruined building which surmounts Gaba Tepe. I then tried to urge the boats to the northward where a good beach was visible – then again to the southward, but efforts in every direction failed. . . . The dawn began to glow and our prominent headland loomed larger and larger against the pale saffron light – the *one* place on the whole coast on which we would have decided *not* to land. However, we were approaching the shore and the dawn was growing so fast that at last in despair I dashed straight for the frowning cliffs now straight ahead.[11] (Lieutenant Commander John Waterlow RN)

Another factor previously held to have contributed to the disruption of the landing was its possible relocation, either deliberately or by mistake, in the hours immediately preceding it. Yet evidence to support this contention has always been extremely confusing. It is clear that the line of battleships from which the tows departed did not eventually anchor where expected, but to the north of this point.[12] A Turkish claim that a navigational buoy which marked the southern flank of the landing was moved on 24 April is unfounded as no buoy was used. The chances of an accidental error seem to be remote and no independent evidence has yet come to light that the landing was deliberately relocated to the north,[13] a move directly contradicted by 'official evidence'[14] that it was moved south on the previous evening. It is also hard to accept that a late change either to the north or to the south could have been made by Rear Admiral Thursby without consulting Birdwood, who by then had embarked in the *Queen*. But there is no hint of such a consultation in either Birdwood's or Thursby's official or private accounts of the night of the landing; Thursby actually claimed that the landing took place close to where he intended, 'a few hundred yards only to the north [of the] assigned position'.[15] From this contradictory and confusing evidence it remains uncertain whether any deliberate change was made and, if it was, in which direction it moved the battleships.

The question of where the landing was supposed to have been located is also overshadowed by the effect of Metcalf's misplaced initiative and the bunching of the tows in the darkness. Had the tows remained spaced 150 yards apart and all moved directly east from whatever starting point, the troops would have landed in their correct order, allowing them to advance inland to their objectives with only a minimum of added difficulty, as was eventually shown by those who landed from the destroyers. In the event by the time the tows were ready for release, the boats on the southern flank had been randomly shuffled. The precise order in which the companies of the 9th and 10th Battalions were intended to land on the beach had been completely destroyed and it is this disruption which remains the single most important factor in the spoiling of the landing's plan, rather than the insoluble question of where it was intended to take place. Once initiated, the resultant confusion continued throughout the day, preventing the successful implementation of the later stages of the plan and helping to shape the position which developed around Anzac Cove and endured with few changes for the remainder of the campaign. No contemporary investigation into these events appears to have been initiated, despite their importance. Perhaps this was because, in an ironic corroboration of Metcalf's instinctive reaction, over the following week as the strength of the fortifications along the beach immediately north of Gaba Tepe became apparent, the mistake which had carried the line away from them was frequently held to be providential.

By the time Metcalf's initial movement of two points to port had taken effect, light was beginning to break above the coastline and after the darkness of the past hour the first signs of the new day were quite distinct. Everything was silent and Private Frank Loud of the 9th Battalion remembered that 'it was rather a peculiar sensation steaming along slowly towards the shore expecting to hear the ping of a rifle every second. Each little movement in any of the boats could be distinctly heard & was quickly hushed.'[16] In the last few moments of the approach, Midshipman Eric Longley Cook RN in No. 5 Tow became aware of a sound from the land. 'As we approached the shore one was amazed that there was no opposition and the first sound that I heard was a bird singing its pre-dawn song. Less than a minute after that we were fired upon.'[17]

Having taken the lead in moving the tows to the north Metcalf inevitably found himself slightly ahead of the rest of the line and was able to release his boats, which held part of the 9th Battalion, before the firing began; a party of the 9th Battalion was later recognized as the first to land, shortly before 04.30, able to reach the shore and take off their packs before coming under fire.[18] But Metcalf was unable to take advantage of his position and open fire on the Turks with his picket boat's Maxim gun because the steam boats had been ordered not to open fire until the gun in No. 3 Tow had signalled that it was safe to do so by opening fire itself.

> There was a bright flare ashore. My Coxswain said, 'I think we're close enough, Sir.' I stopped engines and gave the order 'Slip the tow rope,' and turned to port to give the pulling boats clear water to run on to the beach. I was fascinated by seeing some Turkish troops running along the top of the cliffs from the south, but I had not permission to open fire. No. 3 Tow was now ghosting in close on my port side. There was the sound of feet crunching on the shingle as the first of those brave AIF troops marched up the beach from the leading boat of my tow. I said to my Coxswain: 'Why doesn't No. 3 Tow give us the signal to open fire? Anyway they are ashore alright.' As we were getting away from the beach to go to the nearest destroyer No. 3 Tow gave a short burst of Maxim gun fire, and then everything seemed to open fire, Turks in front and battleships astern. I felt a bullet whizz close past me, then another, a third, and the Turk firing put one through my arm with the fourth. Almost immediately after, my Coxswain received a terrible wound, and the sternsheetmen helped him down to the after cabin whilst I steered and went alongside the nearest destroyer which had crept up behind us and was only a few cables from the beach.[19] (Midshipman J. Savill Metcalf RNR)

Among the first twenty to land, Loud was in the process of climbing out when the Turks opened fire:

> We got right inshore, the pinnace let go & swung around so as to use her machine-gun. As we were directly behind the pinnace

& our pinnace was slightly ahead of the other four, our boat was the first to ground & 8 or 10 were already on shore. I was standing on the seat aft when the first rifle shot was fired. It hit the thwarts just by my ankle. We waited for no more but made for the sides. I went to jump but tripped & hit the briny head first rifle, pack & full equipment. We only had our packs slung on our shoulders, so I quickly lost mine, leaving it in the water. On reaching the beach I quickly loaded & fitted the bayonet on my rifle while staggering across the 40 yards of sand. By that time there must have been at least 100 rifles cracking at us off the cliffs, also at least two machine-guns had opened a hot fire. Things seemed pretty lively and orders to form up in platoons on the beach were ignored & I think every man's only thought was to get to the top of that cliff.[20] (Private Frank Loud)

Behind the tows the destroyers had moved into position as the first troops were landing. Alongside each destroyer strings of lifeboats had been towed from Imbros and while the first wave was disembarking they were filled with men. When the steam boats returned from the beach, after bringing their empty boats alongside so that the remaining men could embark into them, they towed the already full lifeboats back to the beach. Lieutenant Commander Ralph Wilkinson RN, captain of HMS *Ribble*, brought in part of the 12th Battalion and took up a station around 600 yards north of Ari Burnu.

I had a man sounding in the bows; he had just reported 12 feet, & I had rung astern, when they opened fire on us from the cliffs at a range of about 300 yards. I was towing six boats alongside and before we could get them away I had 2 killed and 15 wounded on my decks. Among the latter was my poor sub, Stopford-Sackville, who was shot through the head. . . . I had a bullet through my sleeve and a couple between my legs as I was leaning against the searchlight. The ship's side was ringing from the bullets. The Australians were fine. I felt proud that I was a Briton. They pulled in singing a song 'Australia will be there'. A good many lost their rifles in their eagerness to jump out of the boats, and I could see them scaling the cliffs waving their sword bayonets, and hear them 'cooeeing' like mad. Unfortunately their discipline was poor as they in parties of threes and fours pursued Turks inland until they themselves were scuppered by the Enemy's reinforcements.[21] (Lieutenant Commander Ralph Wilkinson RN)

The *Chelmer* took up a station about 500 yards to the south of the *Ribble* and Thomas Louch embarked into one of her lifeboats. As one of the first to land from the destroyers at around 04.40, his boat was able to approach close to the shore before coming under fire from a Turkish machine gun.

> There were two Turks in the machine-gun nest, and our boat was almost to their direct front. It was not very light at the time, and I must have been very close to them. When they saw us, and other boats approaching, I watched them for a few seconds while they got their gun into action. They fired one or two short bursts, but fortunately not at us, and then the picket boat came in and silenced them. The two men were knocked over backwards, taking their gun with them. The gun crew evidently came from the tents behind them on Plugge's Plateau.[22] (Corporal Thomas Louch)

By the time the final troops from the destroyers were landing, in addition to rifle and machine-gun fire, they were also being hit by Turkish shrapnel fire, which in many cases caused considerable damage to the boats, even causing some to sink.

> We were told to jump overboard. We each had a pick and shovel and I was sharing a box of ammunition with my younger brother. The water was about five or six feet deep and of course we sank. We damned soon dropped the ammunition! Then we tried to wade ashore. I'm afraid I lost my pick, but I still carried the shovel and finally we got ashore.[23] (Private Andrew Kirk)

Once the soldiers of the first wave had landed and dropped their packs on the beach as ordered, despite the fact that it was still barely light and visibility on land was limited to a few hundred yards, it quickly became apparent that something had gone wrong. The men of the 11th Battalion, who had all landed together beyond Ari Burnu, instead of confronting the southern faces of MacLagan's Ridge and Plugge's Plateau found themselves beneath the more hostile, northern face of the plateau and the bleak escarpment of

61

Razor Edge. Most of the tows of the 10th and 9th Battalions had landed together south of Ari Burnu and become inextricably linked. Companies which should have landed in line found themselves dispersed, and platoons and sections became separated from their officers and NCOs. But the men had been firmly instructed that as the covering force they were to push inland as quickly and as determinedly as possible, and, despite what had happened, this they proceeded to do.

The second wave from the destroyers followed on quickly in the correct order and in many cases exacerbated the confusion. In the south the second half of the 9th Battalion moved off across the southern tip of Shrapnel Gully towards 400 Plateau and easily overtook the first half, which had landed from the tows. In the centre the 10th Battalion's second wave was initially slowed down by the more difficult ground of Plugge's Plateau and the jumbled mass of men from the tows. But, having landed in order, it was able to advance inland with greater cohesion, joining up with many men from the first wave. The companies of the 11th Battalion landed behind the companies from the tows and extended their battalion's line further north beneath the western face of Russell's Top and the Sphinx. However, it was the 12th Battalion, which had been dispersed among all seven of the destroyers, that suffered the greatest confusion in the second wave. Having been designated Brigade Reserve, the battalion was supposed to land in separate bodies which would then collect together to the west of 400 Plateau. But seeing the frantic efforts of others to pursue the Turks, as Wilkinson observed, many men of the 12th Battalion simply leapt off the beach and followed the first wave, instead of remaining behind and moving to their collecting point.

The first obstacle confronting the majority of the covering force was Plugge's Plateau. When he finally reached the beach, Louch found himself just beneath the northern face:

As instructed we shed our packs, lay down and awaited orders. Colonel Johnston, who had come in another boat, flopped down beside me and I asked him what we were to do. He said that we had landed in the wrong place, and there was no organization. A bullet spattered into the sand just clear of our noses, and I decided that the beach, where there was no cover, was no place for

dallying; so lugging our box of ammunition – my mate and I –
we climbed the hill in front. Half way up we stopped for breath
in a sandy washaway, and saw the first shell to be fired by the
Turkish battery near Gaba Tepe. . . . We then pushed on to the
top where there were some tents and a wounded Turk.[24] (Corporal Thomas Louch)

When the men reached the summit the scrub thickened and
confusion increased.

Although the Turks were not in evidence you could hear their
bullets cracking like stockwhips all around. A little further on I
reached another line of trenches & as we were about knock[ed]
up we formed a firing line in it after taking the then empty trench.
I am afraid then several of our chaps were shot by their own men
as they pushed on ahead. But of course there was such a mix up
you could not tell as the scrub was full of fleeing Turks & their
snipers were busy.[25] (Private Frank Loud)

After pausing briefly to reorganize, the confused units of the
9th and 10th Battalions set off towards their original objectives just
after 05.00. 400 Plateau could be seen 1,000 yards away to the
southeast and the ultimate objective of Gun Ridge lay just over a
mile beyond it. Moving down into the deep beds of Rest Gully,
Shrapnel Gully and Monash Valley, the men climbed on to the
northern face of 400 Plateau and disappeared into the scrub
beyond. In front of them the troops from the southern destroyers
were already well ahead, with a party of the 10th Battalion under
Lieutenant Noël Loutit having reached Owen's Gully and two
companies of the 9th Battalion the southern slopes of Bolton's
Ridge and Pine Ridge. The Australians' initiative was, on the
whole, commendable; but it eventually led a considerable body of
men to push on too far, too fast. As a result their positions were
unknown and they quickly became isolated. This lack of co-
ordination in the covering force's advance significantly added to the
difficulties of the landing.

To the north of Ari Burnu there was even greater confusion.
The Turkish small-arms fire along the coast there was much fiercer
and hampered attempts to advance up the steep cliffs towards the

northern objective of Battleship Hill. The 12th Battalion's commanding officer, Lieutenant Colonel Lancelot Clarke, led one party up the precipitous cliffs below the Sphinx on to Russell's Top, while another party under Captain Eric Tulloch began to work its way towards the same point along Walker's Ridge. The combined weight of this uncoordinated assault succeeded in driving the Turks back through the Nek towards Baby 700 and by 06.00 the summit of Russell's Top was clear.

Sinclair-MacLagan landed at around 05.00 and after climbing to the summit of Plugge's Plateau was able to see that his brigade was now spread wantonly about the hills and valleys in front of him. With most of the 12th Battalion already engaged, his reserves were limited. Concerned that Second Ridge, particularly along its northern edge, had not yet been adequately secured he sent what few men he had at his disposal in that direction to establish the outposts which subsequently formed the basis of Steele's, Courtney's and Quinn's Posts. One of those sent forward was Captain Hearder with the 11th Battalion's machine-guns:

> I halted just short of the ridge, to enable all my men to catch up, as they had strung out a good deal. Bear in mind we had only advanced a mile as the crow flies, but we had at a conceivable estimate marched three miles, so high and so steep were the hills we had to traverse. . . . We dashed over the ridge, carrying our guns, tripods, belt boxes of ammunition when to my dismay there was no sign of the Company I had come to reinforce. We got under cover of some scrub and set up our guns and opened fire, immediately a terrific fire opened on us, but we were lying pretty close to the ground and they could not actually see us, I think. During the next half hour our boys appeared some distance on our right and then more, and more, kept coming and engaging the enemy, but always on our right. Eventually a small body came up about 100 yards on our left rear and relieved my anxiety a little about that flank, but I did not know what Battalion they were, nor their number.[26] (Captain Dixon Hearder)

Despite the confusion it was clear to Sinclair-MacLagan that the landing had at least been a surprise. The covering force had managed to land and casualties so far had not been severe. The troops were already starting to move inland towards their objectives and the general area around the landing place was relatively secure. The transports of the main body of the 1st Australian Division were beginning to advance through the battleships and would soon be disembarking more troops in support of his brigade. Although the landing had not been carried out as expected, it had not been a disaster.

The disembarkation of the main body was intended to begin little more than an hour after the first tows had landed, and the whole of the 1st Australian Division's infantry was due to be on shore before 09.00. The 2nd Australian Brigade was intended to land first and extend the left flank of the line from Battleship Hill through Chunuk Bair to Koja Chemen Tepe; while the 1st Australian Brigade was to form Divisional Reserve. However, as all of the 3rd Brigade had landed on the northern flank, the ground from the centre of 400 Plateau to the southern tip of Second Ridge was almost devoid of troops. Yet this was precisely the direction from which the Turkish reinforcements were expected to come. Sinclair-MacLagan quickly realized that it was now more important for the 2nd Brigade to extend the right flank beyond the centre of 400 Plateau than take up its intended position on the left, which was already relatively secure.

Colonel James M'Cay, in command of the 2nd Brigade, landed at around 06.00 and was soon in discussion with Sinclair-Mac-Lagan, who explained the way the landing had developed. M'Cay concurred with Sinclair-MacLagan's revision of the plan and, after agreeing a dividing line between their brigades slightly to the north of the centre of 400 Plateau running east–west in line with Owen's Gully, the two brigade commanders moved separately to the plateau, Sinclair-MacLagan going to the northwestern edge and M'Cay to the hill just below the dividing line which was later named after him. From there M'Cay could see that the primary need was to secure the southwestern half of 400 Plateau along Bolton's Ridge and he decided to reinforce it with the first battalions of his brigade as they landed. Independently Sinclair-MacLagan decided that the rough line which had been established by the 3rd Brigade along the northern half of the plateau should now be held until the 2nd Brigade had arrived to support it on the right, with scattered outposts remaining to the east to provide cover for the main line.

Although numerically weak, since the landing of the covering force the Turkish defenders had made good use of the broken ground inland from the beach. The coast to the north of Gaba Tepe had been defended by only two companies of the 2/27th Regiment, with a nominal strength of just over 500, plus a battery of the 8th Artillery Regiment on 400 Plateau. A third company of the 2/27th Regiment was positioned to the south of Gaba Tepe and the fourth was in reserve about a mile inland. The first reports of a landing near Ari Burnu were not received at the headquarters of the 9th Division near Maidos until 05.30, an hour after it had begun, and the divisional commander, Khalil Sami Bey, mistakenly concluded that the landing was a feint to cover a real landing near Bulair. Conscious of his responsibility for the defence of the whole of the southern half of the peninsula, he initially ordered only the remaining two battalions of the 27th Regiment and its machine-gun company to be sent to Ari Burnu to help the hard-pressed defenders.

The 19th Division, commanded by Mustafa Kemal Bey, was also based close to Maidos. Mustafa Kemal was an enigmatic character. Born in Salonika, he was a career soldier who, although an original member of the Young Turks, had subsequently become estranged from them and only obtained release from his position as Turkish Military Attaché in Bulgaria in February 1915. His inspired and expert command at Gallipoli, first of the 19th Division and later of the higher formations to which he was promoted, thrust him forward into a position of national prominence and established a powerful reputation. After the war, he led the revolution that founded the modern Turkish Republic and assumed the name Atatürk, or Father of the Turkish People.

The most reliable regiment of the 19th Division was the 57th Regiment, whose soldiers were Turks rather than Arabs and by chance it had been ordered by Mustafa Kemal to parade at 05.30 on 25 April for a field day; the remaining two Arabic regiments, the 72nd and 77th Regiments, were encamped near Mal Tepe.

When Khalil Sami learned from further reports of the landing that troops were heading inland towards Chunuk Bair, he asked Mustafa Kemal to send one of his battalions to oppose this movement. Instinctively Mustafa Kemal realized that, if successful, an advance up the high ground towards Koja Chemen Tepe would be decisive and rather than a single battalion 'my whole Division would be required to deal with the enemy'.[27] He ordered the 57th Regiment, which was fully mustered for its field day, to march immediately in the direction of the landing in advance of the rest of the 19th Division and set out himself at the head of this regiment.

The first boats of the 2nd Brigade to reach the shore arrived opposite the extreme northern flank of the Australian line and when only about 200 yards from the beach were devastated by fire from Fisherman's Hut, suffering heavy casualties. As a result, for the rest of the day the majority of troops landed on Anzac Cove, between Ari Burnu and Hell Spit.

We lined up on the *Galeka* and waited for the pinnaces and tows to come back. The old bosun of the *Galeka* came along. 'Any of you got any letters to post? Anybody got any of those dirty postcards that you bought in Cairo? If you have, you'd better put them down on the deck because if you get knocked they send them to your next-of-kin.' By this time I was feeling as brave as a ring-tailed possum and I wished I was anywhere but on the *Galeka*. The boats eventually pulled up alongside. We were all done up like sore toes with rifles and shovels and ammunition and packs. How we got down those rope ladders I just don't know, what with the nervousness and the excitement of not knowing what was in front of us. I just felt washed out. As I got into the boat there were about three chaps of the 9th Battalion who had been killed and they hadn't had time to lift them out so we had to walk gingerly over these blokes. Then I heard the voice of the little middie pulling these three boats. It was a child's voice really and I thought, 'If it's good enough for him, it's good enough for me.' Well, we packed in together. The shrapnel was falling. The machine-guns were pelting and as the pinnace hit the shore we boats at the back were pulled up into anything up to three, four foot of water. Somebody said: 'Out you get' and out we got. Lumbering with this shovel and rifle and pack and ammunition we were loaded like blessed elephants. There were dead and wounded of the 3rd Brigade all around. We scampered as hard as we could to a little bit of shelter and dumped our packs and dumped the shovels and picks. We'd had enough of those. Then somebody said: 'Well, up you go' and away we went up the slope.[28] (Private Frank Brent)

Under shellfire close to the shore, the transports were moved further out in an attempt to reduce its effect and as a result the speed of the landing of 1st Australian Division decreased, with the last of its infantry not eventually landing until 13.00. The slow and disorganized way in which the soldiers landed also created chaotic scenes on the beach. Unlike at Helles where they were to land as part of the covering force, at Gaba Tepe the naval beachmasters and military landing officers landed with the main body and did not come ashore until 10.00. The beach personnel had been clearly instructed that the wounded were only to be evacuated by designated medical boats and that the steady work of the tows moving back and forth between the beach and the transports was not to be interrupted to take casualties to the hospital ship. But lack of early authority on the beach prevented strict adherence to this rule and some of the tows, quite understandably, did embark wounded men in their boats, further adding to the slow speed of the disembarkation.

Soon after the 2nd Brigade started to land a rendezvous was selected just inside the entrance to Shrapnel Gully, where units could form up before moving to the right instead of the left as planned. But the lack of any firm revised orders and the fact that the last men of each party often found the first had been ordered forward from the rendezvous before they had arrived, meant that the 2nd Brigade was soon dispersed along 400 Plateau in similar confusion to that which had overtaken the 3rd Brigade.

Major General Bridges landed with Divisional Headquarters at 07.30. After finding it impossible to gain an accurate picture of the situation, he moved to Ari Burnu, where he met Brigadier General Harold Walker, the chief staff officer of ANZAC, who had landed to act as Birdwood's representative ashore. Together they left Ari

Burnu and established Divisional Headquarters at the foot of Plugge's Plateau a short distance inland from the beach.

On the left flank the Australians advanced steadily up the hills towards Chunuk Bair. Although Clarke had been killed, Tulloch led the way forward across Russell's Top to the Nek before continuing northeast towards Baby 700 and Battleship Hill. In the face of the Australian advance the Turks withdrew. But the tenacity of their rearguard defence and the density of the scrub made progress slow and Tulloch's men did not reach the southeastern slopes of Battleship Hill until 09.00. As they were moving forward, Mustafa Kemal arrived near Koja Chemen Tepe. Unable to see anything except the ships out to sea, he ordered his men to halt. On his own he went down the hills in the direction of Chunuk Bair until he could see the northern flank of the Australian attack. There he encountered the Turkish detachment withdrawing from Battleship Hill. Ignoring the men's protests that they had no ammunition, he ordered them to lie down with bayonets fixed. The bluff worked. Tulloch and his men were brought to a halt and never regained their forward momentum up the hills. Tulloch later reported seeing an unperturbed Turkish officer directing the fire across Battleship Hill about 900 yards in front of him. But his attempt to shoot him failed.

After this initial intervention, Mustafa Kemal lost no time in increasing the pressure, and as each successive unit of his division arrived he immediately deployed them on the northern flank. Beginning at 10.00 the whole of the 57th Regiment was gradually brought into action and had soon forced back both Tulloch's forward position and the outpost on Baby 700. Simultaneously, the Turks began to work their way along the seaward slopes of Baby 700. An urgent message was sent back to the Nek, the defences of which had lapsed into a state of complacent calm, warning of the Turks' advance; shortly afterwards Australian parties began to return there. But the situation was reversed by the timely arrival of a fresh Australian company which reached the Nek shortly before 11.00. It immediately entered the fight and, leading a fresh charge, moved the line forward again to retake the summit of Baby 700.

On the southern flank of the Australian line the intensity of the fighting also steadily increased. The reserve battalions of the 27th Regiment had arrived behind the centre of Gun Ridge at around 09.00 and half an hour later attacked the Australians' forward positions along Second Ridge. In response Sinclair-MacLagan ordered forward many of those who had dug in on the northwestern side of 400 Plateau to strengthen the firing line in front of them. Straggling away to the south men began to advance. But the ubiquitous scrub and broken ground prevented any co-ordinated movement and individual parties were soon isolated.

> I heard somebody say: 'This is no good to us. Come on. Heads down, arse up and get stuck into it!' We went into it. We cleared them. Bayoneted them, shot them and the others ran. A little while afterwards a bloke out of the 8th Battalion said: 'Here, look at that bloody bush. It's moving!' We looked at it and it was obviously a sniper and he was done up like a Christmas tree. He'd got branches out of his head and shoulders and he was for all the world like a bush. But he didn't look like a bush when we'd finished with him! One bloke shouted: 'Share that amongst you, you bastards!' The bloke next to me was Robbie Robinson, a corporal in my battalion. He was laughing at the remark and I can see him now grinning all over his face and the next thing his head fell on my shoulder and a sniper had got him through the jugular vein. I really think that was my baptism of fire, because Robbie's blood spent all over my tunic.[29] (Private Frank Brent)

Into this situation those survivors of the covering force who had made the fastest progress off the beach now began to return. Only a small number of men had succeeded in reaching the objective of Gun Ridge, most notably the party led by Loutit which had gained a spur, not marked on their map, running off Gun Ridge to the west. From the spur Loutit and two men had continued to the summit of Scrubby Knoll, only three miles from the Dardanelles, from where they could see the Narrows in the distance. But as the 27th Regiment began to close in around them, these more advanced positions became untenable and the remnants of Loutit's party returned to the northern side of 400 Plateau at around 11.00.

As anxieties along the southern half of the line increased, the sight of the precipitate withdrawal from Baby 700 also alerted

Sinclair-MacLagan to the growing threat to the left. Although he had previously believed this flank to be secure, at 10.35 he was forced to report to Bridges that this was now apparently no longer the case. The 1st Brigade had by this time also started to land and, in common with the pattern of the morning, it had immediately been moved by individual companies into the line along Second Ridge. In response to Sinclair-MacLagan's report Bridges ordered the only two companies not yet deployed to reinforce the line around the Nek. He also reported the situation to Birdwood, who had just been joined on board the *Queen* by Major General Godley. Colonel Francis Johnston, the commander of the New Zealand Brigade, had been judged on 23 April too sick to lead his brigade into action. Yet only now was Godley able to ask Birdwood to appoint a temporary replacement. At Godley's suggestion Birdwood selected Walker and at 10.45 this decision was relayed to Walker at Bridges's headquarters on land. The NZ&A Division, which had arrived off the coast earlier in the morning, had originally been intended to land only after the whole of the 1st Australian Division was ashore. But the first parties of the New Zealand Brigade had in fact started to land soon after 09.00. Bridges now decided to use these New Zealand troops as well to support the threatened left flank. Unfortunately in the process the Auckland Battalion became dispersed along the length of the line from 400 Plateau to the Nek. Despite their limited number, through this unintentional act the New Zealanders turned the position around the beach from an Australian one into Anzac.

By early afternoon, chaos appeared to be rolling forward under a momentum of its own. The Australians and New Zealanders were intermixed and, although from 12.30 to 16.00 there was a hiatus in the landing of troops, the final units of the 1st Australian Division who had landed just before this continued to enter piecemeal into the line. The morale of the Anzacs remained high and many were enthusiastic about closing with the enemy after the tedious months of training. But their high spirits quickly turned to frustration when confronted with the real nature of the fight that had evolved since first light. 'There was no co-ordinated effort about it. We were just a crowd of diggers working with each other, trusting each other blind.'[30]

In contrast the Turks had fared slightly better. Throughout the day their troops had been able to enter the battle with greater coherence and a clearer understanding of what they were expected to do. Two companies had contained a much greater number of Australian troops until reinforcements had arrived and by 10.00, once the numbers were almost equal, the chances of a successful Anzac advance had become very slim. In his account of the fighting Mustafa Kemal clearly identified two reasons for this. Unaware of the unexpected events of the landing which had caused it, he pointed first to the poor position which the invaders had taken up. But then he outlined a second, perhaps even more important factor which the British officers who planned the landing had overlooked. At Gallipoli the Turks were defending their homeland against an infidel invader and this fact gave them an edge in their determination. 'Everybody hurled himself on the enemy to kill and to die. This was no ordinary attack. Everybody in this attack was eager to succeed or go forward with the determination to die.'[31]

The struggle on the northern flank was finally settled by 17.00. During the afternoon Baby 700 changed hands five times and the composition of the attacking troops grew more confused with each new batch of reinforcements, until eventually it included a mixture of Australians and New Zealanders from seven different battalions. At around 16.00 a final Turkish counter-attack forced the Anzac troops to withdraw once again to the southwest, the last to do so being a number of Australians who joined up with some New Zealand machine-gunners digging in at the Nek. The only other troops in the vicinity were two companies of Australians from the 2nd Battalion under Lieutenant Colonel George Braund, who only arrived there at about 16.00 and lay in the scrub around the head of Walker's Ridge. The position was very weak and after dark, at around 20.00, the party at the Nek was forced to withdraw along Russell's Top into Rest Gully. Fortunately the battle for Baby 700 had also exhausted the Turks and they were incapable of following up this late withdrawal. Braund's position on Walker's Ridge remained firm.

Following the final Turkish counter-attack, a significant gap became apparent between the head of Russell's Top and the head of Second Ridge, and Sinclair-MacLagan arranged for part of the

4th Australian Brigade, which had arrived off the coast at around 17.00, to move into position there as it disembarked. A continuous line was not possible but parties from the 15th and 16th Battalions, together with some New Zealanders, established themselves on Pope's Hill, which stood isolated between Russell's Top and Quinn's Post.

At around the same time that the Turks launched their final attack on Baby 700, they also increased the pressure in the south, working out of Legge Valley against 400 Plateau and the southern half of Second Ridge. Well supported by artillery fire, the Turkish attacks soon revealed another consequence of the lack of authority on the beach earlier in the day which had allowed the troops to dump their heavy tools as they landed. 'Towards sundown we tried to dig ourselves into [the] gravelly ground with the aid of an entrenching tool, no shovels or forks or spades or tools of any description being available to us and throwing up what little bit of soil we could in front of us to give a little bit of cover.'[32] The lack of this equipment was a serious hindrance to the Anzacs and their inability to gain protection from the increasingly fierce Turkish shrapnel fire was the cause of further heavy casualties.

In addition, the Anzacs were suffering from a lack of artillery support. Almost no guns had been landed during the day and, because the course of the line was so uncertain, through fear of hitting the Anzacs' own positions, the guns of the ships off the coast had been unable to open fire until the very end of the afternoon when specific requests and accurate co-ordinates had finally been relayed to them. The failure to land guns more quickly arose partly from the use of the boats to clear the wounded and partly from the shelling of the transports in their anchorages. But it was also the result of a decision taken early in the afternoon by Bridges that artillery was not to be landed as the position on shore had not yet been sufficiently well established.

As darkness fell, many of the isolated forward positions on the eastern side of 400 Plateau began to fall back towards the slightly stronger positions in the west. As had been the case on the northern flank, the Turks in the south were in no position to follow up this Australian withdrawal and from 22.00 onwards no further organized attacks were made. The Turks had also suffered heavy casualties during the day, with many Turkish soldiers fulfilling Mustafa Kemal's claim to the letter and all six battalions of the 27th and 57th Regiments had been severely affected. In the line the Anzacs realized that their position was grim, yet there was no sign that they expected anything but to remain where they were and carry on fighting the next day. 'In the Diggers we just trusted each other blind and while one bloke stayed there he could bet his sweet life that the other mate was going to be with him. And if we went we'd all go together.'[33] As he scoured the line for casualties one Australian stretcher-bearer found that this attitude was common among the front-line troops.

> They were determined to stay there. They dug in and they fought and fought. Even some of them were slightly wounded and they still insisted on staying. I bandaged two or three up and they went back to the line and carried on. They had slight wounds of the arms and we'd get a tourniquet or tight bandage on just to stop the bleeding. Eventually they had to give up and come down because the wounds were turning on the gangrene side.[34] (Sergeant Frank Kennedy)

Throughout the day the collection of wounded from the front lines had caused great difficulties. During the planning of the landing the numbers of likely casualties had been severely underestimated by GHQ and the rate at which casualties actually occurred, rising by the end of 25 April at Gaba Tepe to 2,000[35] and at Helles to around 3,000,[36] quickly overwhelmed the inadequate provisions. Only two hospital ships were available, one each at Helles and Gaba Tepe, capable of accepting between 400 and 500 serious cases. To help these ships a number of transports had also been converted into auxiliary hospital ships using the staff of stationary hospitals and field ambulances once the troops they were carrying had been landed. But by early evening the limited number of places available on all ships had been filled to overflowing. As places became scarce, the rate at which casualties could be taken off the beaches became painfully slow and after leaving the beach many tows were forced to make a tedious journey round the ships looking for space.

I was asked by the army to take this lighter load of perhaps 100 wounded men off to the hospital ship. The hospital ship was easily marked and when I got there they just waved me away. I said: 'Well, look, I've got dying men here,' and they were screaming with pain. The hospital ship said: 'We are absolutely full up and cannot take any more wounded.' So then I went to one, two, three, four of the transports. The same story every-where. Eventually, quite late at night, it must have been nine or ten o'clock, I went to my own ship, the *Prince of Wales*, and simply told the officer of the watch and the commander: 'I can't take them any further. These men have got to be taken aboard the *Prince of Wales*.' Everybody turned to. The men were hoisted up the quarter deck and looked after as best we could. We had three doctors and three sick bay stewards, but many of the wardroom officers who had studied first aid knew a little of what to do and they had a whole night's work ahead of them.[37] (Midshipman Eric Longley Cook RN)

Despite that fact that many of the auxiliary hospital ships were full well before the end of the day and their facilities were clearly inadequate for long-term treatment, they were unable to leave immediately for the base hospitals. The General Staff had agreed to allow them to be converted so soon after the landing only on the understanding that they would remain in place for at least forty-eight hours in case the landings failed and the troops had to be re-embarked. Consequently the wounded were forced to remain off the beaches for several days and many wounds, which had been treated only with first aid, putrefied before adequate surgical treatment became available. The added suffering that this caused to those already distressed by their experiences has always been considered to be another strong indictment of the conduct of the landings.

By early evening at the headquarters of the 1st Australian Division, Bridges had begun to call into question the value, for the campaign as a whole, of his troops remaining in position at Gaba Tepe, wondering instead whether they ought to be with-drawn and made available to Sir Ian Hamilton so that he could concentrate all his efforts at Helles, where their additional weight might prove to be decisive. It was clear to him that the landing at Gaba Tepe had achieved little. If the ultimate objective of Mal Tepe had eluded the corps, a subsidiary line along the hills which climbed up from Gaba Tepe to Koja Chemen Tepe would still have been invaluable to the attack on the Narrows. Yet even this had not been reached. The Anzac position was actually so shaky that the strong Turkish counter-attack expected on the following morning could prove to be disastrous. A recognition of the landing's failure and a withdrawal of the Anzac force, under the cover of the ships' guns, appeared to Bridges to be the most sensible course of action.

Examined retrospectively this idea is often considered to be an alarmist reaction to the disappointment and strain of the day; even by some to be an example of panic. But it was seen by Bridges more as a logical, if unpalatable, military response to a difficult situation and the subsequent lack of significant improvement in the Anzacs' situation and the apparent waste of lives and resources in terms of strategic gains to a certain extent later provided some justification for it. Bridges was also following a course of action which had been clearly laid down by both the naval and military commanders before the landing. On 24 April Captain Aspinall had written a memorandum entitled 'Suggested Course of Action in the Event of the 29th Division, or the Australians Failing to Establish Themselves Ashore',[38] in which he had outlined precisely the course of action which came under consideration during the early evening at 1st Australian Divisional Headquarters, and on the same day Thursby had also issued a memorandum entitled 'Re-embarkation' in which he had detailed the naval arrangements for a withdrawal.[39]

Yet despite the logic of the proposal the conditions on and in front of the Anzac beach made it impractical. The shoreline was thoroughly congested, cluttered with both stragglers and wounded, and inland the firing line ran along positions which were often unknown and isolated. It would be impossible to withdraw in an orderly manner. The men in the line were also still determined and in no way expected to be withdrawn. There were no piers or facilities for loading large numbers of men quickly into the boats and the whole area was under shellfire which could be directed incessantly on to the troops if the Turks realized an evacuation was in progress, causing casualties not just to them but to the boats as well, as had happened during the landing. The choice between these difficulties and the logic of withdrawal was a fearful dilemma which divided the officers at Bridges's headquarters. Unable to take such a momentous decision himself, at 21.15 Bridges sent a signal to Birdwood asking him to resolve the critical question.

Birdwood had been ashore earlier in the afternoon and had returned to the *Queen* unaware of the brewing crisis. The signal from Bridges came as a shock and he arrived back on shore at about 22.00. At a crisis conference he considered both sides of the argument and, like Bridges, felt unable to decide what course of action should be followed. He opted instead to lay the dilemma in front of Hamilton and dictated a two-page note. Briefly he outlined the disappointing outcome of the day, stressing the effect of the continual shellfire on the morale of the troops, and ended, 'if we are to re-embark it must be at once'.[40] The note was taken from the beach to the *Queen* for transmission to GHQ. Before this was done it was shown to Thursby, who 'was flabbergasted as I had no idea that things were in such a critical condition. However, a moment's consideration convinced me that to re-embark would be disastrous & couldn't be thought of, at all events until we knew what had happened at Helles. . . . It was quite out of the question.'[41] Thursby decided to go ashore to talk to Birdwood in person and at around midnight embarked in a steamboat. But, as he was about to leave, he heard that GHQ had just arrived in the *Queen Elizabeth*. Instead of heading for the beach he crossed to the *Queen Elizabeth* and finally presented Birdwood's note to Hamilton.

The generals and admirals on board gathered in the battleship's dining room and Hamilton read the note out to them. When he had finished, he asked their opinion and Thursby answered first. He explained his belief that an evacuation during the night was impossible and offered to take a message to Birdwood on Hamilton's behalf. After two senior officers from ANZAC Headquarters concurred, Hamilton was decided. Drawing on his knowledge of Birdwood's character and the fact that GHQ had learnt during the day that the Australian submarine *AE2* had made a successful passage through the Narrows, he dictated a masterly answer to Birdwood telling him to stick it out. On a second sheet of paper he added a characteristic final note. 'PS You have got through the difficult business now you have only to dig dig dig until you are safe.'[42] The tension was immediately dispelled. With determination of purpose restored Thursby left for the beach and, after reaching Birdwood, gave him the long-awaited answer. The effect of Hamilton's message was profound. A decision had finally been taken and attention could now be turned to the task of ensuring that the position was held. Despondency and doubt were cast aside and in its place, as Hamilton had ordered, the digging began.

At Bulair the diversion to threaten the neck of the peninsula and distract the attention of Marshal Liman von Sanders from the main landings further south had begun very early on 25 April. The RND had left Trebuki Bay on the previous evening under the escort of the 3rd Squadron and reached the Gulf of Saros before dawn. An intermittent bombardment began shortly after 05.30 and continued throughout the day, while the division's transports remained inactive off the coast as planned. Only at the very end of the afternoon did the pretence of landing troops finally get under way.

The feint had been planned to take place in two stages. During the first, which was to begin shortly before dusk, the transports were to lower their boats and embark men into tows, which would then be pulled towards the shore by trawlers as if about to land. But as soon as it was dark and the Turks could no longer tell whether in fact the men had landed, the tows were to return to their transports, where the troops would be re-embarked. The second stage, once darkness had fallen, was to be more realistic and include the actual landing of a small party from the Hood Battalion. Originally it had been intended that one platoon would be put ashore to light flares, fire their rifles and simulate a genuine landing. However, during the afternoon Lieutenant Commander Freyberg put forward an alternative. Pointing out the potentially extensive loss of life which a landing might incur, he suggested that as a strong swimmer he could swim ashore to light the flares on his own. His suggestion was accepted and the following day he submitted an official report on what transpired.

> At 12.40 this morning ... I started swimming to cover the remaining distance, towing a waterproof canvas bag containing three oil flares and five calcium lights, a knife, signalling light, and a revolver. After an hour and a quarter's hard swimming in bitterly cold water I reached the shore and lighted my first flare, and again took to the water and swam towards the east, and landed about 300 yards away, where I lighted my second flare and hid among some bushes to await developments. Nothing happening, I crawled up a slope to where some trenches were located the morning before. I discovered they were only dummies, consisting only of a pile of dirt about two feet high and 100 yards long, and looked to be quite newly made. I crawled in about 350 yards and listened for some time, but could discover nothing. I now went to the beach, where I lighted my last flare, and left on a bearing due south. After swimming for a considerable distance I was picked up by Lieutenant Nelson in our cutter some time after 3 A.M. .... It is my opinion that the shore was not occupied, but from the appearance and lights on the tops of the hills during the early hours of the morning, I feel sure that numbers of the enemy were there, but owing to chance of being captured, and as I had cramp badly, I could not get further.[43] (Lieutenant Commander Bernard Freyberg RNVR)

The purpose of the diversion had been to pose a real threat to the neck of the peninsula, where many people had expected the landing to take place, and its principal strength lay in the presence of the soldiers on the transports. The diversionary operations, of rowing the transports' boats towards the shore and landing to light flares, were really only intended to exaggerate and reinforce the threat of the transports. While the overall effect of the diversion was relatively successful and managed to contain Liman von Sanders's reserves for a limited period, both of the feint landings were unrealistic and unthreatening. The original intention to land a complete platoon of the Hood Battalion would have caused Liman von Sanders a much greater degree of anxiety and, although it might have resulted in large numbers of casualties, would have made the diversion more effective as a result.

The landing at Helles was more complicated than the landing at Gaba Tepe and involved a simultaneous disembarkation on five separate beaches. The covering force, formed by the 86th Brigade under Brigadier General Hare, was to land and secure the three main beaches, V, W and X. The 88th Brigade was then to land at V Beach, enabling the British line to advance up the peninsula until its left edge rested on Y Beach and its right in advance of S Beach, these two beaches having been secured independently by two battalions of the 87th Brigade. Once this line had been established, the 87th Brigade, after reincorporating its two detached battalions, was then to advance through the 88th Brigade on to the peak of Achi Baba. The plan was based on a strict timetable and the expectation of inexorable progress. In a report on the landing Lieutenant Colonel Henry Tizard, in command of the Royal Munster Fusiliers, explained that 'it was surmised that by 8.0 a.m. the ground above the beaches would have been won; by noon we should be in the vicinity of the village of Krithia, and have taken the Hill of Achi Baba that night.'[44] But the plan contained no contingency for hold-ups, particularly with regard to the two flank landings. No alternative to sitting tight and waiting for the inevitable advance from Helles was put forward for either S or Y Beaches and no suggestion made as to what they should do if this failed to materialize on time. Such an eventuality was considered unlikely by Major General Hunter Weston.

The first of the individual landings to begin at Helles was at Y Beach. As the whole premise of the landing there was based on surprise, it was to begin shortly before 05.00 without a preliminary bombardment. The overall commander of the troops at Y, Lieutenant Colonel Matthews of the Plymouth Battalion, was given no definite, written orders and was forced to rely instead on imprecise, oral instructions. He was told to advance inland to threaten the Turkish withdrawal, capture a gun which was only believed but not confirmed to be in the area and attract Turkish attention and resources away from the other landings. He was also told to gain touch with X Beach, although it was never made clear whether this was intended to be merely visual signal contact or a definite link forming a continuous line from Y to X.

The KOSB and company of SWB landed at 04.45 on a rocky beach at the foot of a steep, rugged cliff about 150 feet high. The steepness of the cliff and the unlikelihood of anyone trying to land there meant that it was a complete surprise and encountered no opposition. Shortly after the first troops landed the bombardment started around Cape Helles and the fire of the ships' guns, particularly at X Beach less than three miles away, could clearly be heard. The supporting ships at Y also commenced firing at the top of the cliffs above the beach. Within an hour all the troops were ashore and, after climbing the cliffs with relative ease using one of two deep nullahs which ran down to the beach, the leading troops of the KOSB began to work their way out to the centre and both flanks. Behind them the remainder of the KOSB and the SWB reached the top of the cliffs about 06.20, followed in due course by the Plymouth Battalion, which sent half its strength to look for the Turkish gun while the remainder formed a defensive flank facing northeast and carried ammunition and stores up the cliffs from the beach. The first of the landings at Helles was a complete success, achieving, without loss or opposition, its primary intention of lodging a significant force on the flank of the enemy. The *Goliath* reported the success to GHQ at 6.40 and a short while later Hamilton and the General Staff were able to see it for themselves as the *Queen Elizabeth* sailed past Y Beach *en route* from Gaba Tepe to Helles.

The bombardment of the main beaches was intended to last for thirty minutes, during which time the force destined for S Beach was supposed to enter the Dardanelles and complete its preparations for landing. A severe shortage of resources meant that the SWB's tows had to be pulled by trawlers, which were slower and less powerful than naval steamboats, and was also another reason why only three of the battalion's four companies would be able to land there, with the fourth attached to the landing at Y Beach. But an unofficial arrangement agreed on the eve of the landing between the commanding officer of the SWB, Lieutenant Colonel Hugh Casson, and Captain Alexander Davidson RN, the captain of the

Cornwallis, the attendant ship at S Beach, provided a supplementary beach party to supervise the landing of stores and allow the limited number of soldiers to concentrate on storming the beach. The *Cornwallis* was to bombard the area around S Beach until the landing was under way, and under this cover two companies of SWB were to land inside Morto Bay on S Beach, with the naval beach party on their left, while the third landed outside the bay at the foot of the cliffs which rose up steeply from the Dardanelles for around 150 to 180 feet to De Tott's Battery. This company was then to scale the cliffs and take from the rear the trench which overlooked the beach and the landing inside the bay.

Although the SWB's trawlers moved into the Dardanelles entrance as planned at 05.00, they became delayed almost immediately both by the strong current flowing against them and by the mine-sweeping flotilla which had collected there. When at 05.30 the bombardment was due to lift and the tows for the main beaches begin their approach, the trawlers were still a considerable distance from Morto Bay. In an attempt to maintain a simultaneous landing along the coast from X to S Beach, Rear Admiral Wemyss held back the tows for the main beaches and prolonged the bombardment. But shortly before 06.00 it was felt that it would be unwise to hold up the other beaches any longer and the 86th Brigade's tows were ordered to start their approach.

The boats for S Beach continued slowly into Morto Bay, but it was not until 07.30, about ninety minutes later than planned, that the SWB's tows were finally cast off by the trawlers. As the two companies inside the bay approached the beach, Captain Aubrey Williams noticed that the Turks waited until the very last moment before opening fire on the boats, an action he later believed to be mistaken. By delaying their onslaught the Turks failed to inflict heavy casualties on the British troops packed tightly in their open boats. In the deep water at the foot of the cliffs in the Dardanelles, the third company landed unopposed. As soon as the men were ashore they stormed up the cliffs and within a short time had established a position overlooking the Turks who were firing on the troops landing inside the bay. Despite stronger opposition, the companies inside the bay also effected a landing and, once the trench above them had been enfiladed, they were able to storm up the cliffs into the Turkish positions, taking fifteen Turks prisoner. The naval beach party landed about the same time as the other boats and several members of it linked up with the soldiers to join in the assault on the trenches.

> I got a bayonet & rifle & with the Sailors pushed up into the firing line where we potted at the trench for a bit & then fixed bayonets & pushed the Turks out. The Sailors & myself had no packs so we reached the trench easily first & I was nipping along the trench trying to find a Turk to stick when the colonel called us out as they were afraid it was mined, but it wasn't. The Turks were just round the next corner, so it was jolly bad luck. At any rate the Turks surrendered to us very soon afterwards, except for 5 or 6 snipers who kept potting at us whenever they got a chance. So we had to keep under cover fairly well.[45] (Lieutenant Harry Minchin RN)

By 08.30 S Beach was completely secure. The casualties of the landing had been light, totalling only sixty-three killed, wounded and missing,[46] and in due course, once the beach was organized, the wounded were sent off and stores and ammunition landed.

Both of the flank landings had been carried out with great success because neither had been expected. Yet the plan for the three main beaches had dispensed with this very factor, surprise. The bombardment was intended to compensate for it, with the effect of the shelling expected to be so overwhelming that, even if it did not destroy the Turkish defences, it would effectively remove them as a threat; the senior army commanders were more concerned about advancing inland away from the cover of the ships' guns than actually getting ashore. In the event the bombardment was a failure. The main reason for this lay once again in the limited effect of naval gunfire on land targets. A further problem was caused by the inability of the ships to see their targets clearly. The *Albion*, a covering ship anchored 1,400 yards off V Beach, and the *Euryalus*, an attendant ship which was able to approach closer, still remained 1,000 yards off W Beach. From these distances it was clearly difficult to identify individual targets within the narrow confines of the beaches and ensure that they were sufficiently well shelled. In addition, once the bombardment began it created a thick cloud of smoke and dust around the beaches which increased in opacity once the rising sun started to shine through it and eventually rendered accurate shooting impossible.

A third factor which further reduced the bombardment's effect was its deliberate lifting from the area around the beaches to the plateau of land which lay behind the Turkish defences a considerable time before the boats reached the shore. A report by Colonel Mahmut, the commanding officer of the 3/26th Regiment which was defending the area between X Beach and Morto Bay, confirmed that some minutes before the British boats reached the shore 'the enemy's bombardment ... slackened',[47] allowing the front line positions on Hill 141 above V Beach to be visited and the British ships off the coast observed. During the initial, heavy bombardment the front-line troops had withdrawn from their positions to wait for the fire to ease. Once it stopped, they simply returned to their trenches, a forerunner of the tactic repeated on 1 July 1916 at the start of the Battle of the Somme with the same result.

The way in which the bombardment could have been conducted was demonstrated by the attendant ship at X Beach, the *Implacable*. Her conspicuous success was entirely due to the character and initiative of her captain, Captain Hughes Lockyer RN. From the start he expected to take up a station much closer to the shore than 1,000 yards and in conjunction with his gunnery officer, Lieutenant Commander John Scott RN, developed a means of maintaining the *Implacable*'s fire at the beach as she accompanied her tows as close to the shore as possible. Once this point was reached she then continued firing at the bluffs around the cliff top until the actual moment that the boats landed.[48] The effect of this on the morale of the men in the boats as they approached X Beach was immense.

> I have never forgotten the impression which that never to be forgotten run in to the beach made on me, and even more on the soldiers in my boat. They were simply enthralled with the sight of the cliff face being literally blown away by the ship's guns & the spectacle of the ship steaming in firing was magnificent. I think it is no exaggeration to say that the morale of the troops in the boats went up 2 or 3 hundred per cent on that account. I remember it was a beastly cold morning and when the troops embarked from the ship they looked (and evidently felt) anything

but heroes. The change in their attitude towards what lay ahead during that short run in alongside the ship was quite phenomenal. It was a complete revelation to me, & I have often felt that if the other landings had been similarly conducted there would have been a very different tale to tell.[49] (Midshipman Stanley Norfolk RN)

Yet while Lockyer's fire against X Beach was indisputably the most successful, it was also the least necessary. Mahmut deployed his battalion with a company each defending the areas around W and V Beaches. Of his remaining two companies, five platoons remained in reserve and the sixth was placed to observe Morto Bay. No formal defence was mounted of X Beach, its potential as a landing site not having been recognized. There was no wire and only the lightest of entrenchments. Instead the Turks had concentrated their effort along the coast at Gully Beach, which was held by two platoons of the 2/26th Regiment. The defence of X Beach was left to a small picket of just twelve men who were completely stupefied by Lockyer's overwhelming bombardment.

X Beach, the smallest of the three main landings, was a narrow margin of sand about 200 yards long which stood almost a mile up the Aegean coast from Tekke Burnu at the base of steep cliffs around 100 feet high. It was to be assaulted by the Royal Fusiliers, who were given two principal objectives. After securing the beach and the cliff top, they were to take Hill 114 and establish a link with the Lancashire Fusiliers working northwards from W. They were then to protect the northeastern flank of the covering force by establishing an outpost line to the north of and immediately inland from X Beach. With the Turkish garrison mesmerized, the Royal Fusiliers were able to take the cliff top with few casualties by 06.30. But almost as soon as they reached the top Turkish resistance stiffened. Part of the battalion were sent to the left and the remainder moved straight ahead and to the right. For the first 300 yards casualties on the left were relatively slight and the men progressed steadily over the first line of Turkish trenches. But as they continued towards the second line their momentum began to wane and the advance drew to a halt. On the right the attack on Hill 114 also started well. But as the Royal Fusiliers moved forward part of the Turkish reserves positioned inland from X Beach began to counter-attack 'like thirsty lions released from their chains'.[50] At first the Turks were successful. But within a short time the British advance was picked up again and progress resumed towards Hill 114.

W and V Beaches, positioned on either side of Cape Helles, were much more substantial than any of the other three beaches assaulted by the 29th Division. Once the covering force had established itself and secured the area around them, they were to be the two main points of disembarkation for the remainder of the division, starting with the main body of the 88th Brigade at V Beach and the artillery at W. In contrast to Y, S and X Beaches, which were only suitable for landing small bodies of infantry, both W and V, with their wide strips of sand and gradual slopes leading up to higher ground inland, appeared to be ideal for the rapid disembarkation of large numbers of men and guns. Yet, these same features also made them excellent defensive positions. The steep cliffs overlooking both beaches not only completely commanded them but, unlike the other three beaches which ran parallel to their respective cliff-faces, also enwrapped them. It was therefore not surprising that the landings on these two central beaches were the most difficult and least successful. The failure of the planners to anticipate this and attempt to capture them instead with an outflanking movement from the less obvious beaches shows both a distinct lack of imagination and a failure to understand the realities of the formidable defences of these beaches.

The Lancashire Fusiliers, together with 86th Brigade Head-quarters, were to land on W Beach, which was about 350 to 400 yards wide, between 15 yards to 40 yards deep and flanked on either side by cliffs 150 feet high. With the exception of a small gap on the left, the sand had been thickly covered by barbed wire and in the centre a funnel-shaped valley climbed up from the beach to the height of the surrounding cliffs. The whole area had been strongly fortified, with machine-guns embedded in the cliffs and mines laid along the beach and the water's edge. The Lancashire Fusiliers intended to move off the beach on either side of the valley. On the right they were first to attack Hill 138 before pushing across towards V Beach to establish a link with the Munster Fusiliers, and on the left, after securing the left and centre of the beach, push northeast to assist the Royal Fusiliers in taking Hill 114.

The W Beach tows began their approach shortly before 06.00 and as they did so the bombardment advanced according to plan. On the southern edge of the line Midshipman Alfred Williams RN was in command of the *Euryalus*'s steam pinnace, the slowest boat in the line, and sailing east at top speed:

> As we got close in I looked down and found to my consternation rocks underneath me. No sand at all. It continued like that for a few moments and when I slipped my tow, I waved them on to the left towards where the rocks ended and sand began, and got out of it myself as quick as I could. . . . The idea of running aground hard, on rocks, did not appeal to me at that moment, and I only avoided that fate narrowly. Several bullets struck the boat and one or two hit the shield behind which the coxswain and I were standing. I think the bulk of the rifle fire was concentrated on the life-boats rather than on the steamboats, and, as far as I remember it, there were certainly some casualties before the boats grounded.[51] (Midshipman Alfred Williams RN)

After the boats were cast off, when about 50 yards from the shore, they suddenly came under serious fire. 'The first bullet that struck the water brought up loud jeers from our men, but poor devils they little thought what they were in for.'[52] It soon became clear.

> The stroke oar of my boat fell forward, to the angry astonishment of his mates. The signal for the massacre had been given: rapid fire, machine-guns and deadly accurate sniping opened from the cliffs above, and soon the casualties included the rest of the crew and many men. The timing of the ambush was perfect: we were completely exposed and helpless in our slow-moving boats, just target practice for the concealed Turks, and within a few minutes only half of the thirty men in my boat were left alive.[53] (Captain Richard Willis)

Once the firing had started, some men where shot while still in their boats and others killed as they tried to climb out. Orders were given to get into the water, even though the boats had not yet grounded and were still around twenty yards from the shore. The average depth of the water beneath the boats was four to five feet and weighed down by the weight of their saturated equipment many men were drowned.

In the end only two of the twenty-four boats were actually reported to have reached the shore. Lieutenant Talbot reckoned that only a handful of his men got ashore alive, one of whom was his runner, who appeared to have 'a charmed life as he left his rifle on board and ran back for it and never got touched':[54]

> Personally I lost no time in getting ashore and taking what little cover there was. All my boat got knocked out except about 4 and the sand jammed their rifles so we had to lie still without being able to fire back and trust to not being hit; this was maddening with a machine-gun firing at us from under 150 yards away, however thanks to providence I got out all right.[55] (Lieutenant Douglas Talbot)

This frustrating problem was common along the complete length of the beach. Many of the soldiers had dropped their rifles either in the water or in the sand and sometimes both, with the result that the breeches of their rifles became sodden with salt water and clogged by fine sand. Once this was realized 'an astonishing sight was now seen: soldiers on the beach under close fire of the enemy getting out brushes and oil to clean their rifles, a job which would not have been necessary if the Company Commander's request for rifle covers had been listened to'.[56] The other main problem confronting the soldiers was the thick belt of heavy barbed wire which ran along the beach and into the water. Along most of its length the wire had not been damaged by the bombardment and in addition in front of it the Turks had laid a trip wire beneath the surface of the water. The men had been ordered, on first landing, to lie behind the wire until paths had been cut through it by the battalion's wire-cutters. But, in the event, as soon as they reached it 'they were shot in helpless batches while they waited'[57] and further heavy casualties were suffered.

Approaching on the extreme left of the line, Hare was able to exploit the gap in the wire to effect a cleaner landing for the men in his boats.

From where we were behind, we could see nothing. The sun was just above the cliff and the whole shore was in haze. We knew that they must be getting it hot from such a heavy fire at close range but could not see very much except that a lot of men were falling in the water as they got out of the boats. The leading boats were beginning to return empty, evidently with men of their crews hit. We directed our boats towards the cliff just west of the beach, hoping to land under cover. We found the landing was gently sloping rock and got ashore all right, though many were hit in doing so. We started scrambling up the cliff which was a steep earth slope with layers of rock here and there. It was not very steep but was difficult for a man in full kit to climb. There were no Turks on the front edge of the cliff, so we were defiladed from the front, but were getting it pretty hot from the trenches on the east side of the mouth of the glen which formed the beach. When we got to the top we could see that the Lancashire Fusiliers were shoving on straight to their front up the glen but must have been losing frightfully from fire from trenches on both sides.[58] (Brigadier General Steuart Hare)

From the bridge of the *Euryalus* the Navigating Officer, Lieutenant John Godfrey RN, watched this confused scene alongside Hunter Weston and Wemyss. 'The General's and Admiral's immediate reaction was "My God, they haven't got ashore." But they had and what we saw was the boats emptied of soldiers pulling off, some of them with only two sailors at the oars.'[59]

The first movement off the beach was made by the men on the left, who managed to force their way over the wire and up the cliffs, where they joined up with Hare's party. Hare quickly ordered part of them forward in pursuit of the retreating Turks. Having established that the left flank was secure he and one of his staff officers, Major Thomas Frankland, then decided to investigate the landing at X Beach. 'We were just above the top of the cliff not far from Cape Tekke when we found ourselves within about 100 yards of a trench full of Turks. We started to drop over the top of the cliff as they opened fire. I felt a tremendous blow on my calf and just got over the edge of the cliff when I sat down.'[60] Hare had been very badly wounded and his loss so early in the day was to prove a serious setback to the effective command of the landing at Helles.

On the opposite side of the beach the very steep, almost sheer cliffs on the right had also by this time been assaulted and when the summit was reached the Turks withdrew, as they had on the left, leaving the Lancashires to occupy the trenches on top of that side of the valley as well. The seizure of the right summit then enabled the men in the centre to start moving southeast over the head of the beach towards the left flank of Hill 138. By 07.30 a tentative line had been established around the perimeter of the beach. On the left the northward movement to link up with the Royal Fusiliers and seize Hill 114 was progressing steadily. But on the right the line appeared less well defined. Frankland, who had left Hare to wait for stretcher-bearers, and another staff officer, Captain Mynors Farmar, returned to the beach to help push on the attack towards Hill 138 and establish Brigade Headquarters as arranged before the landing in the ruined lighthouse immediately above Cape Helles. Gathering the men who had climbed the cliffs on the right, they led them under cover of the cliffs to the lighthouse and extended their position to the edge of a thick barbed-wire entanglement. But any 'attempt to cut the wire . . . brought an impossible fire to live in.'[61] By 08.00 the Lancashire Fusiliers had formed a complete line around W Beach. For the moment no further progress appeared to be possible and shortly after 08.30 Frankland was killed when attempting to establish contact with V Beach, depriving the 86th Brigade of another capable senior officer. Despite the immense difficulties they had encountered, the Lancashire Fusiliers had succeeded in landing at W Beach. But they had incurred such heavy casualties, totalling 11 officers and 350 men from the landing alone,[62] that they were unable to join up with the landing at V Beach. The only hope for the continuation of the original plan was that the men landing there would be able to clear the defences between W and V Beach from that direction.

Deploying a total force of around 2,800 men, V Beach was intended to be the largest and most important of the landings at Helles. Yet, in the end, due to the gradual expansion of the flank landings it involved only one more company than was landed at Y Beach. Three-quarters of the Dublin Fusiliers were to land first on the beach from tows of boats. Thirty minutes later the Munster Fusiliers, together with the remaining Dublins and half of the 2nd Hampshire Regiment, were to land from the *River Clyde*. The overall aim was to seize the village of Sedd el Bahr and complete the line from there to the right flank of the Lancashire Fusiliers to form a continuous position across the tip at Helles from Morto Bay to X Beach. Yet, even more so than W Beach, V Beach formed a naturally strong defensive position. Tiers of trenches ran across the back of a wide bowl which sloped down gently from the rim to sea level. The bowl was crossed by rows of thick barbed wire on spiked metal stanchions. Originally the Turkish defences had included four 37mm pom-poms but two of these were destroyed by the bombardment, leaving only two in position to the left of centre of the beach. In addition the Turks had four machine-guns, one on the left beneath Fort No. 1, two in the centre and one on the right in the ruins of the Old Fort between Sedd el Bahr and the beach.

The Dublins began their approach like the Lancashires before 06.00. However, being nearer the entrance to the Dardanelles, they encountered the full force of the current and their progress was delayed. When they failed to appear, the bombardment of V Beach was continued by the *Albion* and the other ships supporting the landing until around 06.30. The *River Clyde* also began her approach at about 06.00. Despite having been intended to ground on the beach half an hour after the landing of the Dublins, as a result of their slow progress, she now started to overtake them. To avoid the confusion which would inevitably occur if the second wave of troops landed before the first, Commander Unwin steered her on a circular course through the crowded waters to delay her approach. After turning through 360 degrees the *River Clyde* began her second approach. She was still slightly ahead. But nothing more could be done and at almost the same time that the naval bombardment finally lifted she ran aground.

The Dublins' tows were only a short distance behind and, as the *River Clyde* grounded, the steam boats cast off their pulling boats on either side. One tow made a successful landing with few casualties at the Camber, a small harbour beneath the village just inside Morto Bay; but the men landed there were soon overwhelmed and able to achieve little from this good start. The remaining tows rowed unmolested on the port side of the *River Clyde* until, with the first boats only twenty yards from the beach, a single Turkish shot was fired. Immediately after this, the deluge broke and devastated the Dublins in the open boats. In the *River Clyde* to the men waiting to leave through the sally ports it appeared as if they were being 'literally slaughtered like rats in a trap'.[63] Only around 300 of the 700 men in the boats made the beach, with many of them wounded. The only shelter was a bank about ten yards in from the water's edge which varied in height between five to eight feet. It ran along the length of the beach about twenty-five yards away from the wire entanglements and throughout the day its meagre cover was to provide the difference between survival and complete obliteration for the men who managed to escape the Turkish fire and reach the shore. Captain David French later could not understand 'why the Turks with their vast preparations did not level this bank of earth down. . . . Had they done so not one of us would have escaped.'[64]

Unwin's plan for the grounding of the *River Clyde* had intended the steam hopper to be shot forward on impact into position between the *River Clyde*'s bows and the shore. But when the *River Clyde* ran ashore the hopper actually veered off to port and 'ran aground in the wrong place'.[65] In addition, this mistake was immediately compounded by the fact that the stern of the hopper then swung out behind it, away from the *River Clyde*. It was clear that the hopper could no longer be used to bridge the gap between the *River Clyde* and the shore. Instead Unwin, who had emerged from her holds together with Able Seaman William Williams, decided to connect the *River Clyde* to a spit of rocks that ran out for about forty yards from the beach towards her starboard bow using two of the lighters which had been towed alongside the hopper. Receiving additional help from Midshipman George Drewry RNR, who had been in command of the hopper, Unwin and Williams hauled the lighters into the gap between the *River Clyde* and the spit of rocks. Once in position, Unwin realized that there was nothing suitable on the shore to which the lighters could be secured while the soldiers disembarked. Seeing no alternative, he wound the line round himself and submerged himself in the water, using his own body as a fixing point. Williams then added his own weight to the line to secure it and once this was done Unwin shouted to the *River Clyde* that the landing could begin. Instantly the Munsters began to disembark along the gangways. On the beach, French 'was about 50 yards from where she grounded & as the men ran ashore they were mown down. . . . And still they came down the gangways. It was an awful sight but they were a real brave lot.'[66]

While the first men were landing, Unwin and Williams success-fully held the lighters in position. But it was not long before Williams was hit by a shell and to prevent him from drowning Unwin released the line they were holding. The heavy lighters were quickly caught by the current and pulled away from the spit towards deeper water on the left. As they did so, a second wave of Munsters led by Captain Geddes was just starting to emerge on to the port gangway.

> We got it like anything, man after man behind me was shot down but they never wavered. Lieutenant Watts who was wounded in five places and lying on the gangway cheered the men on with cries of 'Follow the Captain.' Captain French of the Dublins told me afterwards that he counted the first 48 men to follow me, and they all fell. I think no finer episode could be found of the men's bravery and discipline than this – of leaving the safety of the *River Clyde* to go to what was practically certain death.[67] (Captain Guy Geddes)

After dashing down the gangway Geddes discovered that the final lighter was 'adrift, and we were carried broadside on towards the shore'.[68] Nevertheless he pushed on as best he could. Private W. Flynn followed Geddes down the gangway from the *River Clyde*:

> I had a big periscope that I was carrying for him. We had double ammunition, double rations, double everything I think, but he had the sense to tell us to throw our coats off before we made the landing. . . . I followed Captain Geddes down the gangway, along the gunwale of the lighter, lay down in the bow, just enough cover to hide us and he looked back and called for the company, the remainder to come. They couldn't. They must have stopped it. So, he said: 'Well, come on. Over we go.' He goes and falls into the sea. Course I lost him.[69] (Private W. Flynn)

By this time Unwin, who was fifty-one years old, although remarkably still not wounded was close to exhaustion and Drewry had to help him back to the *River Clyde*. 'I stayed on the lighters and tried to keep the men going ashore but it was murder and soon the first lighter was covered with dead & wounded and the spit was awful, the sea round it for some yards was red.'[70] The drifting of the lighter and the congestion of the bodies caused a lull in the landing. In response, Mahmut drew an unfounded but understandable conclusion about the success of his defence:

> The enemy troops were so frightened that they refused to disembark from the large transport which entered Ertugrul cove [V Beach]. Their commanders and officers had drawn their swords and were sending the men down the ladders but they were observed and could not escape the Turkish bullets. Not one of our soldiers' bullets was fired in vain. In fact in many cases one bullet accounted for several of the enemy. The enemy understood how much his landing cost him and how high was the bravery and courage of the Turkish Army.[71] (Colonel Mahmut)

Exhausted by his time in the water, Geddes reached the earth bank and took stock of the situation. Most of the officers who had tried to land had either been killed or wounded and it was clear that it was impossible to advance beyond the cover of the bank. The Turkish defences were still overwhelmingly strong and 'the bombardment by H.M.S. *Albion* was innocuous & failed.'[72] The most immediate threat to the beach came from the unprotected right flank 'where Sedd-el-Bahr Fort ran down to the sea'.[73] If the Turks launched an attack from that direction, there would be no warning and little that could be done as things stood. At around 07.05, Geddes decided to lead a party of men over to the right across a dip in the bank towards the base of the fort to protect this flank. Flynn arrived on the beach just as the movement was getting underway:

> I heard somebody shout out: 'Hoy, Flynn.' I said: 'Yes, sir.' I knew the voice. That was Captain Geddes. He was around the other side of this bit of land that was jutting out and he had about three or four men with him. He said: 'Now, we've got orders to get around near the fort.' I said: 'Oh, that's good.' Because that

was right where the machine-guns was. But he said: 'They tell us
that once we get around about twenty yards, we can get into a bit
of an indent in the bank and we'd be safe.' I said: 'Thank the Lord
for that!' Well, as we was running around – he was in front, I was
behind him and there was another officer behind bringing up the
rear with I think it was three or four men, about seven all told –
the officer got hit on the epaulettes and it turned the bullet down
through his shoulder, only a flesh wound, missed the bone.
Anyway, he got around alright. He didn't stop and we laid
down.[74] (Private W. Flynn)

Geddes confirmed that he 'had a button shot off, and got plugged
through the shoulder, the bullet going clean through, and coming
out of my back – another fraction of an inch, and my career would
have been ended. . . . In the excitement, I felt no pain at the time,
and ran on, and was able to move about all day.'[75] Later he was
joined by some more men from the centre and also fourteen of the
Dublins who had landed at the Camber. A reconnaissance of the
village revealed that it was only lightly defended. But he and his
men were too weak to take advantage of this. Instead he 'reported
to Colonel Tizard by semaphore from the shore that I could do
nothing, as I had no men left. He told me to go for my objective
Fort No. 1 but it could not be done.'[76]

A second wave of troops who tried to land on the beach a short
while later were as unsuccessful as the first. The defences were too
strong and both the men in the boats and the boats' crews again
suffered heavy casualties. A precarious bridge of boats was briefly
established between the bows of the *River Clyde* and the hopper by
Drewry, Lieutenant John Morse RN and Midshipman Wilfred
Malleson RN, both of whom had arrived in the second wave. But
its effect was minimal. Shortly after 08.00 Tizard decided that the
Munsters should make another attempt to land in small parties,
sending only a few men at a time. 'Major Jarrett led off and got
about one platoon over, but a lot were hit in going over as the fire
at once broke out again.'[77] By 09.00 it was clear to both Tizard and
the commanding officer of the Hampshires, Lieutenant Colonel
Herbert Carrington Smith, who was in overall command that the
plan for landing troops quickly from the *River Clyde* had failed.

Unwin's adaptation of the *River Clyde* had inadvertently created one of the most difficult and dangerous of military positions, a defile which opens at close range on to an entrenched enemy position. The narrowness of the *River Clyde*'s pontoon link forced the disembarking soldiers to collect together at exactly the point where the enemy's fire was strongest, with the result that 'more than half those who had left the vessel were either killed or wounded'.[78] In little more than three hours the attempt to land at V Beach had ground to a halt. 'It was a state of impasse. With wire entanglements untouched, compounded by riflemen well dug in ... a reorganization & fresh bombardment were necessary to achieve the objective.'[79] Yet these two essential elements were not forthcoming for over eighteen hours.

The five landings at Helles had met with varying degrees of success and were marked by the award of eleven Victoria Crosses, six to the Lancashire Fusiliers at W Beach[80] and five to members of the Royal Navy at V Beach.[81] At Y and S Beaches the landings had been completely successful, with negligible opposition and surprise allowing the forces to land almost intact. X Beach had achieved a similar success. Then as soon as the troops reached the clifftop, the situation changed. At W Beach the strong defences had been overcome at considerable cost to the strength of the landing battalion, with the result that they were too weak to advance as planned. But at V Beach the defence held. The same determination and courage as shown at W could not this time prevail. Although the Turks had spent as long preparing their defences as the MEF had in preparing their invasion, and from their orders showed 'that they thought it impossible that a landing on the peninsula could be effected',[82] the 29th Division succeeded in breaching their defences and it was only in the light of the overly optimistic expectations of the higher commanders that the landing appeared a disappointment.

From S Beach the SWB could see that the troops at V Beach had failed to make headway into Sedd el Bahr and by 10.00 realized that the expected advance up the peninsula was already seriously delayed. In their isolated position they faced the choice either of remaining in position until the advance got under way or of attempting to work their way round the edge of Morto Bay to outflank the Turks in Sedd el Bahr. Believing the Turkish strength to be much greater than it was, Casson correctly decided to consolidate his position and wait. In reaching this decision he had little real choice. He was in an isolated flanking position, ignorant of the exact progress of the main landing. A breakthrough might have occurred at any moment and by moving his men into an unauthorized position he could easily have prevented its successful exploitation. A salutary reminder of the risks courted by junior commanders adopting too high a degree of individual initiative was also given near by in the sharp criticism meted out to Davidson for allowing his unofficial support of the SWB to distract him from his proper role. Once the SWB were ashore the *Cornwallis* should have moved to V Beach to add her weight to the supporting fire there. But Davidson and the beach party did not withdraw from S Beach until after 10.00. The censure he later incurred overshadowed any recognition of the value of his increased support for the SWB.

The first part of the 29th Division's main body to land was the 87th Brigade at X Beach. Its leading battalion, the 1st Border Regiment, arrived on the beach at around 09.00, along with the brigade commander, Brigadier General William Marshall and Brigade Headquarters. The disembarkation was remarkably civilized and one staff officer, Major Cuthbert Lucas, described how, as they landed, it was 'a bright sunny morning, dead calm sea, not a shot fired. I had a bag in one hand, a coat over my arm, and was assisted down a plank from the boat by an obliging sailor, so that I should not wet my boots. The only thing missing was the hotel.'[83] Once ashore Marshall faced a potentially awkward position as his brigade had effectively been split into two. The KOSB and the SWB had already landed at Y and S Beaches and the remaining two battalions had been designated the 29th Division Reserve. Of the 29th Division's three brigade commanders he was therefore expected to play the least significant role of the day. Although by mid-morning both of the other brigadiers had become casualties, throughout 25 April he was to remain marginalized at X Beach, uninformed of developments on the other beaches and unable to influence events outside the immediate area of his landing.

Soon after reaching the cliff top he received an anxious message from the Royal Fusiliers on the left explaining that they were being heavily attacked by the Turks from Gully Beach and that help was needed to prevent their flank from being turned. He sent what men he could to support the left, but the forward positions were still pushed back towards X Beach. On the right, the opposite flank was making steady progress towards Hill 114. At 11.00 this party took the summit of the hill and established contact with the Lancashire Fusiliers. At around the same time, directly inland from X Beach, a strong Turkish attack drove back the centre of the Royal Fusiliers almost to the clifftop and in the fighting Marshall was slightly wounded. Nevertheless he ordered the Border Regiment to charge the advancing Turks and restore the line. The charge began around midday and forced the Turks back for about 600 yards. Within an hour the line had been re-established and, using the remainder of the Border Regiment and part of the 1st Royal Inniskilling Fusiliers who had begun landing after them, Marshall was able to establish a secure bridgehead around the beach.

The first part of the 88th Brigade to land was the Essex Regiment, which had been intended to follow up the covering force at V Beach. But at 08.30 Hunter Weston unexpectedly diverted it to support the Lancashire Fusiliers at W Beach. For the Essex this was a fortunate decision and it represented one of the few significant interventions by Hunter Weston on 25 April in the original plan. Hunter Weston and his staff officers were only able to see for themselves a very limited part of the battle on land, almost wholly restricted to the area around W Beach and they were completely reliant on the reports they received from each of the individual positions for any appreciation of how events there were progressing. Inevitably some of these reports were inaccurate or misleading. At 07.30 29th Division Headquarters received a report stating that the troops from the *River Clyde* 'appeared to be getting ashore well'[84] and at 07.50 the battleship HMS *Lord Nelson* sent a confusing signal which stated that British 'troops are now in Sedd El Bahr village',[85] suggesting the men from V Beach but probably referring to the survivors of the landing at the Camber. When combined with the good reports he had also received of the landings at Y, S and X Beaches, Hunter Weston felt that resistance around

Cape Helles would soon be overcome and that the original plan was only temporarily delayed.

He also believed that only hostile shellfire was preventing an advance at V Beach and at 09.00, in an attempt to support the attack on Hill 138, he urged the landing there to be continued. Around 09.30, Carrington Smith tried to land a platoon of the Hampshires. But the result was unchanged and only a handful of men reached the beach unscathed. At almost the same time a single tow, containing the commander of the 88th Brigade, Brigadier General Henry Napier, his Brigade Headquarters and parties of the 4th Worcestershire Regiment and the Hampshires, began to approach the stern of the *River Clyde*. From the bridge Carrington Smith directed the leading boats to the port bow. After jumping on to the lighters clustered there, Napier and his staff led the way forward towards the deep water into which Geddes and Flynn had jumped earlier in the morning. The Worcesters who followed were forced to throw themselves flat on the lighters. The Hampshires who landed on the starboard bow of the *River Clyde* were relatively successful in getting ashore, with thirty-five out of the fifty men actually reaching the earth bank. After briefly returning to the *River Clyde*, Napier made his way once again on to the lighters and soon after this was shot dead, together with his Brigade Major. The second concerted attempt to land from the *River Clyde* had also failed with the loss of two more senior officers. At 10.21 Hamilton, who had arrived in the *Queen Elizabeth* at the entrance to the Dardanelles at around 07.00 and actually seen V Beach for himself by 08.30, unequivocally instructed the *Albion* 'not to send more men on to V Beach'.[86] No new troops were landed there on 25 April, all being sent instead to W Beach.

After being diverted there, the Essex Regiment began to land on W Beach shortly after 09.00. Once ashore, its commanding officer, Lieutenant Colonel Owen Godfrey-Fausett, ordered an attack against Hill 138. But the attempt failed, mainly because Hill 114 had not yet been taken and the men on the left were still vulnerable to the fire of the Turks behind them, while the men on the right were stopped by the fire from the redoubt on Hill 138 itself. By the end of the morning the situation at Helles was not good and had improved little since the landing of the covering force. The line around W Beach was stronger, but only because three companies of the main body had been drawn into it. A link had been established from there to X Beach, but in the process had so weakened the line further to the north that more companies of the main body had been forced to make a bayonet charge from the cliff top to restore it. At V Beach there was still no sign of any movement at all. The landing had now fallen well behind its ambitious timetable and if there was to be any realistic chance of reaching Achi Baba before nightfall an objective reassessment was needed to identify those parts of the plan which had succeeded and direct all the remaining resources at them.

The successes of the two flank landings were known both at 29th Division Headquarters and at GHQ in the *Queen Elizabeth*. But Hunter Weston appears not to have considered the alternative possibilities that they offered. In contrast Hamilton had begun to look into them soon after passing Y Beach earlier in the morning. Although the exploitation of these landings had not been envisaged in the original plan, he now saw that better results might be achieved if troops intended for the main beaches were diverted to the flanks, Y Beach in particular. But reluctant to interfere with Hunter Weston's conduct of the landing now that it was under way, all he felt able to do was suggest a possible alternative and at 09.21 he sent a signal to 29th Division Headquarters asking if they would like to land more men on Y Beach. At 10.00, after no reply had been received, he repeated the signal, ordering Hunter Weston this time to acknowledge it. Hunter Weston still believed that progress at Helles was just delayed. No reports had yet reached him about V Beach and he had already taken action to support W Beach. When he received this second signal, he apparently failed to appreciate the significance of its polite suggestion and, after consulting Wemyss, at 10.35 he declined the offer. Faced with this reply, there was nothing more that Hamilton could do.

The conduct of the two flank landings, the subsequent failure to exploit them and all the misunderstandings and disagreements associated with them reveal a number of important failures in the command of the landings at Helles on 25 April. Inherent in Hunter Weston's approach was a lack of flexibility. Throughout the landings he showed no inclination to depart from the original conception of a strong landing at Helles and a subsequent advance to Achi Baba, with no attempt being made to look for alternatives to pushing hard on the front door in the hope that it would open. Yet Hamilton was equally at fault. His belief that the Commander-in-Chief should not intervene, except in the direst emergency, meant that he was unable to act when decisive action was clearly needed. During the day, in the fastest and best-equipped ship in the EMS, he was uniquely placed to co-ordinate all of the widely spaced landings and his failure to do this was conspicuous. Hamilton and Hunter Weston, for different reasons, were both guilty of serious errors of judgement on the day of the landings and, through these errors, they must be held responsible for the failure of the 29th Division to exploit the opportunities that arose at Helles.

The landing of the French at Kum Kale, which was supposed to take place concurrently with the British landing around Cape Helles, was several hours late getting underway. Like the RND diversion at Bulair, its principal purpose was to prevent Turkish forces being moved across the Dardanelles to face the real landings at Helles and Gaba Tepe. However, unlike the RND, the French were to land both an infantry regiment and an artillery battery and maintain their position until Helles was completely secure. Encountering the same problem with the current that had delayed the landings at V and S Beaches, the French did not reach the shore until shortly before 10.00. But once on land they made good progress and Kum Kale was captured by 11.15. Unlike the resistance offered at both Helles and Gaba Tepe, the Turkish troops who were defending the Asiatic coast failed to contain the landing close to the beach but withdrew and it was not until later in the afternoon that they returned to counter-attack the French landing. During the night the Turks pushed heavily against the French position, making four concerted attacks; but the line was maintained and the attacks driven off. However, it was evident that no further advance would be possible without the landing of more troops.

The disembarkation of the 88th Brigade continued uninterrupted at W Beach and the remainder of the Worcestershire Regiment started to arrive there at around 12.00. Forty minutes earlier 29th Division Headquarters had been asked to send someone ashore to take command of operations at W Beach, and after landing at 12.30 Colonel Owen Wolley Dod, the division's senior staff officer, quickly realized the importance of capturing Hill 138 in order to advance from W Beach to V Beach. He organized an attack on Hill 138, preceded by a successful naval bombardment, which began soon after 14.00. On the left the Essex quickly seized the summit and its redoubt, while across to the right the Worcesters moved on to the southeastern slopes of the hill, and by 15.00 a new line was in place along the whole of the inland edge. But any further British advance was for the moment prevented by thick banks of barbed wire and heavy fire from Turkish positions in a second redoubt a few hundred yards to the southeast which had not been featured on the British maps.

The map used by GHQ to plan the landing and issued to the troops in conjunction with their orders was later found to be remarkably unreliable. Several important features encountered both at Helles and at Gaba Tepe were misleadingly portrayed, but the most significant failure was revealed after the capture of Hill 138. The map showed only one hill, 138 feet high, on the tip of the peninsula. However, 400 yards to the southeast, there was a second, unmarked hill, known to the Turks as Guezji Baba, which at 159 feet was actually the highest peak in this locality. The fortifications around Guezji Baba were of even greater strength than those on Hill 138 and the two summits were connected by a trench running along the top of a shoulder of raised ground which linked them and showed them to be part of the same topographical feature. Yet as Guezji Baba was absent from the map, it did not feature in the objectives allocated to the troops landing at either V or W Beach. The failure to distinguish correctly between the hills also produced many confused reports towards the end of the day once Guezji Baba had eventually been captured.

Although the first hill was now secure the attack would clearly need to be continued to capture the second as quickly as possible and preparations by the Worcesters began immediately. The extensive wire network which encased Guezji Baba first had to be penetrated, but heavy fire from the hill made progress very slow. To overcome this the Worcesters launched a simultaneous attack from the southwest near the lighthouse. As both flanks of the

Worcesters closed on the main redoubt, the Turks started to withdraw. Once sufficient men had filtered through the wire, the final British assault began and by 16.00 the summit of Guezji Baba had also been taken. Watching from the *Queen Elizabeth* the continual, determined drive which achieved this, one of Hamilton's General Staff concluded, 'I think this was the finest sight I have ever seen.'[87]

The movement towards V Beach first became apparent to those on board the *River Clyde* at the beginning of the afternoon. Shortly before 15.00 Carrington Smith was killed on the bridge by rifle fire and command of the troops devolved on Tizard. When reports began to reach him that the attack from W Beach was making progress, he 'sent a message by Lieutenant Nightingale who had remained on the vessel to take the remainder of "Y" Company on the shore and ask Major Jarrett to work one Company along the shore to the left and get in touch with the Worcestershire Regiment, who had taken Hill 138'.[88] Nightingale had first landed with Jarrett earlier in the day, and for the second time, at about 16.00, he left the *River Clyde*. 'We jumped into the sea and got ashore somehow with a rain of bullets all round us. I found Jarrett and a lot of men but very few not hit.'[89] Despite the approach of the troops from W Beach the situation was still hopeless and Nightingale was forced to join the other men on the beach, where 'the groans and cries of the wounded and dying were awful'.[90]

After the Worcesters had cleared Guezji Baba they found themselves under fire from the Turkish position on Hill 141. At around 16.35 Wolley Dod ordered their commanding officer, Lieutenant Colonel Douglas Cayley, to halt on the line he had reached. But Cayley, having seen V Beach for himself, decided to keep his men moving slowly forward for as long as he could. This decision was vindicated shortly afterwards when Hunter Weston, who had finally realized what had occurred at V Beach, ordered only limited detachments to be retained to consolidate the positions won during the afternoon. The remainder of the troops on the right of W Beach were to push on towards Hill 141 as rapidly as possible. Although this order reached Wolley Dod at 17.00, it was not received by Cayley for another ninety minutes, by which time it was too late. Dusk was beginning to fall and, although the right flank of the Worcesters eventually reached the ruins of Fort No. 1 and the cliff tops overlooking V Beach, it could advance no further.

At Y Beach, throughout the morning all remained quiet. After failing to find the Turkish gun, at around 11.00 the Marines returned to the beach and at about the same time the KOSB's forward positions were withdrawn in anticipation of the advance from the south. At 11.45 the commanding officer of the KOSB, Lieutenant Colonel Archibald Koe, sent a message to X Beach, which subsequently proved to be the only direct contact between Y Beach and the main landings all day, explaining that the force had landed and asking if it should remain there or advance to join up with the troops further south. From X Beach, the signal was immediately forwarded to 29th Division Headquarters, where it was received by 12.00. Just less than two hours later, at 13.45 the details that the KOSB had established themselves at Y Beach but had not yet got in touch with X Beach were again repeated to 29th Division Headquarters. The original signal was also received at 86th Brigade Headquarters at 12.35, and at 14.30 they too repeated the gist of it to Divisional Headquarters. However, in writing out the signal Farmar apparently made an easy mistake. After first describing the position at Y Beach, he went on to describe that at X. But, instead of stating the true fact that by 14.00 the Royal Fusiliers were in touch on their left with one company of the Border Regiment, he erroneously wrote 'one Co: Borderers'.[91] When the signal was recorded at Divisional Headquarters at 15.00 it reported unequivocally that by 14.00 the Royal Fusiliers were in touch on their left with the KOSB and the same observation was passed to GHQ shortly afterwards. The implication that a continuous line ran from X to Y was to prove a serious mistake.

In fact, by 15.00, the line around Y Beach had been withdrawn even closer to the beachhead and formed a rough salient round the head of the two nullahs which led down to the beach. Even though Koe's signal had twice been successfully relayed to 29th Division Headquarters, no word was sent back either to him or to Matthews to explain the non-appearance of the main body. By mid-afternoon at Y Beach it was clear that there would be no advance before nightfall and that the position would probably have to be defended overnight until the original plan could be resumed on the following morning. Five hours had elapsed since the same conclusion had been reached at S Beach and this valuable time, which the SWB had used to prepare their defences, had unfortunately been squandered.

Although unknown at the time of the landing, the number of Turkish troops in the vicinity of Y Beach had actually been very small and the force landed there was greater than the combined strength of all the Turks between Achi Baba and Helles. Above Y Beach there had been no garrison at all. The nearest detachments had been the two platoons of the 2/26th Regiment at Gully Beach and a third platoon to the north of Y Beach at a point called Sari Tepe. Beyond Sari Tepe lay the 1/26th Regiment, but they were restricted to defending the coast, and the main Turkish reserve, the 25th Regiment, was a considerable distance inland from there, five miles to the northwest of Krithia at Serafim Farm. Sporadic Turkish attacks from the north and the direction of Krithia had first begun against Y Beach towards the end of the morning; but they represented little serious threat to the position. However, at 13.00 a substantial body of reinforcements, including one battalion of the 25th Regiment, a field artillery battery and a machine-gun section, had been despatched from Serafim Farm to Y Beach.

As soon as it was realized that they might have to defend their position, the British troops began their first serious attempts to dig in. But it was already too late. The soil was very hard and full of roots. The men had no decent tools to help them dig, only light entrenching implements, and desultory Turkish rifle fire further inhibited their progress. By late afternoon the trenches were still only about eighteen inches deep and the men's packs had to be brought up to form a haphazard breastwork. The line was drawn up with three-quarters of the Plymouth Battalion on the right, the SWB and most of the KOSB in the centre and the final portion of the Plymouths on the left. The Turkish reinforcements moved up quickly from reserve and shortly after 17.30 they began their first concerted attack, which the ships off the coast helped to beat off decisively. But after dark the ships would no longer be able to fire, 29th Division Headquarters had sent no message of encouragement or support all day and for the first time the complete isolation of the position at Y became apparent.

At X Beach Marshall too received no fresh instructions and at

15.43 he signalled to Divisional Headquarters his intention to dig in at X Beach on his present positions to await an advance from Sedd el Bahr. As the afternoon ended, the sound of the fighting at Y became distinctly audible at X Beach and Marshall grew increasingly anxious about the position there. At 18.00 he asked Divisional Headquarters for advice over whether he should take action to help Y Beach by advancing independently to its assistance and so risk weakening the defences of X Beach, or whether he should stay where he was and wait. It was two hours before he received a reply. Hunter Weston instructed him to remain where he was and wait until the morning when the advance would continue as originally planned. At about the same time, he also received a contradictory answer from Wolley Dod at W Beach, who ordered him to get the Y Beach force to extend its line southwards and establish firm contact with X Beach. But events had already gone too far. Marshall's patrols were unable to establish contact and at Y Beach, now that it was dark and the ships had been forced to stop firing through fear of hitting the British positions in error, the ferocity of the attacks had significantly increased.

At V Beach towards the end of the afternoon Tizard ordered the remaining men of the Hampshires under Major Arthur Beckwith to land in small groups if and when opportunities arose, and shortly before dusk 2nd Lieutenant R. B. Gillett led his platoon out of the *River Clyde*.

> The sight that met our eyes was indescribable. The barges now linked together and more or less reaching the shore were piled high with mutilated bodies – and between the last barge and the shore was a pier formed by piles of dead men. It was impossible to reach the shore without treading on the dead, and the sea round the cove was red with blood.[92] (2nd Lieutenant R. B. Gillett)

As the light started to fail, Geddes and the men he had led across to the Old Fort formed a natural focus for the men on the beach. Once the Hampshires had finished disembarking, they were followed at around 19.30 by the remaining Munsters and finally the last of the Dublins. While they were landing Beckwith joined up with Geddes who, after discussing the situation, went off to have his wound dressed. Beckwith was now the most senior officer on the right flank of the beach and he ordered part of his men to secure the exit from the Old Fort which led north towards the village and the rest 'to advance through the barbed-wire entanglements on the west side of Fort Sedd-el-Bahr and take up a position in the open to protect the beach from any attack made during the night'.[93] Conditions soon became very uncomfortable.

> The night was dark and very cold. My Platoon were lying in the open in extended order. At intervals throughout the night search lights flashed hither and thither searching for us, for the Turks knew we were there but not quite where. Also throughout the night machine-guns were searching for us. On one occasion they got our range and a bullet spat into the sand nicely placed one between each man. Once when I raised myself on my elbow a bullet struck the sand just beneath my chest. None of us had had much sleep since Friday night, and fearful that the men might fall asleep I kept a fairly continuous stream of messages passing up and down the line.[94] (2nd Lieutenant R. B. Gillett)

Nightingale, who was near by, remembered that 'it was pouring with rain too'.[95] Across the whole British position these miserable conditions added to the suffering of the wounded as they were brought in by stretcher-bearers like Private Cecil Tomkinson of the 87th Field Ambulance:

> There were quite a few wounded soldiers which were brought down to the beach – I think I brought two stretcher loads in – and these poor fellows with their wounds, there wasn't any barges to take them back to the hospital ship. It had been hot during the day, but it was freezing cold at night. These poor fellows with their wounds were lying there stone cold, freezing cold, crying out for some attention. 'Just a minute, soldier. We'll have you off soon.' But it was very slow. The doctors were very, very busy and, while we could give them first aid, we couldn't help with the bleeding and patching up. . . . It was bad. We were sensitive young lads, sensitive to the screams and moanings of the wounded. They had a right to moan. They didn't appear to be getting attention.[96] (Private Cecil Tomkinson)

At about 02.00 on 26 April the hard-pressed Turks of the 3/26th Regiment were finally reinforced by two-and-a-half companies of the 1/25th Regiment who had been moved up from the Turkish reserve. But even before this, the Turks had begun a series of probing attacks along the length of the British line. The attacks were fiercest against Y Beach, where, after beginning at around 19.30, they continued throughout the night, skilfully executed and spearheaded by machine-guns and relentless bombing. During the last hours of 25 April, when the almost full moon lit up the previously dark sky, one KOSB officer, Captain Robert Whigham, was able to observe them clearly:

> One could see line upon line of Turks advancing against our position. They fought with extraordinary bravery and as each line was swept away by our fire another one advanced against us and the survivors collected in some dead ground to our front and came on again. The attack worked up and down our whole front as if they were looking for some weak spot to break through our line. I saw one man, during one of these advances, continue to run towards us after all his companions had stopped. He ran at full speed towards [us], dodging about all over the place. He got up to within about fifty yards of the trench and then I saw him drop. Four times during the night they got right up to my trench before they were shot and one Turk engaged one of my men over the parapet with his bayonet and was then shot.[97] (Captain Robert Whigham)

At 23.55 Matthews sent a signal via the *Goliath* to Divisional Headquarters reporting the serious nature of his position and asking for reinforcements. The signal was received within twenty minutes but, as had been the case throughout the day, neither reply nor acknowledgement was sent in return. It was now over eighteen hours since the Y Beach force had landed and twelve hours since their only direct signal had been received. Yet still they remained isolated. In part this can be explained by the mistaken belief at Divisional Headquarters that a continuous line existed from Y to X Beach, a belief still held by Hunter Weston when he visited Hamilton at 21.00. Yet by 20.30 it had been clear to others, such as Wolley Dod at W Beach and Marshall at X Beach, that Y Beach was in serious trouble. Over a period of twelve hours, beginning at 21.00, a series of messages from several different sources arrived at 29th Division Headquarters asking for help and stressing the increasingly difficult situation at Y. During the night Hunter Weston sent one of his staff officers to V Beach to liaise with the commanding officers there, but no such action was taken to help Y Beach. Although a request from Matthews for more ammunition was received at Divisional Headquarters at 00.25, no action was taken and it was left to the *Queen Elizabeth*, which had intercepted the signal, to order the *Goliath* to land what was required. Y Beach was a late addition to the Helles plan, originally conceived by Hamilton, which did not fit into Hunter Weston's scheme of things. Throughout 25 and 26 April his actions suggest that he had little interest in it, even that he did not care.

The sequence of events which led to the final abandonment of Y Beach was very confusing. Shortly after dawn, at 05.30, Matthews sent his first signal of the new day to 29th Division Headquarters reiterating his plea for reinforcements and ammunition. But, although the signal was received at 06.00, it still elicited no response. As soon as it was light the warships recommenced their supporting fire and for the first time the intense overnight pressure began to ease. Unfortunately, at 06.00 a number of naval shells fell short and landed among the hard-pressed British defenders. On the extreme left of the line these shells had a particularly devastating effect on the Plymouth Battalion and parties of them suddenly started to stream back to the cliffs, heading for the beach. Thirty minutes later, in circumstances which remain unclear, from an isolated position 500 yards to the south of the main beach an unidentified young officer of the KOSB appears to have sent a request for assistance in removing his wounded and in response boats were sent to take them off. The consequences were profound. The sight of men being removed in boats is held to have started a rumour, which quickly spread, that a general evacuation of the position had begun; a conclusion apparently supported by the sight of the Marines scurrying back to the beach.

Unaware of what was happening, Matthews was preoccupied by the signs of an impending Turkish attack which had been building up for over an hour. When it finally broke against the right flank, it was made in great strength and succeeded in breaking through, first on the right and then in the centre. On the left, Whigham watched as this second breakthrough occurred.

> I saw the men in the trenches begin to crumple up but the Turks were right on our flank and nothing could stop them and our men began to retire right on top of us, many of them jumping into the trench in [which] we were and if we had not retired we would have been trampled to death. We got out and ran for the gorge [at the top of one of the nullahs] and here I managed to stay a few of the men and lined them up to try and keep back the Turks and here we got all mixed up with the RMLI who began to stampede. If I live to be a thousand I shall never forget that fearful stampede into that gully. I fell over the point of a bayonet which went through my boot and puttees but fortunately only just pricked me. The only thing I could do was to collect as many as I could and get them on to the top of a bluff to my right and then I made them lie down and open a heavy fire on the Turk.[98]
> (Captain Robert Whigham)

Fortunately the remains of the left flank held firm and, from a line established on the top of the cliffs, a hard counter-attack was launched. The Turks were pushed back again towards Gully Ravine and remained there for the rest of the morning. No further attacks were made against the British line; the position had been secured.

While the attack was at its height, a number of signals passed between the beach and the ships referring to the desperate nature of the situation and asking again for boats to be sent to help out. As the attack began to ease off, it appears that Matthews came to the decision that the force at Y Beach should withdraw from its isolated position and work its way down the coast towards the main body of the 29th Division in the south. After receiving an order to this effect, the senior surviving officers of the KOSB pointed out to Matthews that such a course of action was wholly impractical as it would take too long to remove the wounded. The only alternatives were to remain in position or evacuate completely. Recognizing the sense of their argument, Matthews cancelled his order. Shortly afterwards, at 07.45, he sent another important signal direct to Hunter Weston: 'Situation critical. Urgent need reinforcements and ammunition, without which cannot maintain ridge at Y. Alternative is to retire on to beach under cover ships' guns.'[99] It was the final statement of his position and in it he made it clear that without assistance the force at Y Beach would have to retire. Yet, interested only in the problems of Helles, where he felt the decisive success was still to be achieved, and unconcerned with the potential of an uncertain side-show, in a microcosm of the relationship of Gallipoli to the Western Front, Hunter Weston remained silent.

Since dawn he had been engaged in procuring reinforcements to continue the advance of the previous afternoon and release the force pinned down at V Beach by taking Hill 141 from the west. The only men available were the French troops who had not been landed at Kum Kale but remained in their transports off Besika Bay near Tenedos, and at 06.25 Hunter Weston asked Hamilton if a French regiment could be landed at W Beach to strengthen the British right and ensure that an immediate advance towards Achi Baba could begin once Hill 141 had been taken. His request was delayed and did not arrive at GHQ until 08.15. But Hamilton had already embarked on an alternative course of action. At 07.15 he had independently offered Hunter Weston a French brigade, twice the number of troops he had originally requested. Twenty minutes later 29th Division Headquarters forwarded to GHQ a signal explaining that the position at Y Beach was desperate and needed reinforcements, with the additional comment that the 29th Division had no men available. Hamilton was largely unaware of the way things had developed at Y Beach and in contrast to the measured indifference of 29th Division Headquarters this signal prompted an immediate reaction. He decided to use the French brigade, which he had just offered as reinforcements to Hunter Weston, to help Y Beach and at 07.40 he ordered General d'Amade to send the Brigade Métropolitaine immediately to X Beach, forwarding this change of plan without delay to 29th Division Headquarters. At 08.11 Hunter Weston replied positively to Hamilton's original offer. The amendment was received only nine minutes later but, in a clear example of incompetent staff work, it was not shown to him for almost two hours and consequently once again no action was taken. Hamilton's second attempt to intervene in the landing at Y Beach had also failed.

At Y Beach, once the Turkish attack had died away, its consequences soon became clear. British and Turkish losses had both been severe and the position was now covered with dead and wounded. On the beach the number of men returning without authorization was still growing and the momentum of evacuation was strong. To remain in position seemed hopeless and at 09.30 the men still in the line were ordered to begin re-embarking. The wounded were slowly removed from the line and successive parties of men withdrew to the beach to be taken off to the covering ships. Throughout this time there were no signs of opposition and the support of the warships appeared to keep the Turks subdued.

Shortly after 09.00 Hamilton was shocked to learn from signals still emanating from Y Beach that his actions had been unsuccessful. The *Queen Elizabeth* sailed from Gaba Tepe as quickly as possible and, arriving soon after the evacuation had finally been ordered, Hamilton and GHQ were greeted by the sight of men being taken off the beach to the *Goliath*. Although he had had doubts about the possibility of being able to land, Hamilton had never considered that once ashore the force would not be able to hold out. No response could be gained from 29th Division Headquarters and he could only assume that Hunter Weston had authorized the evacuation. Contrasting this to Birdwood's actions during the night, he was irritated by Hunter Weston's apparent lack of consultation. As all attempts by GHQ to establish contact either with the beach or with the supporting ships failed, there seemed little more they could do and the *Queen Elizabeth* continued south to Helles, where she arrived at 10.30. GHQ then discovered that the evacuation had not been authorized by 29th Division Headquarters and Hunter Weston knew nothing about it. An attempt was made to see if it could still be halted. But the answer, received at 11.15, made it clear that it could not. The wounded had all been embarked, the other troops were now following and only a rearguard remained holding the ridge. Returning to Gaba Tepe shortly after midday the *Queen Elizabeth* again passed Y Beach and the quiet, uncontested evacuation. Hamilton and his staff felt sick with disappointment.

By mid-afternoon on 26 April the position at Y Beach had been completely relinquished. Within forty-eight hours its value would become startlingly clear, but it was to be over two weeks before it could be recaptured. To the men evacuated to the warships at first there seemed little consolation for their struggle. 'Our casualties were enormous and as far as we could see no object had been gained. However we heard afterwards that we had kept a good large body of Turks which might have gone down to help repel our main landing in the toe of Gallipoli. They say we had not less than thirteen thousand Turks against us.'[100] Unfortunately, although Y Beach did successfully divert Turkish troops from the main beaches, their numbers were nothing like this huge figure, being in fact nearer 1,600.[101] Yet to achieve this limited success the British had suffered a total of almost 700 casualties from the 2,000 men who had landed. A great opportunity to circumvent the strongly fortified positions at Helles, particularly those at Sedd el Bahr and V Beach, had been lost and the damage to the campaign would prove irreparable.

In direct contrast to the events at Y Beach, from an initially poor start, 26 April went increasingly well at V Beach. The last men from the *River Clyde* landed shortly after midnight. An attempt by Tizard earlier in the evening to co-ordinate an advance off the beach had by then already started to falter and from this point on he gradually lost control of events on land. Just before midnight Hunter Weston had despatched Captain Garth Walford from Divisional Headquarters to the *River Clyde*, where he joined the two officers attached by GHQ to the V Beach landing, Lieutenant Colonels Weir de Lancey Williams and Charles Doughty Wylie. Together with Beckwith, who was already on shore, these three staff officers now took over effective command at V Beach, leaving Tizard out of touch on board the *River Clyde*. Doughty Wylie learned from Beckwith that he did not consider an attack out of the Old Fort to be possible before daylight, but he hoped to begin one at about 05.30 after a thirty-minute naval bombardment of the village and the Old Fort. After returning to the *River Clyde* Doughty

Wylie discussed Beckwith's intentions with Williams and they decided that Williams should return to the beach to collect all the men he could find to support the attack, while Doughty Wylie remained on board. Beckwith was to lead the main attack into the village through the centre of the Old Fort and along the clifftops to the east, with Williams moving in support along the west of the Old Fort. Despite a certain amount of confusion over the bombardment, the attack inside the fort progressed well and by 10.00 had fought its way across the ruins to the postern gate in the northeastern corner. The supporting attack on the western edge, however, fared less well. Watching from the *River Clyde* Tizard noticed one party working its way along a path under the fort wall:

> When about halfway up this path and opposite to the abutment of the fort that had two windows in it a machine-gun opened on them from the nearest window. None of them were hit and they jumped over a low wall on their left and took cover. I happened to be watching the party and immediately sent a message to HMS *Albion* with the help of Captain Lambert to open on this abutment, and which was done very smartly and with good effect, and the machine gun troubled us no more.[102] (Lieutenant Colonel Henry Tizard)

The *Albion* had moved in before dawn from the position she had occupied throughout 25 April and by 05.30 had taken up a station close to the beach which enabled her to support operations on land much more effectively. The success of her support on 26 April stands in clear contrast to her failure on the previous day and her ability to destroy from a range of only 600 yards this concealed machine-gun post, which could not even be seen from her previous position, confirms that a similarly close station on 25 April might well have provided material assistance to the troops who sheltered during the day under the earth bank. However, despite this support the attack along the western edge of the fort was driven back to the beach.

Williams 'sent back to Wylie to say I was going over to [W] beach to see the conditions there, as further progress at V seemed impossible'.[103] Whether Doughty Wylie received Williams's message is hard to ascertain for at about 09.00 he decided to land with the

Military Landing Officer, Captain George Stoney. Leaving Stoney to organize the troops along the centre of the beach, Doughty Wylie himself moved across towards the Old Fort and started to assist Beckwith by leading up stragglers and reinforcements. Once through the fort, on leaving the postern gate, which led out near the point that the path climbed up from the Camber, the attack was held up by fire from the village. Immediately Beckwith sought to renew the momentum and, under the cover of some machine-guns that had been brought up, Walford and Captain Alfred Addison of the Hampshires led a movement out of the gate into the battered houses of the village; both officers were killed soon after. At about 12.00 Doughty Wylie moved across to the left to take command of the attack there as it slowly moved uphill towards the inland edge of the houses. It was not until 13.00 that the village was finally cleared and throughout this time the fighting was tense and difficult.

> The village was an awful snag. Every house and corner was full of snipers and you only had to show yourself in the streets to have a bullet at your head . . . we lost a lot of men and officers in it. It was rotten fighting, nothing to be seen of the enemy but fellows being knocked out everywhere. I got one swine of a Turk with my revolver, when searching a house for snipers but he nearly had me first.[104] (Lieutenant Guy Nightingale)

Once Sedd el Bahr had been consolidated, preparations for the final attack against Hill 141 began immediately. Stoney, whose task of sorting the effective men from the wounded along the beach had been made more difficult by their wide distribution, 'received a written order to take all I could find on the beach and advance with them. That made it quite clear to me what I was to do. I warned each party what they were to do and went up myself with a party of Munsters.'[105] From the *River Clyde* Tizard observed that Stoney's advance began at about 13.30 'and it was now that Corporal Cosgrove RM Fus, greatly distinguished himself in clearing a way through the wire entanglements and leading a charge after Sergeant Major Bennett had been killed'.[106] Under a fierce fire from the houses on the right, Cosgrove and the leading men rushed to the edge of the wire and started to try to cut it with wire-cutters, but found it too strong. Brought up short, instead Cosgrove attacked the stanchions on which it was hung. 'I threw the pliers from me. "Pull them up," I roared, "put your arms round them and pull them out of the ground." I dashed at the first one; heaved and strained, and then it came into my arms the same as you'd lift a child.'[107] As soon as a path was cleared, the assault continued and the Turkish trenches on the west of the village were taken.

Watching from the *Albion* Commander Gibson became aware of mounting preparations for the main attack from the village at about the same time:

> It was the most wonderful sight I've ever seen & I enjoyed it more than anything. They never signalled off they were going to attack but suddenly a firing line began to form in the open & men dashed by ones & twos to a little wall about 40 yards above [the] beach. We opened a heavy fire on the trenches & houses & old fort & I'm thankful to say kept the fire down. It was topping to watch. We in [the] foretop 130 feet up, only 1150 yards from the objective . . . on Hill 141 (feet high) & looking right down on it all. The only thing was I was so frightfully anxious some maxim would suddenly open on our men. Our gunlayers shot well & we went on firing until our soldiers were close up. . . . We didn't quite know when to stop firing . . . after we heard they were waiting a little for us to stop. However, it was better than not supporting them enough.[108] (Commander Worsley Gibson RN)

The final attack began at around 14.00 and developed in two separate directions. Led by Beckwith, the men on the right flank charged northeast, parallel with the cliffs above Morto Bay, towards the edge of the village. At the same time the left flank, led from the front by Doughty Wylie, moved directly to the north against the redoubt on Hill 141 and linked up with the men led by Stoney.

> We did not come under any heavy fire only losing about 4 men wounded. We rushed the line of trenches and saw the Turks clearing out. Not many getting away alive. The place proved to have been held by only a very few men – certainly if there had been more we could not have got up as easily as we did. This hill gave us the command of all the surrounding country, and gave us a real footing. It also gave us a certain amount of safety on the beach.[109] (Captain George Stoney)

During the final stages of the attack Doughty Wylie was killed.

> We went through the fort, through Sedd el Bahr village and we took Hill 141. And after we took the hill we dug in a bit of a trench and laid down there and Colonel Doughty Wylie was with us. He went all through the village. I never forget him because he had one puttee on and all he had was a walking stick. I didn't see a revolver and he come all through the village with us and, he was stood up – I was laid down here with the company – and he was stood up alongside of me, and his orderly and they were shouting to him to get down. 'Get down, sir, you'll get [hit].' Because there was sniping. And he wouldn't and an explosive bullet hit him right here, just below the eye, blew all the side of his face out. And his orderly got killed.[110] (Private W. Flynn)

Doughty Wylie's death was not without its consequences, removing yet another senior officer. But his reckless disregard for his own personal safety was perhaps the determining factor of his decisive leadership. For their actions on 26 April Doughty Wylie, Walford and Cosgrove were all awarded the VC, bringing to fifteen the number awarded to British servicemen for deeds performed at Helles within the first thirty-six hours of the campaign.[111]

At 14.32 29th Division Headquarters sent a signal to Wolley Dod at W Beach informing him that 'our men from V now swarming into old castle on top of Hill 141. Push forward your right to join up with old castle and consolidate your position'.[112] The news of the capture was quickly signalled to GHQ. But their relief was tempered by the news that Doughty Wylie, one of their number, was dead. Once it was clear that the attack was going to succeed, Tizard left the *River Clyde* to establish his Headquarters on Hill 141.

> On getting to my new position I found that the Munsters and Dublins were in possession of the hill and the Hampshire companies were on the right at the end of the village on a small hill. The Worcester Regiment from W Beach were advancing slowly clearing the ground between the hill 138 and the ruined hospital. The enemy were falling back slowly towards the Krithia Road and they were under shrapnel fire from the ships from 'W' Beach.[113] (Lieutenant Colonel Henry Tizard)

The Turks had begun their final withdrawal once the naval bombardment lifted immediately prior to the attack. Moving inland for about half a mile along the rear slopes of Hill 141 they had descended to the plain alongside Morto Bay and entered the relatively secure beds of the nullahs which reached up from there to Achi Baba. The advance of the Worcesters finally drew into line with the position on Hill 141 at about 16.00. Nightingale reckoned 'it was 6 by the time we finished firing on the Turks and we dug ourselves in, in an outpost position'.[114] The landing at Helles had finally made good a single, continuous position. However, the laurels of victory rightly belonged not to the British 29th Division but to the Turkish 3/26th Regiment. Like the successful defence of the hills around Ari Burnu by the 2/27th Regiment, the actions of the 3/26th Regiment in opposing so resolutely the main British landings around Cape Helles had been decisive and its commanding officer was fully justified in concluding modestly at the end of his report that they had done well for their country:

> I acknowledge that a battalion is the most trifling element of an army and that it did not do anything else but its duty and that to stop the enemy's intention in spite of his superior numbers and armaments was due to the grace of God. I consider, however, that its resistance and tenacity on the Seddulbahir shore on [25/26] April ... is a fine example of Turkish heroism.[115] (Colonel Mahmut)

4

The End of the Battle
of the Beaches

Once Hill 141 had finally been taken the time would then have
been propitious for the British line to advance in pursuit of the
retreating Turks and link up with the SWB at S Beach. But this was
not possible. Earlier in the morning Major General Hunter Weston
had ordered the left and centre of the line to consolidate their
positions until the arrival of the French troops from Tenedos. As,
by mid-afternoon, the French had still not arrived and fearful that
any further advance without them would render the British vulnerable to a concerted Turkish counter-attack, Hunter Weston ordered
the 29th Division to dig in where it was. 'There must be no retiring.
Every man must die at his post rather than retire.'[1]

Unabated by the fighting at Sedd el Bahr, at W Beach the
disembarkation of the 29th Division progressed slowly throughout
the day. Little more than twenty-four hours after the first landing,
Private Denis Buxton of the 88th Field Ambulance found the beach
already teeming with men and equipment:

> The shore is covered with men asleep and awake, mules, horses,
> GS wagons, limbers, Maltese carts, bykes, motor bykes (with
> despairing riders!), barrels and cans of water, boxes of beef, jam,
> bacon, cheese and potatoes, dixies, ammunition, rifles, and large
> coils of Turkish barbed wire, cut and piled in heaps. The rising
> ground is spattered with bits of equipment, etc, and a few dead.[2]
> (Private Denis Buxton)

During the afternoon the Drake Battalion of the 1st Naval Brigade,
RND landed and was attached to the 87th Brigade at X Beach to
provide additional support to the 29th Division and to relieve the
Anson Battalion, RND, which had landed with the covering force,
from its work on the beaches. The Brigade Métropolitaine also

119

finally arrived off Cape Helles at 19.00. But a shortage of boats once again made its disembarkation extremely slow and the leading troops did not begin to land on V Beach until 22.30. Earlier in the day General d'Amade had visited Hamilton on board the *Queen Elizabeth* and obtained his permission to withdraw the troops from Kum Kale. However, shortly after this was agreed, Turkish resistance on the Asiatic shore suddenly crumbled. A late attempt by Hamilton to halt the withdrawal failed and by the following morning all the French from Kum Kale had been re-embarked, together with 450 Turkish prisoners.

The late arrival of the French meant that the troops who had fought their way through Sedd el Bahr had to remain in position between Hill 141 and Morto Bay overnight. At 04.00 on 27 April General Vandenberg, in command of the Brigade Métropolitaine, finally reached Lieutenant Colonel Tizard's headquarters on Hill 141 and three hours later the British troops were able to leave their forward positions. During the night Tizard was also ordered to return to 29th Division Headquarters where, in the morning, he was relieved of his command for his apparent failure to achieve a quicker success at V Beach. Hunter Weston had hoped to resume the advance on Achi Baba at midday on 27 April, once the French had completed their landing. But by early morning, with only two fresh battalions landed, it was clear that the day would have to be used instead merely to prepare for a larger attack on the following day. It was agreed that until d'Amade landed, the French troops would be placed under the tactical command of the 29th Division and, as Hunter Weston felt that he would be better able to command this extended force from the central point of the *Euryalus*, Brigadier General Marshall was temporarily appointed to command the British troops on shore.

At 10.00 on 27 April 29th Division Headquarters issued orders for the present line to advance at 16.00 and establish a new line across the toe of the peninsula from Hill 236, a quarter of a mile northeast of S Beach, to the mouth of Gully Ravine. The French were to take over the right flank of the line, from the edge of the Dardanelles to a telegraph line which ran northeast from Sedd el Bahr. The 29th Division would then continue the line to the Aegean coast, with the 88th Brigade on the right, the 87th Brigade on the left and the remnants of the 86th Brigade in reserve. Reconnaissance patrols sent out during the day indicated that the ground in front of most of the British line was empty. The Turks, having suffered almost 1,900 casualties at Helles since 25 April,[3] had withdrawn from the hills around the coastline, which represented their first line of defence, to their planned second line of defence which ran northwest and southeast of Krithia from a point a few hundred yards beyond Y Beach to the high ground west of Kereves Dere a short distance inside the Dardanelles. The advance began as planned and the new line was reached by 17.30. But the left flank of the 87th Brigade remained in position 500 yards southwest of Gully Beach, creating a difficult bend near the centre of the British line.

Throughout the night the need to dig in once again meant that few of the troops were able to get any sleep as further vigilance was required against Turkish patrols. The advance of the French meant that the SWB were finally relieved at S Beach and able to rejoin their brigade.

> We were ordered to move across the peninsula immediately to X Beach, and report to the remainder of our Brigade, the 87th. We had no idea where they were, but Lieutenant Colonel Casson did have a map with a small 'x' marked on it. I took the map, and with my Intelligence Officer, Desmond Somerville, we took a rough compass bearing and moved off. Luckily we appeared to strike the small gap between our general line and the Turks, so all was well.[4] (Captain Aubrey Williams)

At 29th Division Headquarters during the evening of 27 April Hunter Weston drew up plans for a British and French advance on the following day. His scope was limited by a number of important factors, the most significant of which was the weak state of his division as a result of its heavy casualties. Of the three brigade commanders Marshall alone had survived; only seven out of the twelve original battalion commanders remained and three of these had been temporarily appointed to command infantry brigades, leaving just four still with their battalions. Although the casualties of most of the battalions of the 87th and 88th Brigades had not yet been severe, with the Border, Worcestershire and Essex Regiments sustaining less than 100 casualties each on 25 April, those of the 86th Brigade had been very high. Both the Lancashire and Royal Fusiliers had lost about half their officers and men. The Dublins and Munsters had lost slightly more men, and in addition the Munsters had lost seventeen officers and the Dublins twenty-four. The number of French troops landed by the evening of 27 April was still insufficient to compensate for these losses. Other factors, such as a shortage of both food and water and the fact that the number of guns ashore by the evening of 27 April still totalled only twenty-eight, imposed severe constraints on the offensive capability of the 29th Division. Had it been possible, it would undoubtedly have been better to suspend further attempts to advance until the division had been reorganized and more substantial reinforcements, such as the remainders of the French and Royal Naval Divisions, landed in support. But it was essential to proceed as quickly as the meagre resources allowed.

> Delay meant that the Turks would gain heart, and also more guns and reinforcements. It was a big risk to advance without reconnaissance and without artillery support, the thin line of infantry stretching across the peninsula, and no weight anywhere with which to carry through an assault. The guns of the ships could not give the close support necessary for infantry owing to the flatness of their trajectory. But it was necessary. Ground had to be gained to give safety in disembarking stores, men, and guns, and to support other landings.[5] (Captain Mynors Farmar)

Unable, as a result of these limitations, to fix Achi Baba as the final objective for the attack, Hunter Weston decided instead to move his troops into the requisite position for a final assault. He had always intended to attack Achi Baba from the west, advancing towards it from a line running just beyond the eastern outskirts of Krithia and this line was the objective he set for 28 April. Beginning at Hill 236 it was to run north to a point one-and-a-half miles beyond Krithia called Yazy Tepe, where it would turn back through almost 90 degrees towards Sari Tepe on the Aegean coast. The plan to achieve this was ambitious and involved a sweeping right wheel which, despite the weakness of the troops, would result in a final line over three miles longer than that held at the start of the battle.

On the left flank the 87th Brigade was to move forward on both sides of Gully Ravine for about four miles, advancing past Y Beach to form an acute-angled triangle with its apex fixed on Yazy Tepe. In the centre the 88th Brigade was to swing right through more than 45 degrees to capture Krithia before advancing a further 200 yards to the east to form a rough north–south line connecting the 87th Brigade with the Brigade Métropolitaine, whose right flank was to remain in position on Hill 236, while its left swung round to conform with the 88th Brigade as it advanced.

It was a complex manoeuvre to be carried out largely by tired troops over unknown ground. The poor maps and inadequate reconnaissance made before the landing suggested that the ground climbed evenly from the beaches up to the summit of Achi Baba. But this was not the case. Branching off the two main nullahs which ran southwest from the hill, Kirte Dere (or Krithia Nullah) and Kanli Dere (or Achi Baba Nullah), a series of smaller streambeds dissected the ground to form a complex network of strong natural defensive positions which were completely unappreciated by Divisional Headquarters. The depleted defenders of the landing had now been reinforced by four new battalions and, after regrouping along their second line of defence, the Turks had also established several interlocking posts across the rough terrain around the upper reaches of the nullahs half a mile in front of this.

The orders for the battle were issued by 29th Division Headquarters at 22.00 on 27 April. The attack was due to begin less than twelve hours later at 08.00 on the following morning. Orders could not be issued by the two British brigades until the early hours of 28 April; battalion commanders were not briefed until daybreak, with some battalions not receiving their final orders until less than an hour before the start of the attack, and the SWB, who had not finally rejoined the 87th Brigade until around 05.30, being immediately told that they were to form the brigade reserve for the attack, together with the two battalions of the RND working at X Beach for further support if necessary.

The preliminary bombardment against Krithia began on time and was followed shortly afterwards by the start of the infantry attack. Initially the advance was successful; but confusion in the centre of the line and the inability of the tired troops to maintain their early momentum soon brought it to a halt. An attempt by the Brigade Métropolitaine to advance its right flank from Hill 236 to the mouth of Kereves Dere in order to dominate the advanced Turkish positions there was unsuccessful and as a result the campaign suffered the first clear example of what might be termed the 'domino effect', a sequence of events which was to become familiar at Helles over the coming weeks and play a significant part in all of the general actions fought there.

The left flank of the French had been intended to keep pace with the 88th Brigade in the centre. But, instead of beginning its advance at the same time as the British right, the French left was ordered to wait until its right had established itself at the mouth of Kereves Dere; the failure to achieve this held up the left for over ninety minutes. Consequently, the adjoining battalion of the 88th Brigade was also forced to delay its initial advance, leaving the brigade's centre to go forward alone. In addition the 88th Brigade's left flank was holding the awkward, crooked section of the over-night line. The centre failed to wait for the troops on the left to make up the difference of over 600 yards before beginning its advance and when it moved forward its left flank was soon exposed as well. In due course, both flanks eventually caught up and the 88th Brigade succeeded in advancing a considerable distance, reportedly coming to within a mile of Krithia. But the disorganized start prevented the battalions from co-ordinating their advance and as the Turkish defence stiffened the fighting degenerated into a series of disconnected local actions which quickly drew in the brigade supports.

On the far left the 87th Brigade made a promising start and for the first three hours it advanced steadily astride Gully Ravine. But by 11.00, when still half a mile from Y Beach, the British troops had reached the Turks' forward posts and heavy rifle fire from these positions finally exhausted what little of the brigade's strength remained. By that time its two leading battalions had started to diverge and two SWB companies were ordered up to fill the gap, one on either side of Gully Ravine. Yet, although they were able to reunite the line, the SWB were unable to restart the advance. Many of the British soldiers had now been fighting almost continually for over three days and were nearing exhaustion. Across the line, once it had finally begun, the advance of the Brigade Métropolitaine at first also made good progress. But as feared the Turkish positions at the mouth of Kereves Dere levelled a fierce enfilading fire against the French left flank as it moved past them. Under this fire the ground seized proved impossible to hold and towards midday the French were forced to return towards their starting position.

Soon after the start of the battle, following the arrival of d'Amade, Hunter Weston landed from the *Euryalus* and resumed command of his division. He sent Marshall forward to reinvigorate the attack and Marshall arrived behind the front line just as the first advance was drawing to a halt. Supplies of ammunition, particularly within the 88th Brigade, were also beginning to run very low and he attempted to use the divisional reserve, the 86th Brigade, to solve both problems at once.

> The 86th Brigade received orders to take forward ammunition for the 88th, and to carry the latter on in the advance to the objective given. This was a spur lying northeast of Krithia, and involved the capture of the village. The Royal Fusiliers and the Lancashire Fusiliers were given written orders; and the firing line and supports for the attack were organized in a nullah, under cover, and launched under the command of Major Bishop. The Royal Munster Fusiliers and the Royal Dublin Fusiliers formed the reserve.[6] (Captain Mynors Farmar)

Marshall also visited 87th Brigade Headquarters and urged Lieutenant Colonel Casson, who was temporarily commanding the brigade, to start his left moving again. A third company of SWB was sent forward on the eastern side of Gully Ravine to support the brigade's right flank and parties of the Anson and Drake Battalions were directed to the opposite side to support the left. Aubrey Williams was also sent across the Gully to bolster the SWB, who had been directed there earlier in the day.

> General Marshall said to our Commanding Officer: 'Send your Adjutant over to the left to see there is no withdrawal, most important to hold our left'; so away I went running as fast as the ground would allow in full kit. . . . Then I decided to dump my pack as I could not go fast enough under the weight. Down I

125

went across the gully and up the other side, and finally reached some of our men of 'B' Company. By then I was too puffed to run. Company Sergeant-Major Alabaster shouted out: 'Run sir, run,' to which I replied: 'Sergeant Major, if the whole Turkish army was after me I could not run another step.' Anyhow I continued to walk slowly behind the line, speaking to the men, and telling them that if the Turks came too close they were to fire rapid at them, and then charge with the bayonet. The Turks all the time were firing at us with rifles and the odd artillery shell came over. One or two men started to move back, but I ordered them back into the line again and I shouted out that I would shoot the next man that left the line. Not long afterwards a man, I don't know which regiment he was from, jumped up and started to run back. I was just taking aim when a rifle cracked just near me and the man rolled over. The man who fired was one of my own men who had attached himself to me as my orderly. I said: 'What did you do that for?', to which he replied: 'I knew you wouldn't like to do it, Sir.'[7] (Captain Aubrey Williams)

Following receipt of Marshall's orders the forward battalions of the 86th Brigade moved up quickly towards the left centre of the overall line, taking, as their 'point of direction ... a prominent white mosque at the western edge of Krithia village'.[8] Advancing in short rushes they reached the edge of a small wood, later known as Twelve Tree Copse, immediately due north of a larger one called Fir Tree Wood, where they halted. Farmar and a small party continued through Twelve Tree Copse until they emerged on the far side on a slope which led forward to Krithia.

The buildings on the outskirts could be clearly seen, and Turks running back and jumping into some small quarries. Shouts for the line to come forward met with no response. Probably the men who had made the rapid advance were exhausted, carrying heavy packs and 200 rounds of ammunition. Officers had been wounded, and it is probable that no one responsible was left unwounded who knew that the little party had gone beyond the wood to reconnoitre while reorganization was taking place.[9] (Captain Mynors Farmar)

126

All efforts failed to bring the men forward from the southern edge of the copse and gradually the forward party was reduced in number to only three. In frustration they watched the Turks starting to return towards them.

> The Turks came up quite close, and a machine-gun opened fire some forty yards away, firing obliquely under cover of the wood and making use of the depression in the ground. The party of three decided to bolt; they crawled into the wood, and did what was possible to find if there was any one left there alive, but apparently the wounded had got clear. Both sides were now firing at the wood, and nothing could be seen of the British, every one had gone back. . . . It took more than a month and many lives to regain the ground which was ours on this day, and all this time the Turks were digging and transforming the slopes of Krithia into the outworks of the Achi Baba stronghold.[10] (Captain Mynors Farmar)

The extreme left of the 87th Brigade resumed its advance along the Aegean coast at about 13.00. But when the line started to approach the nullahs which ran down to Y Beach and the trenches which had been dug around them by the British on 25 April, a strong Turkish counter-attack succeeded in driving it back again. On board the *Queen Elizabeth*, which had moved down from Gaba Tepe and been in position close to the shore on the left flank of the British line since mid-morning, one of Hamilton's staff, Captain Guy Dawnay, witnessed the subsequent sequence of events:

> We suddenly saw line upon line of Turkish infantry come streaming across the open towards a big ravine running down to the sea, which lay across the line of advance of the extreme left of our troops. They got under cover in a big depression before the ship's guns could get on to them, and we all waited rather breathlessly to see what was going to happen. Our people were coming steadily up with their left on the top of the cliffs over the shore, while the ships were shelling the ravine with apparently no effect. When our troops had got to within about 500 or 600 yards of the ravine, suddenly a mass of Turks leapt out and charged! It was a magnificent counter-attack, and we had a most

127

wonderful view of it. The Turks came on in quite a dense mass, bayonets fixed, and only stopping now and then to fire standing, while our men had lain down and were firing away at them like mad. Oddly enough, the Turks did not seem to be suffering any great loss as they came on, though they came very thick and bunched together. As soon as they appeared the *Q.E.* trained her 15-inch guns on them – but it takes a terrible time (or so it seems at a moment like that) to get naval guns going. But just as it began to look as if they must get right into our line – the Turks can't have been 200 yards distant – the 15-inch spoke. . . . Never was shell better aimed or more timely. Everything was covered with a great burst of black & white smoke, and dust & earth flying into the air. Then as it cleared away – nothing but a few of the Turks racing back to the ravine for cover. It was rather awful, really![11] (Captain Guy Dawnay)

The British retirement in the face of the Turkish counter-attack was followed with some concern by those in the *Queen Elizabeth* and in response to the sight of some men starting to scramble down the cliffs to the beach Hamilton sent Captain Aspinall ashore to rally them and restore the line. During the afternoon a similar retirement began further across to the right above Gully Ravine after an unauthorized order to 'retire' spread among the men, apparently as a result of the sudden recall of the RND men to X Beach, which caused others in the line to follow suit. The remaining officers in the area were hard pushed to counter the momentum of the retirement, but eventually succeeded and returned the line to a position about 200 yards south of the old Y Beach position.

On the far right, after the Brigade Métropolitaine had been driven out of its forward positions, Vandenberg attempted to restore the line during the early afternoon by deploying his final reserves. But a reinforced Turkish defence repulsed the attack and the French ended back on their original line which again exposed the right flank of the 88th Brigade. At almost the same time the left flank of this brigade also started to withdraw from its forward position and the circumstances in which the brigade began the battle were repeated, with only the centre pushed forward. Eventually this too was ordered to conform with the positions on either side. Many of the men fell back over a considerable distance and felt very frustrated at having to do so. Just over a fortnight later Lieutenant Henry O'Hara, a subaltern in the Dublin Fusiliers who by the end of the day was in command of the battalion, described 28 April in a letter to Captain French as 'the day of the big retreat – a most awful show it was – the whole division simply took to their heels and ran – if the Turks had followed us up we would have been driven into the sea I think'.[12]

By the end of the afternoon there was little chance of further improvement. At 17.15 Marshall signalled to Hunter Weston that, unless specifically ordered to do otherwise, he proposed to hold his present line until dusk and then to dig in a short distance to the rear of this position. Throughout the afternoon Hunter Weston had received many anxious messages about the vicissitudes of the battle. But he had remained unperturbed and at 18.00 he told Marshall to entrench as he proposed. After dark the units in the line were sorted as best as possible and defensive positions established along what became known later as the Eski Line.

The First Battle of Krithia had been a disappointment. The 29th Division had proved too weak and too tired to prevail and the Brigade Métropolitaine had been unable to make headway against the hidden Turkish artillery and well-sited defensive positions above Kereves Dere. In contrast the Turks had once again used the natural advantages of the landscape well. At key points during the battle they had also been significantly reinforced. At 11.00 the Turkish line facing the 88th Brigade had appeared to break and an order had been issued for a retirement to Achi Baba; but the opportune arrival of fresh troops prevented it. Although they were extinguished by the *Queen Elizabeth*'s shell, the Turks who attacked the 87th Brigade had also recently been reinforced and the final attacks made by the Brigade Métropolitaine were again directed against new troops. Between the morning of 27 April and the afternoon of 28 April the Turks received eight reinforcing battalions. But to the strength of the attacking force the Brigade Métropolitaine added just five complete battalions and those sections of the Anson and Drake Battalions which were also drawn into the line were too small to have any significant effect.

The central unit in the attack, the 29th Division, had received no direct reinforcements since the start of the landing. The mistake of sending the division 3,500 miles from Great Britain without the standard 10 per cent draft that had accompanied the divisions of the BEF to France in August 1914 was now trenchantly clear. 'Today each Battalion of the 29th Division would have been joined by two keen Officers and one hundred keen men – fresh – all of them fresh! The fillip given would have been far, far greater than that which the mere numbers (1,200 for the Division) would seem to imply.'[13] Yet even these reinforcements, had they been available, would not have made up the division's loss. By the end of 28 April the 29th Division had been more than decimated. In the first five days it had lost a total of 187 officers and 4,266 men.[14] From an approximate strength of 104 officers and 4,000 men, the infantry of the 86th Brigade alone had been reduced to 36 officers and 1,850 men,[15] with the Royal Dublin Fusiliers down to just 374 men and Lieutenant O'Hara. Yet for these losses they had gained a position which at its maximum was only three miles deep. Although this should be acknowledged as a significant achievement, it cannot be claimed as a success.

Along the Gaba Tepe front line the question of withdrawal which had so preoccupied the generals during the night of 25/26 April had never been contemplated by the men in touch with the Turks. After dark the Turks' guns had ceased firing and their sniper fire lost its former accuracy. Although the Anzacs' line continued to be probed, forcing them to keep up a steady fire to hold off the Turks, the intense pressure of the late afternoon abated and, after returning to collect the picks and shovels which they had dropped as they landed, the men began to dig their first deep trenches. Wherever possible, gaps which had been reported in the line were filled by the remaining companies of the NZ&A Division as they slowly disembarked, and gradually it became relatively secure. As the sun rose on 26 April, Rear Admiral Thursby, who had by then returned to the *Queen*, closed his ships in to the shore and opened fire. From the sea the bombardment appeared to be devastating, but on land the men in the line, such as Captain Kenneth Gresson of the Canterbury Battalion, soon realized this was not the case:

During the night the Turks had been strongly reinforced and early in the morning they made the most determined attempts to drive us from the position we had won. As soon as the Turkish masses were sighted creeping forward to the attack, rifle and machine-gun fire increased until every available rifle and machine-gun were in the firing line. The hills over which the Turks had to advance were plastered with shells by the warships, each of which had a certain sector allotted to it. . . . In the firing line the din was terrific. Behind the roar of the ships' guns – the snapping bark of the *Bacchante*'s six inch mingled with the boom of the twelve inch and the still deeper and louder boom of the *Queen Elizabeth*'s fifteen inch. In front the hills ablaze with bursting shells, dense clouds of smoke rising as pieces of hill were hurled skywards. Above, the sky filled with puffs of white smoke which marked the bursting of Turkish shrapnel and higher still, far up aloft seaplanes circling and soaring as they observed the effects of the warships' fire. Yet throughout it all the Turks came on and it was only after repeated bayonet charges on our part that they were finally checked and fell back to entrench themselves, leaving us free to improve our trenches and communications.[16] (Captain Kenneth Gresson)

Despite its limitations, the effect of the bombardment on the morale of the Anzacs, who had been without artillery support during most of the previous day, was still good and on the Turks correspondingly bad. Once the Turkish attacks had been success-fully repulsed, the position continued to stabilize and the anxiety and tension which had hung over it for the past twenty-four hours gradually dispelled. As the front line became more clearly defined, the warships were able to provide supporting fire with greater ease and, when the landing of field artillery resumed, the number of guns ashore also began to increase steadily, helping to consolidate the position and reduce the pressure on the infantry alone to fight off Turkish attacks.

During the day, wherever possible a start was made in with-drawing the scattered units of the 3rd Brigade from their positions along the line to return them to the beach for reorganization. Until this had been completed and the two Anzac divisions supplemented by fresh reinforcements, no serious attempts could be made to enlarge the Anzac position. Yet despite this, Mustafa Kemal Bey, who had been in overall command of the Turkish forces in the area since the previous afternoon, remembered it as a critical day. His difficulties arose largely from the heavy casualties that the 19th Division had suffered in containing the landing. He found himself in the same position as Birdwood, forced to wait for reinforcements before the offensive could be resumed. His arrived first. Towards the end of 26 April he heard that he was to receive two further regiments and more mountain artillery on the following morning and he decided to use these new regiments, together with the one unused regiment of the 19th Division, to launch an immediate, concerted attack against the whole Anzac line in order to 'drive those in front of us into the sea'.[17]

Yet when his troops began to deploy on 27 April they encountered many of the same problems that had thwarted the Australian attempts to advance two days earlier. Before the start of the battle the Turkish regiments became dispersed among the broken ground to the east of the Anzac line and as a result they were late arriving at their starting points. This confusion was then exacerbated by the fire of the British warships, which began even before Mustafa Kemal had issued his final orders and not only caused serious casualties, but also had a deleterious effect on their morale. The combination of these problems made the attacks so disconnected and irresolute that when they finally got under way at ANZAC Headquarters it was not even realized that they formed part of a determined attack. The same level of detachment was not felt in the front line, even though the attack was eventually defeated.

> After a heavy bombardment all the morning, attacks were made in force on our right and left. First the right wing broke and we had the mortification of seeing our boys retire at a double. I ordered my gun to swing round and we checked the pursuit by pouring in a heavy enfilade fire on the pursuing Turco. This broke him up and gave our boys time to collect and take up a fair position which their supports had managed to get ready. Just then we noticed that the new line was in the rear of us, so that our position, which had been isolated all through was now liable to a daring enfilade on the right. We at once started digging and

throwing up a parapet to meet this new danger, when I was thunderstruck to see our left, which had been really well reinforced, give way and retreat. You can guess our opinion of our chances. There we were, out in front, dug right in, no protection on our right or left and enfilade fire coming on us and our retreating troops. When suddenly the 'Lousy Liz' lost her name for ever. She is now 'The Lady'. Like a bolt from the blue a 15″ shell fell fair in among the pursuing enemy. Before they could rally another fell, then another. A panic set up and the momentary triumph of John Turco was over.[18] (Captain Dixon Hearder)

With the extreme left of the Anzac line around Russell's Top and Pope's Hill clearly the weakest and most vulnerable point, the Turks made their strongest attack against it from Baby 700. The head of Walker's Ridge was still held by Lieutenant Colonel Braund with a mixed party of New Zealanders and Australians. Despite the exhaustion of these men, at 08.00 Braund led them forward in an attack intended to close off Russell's Top before the Turkish attack could force its way through the gap which existed there.

A confusing fight developed in which the line moved backwards and forwards around the position Braund was trying to estabish and he called for reinforcements. Despite the protests of its commanding officer, Lieutenant Colonel William Malone, part of the Wellington Battalion was sent forward. The New Zealanders were not able even to move into position before being hit by fire from the higher ground to the northeast and, unabated, the fighting continued all day. Towards the end of the afternoon the number of Turks moving forward from Baby 700 increased. But their massed formations were effectively dispersed by the fire of the ships, which prevented them from developing an attack against the disorganized Anzac position. By evening a precarious line had been formed across the head of Russell's Top in touch with the outpost on Pope's Hill. But once the Wellington Battalion had relieved the remnants of Braund's party at 18.00, Malone repositioned the line where it would be less exposed. Braund's decision to meet the Turkish attack head on in a charge was extremely risky and nearly failed. Malone, in particular, was vehement in his criticism, believing Braund should have been court-martialled. But, in mitigation, it must be recognized that Braund's stolid defence of Walker's Ridge had successfully secured the left flank since the afternoon of 25 April. While at rest in Shrapnel Gully on 4 May, Braund, who was slightly deaf, was killed by a sentry whose challenge he failed to answer.

The gradual reorganization of the Anzac units brought a degree of unity and order to Gaba Tepe and on 27 April Birdwood was able to divide the position into two divisional sectors. In the south the line was allocated to the 1st Australian Division. Beginning at a point about 2,000 yards north of Gaba Tepe near the centre of Z Beach, later known as Brighton Beach, the line climbed up Bolton's Ridge, crossed the western half of 400 Plateau and continued north along Second Ridge to Courtney's Post, a short distance beyond MacLaurin's Hill where the commander of the 1st Brigade, Colonel Henry MacLaurin, and his Brigade Major were both killed by sniper fire on 27 April. In turn, this section of the line was subdivided between the 2nd Brigade in the south and the intermixed 1st and 3rd Brigades in the north.

To the north of Courtney's Post, curving round the head of Monash Valley and then falling back down Walker's Ridge to the sea about 500 yards to the north of Ari Burnu, the line was allocated to the NZ&A Division. Of this division's two brigades, the 4th Brigade, commanded by Colonel John Monash, held the northern spine of Second Ridge as far as Quinn's Post and the outpost on Pope's Hill, embracing the exposed, inland slopes of Monash Valley. From the summit of Russell's Top to the end of Walker's Ridge and the outposts which had been established beyond it to secure the coast from the north, the line was held by the New Zealand Brigade. Both divisional headquarters, along with ANZAC Headquarters, were established above Anzac Cove along the lower slopes of Plugge's Plateau.

Following the landing of the Drake Battalion at Helles on 26 April the remainder of the RND had also sailed south from Bulair later that evening. But congestion at W Beach on 27 April prevented any further battalions from landing and instead they were forced to wait aimlessly off the coast. In the early hours of the following day, after reporting the successful repulse of the latest Turkish attacks to GHQ, Birdwood asked for reinforcements to help secure his line and at 11.00 the transports of the RND were ordered to sail north once again, this time to Gaba Tepe. The divisional commander, Major General Archibald Paris, landed and agreed with Birdwood that four battalions from the 3rd Royal Marine and the 1st Naval Brigades would begin landing later that day. During the late afternoon of 28 April the Chatham and Portsmouth Battalions began to disembark and on reaching the shore the Chathams moved directly inland to relieve the Australians on MacLaurin's Hill.

> Landing in horse boats on the open beach at dusk, we were led by an Australian guide up the bottom of a deep ravine. This was our first experience of being in enemy country. It was all rather eerie. In the darkness, the guide lost his way, which led to counter-marching and some confusion. He eventually brought us to a very steep slope, at the top of which the Australians were entrenched only a few yards from the edge of the ravine. We took over the trenches and they withdrew into rest. For four days the Battalion held this precarious line wholly devoid of depth against spasmodic attacks, and suffered grievous casualties.[19] (Lieutenant Arthur Chater)

The arrival of the Portsmouth and Chatham Battalions helped to speed up the reorganization of the Anzac brigades into the new divisional sectors, particularly among the most intermixed units of the 1st and 3rd Australian Brigades, whose line from Courtney's Post through MacLaurin's Hill to the northern half of 400 Plateau the Marines now took over. The line at this point surrounded Wire Gully, a watercourse which led steeply down from the narrow crest of MacLaurin's Hill towards the Turkish lines, and at the bottom of Wire Gully a series of advanced battle posts, each held by only a handful of men, had been established in front of the main line by the first Australians. Many of these posts had been lost in the days following the landing after the occupants had been killed; but others remained precariously held and these the Marines also took over.

To the north of Wire Gully and MacLaurin's Hill the line was formed almost entirely by isolated posts. There had been little opportunity along Second Ridge to develop these cramped, overlooked positions into a continuous trench line and conditions there remained very poor, providing a harsh introduction for the Marines, who moved in the space of only a few hours from their transports to the sordid conditions of the front line.

> We took up these positions in the dark. We were along the top of this ridge and there was what you might call a ditch about two feet deep which the Australians had dug along the top and made a kind of trench. But there was very little protection there. Every few yards lay a dead man. So you had to crawl over him to take up your position. There were quite a number of dead men there. You could feel them and see them – that's not a very nice experience. Self preservation was the main thing and you had to keep your head down as much as possible. The lower you could get, the better it was. I can assure you it was very steep, just like a railway embankment, all around, with scrub and bush and trees – not very big trees – but oddly enough quite a few that were like Scots firs. They hadn't managed to clean up all the snipers. There were still snipers in this bush behind the front line. They used to pick quite a number of men off before they got wiped out because they couldn't get out once they were behind the front line and we picked them off gradually. What you used to watch for in the dark was to see where the flash came from which betrayed where they were and we picked up quite a number like that.[20] (Private Harry Baker)

The first two battalions of Marines were followed on 29 April by the Deal Battalion RMLI, which relieved part of the 2nd Australian Brigade and extended the Marines' line further south across 400 Plateau, and the Nelson Battalion, which was placed in reserve; Brigadier General Charles Trotman, in command of the 3rd Royal Marine Brigade, assumed command of the northern half of the 1st Australian Division's line.

As the scattered Australians were relieved, the exhausted, bedraggled men made their way back to the mouth of Shrapnel Gully. Hearder learnt from a note thrown into his isolated position on the morning of 28 April that he and his men were to be relieved that night:

We had quite a happy day and engaged every Turk we saw in a most lighthearted way and that night we left our little home and despite much sniping we reached the Beach about midnight. Next day I looked up a lot of pals along the Beach and saw Jack Booth. I scribbled a note to Mother and enclosed the note of relief. . . . I sought out my Colonel and reported to him. He was most pleased to see me and to hear I still had a few men. It seems I and all my boys had been reported as wiped clean out. No one had seen us and so complete was our isolation that the inference was a fairly safe and obvious one.[21] (Captain Dixon Hearder)

In countless similar incidents men were now reunited for the first time since 25 April. But as often they found that others they had hoped to find again were not there. By midday on 30 April the 3rd Brigade had suffered total casualties of killed, wounded and missing of 62 officers and 1,803 other ranks and the 1st Brigade 60 officers and 1,325 other ranks. When the final battalions of the 2nd Brigade were relieved the total casualties of the 1st Australian Division were found to be 179 officers and 4,752 other ranks, nearly 500 more than even the 29th Division.[22]

At the same time as the battalions of the RND moved into position in the centre of the Anzac line, Mustafa Kemal too received reinforcements. On almost every night the Turks made local attacks against different parts of the line; but after being strengthened by five new battalions Mustafa Kemal decided to make another concerted push against the centre of the line on 1 May. The success of the naval fire in breaking up his formations on 27 April convinced him that he should attack at dawn, with the attacking battalions moving into position well in advance under the cover of darkness. Shortly before the opening of the battle he called his commanders to his headquarters on Scrubby Knoll, known by then to the Turks as Kemalyeri, and addressed them:

I am of the wholehearted opinion that we must finally drive the enemy opposing us into the sea if it means the death of us all. Our position compared to that of the enemy is not weak. The enemy's morale has been completely broken. He is ceaselessly digging to find himself a refuge. . . . I simply cannot accept that there are among us and among the troops we command those who would not rather die here than experience a second chapter of Balkan disgrace. If you feel there are such people let us shoot them at once with our own hands.[23] (Mustafa Kemal Bey)

In preparation for the attack the Turks began to collect in Wire Gully towards the end of the afternoon of 30 April.

The second day the Turks began to attack in the afternoon in huge numbers en masse. They came out of this scrub like rabbits towards you and – Oh my word! – we had a tough time repelling that. I'd got two men loading for me and I kept firing these rifles and they didn't get within fifty yards finally. I reckon if you missed one you'd probably have the next man. Mind you, you didn't get too much time to aim. You'd got to get on with the job. It was all over in minutes. They were heaped up wounded and dead.[24] (Private Harry Baker)

During the attack the battle posts in front of the Marines' line were surrounded. The following morning a stretcher-bearer from the Portsmouth Battalion, Lance Corporal Walter Parker, succeeded in reaching one of the isolated posts at the bottom of Wire Gully and helped to deal with the wounded until he himself was hit. He was the first soldier to win the VC in the Anzac operations.[25]

The attack, made by a battalion of Turks, developed in earnest at 04.00 on 1 May and, despite the Marines' weak position above Wire Gully, it was successfully defeated. During the attack Private Joseph Clements of the Deal Battalion used his machine-gun to devastating effect:

There was flags flying and bugles blowing and they were coming over in droves. I'd got our gun fixed up and I sat there and I was shooting, swinging it backwards and forwards, not taking aim but you couldn't miss. No more than two hundred yards, there was so many, they weren't spread out because there wasn't the room for them to spread out owing to the rocky nature of the ground. There was a kind of an opening through which they were coming. We had this end and they were coming through the other end. I was firing, the No. 2 he was seeing the belt ran and getting a belt out of the box ready. The others were taking a pot shot now and again with their rifles. You couldn't see the effects, you were just firing into a kind of a big object. It didn't look like individual people. It finished all of a sudden. They just turned and there wasn't anybody there any more.[26] (Private Joseph Clements)

Once again Mustafa Kemal's tactics of a strong frontal assault against the Anzac line had failed. Even without the fire of the ships and when attacking one of the most vulnerable points, the Turks were unable to prevail and gained only further heavy casualties.

In addition to allowing the Australian brigades to be reorganized, the arrival of the four RND battalions also reintroduced the possibility of an Anzac attack. During the last days of April Turkish artillery fire against the northern half of the Anzac line was relatively quiet and this created a mistaken impression that many of the Turks had been withdrawn for transfer to Helles. An ambitious plan was drawn up by Birdwood for an attack on 1 May with the dual aim of capturing Baby 700 and throwing the whole of the Anzac line forward on to the eastern edge of 400 Plateau and Mortar Ridge, which lay around 400 yards inland of the northern half of Second Ridge. Principally the attack was to be carried out by the NZ&A Division. But after relieving the Marines the 1st Australian Brigade was to form the right flank of the attack on 400 Plateau. Following the death of MacLaurin and the resumption of command of the New Zealand Brigade by Colonel Johnston, the 1st Brigade had been placed under the command of Brigadier General Walker, who felt that his brigade was too weak to advance as required by the plan. Only hours before the attack was due to start Walker convinced Major General Bridges that, as the 1st Australian Division had only partially completed its reorganization, it was not in a fit state to take part, and when these views reached Birdwood he was forced to cancel the operation along Second Ridge.

However, Major General Godley still believed that the NZ&A Division was capable of carrying out its part of the plan concerning the capture of Baby 700 and, with the date simply postponed by twenty-four hours to the evening of 2 May, it was agreed that it would still be made. Godley and his staff decided to attack at night after the most concentrated bombardment yet seen at Gaba Tepe. At 19.00 the guns both on land and at sea were to fire for fifteen minutes before lifting on to Battleship Hill and Chunuk Bair. Three battalions, two Australian and one New Zealand, were then to advance from Monash Valley to assault Baby 700. Once they had seized the hill, a company of the Canterbury Battalion would then move through the Nek and extend the line along the northern side of Malone's Gully to No. 1 Outpost. The Nelson Battalion of the RND was to act as support and the three battalions of Marines, who were to be relieved on the night of 2 May, were also to be available as a reserve if necessary.

It was a complicated plan that was entirely dependent on the simultaneous and co-ordinated movements of the three attacking battalions. Yet such a level of co-ordination had been noticeably lacking in all the operations carried out to date, both by the Anzacs and against them by the Turks, and the attack on Baby 700 proved to be no exception. The bombardment opened on time and the shells appeared to be having great effect on the Turkish positions. But, when it advanced, almost immediately the attack began to falter. The New Zealanders of the Otago Battalion had not yet reached their starting position, leaving the Australians to move off alone. The Otagos had been in position on Walker's Ridge when word reached them that they were to take part in the attack and had been forced to march down Walker's Ridge, along the beach to Hell Spit and then up Shrapnel Gully and Monash Valley to reach the foot of Pope's Hill. Their commanding officer left insufficient time to move along the heavily congested route and they did not arrive at Pope's Hill until 19.45, thirty minutes after the intended start. Despite this, the Australians initially managed to make some progress. But the strength of the Turkish fire which met them showed that, despite its impressive appearance, the bombardment's effect had once again been limited and they were prevented from reaching their objectives. By the time the Otagos were ready to begin their attack at 20.45, the Australian advance had been completely held up on the exposed ground surrounding Pope's Hill, Bloody Angle and Quinn's Post, later known as the Chessboard after the network of trenches which evolved there, and the men were forced to dig in wherever they could. Once in position the Otagos also moved off. With the Australians already halted the Turks were able to concentrate all their fire on the New Zealanders.

Casualties were immediately heavy and all they could do was to work their way into a position roughly in line with the Australian left.

After three hours it was clear to those engaged in the attack that it had not succeeded. Yet at his headquarters Godley believed that the Otagos had at least reached the inland side of the Nek and in accordance with the plan he ordered forward the company of the Canterbury Battalion who were to push through it from Walker's Ridge. Gresson had been informed at 17.00 that his company was to carry out an attack that night:

> On receiving these orders I immediately went up to the top of Walker's Ridge with the officers and made a reconnaissance as well as I was able through the periscope. As soon as it was dark I took the Company into the Wellington trenches and led them over the parapet into the dense scrub in front. The ground was thickly covered with Turkish dead and the stench was horrible. As soon as I had got all the Company out and lying down in the bushes I went forward with two scouts to examine the ground in front which was entirely unknown to me. I found as I expected a narrow neck or saddle connecting the ridge we were on with the hill which was our objective and across this ran a track about two feet wide. It had evidently been used by the Turks on returning for it was well worn and strewn with corpses. On advancing along this I found that the other end was commanded by two Turkish trenches one of which was firing but not in our direction though a few stray bullets came across occasionally. It was at once evident to me that any attempt to take the Company across this narrow track must result in failure as the neck would be swept from these trenches either with rifle fire or by machine-guns and men could not be put across in sufficient numbers to assault. I consulted two of my officers and found they supported me in my opinion. I accordingly returned to Walker's Ridge and making my way to Brigade Headquarters informed the Brigadier that I considered it would be foolish to attempt the crossing. Although obviously reluctant to abandon this scheme he left the matter in my hands and I returned to the Company and ordered them to retire which was accomplished without any confusion.[27] (Captain Kenneth Gresson)

141

Throughout the night the attack continued to the east and first part of the Nelson Battalion and then two more companies of Australians were thrown into the fight. During the early hours of 3 May Godley told Monash to use the Chatham and Portsmouth Battalions, who had only left their section of the line on the previous evening, to consolidate the ground that had been taken. To the two battalions of Marines, who were expecting twenty-four hours' rest, the order came as quite a shock.

> As the Battalion reached the foot of the slopes to the crest, 'A' Company was for some reason diverted to the right. From our position near Quinn's Post, we watched the remainder of the Battalion struggling up the steep slope. As the leading waves reached the crest, they were caught in machine-gun fire from the flank. Many of the bodies rolled back down the hill they had so laboriously climbed; some lay where they fell until two days later we sent out in darkness and pulled them down, Monday 3rd May was a black day for the Chatham Battalion.[28] (Lieutenant Arthur Chater)

Among the men who moved under Chater's gaze on to the slight ridge which lay a short distance to the east of Pope's Hill, and later became known as Dead Man's Ridge after the bodies of the Marines who remained there after the end of the battle, was Harry Baker:

> Our officer ordered us to scale this steep rise to the top of the toe of the position and we lay there at the end. He said: 'Open fire at 200 yards,' and he stood up in full view of the enemy. Suddenly I saw him with a huge triangular cut below his right shoulder blade. His shirt opened up and he came back. He was twenty yards forward of our position and he ordered me to move to the left which I did. He lay where I was lying. He was still shouting: 'Open fire at 200,' to all the men and we lay there shoulder to shoulder. After Captain Richards had ordered me to move to the left we fired away at all the Turks who kept advancing. They were then about one hundred and fifty yards away and they came in almost mass formation so we had very easy targets. Next to me there was a space and an Australian came and lay next to me and on his right another man scaled this steep slope and it turned out to be Major Armstrong of the Portsmouth Battalion, Royal

Marines. Why he was there I don't know. Captain Richards was next to him and all the way to the right were men shoulder to shoulder lying on the ground. No cover at all, just lying on the very ridge. Suddenly a machine-gun crackled away at right angles to us; we were firing ahead and it was even behind us, on the right. He had a good view because he was higher up and he could see exactly what he was doing. It was like mowing grass I should think for him. This machine-gun went along and killed every man on the ridge except the Australian and me. We were the only two left on the ridge. The Australian said: 'The bastards can't kill me. They've had lots of tries. They can't kill me.' I looked again. The machine-gun started barking again behind us and came along. It was knocking the sand up and covered every man again, every man. It came right along. I felt the bullets thud into the Aussie and he never spoke again. . . . I had a bullet through the right foot and I felt as though I'd been hit by a donkey. When I saw those bullets coming along, I knew that it would be the end of me if they came along far enough. . . . They say your past comes up, but I can say truthfully that I hadn't got much past at nineteen and all I thought of was, 'Am I going to live?' That's all I thought; that's what struck me. 'Am I going to be lucky?' Because I couldn't see how I could be with all these bullets coming along and I waited for it. It was inevitable. But for some reason the gun stopped at the Aussie and my right foot.[29] (Private Harry Baker)

The attack had been a failure, and for Godley and the NZ&A Division, whose first independent operation it had been, it proved a severe disappointment. Over-ambitious and poorly prepared, it had finally been ruined by the late arrival of the Otagos, among whom a discernible sense of culpability spread about their part in the ruin of the plan. The battle was already beyond salvation by the time the first units of the RND were sent forward. The sharp criticism of these troops, many of whom had already been in the line for four days and defeated a concerted Turkish attack, which has frequently been directed against them, is unfounded and in fact, despite moments in the line on MacLaurin's Hill when their inexperience showed, the RND's time at Anzac was not discreditable.

By mid-morning on 3 May the situation was once again a stalemate. The Anzacs had shown on numerous occasions that their line was now secure. But the latest attack had also shown the same was true for the Turks. When Hamilton visited Birdwood on 29 April they had discussed the question of what the beach on which the Australians had landed, and which ever since had been the main point of entry for all the troops and stores, should be called. They agreed that it should be known by the acronym which had first been applied to the Corps in Egypt, and a few days later Hamilton formally announced it was to be named Anzac Cove, a name which has endured ever since. Both Australia and New Zealand had now made their first mark upon the war.

5

Deadlock

By the start of May the position at Helles had started to show some improvement. Already the early casualties were beginning to return to their units after a week of treatment and recovery and two days of relative inactivity allowed the surviving infantry to regain their equilibrium. On 29 April the Hood and Howe Battalions of the RND's 2nd Naval Brigade, which had not disembarked at Gaba Tepe, landed at Helles, followed four days later by Major General Paris and Divisional Headquarters, and all five of the RND battalions at Helles were collected as a general reserve near Hill 138. By 1 May the Brigade Coloniale had also completed its transfer from Kum Kale and the French Division under the command of General Masnou was placed on the right flank of the Allied line.

The landing of transport wagons and animals was still proceeding slowly and the organization of supplies remained confused. During a visit to Helles on 30 April, while preparations were being made to move GHQ from the *Queen Elizabeth* to the transport *Arcadian*, Sir Ian Hamilton learned from Major General Hunter Weston that he estimated that over half the troops at Helles were involved in manual work, landing stores or animals, unloading lighters or building roads from the beaches to the camps. Hamilton cast his mind back to the troops he had previously commanded in Central Force and wistfully concluded, 'Had we even a brigade of those backward Territorial reserve battalions with whom the South of England is congested, they would be worth I don't know what, for they would release their equivalent of first-class fighting men to attend to their own business – the fighting.'[1]

However, the first units of reinforcements were already heading to Gallipoli from Egypt. Following Hamilton's earlier requests, the

29th Indian Infantry Brigade under Brigadier General Vaughan Cox had been ordered to prepare for Gallipoli in the middle of the second week of April. But the brigade took over a fortnight to complete its preparations and was not ready to leave Egypt until after the landing had begun. Initially, GHQ had intended to use it to bring the strength of the NZ&A Division up to three brigades. But this idea was changed in the light of the failure of the 29th Division to make headway on 28 April, and on the following day it was decided that the 29th Indian Brigade would not go to Anzac but to Helles. Cox finally arrived on 1 May and reported to Hamilton. 'Better late than never is all I could say to him: he and his Brigade are sick at not having been on the spot to give the staggering Turks a knock-out on the 28th.'[2] Had the brigade been ready to land on that day at Helles its presence during the First Battle of Krithia might have been decisive.

Almost as soon as the Indian Brigade had begun to disembark at Helles complications arose over its two Punjabi regiments, which both included two Muslim companies. Despite voicing no reservations during the long preparations in Egypt, Cox now made it clear that he was not prepared to guarantee the resolve of these companies in battle against their fellow Muslims. Others believed that the Muslim soldiers would have been perfectly sound. But it was decided to replace both Punjabi regiments with two more battalions of Gurkhas, bringing the total number of the latter to three with the brigade's fourth battalion composed of Sikhs.

Competition between Hamilton and Lieutenant General Maxwell for the limited resources available in Egypt also overshadowed the despatch of the 42nd Division to Gallipoli. By successfully deflecting Kitchener's telegram of 6 April Maxwell had been able to retain the 42nd Division and keep Hamilton in ignorance of Kitchener's attitude towards the troops in Egypt. Apart from his diffident requests for the 29th Indian Brigade, to which he had received no immediate reply, Hamilton had therefore made no attempt to increase the size of his force before the landing. After the landing his belief that he had knowingly undertaken to carry out the campaign with only the limited resources placed at his disposal initially made him feel obliged to honour this commitment and the sanguine reports he sent to Kitchener, which deliberately played down his difficulties, contained no pleas for further troops.

However, on 27 April Kitchener received more anxious reports of the operations both from Winston Churchill, who took Vice Admiral De Robeck's latest report to the War Office in person, and from the French government, which forwarded a signal from Admiral Guépratte, in command of the French naval forces, asking for immediate reinforcements. In response to these reports that evening Kitchener sent a signal to Hamilton explaining that 'if you want more troops from Egypt Maxwell will give you any support from Egyptian garrison you may require'.[3] Hamilton was puzzled. Having not seen Kitchener's telegram of 6 April he was unaware that this was the case. But after receiving this latest signal, during the night of the 27/28 April he finally felt able to send a formal request to Kitchener for the 42nd Division. In response to Guépratte's signal, Kitchener had already suggested to Maxwell that he should send the division to Gallipoli and when Kitchener received Hamilton's formal request he ordered the division to be embarked as quickly as possible. Despite Maxwell's natural reluctance to give up the division, its first unit, the 125th Brigade, started to embark on 1 May and within a week of Kitchener's order the complete division was *en route* to Gallipoli, significantly quicker than the time it had taken the 29th Indian Brigade to leave a few weeks earlier.

A further consequence of Guépratte's plea was the decision taken by his own government on 30 April to send another division from France to join the CEO. In line with the division already there the new division was designated the 2nd Division and, under the command of General Maurice Bailloud, it began to depart from Marseilles two days later. In addition to this promise of increased infantry strength the level of Allied artillery cover at Helles was also gradually increasing. By the beginning of May most of the guns of the 1st French Division had landed and the main French artillery weapon, the 75mm field gun, soon became popular with the British as a result of its accuracy and the rapid rate of its fire. In addition, between 30 April and 4 May General d'Amade ordered four 14cm and two 10cm naval guns and their crews to be landed and positioned near Sedd el Bahr to carry out counter-battery work against the guns in Asia, which were already posing a serious threat to the French area on the right flank.

The artillery of the 29th Division was also complete by the start of May. Yet, despite the increased number of guns, British artillery cover remained poor due to a shortage of shells. In contrast to the French, who were well supplied, the stock of British artillery ammunition was already beginning to run low and by 4 May had been reduced to half of its original level. Since 25 April 23,000 18-pounder shrapnel and 5,000 4.5-inch howitzer shells had been fired, leaving stocks of only 48,000 and 1,800 respectively.[4] On 4 May Hamilton began protracted negotiations with the War Office for an urgent increase in the level of his artillery ammunition stocks. The authorities in London were reluctant to agree and once again compromised. In the middle of the next attempt to advance at Helles they informed him that 10,000 rounds of 18-pounder shrapnel and 1,000 rounds of 4.5-inch high explosive would be sent out 'in the next relief ship',[5] making it unlikely to arrive much before the end of the month.

Additional artillery cover was still being provided by the ships' guns. But they too were short of ammunition. The covering fire for the landings had expended much greater quantities of it than De Robeck had intended. As the purpose of the military operations remained the admission of the EMS into the Sea of Marmara, he was concerned that, if too great a quantity of naval ammunition was used merely to admit the fleet, once it was through it would be unable to carry out the next stage of the operations, the engagement of the Turkish Navy and domination of Constantinople. Consequently, on 1 May it was decided that only one-third of the remaining naval stocks could be used to support the military operations. Most of the Allied troops had by this time moved away from the coastal area which was directly visible to the ships and consequently only indirect naval fire could be brought to bear. Yet the nature of the country southwest of Achi Baba made the Turkish positions very hard to locate and the limited aerial reconnaissance was unable to provide the naval gunners with accurate targets. To be effective the naval guns needed to make a concerted sweep of a wide area to be sure of hitting a specific target. But with the need to conserve ammunition paramount, this was clearly not possible and although, when successful, the material impact of the naval fire was still considerable, its growing inaccuracy soon began to reduce its additional effect on the morale of the Turkish troops.

The strength of the Turkish defences was also increasing fast, with troops being moved to the southern end of the peninsula both from Bulair and the Asiatic coast and from further afield. Two divisions had arrived from Constantinople by 1 May and another from Smyrna was expected within five days. With his force growing rapidly Marshal Liman von Sanders reorganized it to reflect the two distinct areas which had been created by the Allied landings, forming one group in the north opposite to the Anzac line under the overall command of Essad Pasha and a second in the south under the command of Colonel von Sodenstern. On 30 April Liman von Sanders was ordered by Enver Pasha in Constantinople to launch a decisive attack against the Allied forces in the perpetual hope that it would drive the invaders into the sea. As an attack was already in hand at Gaba Tepe, he decided to make this fresh assault at Helles. Conscious of his own shortage of artillery ammunition and wary of the potential of the British naval guns, he decided on a night attack and ordered von Sodenstern to carry it out on the night of 1/2 May using all the troops he had to hand. The attack was to be a closely fought, hand-to-hand battle and in case the initial attack failed to achieve the absolute destruction of the Allied force, it was to be supported by special incendiary detachments whose task was to burn any boats they found on the beach to prevent escape.

The day and early evening of 1 May were quiet, despite a certain amount of Turkish artillery fire. But at 22.00 a violent bombardment presaged the start of the attack. The first column of Turks reached the British line at the point where it crossed Krithia Nullah and was held by the remnants of the Dublin and Munster Fusiliers, who had been temporarily amalgamated on 30 April to form a composite battalion of 8 officers and 770 men known as the 'Dubsters'. Despite the strength of the bombardment the start of the infantry attack caught the 'Dubsters' unaware. 'The big night attack went on from 10.30 pm till dawn. The Turks attacked again and again shouting "Allah! Allah!" It was most exciting hearing them collecting in a dip in the hill about 40 yards away waiting for their next charge.'[6] During the attack several British regiments recorded incidents in which commands were called out by the Turks or their German officers to deceive them, with a number of British officers being killed as a result.

The heaviest parts of the attack fell against the French. At one point during the night one of the Senegalese battalions of the Brigade Coloniale broke from their forward positions and a party of British gunners had to move forward to hold the line until a company of the Worcestershire Regiment could take over. At 02.00 on 2 May Masnou asked Hunter Weston for two British battalions in support. Hunter Weston, anxious about the attacks being made against his own line, sent forward the Hood and Howe Battalions to support the 29th Division, moving them along the Krithia Road where the British and French lines met, in the hope that they would be able to assist the latter if necessary. Masnou's request also reached Hamilton, who ordered Hunter Weston to send a battalion of the RND specifically to help the French; accordingly the Anson Battalion was moved up, entering the French line on the extreme right.

Despite the anxieties of the night, the Allies maintained their line and the defeat of the Turkish attacks reassured Captain Aubrey Williams. 'From that night I knew quite well that the Turks would never drive us into the sea or from any position which we intended to hold.'[7] By daybreak on 2 May the Turks had gained only heavy casualties. On the previous day Hamilton had discussed with d'Amade the need for him to advance the French right flank on to the crest overlooking the Kereves Dere in preparation for the next attack against Krithia and, as the last of the Turkish attacks were driven off, d'Amade felt it was an opportune moment to attempt this. Supported by the British troops on their left, at 10.00 the French moved forward. On the extreme right the Brigade Métropolitaine was successful. But further across to the left the haste with which the attack had been organized prevented the Brigade Coloniale from following suit, and the Hood and Howe Battalions, who moved forward on its left, were unable to advance more than 400 yards before undiminished Turkish fire brought them to a halt.

As a result of the Turks' attack and their subsequent attempt to advance, the French suffered over 2,000 casualties; in comparison the British lost less than 700, but among this smaller number were five more battalion commanders and four adjutants. By the end of the day the French sector was in a very weak state, and morale, particularly among the Senegalese, was extremely low. The Turkish attack had placed significant strains on relations between the British and French commanders and this tension was exacerbated by further attacks against the French line, particularly during the night of 3/4 May, when the Senegalese again deserted their line, forcing it to be restored by French cooks and orderlies from their base lines. On the afternoon of 4 May Hamilton discussed the situation with d'Amade and Hunter Weston. D'Amade explained that his men were exhausted and had suffered severely over the past week. Many of his units were now clearly unreliable and needed to be relieved. But Hunter Weston felt that his men were little better off and Hamilton had to arbitrate. He decided to lend the 2nd Naval Brigade to the French on a more official basis and that evening its commanding officer, Commodore Oliver Backhouse, was ordered to take command of the Brigade Coloniale.

Although the spate of Turkish attacks inevitably caused a delay in the resumption of a general advance against Achi Baba, the steady rate at which the Turks were being reinforced made it essential that this should begin again as soon as possible and on 4 May, somewhat superfluously, Hamilton was reminded by Kitchener that 'any delay will allow the Turks to bring up more reinforcements and to make unpleasant preparations for your reception'.[8] On the previous day Hamilton had agreed with Lieutenant General Birdwood that, following the unsuccessful attempt to advance at Anzac on the night of 2/3 May, the line there should be placed on the defensive and two Anzac infantry brigades withdrawn and sent down to Helles to support the next attack, together with one New Zealand and four Australian field artillery batteries which had not yet been able to land there. The time needed to transfer these Anzac troops would bring them to Helles shortly after the 125th Brigade of the 42nd Division.

In anticipation of their arrival the troops at Helles were reorganized. The focus of the Allied force remained the 29th Division. But, as a result of their heavy casualties, the battalions of the 86th Brigade were divided among the division's other two original brigades, with the 'Dubsters' being attached to the 87th and the Lancashire and Royal Fusiliers to the 88th. To compensate the 29th Division was allocated the 29th Indian Brigade and, as it was due to arrive in advance of the rest of the 42nd Division, the 125th Brigade as well. This brought the nominal strength of the 29th Division up to four brigades. As the 2nd Naval Brigade had already been added to the 1st French Division, a temporary Composite Division was now to be formed from a Composite Naval Brigade, incorporating the Plymouth and Drake Battalions, and the two brigades that were to be sent down from Anzac, the 2nd Australian Brigade and the New Zealand Brigade. This temporary division was to be based around the headquarters of the RND. All of these troops were due to be in place by the morning of 6 May and Hamilton selected that day on which to launch his next attack. As it had done before the landing, consideration turned to whether the first movement of the attack should be made at night. Once again Hamilton was in favour. But both Hunter Weston and d'Amade disagreed. The recent attack at Anzac had clearly demonstrated the potential dangers of attacking at night. Yet at Helles neither the attack along a single line nor the ground over which it was to take place was as complicated as the Anzac attack. Despite this, a standard, unimaginative frontal assault in daylight preceded by a bombardment was selected for the next attack at Helles.

As it was to be made with a much stronger force than on 28 April, the capture of Achi Baba once more became the ultimate objective. The plan divided the advance into three distinct stages, the first two of which were effectively a renewed attempt to reach the objectives of 28 April. During stage one the Allied line would advance directly forward for about a mile and carry the extreme right flank of the French across the mouth of Kereves Dere on to the high ground which lay to the northeast, to form a new line running northwest from there to a point on the Aegean coast about a quarter of a mile beyond Y Beach. With the French remaining static in their new position, during the second stage the British would then wheel right using the junction of the French and British lines on Achi Baba Nullah as a pivot. Passing through and capturing Krithia, the British would come to a halt to the east of the village, with their line running north from the pivotal point to Yazy Tepe before cutting back to Sari Tepe. The final stage would then see two British brigades advance through the left centre of this second line to attack Achi Baba from the west and southwest, while the French moved forward almost two miles to prolong the southern tip of the final line to the edge of the Dardanelles.

Although the Allied force was numerically stronger than on 28 April, many of the underlying factors which had so seriously impaired the earlier battle were still present. The original troops were still tired and faced their second week of almost continual fighting. Of the two fresh brigades, the 29th Indian Brigade had already lost a quarter of its strength through the decision not to use the four Punjabi Muslim companies, and the 125th Brigade, which had never been in action before, would not arrive at Helles until the afternoon before the battle. The orders were again issued late and reached the front-line units only hours before the battle's start, giving the commanders very little time to absorb them and organize the men.

The attack was to be preceded by a bombardment lasting just thirty minutes. But the shortage of ammunition meant that even this could only be light and the British 18-pounder guns had no high explosive, only shrapnel. Knowledge of the ground over which the attack was to take place had barely improved; only two daily aerial reconnaissance flights had been possible with one camera. The interpreters of the few photographs that had been taken had not yet developed the skill needed to discern accurately the newly dug Turkish positions and only a few isolated trenches had been identified. These were believed to be the Turks' advanced positions. But in fact, although by 6 May still not connected, they actually formed part of the main Turkish line, which now ran southeast across the peninsula approximately half a mile in front of Krithia. Unknown to the British, in front of this line a series of outposts had also been established based on hidden machine-gun posts. Although these outposts were geographically isolated, their fields of fire created an almost impenetrable defensive line which was virtually invisible from the air and therefore vulnerable only to random artillery fire. Only on the left of the Turkish line opposite the French, where the Turks' forward posts were much closer to their main line and had been developed in greater strength, were definite positions correctly located.

By 6 May the Turkish strength was thirty-one battalions,

totalling around 20,000 front-line troops, but only a small proportion of these were needed to hold the outpost line. After the failure of the night attack, in the first example of Liman von Sanders's more ruthless attitude towards his subordinate commanders, von Sodenstern, who had been slightly wounded, was replaced in command of the southern group of Turkish forces by Weber Pasha, a German officer who had previously commanded the forces on the Asiatic shore. On taking over on 5 May, Weber had not been impressed by the state of the Turkish defences and suggested to Liman von Sanders that the line should be withdrawn behind Achi Baba. But Liman von Sanders rejected this idea, insisting instead that no ground be relinquished voluntarily and every piece of it contested. This Weber and his Turkish divisions proceeded to do.

The order for the two Anzac brigades to move to Helles reached the battalions in the line early on 5 May and they embarked that night on destroyers for the journey south. They arrived shortly before dawn on 6 May and soon after landing it became clear to Captain Gresson that it was going to be a magnificent day:

> Day dawned just as we were marching past the now destroyed fort of Sedd el Bahr and the scene then lacked nothing in beauty ... the fields of the peninsula for the most part open pasture land with cottages and fig trees dotted about here and there. The whole countryside was a blaze of colour as the meadows were thick with wild flowers all in bloom – the red poppy predominating. It was a wonderfully peaceful scene and except for the fitful stutter of a machine-gun somewhere in front and an occasional burst of rifle fire it was difficult to realize that here lay a battlefield where had taken place one of the fiercest struggles British soldiers have ever been engaged in.[9] (Captain Kenneth Gresson)

Over this landscape, at 10.30, the bombardment opened to mark the start of the Second Battle of Krithia. But the lack of ammunition and ignorance of the Turkish positions meant that by 11.00, when the infantry started to move forward, its effect had been minimal. For the first stage of the attack the 29th Division, which formed the British line, deployed the 125th Brigade on the left between the Aegean and Gully Ravine, a strip of ground called for convenience after the war Gully Spur, and the 88th Brigade on the right between Gully Ravine and Krithia Nullah, later called Fir Tree Spur. Between Krithia Nullah and the east bank of Achi Baba Nullah where the British line joined that of the French, an area later called Krithia Spur, no advance was to be made, the open ground being considered too difficult to cross. Instead the Composite Naval Brigade was simply to hold Krithia Spur until the first objectives on either side had been reached, at which point it would advance up the spur to link the right of the 88th Brigade to the left of the French. To safeguard this important link the 1st Lancashire Fusiliers had been detached from the 88th Brigade and placed on the right of the Composite Naval Brigade with orders to keep touch with the French line as it advanced.

The 1st French Division, forming the line from Achi Baba Nullah to the Dardanelles across Kereves Spur, placed the Brigade Coloniale on the left and the Brigade Métropolitaine on the right. Unfortunately, in a further echo of the previous battle, the start of the French advance was delayed by over thirty minutes because of confusion over the precise role of the 2nd Naval Brigade, which was to support the French left flank, and it was not until 11.40 that it finally got under way. Initially the Brigade Métropolitaine made some progress and reached the high ground above the mouth of Kereves Dere. But there it was halted by heavy fire from the corresponding high ground on the opposite bank. To the left the Brigade Coloniale advanced more slowly and by the early part of the afternoon had built up a strong line of Senegalese troops opposite the entrenched Turkish positions. Yet in spite of apparently effective artillery support the Senegalese did not actually attack the positions in front of them.

From the outset the left flank of the Brigade Coloniale started to pull away from Achi Baba Nullah, where it was intended to keep touch with the British line, and the 2nd Naval Brigade was moved up almost immediately to maintain the link. But as the leading troops pushed forward, the Turks on the raised ground to their right levelled an increasingly heavy fire against them and their momentum soon began to falter.

> I remember, Yates was just a little ahead of Don [Townshend] and I. We crawled up more or less line abreast, but the bullets were hitting the sand, spraying us, hitting our packs. So we

decided: 'How about another dash?' Off we went. Near enough fifteen yards, one drops, everybody drops. We got down again. Then we decided to go a little bit further. We'd got to keep bearing to our right slightly, because we seemed to be dodging the line of fire. But it was still whinging overhead and flying about, hitting the ground. I think it must have been a machine-gun. But there's a tendency for a man, if he's being fired on by two or three men at the same time, to think it a machine-gun. You couldn't see them and there was a rattling going on, not only in our section but all over the place. Rapid fire was going on. We decided to go a little bit further and all four got up together. Yates was in front and all of a sudden he bent down. He'd been shot in the stomach, maybe the testicles, but he was dancing around like a cat on hot bricks, fell down on the ground. We decided to ease up a little bit. But as soon as we got somewhere near him he got up and rushed like hell at the Turks and 'Bang!' Down altogether, out for the count. Horton and I were more or less together. Townshend was on the other side and there was a gap where Yates had been. Young Horton, he was the first to get to Yates and he got a hold of him and sort of pushed him to see what was wrong when a bullet struck him dead centre of the brow, went right through his head and took a bit out of my knuckle. Poor old Horton. He kept crying for his mother. I can see him now. Hear him at this very moment. He said he was eighteen, but I don't think he was sixteen, never mind eighteen. He was such a frail, young laddie. He was a steward on the Fyffe banana boats in peacetime. Yates was dead. Horton was dead. Only Don and I left.[10] (Ordinary Seaman Joe Murray)

Towards the end of the afternoon, because the Brigade Coloniale on their right had not advanced as far, the leading battalions of the 2nd Naval Brigade were forced to withdraw from their advanced positions to establish a continuous line with the left flank of the French. By the end of the day the French line had made an average advance of only 400 yards.

In the centre of the Allied line, preceded by advanced parties of scouts, the 88th Brigade had also only been able to move forward very slowly. After advancing about 400 to 500 yards the scouts were held up by the advanced Turkish machine-gun posts and by shrapnel fire, and within about an hour of the start the brigade's line had ground to a halt just short of Fir Tree Wood. During the afternoon a renewed effort managed to push the line a short distance further forward. But by 16.00 it was clear that no more ground would be gained and the 88th Brigade began to dig in on its new line. A few hours later the Drake Battalion of the Composite Naval Brigade conformed with this new line and linked its right flank with the Lancashire Fusiliers on the left of the French.

The 125th Brigade, on the extreme left, had arrived at Helles only at the end of the previous day. Its leading battalion, the 1/6th Lancashire Fusiliers, moved up immediately from W Beach to Gully Spur where it was to take over the line. But it did not arrive in position until 02.00 on the day of the attack and within nine hours faced an advance across unreconnoitred ground against unknown positions. Owing to a mistake in the transmission of the battalion's orders, it did not start its advance until 11.30 and, although it reached its first objective on a ridge 400 yards ahead of its starting line, a Turkish post of at least five machine-guns at the head of the nullahs leading down to Y Beach prevented it from making further progress. The battalion had been ordered to post a man carrying a blue and white flag on its left flank to indicate to the ships off shore how the attack was progressing. Despite this, the ships' guns were unable to subdue the Turkish machine-guns and for the rest of the day the battalion remained in position on the crest of the ridge.

Although along the length of the whole line an advance of 400 to 500 yards had been made, the expected breakthrough had not materialized and the Allied troops had not even reached the Turks' forward positions. Having spoken both to Hunter Weston and d'Amade during the afternoon and ascertained that the day's casualties had been relatively slight, Hamilton ordered the attack to be renewed against the same objectives on the following morning. Additional reinforcements, in the shape of the first brigade of the 2nd French Division and the 127th Brigade of the 42nd Division which was to be attached to the Composite Division, had also just begun to disembark. At 22.00 the 29th Division issued orders that the advance was to continue at 10.00 on 7 May along the lines of the original plan, but with the first and second stages amalgamated, and implemented without a pause at the end of the first stage. The circumstances surrounding the attack had changed little in twenty-four hours and, if anything, had deteriorated. All the front-line troops had now been engaged and suffered casualties for minimal gain. The already low stocks of artillery ammunition had been further depleted by the first day's fighting and nothing but a desultory bombardment against the still unlocated targets would be possible before the next attack.

At 09.45 on 7 May this meagre bombardment began. On the left flank in an attempt to supplement it and destroy the machine-gun post above Y Beach, two ships were sent to shell the top of the cliffs with the aid of a ship towing an observation balloon. Directly the naval bombardment lifted, one battalion of the 125th Brigade was to seize the machine-gun post and, once this had been successfully accomplished, the remainder of the brigade was then to advance along the coast to capture Yazy Tepe over two miles to the northeast. To make its attack the 1/5th Lancashire Fusiliers had to move forward from their position in the support trenches to the front line. But, as 2nd Lieutenant Horridge discovered, even this preliminary movement was fraught with difficulty and before he and his platoon had even reached the front line to begin their attack they became dispersed among the scrub.

We were told we would advance by platoons in extended order. The order for the companies was 'D', 'C', 'B' and 'A'. I was in 'A' Company, No. 3 Platoon. So that meant I was the last platoon but one in the advance. As the distance between Gully Ravine and the sea is some 300 yards, I had to extend my platoon in two lines, thirty men in each line at ten pace intervals. The scrub was so thick that it was impossible to keep in touch with all the men and one merely had to blow the whistle and hope that everybody advanced. You had to follow the people in front of you. When you found the line in front lay down, you lay down. When they got up, you got up and continued the advance. And so we started. There were a few hisses of bullets and as we went further these got more and more. We came to a trench. Then we advanced still further and the amount of rifle fire we were under seemed to get bigger still. I began to lose control of the platoon because I simply couldn't see them in the scrub. All I could do was blow my whistle and we would advance with the line in front of us and I hoped that the NCOs were doing their job. Eventually we got to one trench behind the front line. Next to me was an old soldier called Collinson. We got out of the trench and we had to go at the double because fire was very heavy. The bullets were hissing round, swish, swish, swish, swish, swish. We ran halfway and then we got behind a mound. After a minute or so's rest, I said to Collinson: 'Look. We've got to go on,' and off we set again. I wasn't too bad a runner and I outstripped Collinson and eventually leapt into the front line trench. I'm sorry to say that Collinson, in the last ten yards, got hit through the chest or stomach. We got him in, but he died later.[11] (2nd Lieutenant George Horridge)

When they finally reached the front line, the men who had held the line overnight helped them begin their assault. 'We had to lift the Fifth Lancashire Fusiliers up to go over the top to start advancing. But instead, when we lifted them up, they just dropped dead. I think every man had a machine-gun. There seemed to be so many machine-guns, not rifles, cutting the top of the trenches off.'[12] Already depleted by the chaotic advance to the front line, when Horridge finally took his men into the real attack he saw his platoon disintegrate even further. But, as was often the case, his casualties were actually less severe than they first appeared.

Captain Milnes, the second in command of the company, was shouting: 'All people from the 5th Lancashire Fusiliers, come to the left.' He was only about twenty yards from the edge of the cliff leading down to the sea. I made my way there, not knowing where a lot of my platoon were by this time, but realizing that the attack had to go forward. The order was given and we got out of the top of this trench. The fellows were firing from the parapet, presumably at the Turks who I hadn't seen hidden in the bush. But the fire was very, very heavy. We didn't get more than ten or fifteen yards before it was quite obvious that if we didn't lie down we were just going to be hit. We lay down. You could see the bullets cutting the grass in places. I said to Captain Milnes: 'Sidney, d'you think we should stop here? What about going down to the cliff?' He said: 'Yes. I think perhaps we'd better. It's no good stopping here. We can't go on against this fire. You go first.' So I got up and ran to the cliff edge. A fellow called Hudson followed me and he was hit in the neck. What happened to the others, I really don't know. We got under the cover of the cliff edge, got Hudson down to the shore. A naval cutter came and gave us some water which had some rum in it which tasted very nice. They took Hudson off and we just waited for orders because what we had to do then didn't concern me as a 2nd Lieutenant. I had to wait for what the company commander told us to do. I ended the day more or less under the cliffs. My platoon had stopped at various places on the way, some at the trenches, some hadn't gone forward. I just didn't know where any of them were. When the battalion was eventually formed up in the dark to go back of course they all began to appear. I thought they must have got hurt, killed or injured, but it turned out in the end I'd lost three killed and three wounded out of sixty which, after all, is decimation.[13] (2nd Lieutenant George Horridge)

Along the rest of the Allied line from Gully Ravine to the Dardanelles the previous day's events were repeated in similar fashion. Individual units, notably the 1/5th Royal Scots opposite Fir Tree Wood and part of the 2nd French Division in the centre of their line, did succeed in making limited advances. But the failure of the line on either side to conform left them isolated and they were eventually forced to withdraw towards the positions from which they had begun. All further efforts met with the same lack of success and effectively the day was a waste, with barely a couple of hundred yards gained on the left centre. After the war it became known that the Turks did not even realize that a general attack had been made on 7 May. The chances of a third day's fighting resulting in significant gains did not seem likely. Artillery ammunition was almost exhausted, as were the bulk of the Allied front-line troops. The Turkish forward posts had still not been reached. The main line which lay beyond them had been little affected by the fighting and the Turks had gained two further days of digging and consolidation. The already strong position facing the left flank of the French line was now even stronger. Yet, with more troops due to arrive shortly, Hamilton was still convinced that a further effort was justified. At 22.25 GHQ issued orders for the attack to be resumed on the following morning at 10.30 and 'pressed with the utmost possible vigour'.[14]

The 125th Brigade, which since the morning of 6 May had lost 23 officers and 626 men, was withdrawn during the night from the left flank and sent to join the Composite Division in reserve. It was replaced by the 87th Brigade. In turn the New Zealand Brigade, which had been moved out of reserve to support the attack in the centre, joined the 29th Division and established itself in the original trenches from which the 88th Brigade had launched its attack on 6 May. With the arrival of the 127th Brigade, despite these changes, three unused brigades remained in the Composite Division, and the 2nd Australian Brigade moved into position behind the Composite Naval Brigade, which had taken no active part in the fighting on 7 May.

Mistakenly believing the French left to have advanced further than it had and actually to have taken the key pivotal point, GHQ ordered d'Amade to consolidate this point and restrict his offensive efforts on 8 May to pushing his right flank across the Kereves Dere. The main thrust of the advance was to be made by the 29th Division as it attempted once again to execute its elusive right wheel through Krithia. The New Zealand Brigade was to form the right flank of the division's attack and advance through the 88th Brigade to capture Krithia. On the left the 87th Brigade was to advance along Gully Spur. But for the first time no direct frontal advance was ordered. Instead one battalion was to work forward on the edge of the cliffs above the sea in an attempt to overcome the Turkish machine-gun post above Y Beach, while a second worked along the western edge of the gully with a screen of scouts moving forward in conjunction on the eastern edge to protect the left flank of the New Zealanders.

Hunter Weston issued a warning order at 23.25 on 7 May to allow the commanders of the brigades that were to carry out the attack to make tentative arrangements. But formal written orders were not issued by Divisional Headquarters until two hours before the start of the attack and the attempt to forewarn the brigade commanders was unsuccessful. Colonel Johnston did not confer with the battalion commanders of the New Zealand Brigade until

09.00, after he had received the division's written orders, and his four commanding officers did not return to their battalions for over an hour, by which time the bombardment had started. Before each attack the bombardment had become progressively weaker. After just fifteen minutes the firing ceased and at 10.30, almost the same time as on the previous two days, the familiar pattern began all over again.

On the left, unable to locate the Turkish machine-guns the 87th Brigade could not advance. To its right, across the gully, because the New Zealand battalion commanders had only been able to give their officers a cursory warning of the attack, their advance began in inevitable confusion. Advancing with its right flank first, the whole New Zealand line moved through the British forward positions, but immediately came under the same heavy shrapnel and machine-gun fire which had frustrated the attacks there for forty-eight hours. On the right and in the centre gains of around only 200 yards were made. On the left, despite fierce fire from across Gully Ravine, the line advanced a further 100 yards. Yet, by early afternoon, it was clear that the attack had not succeeded.

During the first two days of the battle GHQ had remained on board the *Arcadian* in touch with Hunter Weston's and d'Amade's Headquarters by cable. But for the final effort on 8 May Hamilton and his staff came ashore and established themselves on Hill 114. From there in the mid-afternoon Hamilton 'resolved firmly to make one more attempt'[15] using some of the troops who still remained in reserve and at 16.00 he ordered an advance along the line from the Aegean to the Dardanelles, including this time the French, at 17.30 in what would clearly have to be the final attempt. Every gun was to use as much ammunition as could be spared in the preceding fifteen minutes and every effort was to be made to move the line as far as possible.

Despite the repeated success of the Turkish machine-guns in preventing any movement towards Y Beach, at 16.30 Hunter Weston ordered the 87th Brigade to advance directly ahead with the upper reaches of Gully Ravine and the lower slopes of Yazy Tepe as its ultimate objective. The New Zealand Brigade was to renew its attack and capture Krithia. On their right, for the first time since the start of the battle, an advance was also to be made across Krithia Spur. Without warning the 2nd Australian Brigade was ordered to advance from its reserve position 1,000 yards behind the Composite Naval Brigade, cross the line which this brigade had held since the end of 6 May and continue up the spur as far as possible.

At 17.15 the most concentrated bombardment of the campaign so far began and five minutes later the first two battalions of Australians started to move up beneath it.

> It was indescribable. The noise, the dust. You just couldn't hear each other speak. That went on for about quarter of an hour. Then everything was as silent as the blessed grave and that was the time we had to hop out. The barrage had been so heavy that we thought: 'Well, this is going to be a cake walk. There's nothing to stop us.'[16] (Private Frank Brent)

But although the bombardment appeared to be impressive, the lack of knowledge about the location of the Turkish positions rendered it futile. When, at 17.30, it stopped and the attack began, the fire from the advanced Turkish posts and their supporting artillery showed that nothing had changed. On the left, exactly like the 125th Brigade on both of the preceding days, despite making every effort and suffering significant casualties, the 87th Brigade was unable to advance even a short distance. Across Gully Ravine, the New Zealanders again crossed the ground in front of Fir Tree Wood, which they knew as the Daisy Patch, but were forced back, leaving only the Canterbury Battalion on the right able to push forward slightly from their starting line. Gresson's company had been left in reserve when the rest of his battalion had advanced during the morning and he had spent the day lying 'on my back in the sun . . . listening to the whiz of bullets'.[17] His tranquillity was shattered by the end of the bombardment:

> It ceased abruptly and we were ordered to advance through the foremost trenches held by the Munsters. To accomplish this we had to come out from behind our knoll, leap across a Worcester trench just in front and race across about a hundred yards of flat open ground before reaching the Munster trench. I had covered about 75 yards at my top speed when my legs suddenly went from under me as if struck by a hammer and I fell over and lay

still among the daisies. After a few seconds perceiving that I was not dead but had merely been shot through both legs I raised my head cautiously and looked about me. The ground all round me was plentifully dotted with khaki clad figures, for the most part ominously still, though here and there was to be seen some one endeavouring to crawl to the trenches in front. Just in front lay the Munster trench and as I looked one of the men in it beckoned to me with his finger. The suggestion conveyed by this action awakened me to the fact that I stood a very good chance of getting further bullets where I lay as the ground was swept from all sides so I made ready to act on it by unfastening my equipment and allowing it to fall off. As I was unable to get up I had no alternative but to shuffle along as best I could and using this mode of progression I reached the Munster trench and lay there in great pain but sheltered from the constant stream of bullets.[18] (Captain Kenneth Gresson)

To the right the Australians had come under artillery fire even before they reached the Composite Naval Brigade, by which time the New Zealanders had been brought to a halt. But having now reached the British front-line trenches, under fire from their front and both flanks, the leading Australians launched a charge regardless.

You could see your mates going down right and left. . . . You were face to face with the stark realization that this was the end of it. That was the thought that was with you the whole time. Despite the fact that you couldn't see a Turk, he was pelting us with everything he'd got from all corners. The marvel to me was how the dickens he was able to do it after the barrage that had fallen on him. . . . I copped my packet and, as I lay down, I said: 'Thank Christ for that.'[19] (Private Frank Brent)

After 500 yards, unable to continue, those in front formed a line and soon the remaining men arrived to help them consolidate. By 18.00 the charge up the barren spur, which lasted longer and sustained heavier casualties than the charge of the Light Brigade, was exhausted. Over 1,000 out of the brigade's 2,000 men had been lost.[20] But for the first time since the start of the battle the main Turkish position was in sight, only 500 yards ahead.

As the Australian attack was ending, the French was just beginning.

> The French general had given orders for his line to advance with drums beating and bugles blowing, and we could see their battalions streaming up the spurs leading towards the Achi Baba position. They went forward in great force and with tremendous dash, right up the spur; and, in spite of the bitter shell fire that met them as they topped the rise in front of them, they got right up to the Turkish trenches and drove the enemy out. We could see the Turks streaming away over the rise in hundreds, with the French at their heels – a most stirring sight! Things began to look as if we should be able to get even further forward than we had expected. But as it happened the French ran right over the Turkish trenches and on in pursuit into very difficult country – precipitous ravines swept by machine-gun fire – and were forced back after some heavy fighting. After this they were not able to do more than maintain the ground they had won.[21] (Captain Guy Dawnay)

On the left of their line the French finally captured the entrenched Turkish position which later became known as La Redoute Bouchet. But their overall gains were disappointing.

By 19.00 the battle was finally recognized as over. In three days for losses of about 6,500[22] the Allies had nowhere gained more than 600 yards. The New Zealanders proceeded to establish touch with the left flank of the new Australian line and the 1st Lancashire Fusiliers and Drake Battalion of the Composite Naval Brigade were sent up to link the Australians' right to the 2nd Naval Brigade on the French left. By 9 May there could be no lingering doubts that, despite every effort having been made, in real terms the Allied position at Helles had only marginally been improved and the Turks had again succeeded in preventing a general advance towards Achi Baba. Having made no entry since 5 May, on 9 May GHQ's Cipher Officer, Captain Orlo Williams, returned to his diary with a reluctant recognition of this fact:

Perfect spring day. Cool breeze, warm sun, everything lovely but the war. The great attack went on for 3 days and by the end of yesterday evening was brought to a standstill with a small advance on the part of our troops, but no real impression made on the Achi Baba position. There is no concealment on anybody's part that the attack has been a failure and that if we are to get on at all, we must have more troops, guns & ammunition. Late last night a telegram to that effect was sent to Lord Kitchener which will not make very pleasant Sunday reading for him.[23] (Captain Orlo Williams)

In the telegram Hamilton explained to Kitchener that 'our troops have done all that flesh and blood can do against semi-permanent works, and they are not able to carry them. More and more munitions will be needed to do so. I fear this is a very unpalatable conclusion, but I see no way out of it.'[24] After quoting Hamilton's closing sentence, Williams concluded, 'No doubt the General is anxious & disappointed & the General Staff too. Events can only be waited for, but it seems that now we have let ourselves in for it we cannot possibly draw back and troops will have to be sent.'[25]

In response to Hamilton's despondent conclusion, Kitchener showed his own disappointment over the way in which the campaign had unfolded. From the outset he had made it clear that military operations at Gallipoli were to be carried out by the smallest possible force. The events of the past two weeks had shown this to be unrealistic and he now asked Hamilton to tell him what future operations he felt would be necessary to continue the attack in co-operation with the navy. After twenty-four hours of reflection, Hamilton's natural confidence returned and his answer was once again more positive. Although no large-scale attack would be possible in the immediate future, he hoped to maintain the pressure against the Turks through minor operations at Helles and in the process improve the position there in preparation for a resumption of a full-scale offensive. To do this, despite the promise he had made to Kitchener on his appointment not to press for reinforcements, he felt that the strength of his force must be increased. 'If two fresh divisions organized as a corps could be spared me I could push on from this end and from Gaba Tepe with good prospects of success, otherwise I am afraid it will degenerate into trench warfare with its resultant slowness.'[26] Demands for resources from other concerns meant that Kitchener was unable to meet Hamilton's request in full at that point. But on 10 May he informed him that the 52nd Division was to be sent out as immediate reinforcements.

In the weeks between 18 March and 25 April, when plans had been drawn up for the landing, it had always been intended that the navy, using a cruiser squadron supported by two battleships, would renew its attack on the Dardanelles on the second day of the landing, by which time the Kilid Bahr Plateau was expected to be under attack from the military force. But the successful containment of the landings by the Turks close to the beaches had prevented the army from even threatening the plateau and the landing appeared to have made little difference to the naval situation. Despite this, by the beginning of May many senior naval officers believed that the attack should be renewed. Those in favour of a renewal believed that the landing did appear to have diverted many of the mobile Turkish guns away from the Dardanelles and that a reorganized mine-sweeping force based on destroyers in place of the ineffective trawlers could now succeed in making headway. Vice Admiral De Robeck remained unconvinced and, after referring the question to the Admiralty on 10 May, his scepticism was supported by their conclusion. Until the shoreline around the Narrows had been captured there was to be no renewal of separate naval operations.

Hamilton's view that he needed significant troops to push on against the strong and well-established Turkish defences and the Admiralty view that the naval attack should not be resumed until this had been done were both presented on 14 May to the War Council at its first meeting since 19 March, when it had agreed that De Robeck should continue his attack. In the intervening eight weeks the war had changed immeasurably, not just in the eastern Mediterranean but across the rest of Europe as well. The Italians were about to declare war in support of the Entente, the Battle of Aubers Ridge fought in France on 9 May had been a costly waste of resources for no gain and the Russian situation in Galicia was very poor, making any assistance from the Russians in the campaign against Turkey unlikely; Kitchener was also still fearful of a German attack on the east coast of Britain. At Gallipoli, the balance between the army and the navy had been reversed and the military campaign was now predominant. Yet there had still not been any discussion by the War Council of the relative merits of the operations in the eastern Mediterranean versus those on the Western Front. Whichever campaign was felt by the middle of May to be more important and more promising of results should have been clearly identified and the other campaign suspended and placed on the defensive. But this was not done and the failure to do so eventually precipitated the demise of the campaign at Gallipoli.

Faced with the new situation at Gallipoli the War Council had to decide between a number of options. They could either abandon the military campaign on the grounds that it could not be adequately supported or they could continue it. If they opted for the latter course, they could attempt to finish it quickly by sending strong reinforcements or slowly using fewer men through protracted siege operations. In a paper written on 13 May Kitchener, citing the fact that he had only undertaken to support the campaign in the belief that the navy would be able to carry it to a successful conclusion alone, showed that he favoured its abandonment. But at the War Council's meeting he admitted that a withdrawal was politically unacceptable. He also stated that in the light of Hamilton's latest communication he believed that two divisions would be insufficient to overcome the Turkish defences. Although he was unenthusiastic about a significant increase in the size of the MEF, this was the option towards which the majority of the War Council inclined. But they felt unable to reach a definite conclusion. With the 52nd Division already ordered out to allow the position to be consolidated, they asked Kitchener instead to obtain from Hamilton a more detailed appreciation of the situation, including an estimate of the size of the force he felt would be necessary to produce a rapid, decisive victory.

Kitchener's telegram to this effect was received by Hamilton with some surprise. Three days later, on 17 May, he forwarded his reply. He outlined two possible courses. If assistance was forthcoming either from Russia or from the Balkans, notably from Greece or

Bulgaria, then he would need one army corps of two divisions. However, if he was to proceed unassisted, then he would need two army corps totalling four divisions. Kitchener was fully aware of the strain that two simultaneous campaigns would place on Britain's limited military resources and his reaction to Hamilton's reply was a mixture of disappointment that he should need so much and a terse reminder that he hoped he would bring 'the present unfortunate state of affairs in the Dardanelles to as early a conclusion as possible'.[27] In this reply Hamilton quickly perceived Kitchener's increasing political difficulties in reconciling the growing demands of the war and in response he tried to allay Kitchener's fears. 'Although I have made requests for certain additional troops, I am sure you will realize that does not imply that I am not doing all I possibly can with the force at my disposal, and every day sees some improvement in our position.'[28]

Other than to explain that the 52nd Division was on the point of departure, Kitchener gave Hamilton no further details of what reinforcements were to be sent to him in response to his appreciation and it was to be three weeks before a full decision was reached. The delay was caused by the dissolution of the Liberal government and the length of time it took to form a wartime coalition of Liberals, Conservatives and Labour in its place. Political pressure had been growing on Asquith, who managed to remain as Prime Minister, for some time and it came to a head in the middle of May. One final blow to the government was the eruption of a public outcry, orchestrated in particular by the newspapers owned by Lord Northcliffe, over a shell shortage which was felt to have played a significant part in the débâcle at Aubers Ridge. Another was the abrupt resignation of Lord Fisher, who felt he could no longer either support the campaign at the Dardanelles or work with Churchill. Churchill himself was one of the chief casualties, as well as causes, of the change of government. Demoted to the post of Chancellor of the Duchy of Lancaster, he was replaced as First Lord of the Admiralty by the former Conservative Prime Minister, Arthur Balfour. While the politicians procrastinated in this way, at Gallipoli the men in the line continued to dig in.

*

At Anzac the first deep trenches, begun to protect the beach on the morning of 26 April, had soon been well established. On 29 April Hamilton and a party of officers from GHQ landed to inspect the Anzac position. 'The trenches were a wonderful sight. Gallery after gallery with dugouts in the sides, & long communication trenches (some of them the Turkish trenches now used by us) – and all the time a ceaseless whistle of Turkish bullets coming over. But people in the trenches are quite safe so long as they keep their heads down.'[29] Throughout May wherever possible along 400 Plateau and across Russell's Top similar trenches were dug to secure the fragile position that had been so desperately seized. But the original boundaries remained unchanged, with the troops tightly hemmed in around the beachhead. Forming a rough triangle of less than 400 acres, with its base one-and-a-half miles long and the front line only 1,000 yards from the sea at its deepest point, the position was cramped and claustrophobic. Every feature seemed to be overlooked and no gully was completely safe.

The transfer of the two brigades to Helles left only three Australian brigades and four battalions of the RND at Anzac. With a combined strength of only 10,000 rifles, it was a small number for the many demands of the developing position and it added to the overall sense of strain which characterized Anzac at this time. But over the ensuing weeks numbers slowly rose. On 12 May 3,000 men of the Australian Light Horse and the New Zealand Mounted Rifles arrived from Egypt after volunteering to serve on the peninsula as infantry and towards the end of the month the two infantry brigades returned from Helles. Yet the tension remained. The terrain which surrounded the beach was fantastically complicated and presented considerable difficulties in the construction of continuous defences. However, in many ways it was only because of its unevenness and irregularity that the position could be defended at all. Had the ground sloped gently down from the perimeter to the sea it would have been untenable.

On the outer flanks of the line the opposing lines were relatively widely spaced and the presence of the ships off the coast and the continual threat of their supporting fire helped to keep the Turkish numbers down. Lieutenant Commander Hugh England RN, captain of the *Chelmer*, explained that she was posted off the southern flank of the line:

> After we had become established at Anzac my main job was guarding the flanks at night and burning searchlights, bombarding enemy trenches when this was called for. An example of the *sang-froid* of the Australians was when an officer of the Queensland Light Horse regiment, who I knew well, asked me to bombard some Turkish trenches which were giving him trouble near Chatham's Post on the extreme right of our line opposite Gaba Tepe. He told me I should have no trouble in recognizing them as the parapets were lined with speckled sandbags and when I went in that night they were clearly visible in my searchlight. After firing about 40 rounds from my 12 Pounder gun and when for some reason the Turks at Gaba Tepe were slow to open fire at us, I signalled to him, asking: 'Is that enough?' He replied, to my great astonishment: 'Wait a bit while I go over and see.' After what seemed much longer but was really only a few minutes as our trenches were only a few yards from the Turks, he signalled: 'Quite enough. You have blown the place to Hell!'[30] (Lieutenant Commander Hugh England RN)

In the centre of the line a similar degree of close support was not possible. To prevent exactly this kind of naval gunfire Liman von Sanders had ordered Essad to push the Turkish positions as close to those of the Anzacs as possible and so increase the risk of any fire hitting the latter as well as the former. Along the crest of the narrow spine which formed the eastern wall of Monash Valley and on Pope's Hill the posts which had evolved there remained isolated. Throughout May a great deal of work was devoted to developing their strength and establishing a margin of safety in case of a major Turkish attack. As it was impossible to create a single, continuous line, like those on either flank, tunnels and deep communication trenches had to be carved out to link the posts. Increasingly the Turks began to rely on a steady supply of bombs, a weapon with which the MEF had not been provided and which the Anzacs now had to learn to improvise from jam tins, and overhead cover became a priority to reduce the drain of casualties they caused. A mutually supporting network of enfilade fire was also developed to overcome the difficulty of firing directly to the front.

Central to this part of the line was Quinn's Post, which probably had the most evil reputation of all. The situation at Quinn's verged on the surrealistic, with the Anzac front line wedged between an almost sheer drop which cascaded down into Monash Valley, a mere five yards behind the rear of the trench, and the Turkish front line, which lay only a matter of a few feet in front. In isolation Quinn's would have been indefensible. But enfilade fire from Pope's Hill to the west and Courtney's Post to the south prevented the Turks from overrunning it. Yet, likewise, Turkish fire from Dead Man's Ridge alongside Pope's Hill and German Officer's Trench beyond Courtney's Post prevented the Anzacs from pushing their position further inland. As the weeks went by, raids and constant bombing created wretched conditions and the fear of death became ubiquitous. After returning from Helles on 20 May the Auckland Battalion, including Rupert Westmacott, who had been commissioned since his early days in New Zealand, relieved part of the 4th Australian Brigade at Quinn's.

> We were told that the battalion was to go up and take over Quinn's Post. All the way up the track there were sandbags placed to stop the bombs rolling down the hill. There were men coming and they said to us, 'You're going to absolute hell and you'll probably never come back!' We crawled up on this track to Quinn's Post which was a ghastly spot – hot and barren, all sorts of holes and trenches, in one place literally within inches of the Turkish trench. In fact there was one place where you could put your hand round the corner and shake hands with a Turk as he put his hand round. I was determined to see what the Turkish trenches were like, and in daylight I popped up over the top of the trench and had a look round, and down again. I got into trouble for this, blasted by the Colonel who said I was 'a perfect bloody fool' and 'what on earth did I do that for?'[31] (2nd Lieutenant Rupert Westmacott)

The attack on Baby 700 had shown that any attempt by the Anzacs to move directly forward out of their restricted position was futile, and the complete failure of a raid on Gaba Tepe on 4 May by 100 men of the 11th Battalion simply helped to confirm the strength of the surrounding Turkish defences. Two days earlier fifty men of the Canterbury Battalion had made a successful raid on the southern arm of Suvla Bay to destroy an observation post suspected of overlooking the Anzac area, killing two of the Turkish garrison and taking one officer and twelve other men prisoner for no New Zealand casualties. The raid was repeated on 14 May by a hundred men of the Canterbury Mounted Rifles to see if the post had been reoccupied. Lieutenant Commander Wilkinson, who landed the New Zealanders from the *Ribble*, explained that they 'worked the land like beating for birds, hoping to find the men who spot for the fall of shot, but there were none there. Our bag consisted of three sheep.'[32]

During the first fortnight of May the Turks suspended their attempts to break through the Anzac line, having suffered over 14,000 casualties there since 25 April.[33] But the Anzacs' presence represented a potentially significant threat to Turkish communications, as only a small Anzac advance would have taken them on to the crest of Gun Ridge and given them the clear view across to the Dardanelles that Lieutenant Loutit had on the morning of 25 April. Following a personal visit to the peninsula in the middle of May, Enver Pasha ordered a new attack to be launched as soon as possible. After the 2nd Division arrived fresh from Constantinople on 16 May to reinforce the three divisions already holding the line, it was decided to use it to spearhead an assault two days later with the aim of splitting the Anzacs' line and driving them back to the beach, where they could be overwhelmed. On 18 May reports of a cessation of firing in the centre of the line alerted ANZAC Headquarters to the imminence of an attack and aerial reconnaissance flights confirmed that large numbers of Turkish troops were building up inland. An order was issued warning the troops to be vigilant, and at 03.00 on 19 May they stood-to along the front line. Twenty minutes later the Turks began to stream along Wire Gully towards the isolated posts on Second Ridge and on to 400 Plateau to the south.

They came over in two great waves from their trenches, great hulking masses shouting 'Allah' and blowing trumpets, whistling and shouting, like schoolboys. As they got closer within nice rifle range we had the order to fire. We opened with rapid fire and brought them down in hundreds. Hundreds fell. The attack slackened off and they got back into their trenches. I should think when the attack was over there would be anything from 2 to 3,000 dead or dying in front of our brigade.[34] (Private Walter Stagles)

The interconnecting fire pattern established between the posts proved to be successful and inflicted terrible casualties on the Turks, which totalled 10,000.[35] The main thrust of the attack was defeated by 05.00, but further smaller-scale attacks continued as late as 11.00. In places, such as Quinn's Post, the Turks came very close to breaching the line.

There was one he came over bawling some Moslem phrase and he was shot by me and the fellow next to me – two or three shot at the same time – he came through practically on top of my bayonet, right on top of me. He was a very big man and none of us could lift him out. He was too heavy to lift three feet while you kept down out of fire. Literally I sat on that Turk for two days, ate my lunch sitting on him![36] (Private Henry Barnes)

At Courtney's Post a group of seven Turks actually succeeded in breaking through. But they were outflanked by Lance Corporal Albert Jacka of the 14th Australian Battalion. After working his way behind them and storming the trench which they had captured, Jacka then bayoneted five of the Turks before shooting the remaining two. For his actions he was awarded the first Australian VC of the war.

As the sun rose on 20 May, the heaps of Turkish dead lying in no-man's land posed a new threat to the Anzacs. The sheer stench and miasma of corruption emanating from the rapidly decaying corpses threatened to make life in the front line unbearable.

On the following morning they came out with their Red Crescent flag but they were fired on and told to get back as they were massing their troops in the trenches again. They were lying there for three or four days. The smell got so awful that we prayed that the wind would blow in from the sea and take the stench of the dead over the Turkish trenches instead of our own. Then there was an armistice arranged on the 24th. About 7.30 in the morning the Turks and ourselves went forwards under the red cross flag to bury the dead. In the groups where there was a lot of dead lying, there was a grave or trench dug and they used broom sticks or rifles with meat hooks tied on the end and pulled the dead into the trenches they had dug.[37] (Private Walter Stagles)

Formal negotiations on 20 May between Hamilton and Liman von Sanders had resulted in an agreement for an armistice to last for nine hours, strictly to allow for the removal and burial of the dead. At last the adversaries were able to get the measure of each other.

The Turks had a very big man, he must have been about seven feet tall and our own man was nearly as big. I suppose it was prestige that made them choose big men. They both had white flags and they stood in the middle. . . . I wasn't one of those burying the dead but I sat on the parapet and after a while walked over and offered bully beef to one Turk. He smiled and seemed very pleased and passed me a whole string of dates. Jacko, as we called the Turkish soldier, was very highly regarded by me and all the men on our side. I never heard him decried, he was always a clean fighter and one of the most courageous men in the world. When they came there was no beating about the bush, they faced up to the heaviest rifle fire that you could put up and nothing would stop them, they were almost fanatical. When we met them at the armistice we came to the conclusion that he was a very good bloke indeed. We had a lot of time for him.[38] (Private Henry Barnes)

After the Turkish attack the situation settled down as both sides recognized the inherent strengths of their opponents' position. Small attacks to achieve marginal improvements became increasingly expensive in lives and were gradually phased out. Only diversionary operations in conjunction with the attacks at Helles were made and the repercussions of these sometimes reverberated for days afterwards. On 4 June the New Zealanders launched a raid from Quinn's Post. Inevitably it was a demoralizing failure. But three days later a second raid was ordered to recover material lost during the first and destroy the Turkish trench directly in front of Quinn's.

> The attack was not by my Hauraki Company, it was the 3rd Auckland Regiment Company who had two well trained English sergeant majors, both married men with families. They didn't want to risk their lives and I was the most useless person that they had – they didn't care whether I was killed or not because I was more untrained than any other officer – but I could lead men and I must take their platoon over the top. I was told that we were to go over the top at ten o'clock and capture the Turkish trench. Well, my wrist-watch had gone bung on me so I borrowed a watch from a chap called Johnstone, so I could go over punctually. We sat in the trenches while the Navy bombarded, you could see the shells coming over from the ships, wondering whether any would fall short and take me with it. At 10 o'clock I gave a 'View-Halloo! Come on Boys!' and went up over the top. I got to the edge of the Turkish trench and flung myself down, just to crawl in and a bomb came and blew my leg off. I couldn't do any more. I lay there for a bit and then crawled back to our own trenches. I heard a voice saying: 'Where's Westy? Westy, you've got my watch. Let me have it back will you?' I said: 'Yes,' and he took the watch. Johnstone said: 'I'm going to take you down.' I said, 'There's been orders that no wounded are to be carried back.' 'Balls to that!' he said, and hoisted me on his back and carried me down this awful track. My wounded leg, hanging on by puttees and boots, caught on the sandbags all the way down.[39] (2nd Lieutenant Rupert Westmacott)

A concerted Turkish attack on 29 June, the last made against the line at Anzac, failed in the same way and life degenerated into a monotonous routine of digging, tunnelling and mining. Yet the enervating tension persisted. As June turned into July these factors combined to produce a lethargic fatalism which bitterly contrasted with the enthusiasm and energy of the landing.

> Three months continuous trench fighting is a big strain on any man & I notice even the toughest among us are beginning to show signs of nerves & everyone is heartily sick of the game of

The British Commanders: General Sir Ian Hamilton (left) and Vice Admiral John de Robeck (right).

Winston Churchill, First Lord of the Admiralty, October 1911 to May 1915.

Lieutenant General Sir William Birdwood (right) and Field Marshal Lord Kitchener (centre) at Mudros on 11 November 1915.

Lieutenant General Sir Aylmer Hunter Weston (centre) outside VIII Corps Headquarters at Helles.

Lighters clustered round the bows of the *River Clyde* on the morning of 25 April. On the shore troops can be seen sheltering under the earth bank.

Lancashire Fusiliers of the 42nd Division waiting to land on the peninsula from a trawler at the start of May.

Photographs taken by Captain Orlo Williams, Cipher Officer at GHQ and one of the Staff Officers who observed the landing from the *Queen Elizabeth*.

Left: The *River Clyde* seen from the aft torpedo control of the *Queen Elizabeth* on the morning of 25 April.

Below: Hunter Weston (left), Hamilton (centre) and his Chief of the General Staff, Major General Walter Braithwaite (right), at 29th Division Headquarters above W Beach on 30 April.

Above: V Beach, Sedd el Bahr, and the Old Fort from the cliffs beside Fort No. 1 on 30 April.

Right: The ruins of Sedd el Bahr on 2 May.

The Hood Battalion, RND, rest at the White House on 6 May during the first day of the Second Battle of Krithia.

The advanced dressing station of the 1/1st East Lancashire Field Ambulance, 42nd Division, located at Clapham Junction, a fork in Krithia Nullah, on 4 June during the Third Battle of Krithia.

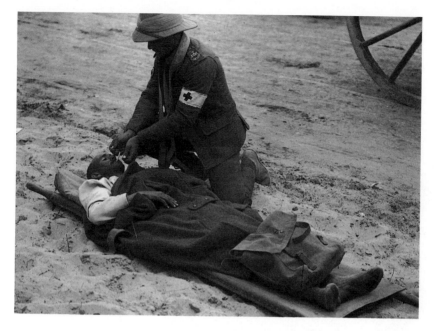

A territorial stretcher-bearer lights a cigarette for a wounded soldier awaiting evacuation.

Chaplains of three denominations attend the burial of four British soldiers at Helles.

Marshal Otto Liman von Sanders, the German commander of the Turkish Fifth Army.

Mustafa Kemal Bey, later known as Atatürk, who played a key role in the defeat of the attacks at Anzac in April and against Chunuk Bair and Suvla in August.

war. I myself if I ever get back think I will take up a small block of orchard land & take things easy but [I] am afraid it will be some time, if ever, I see Australia again. But whatever 'kismette' holds in store for me I do not know so hope for the best.[40] (Private Frank Loud)

The position at Helles was larger and less claustrophobic. By the end of the Second Battle of Krithia the front line stretched for two-and-three-quarter miles across the toe of the peninsula, and the distance from there to the beaches was about three miles. In the reverse of the situation at Anzac, it was on the outer flanks at Helles that the British and Turkish lines were closest and in the centre they remained a considerable distance apart. The countryside at Helles was also different. Before the war it had been an agricultural area with orchards, vineyards and fields of golden crops. Although the ground was cut up by deep ravines, the extreme undulations of Anzac were not present. With the sea surrounding it on three sides and many of the sights of the mythological world of Ancient Greece in view, at the start of May it was a beautiful, almost romantic, place and its charm struck many of the soldiers, including Lieutenant Colonel John Patterson, the commanding officer and founder of the Zion Mule Corps:

Away to my left stood the quaint old ruined walls and towers of Sedd-el-Bahr, thrown into bold outline against the rippling waters of the Dardanelles, while further on the eye was caught by the green plains of Ilium, set in a tangle of hills, on the picturesque Asiatic coast. Ahead of me . . . glittered the soft sea, with Cape Helles jutting into it like a rough brown hand thrust into a basin of shimmering quicksilver. . . . Away on my right sparkled the Aegean, with the Isles of Greece jutting out of it, like rugged giants rising from their ocean lair. To crown all the sun was going down in a perfect blaze of colour, tipping the crests of Imbros and Samothrace with a glint of gold as it sank behind them into the sea. . . . Never have I seen anything to equal the gorgeous lights and shades which at sundown are painted on the Aegean sky. If I were an artist my ambition would be to . . . try to put on canvas the perfectly gorgeous but harmoniously blended rose,

177

pink, scarlet, red, yellow, purple, green, amber and blue – a perfect intoxication of glorious colours which the imagination would be unequal to, unless they were absolutely thrown on the sky before one's own eyes.[41] (Lieutenant Colonel John Patterson)

From the hills around the beaches the ground dropped down to the plain which ran inland from Morto Bay before rising slowly to the dominating height of Achi Baba. Initially the plain was a fertile area, swathed with crops and spring flowers and in his account of the Second Battle of Krithia the official British war correspondent, Ellis Ashmead Bartlett, described a profusion of vivid colours which covered the ground at that time:

> On the cliffs are great bunches of yellow plantagenasta and yellow poppies. You ride over fields and through gardens in which flowers abound in a reckless and beautiful profusion. There are white orchids and rock roses, while mauve stock and iris abound. There are fields of poppies, white marguerites, and blue borage, intermingled with deep purple vetches, brick red pea and yellow clover, pink and white campions, and asphodel.[42] (Ellis Ashmead Bartlett)

Denis Buxton, a keen ornithologist, noted in his diary entries at the beginning of May the presence of a multitude of birds.

> A Woodpecker (like our greater spotted), Magpies (whiter than ours I think), Jays (heard, not seen), Hoodies and Jackdaws, Lesser Kestrels, Great Tits, and several kinds of Warblers, which I am afraid cannot be identified. . . . There was also a Roller about, or he may have been a big Bee Eater (green and black, no red). Also a pair of Great Tits (they looked smaller than ours) and a Flycatcher (spotted) and I think a pair of Black Caps. . . . It was strange to go to sleep, and to wake up, about a mile from our trenches, and hear no rifles nor guns and only the birds singing in the fig tree over our heads.[43] (Private Denis Buxton)

Many soldiers, including Sapper Thomas Rowatt of the Signal Company, RND Engineers, did not greet the burbling song of the local fauna with the same degree of enthusiasm:

The frogs began as soon as it was dark and kept it up for hours making it impossible to sleep. . . . Then the nightingales started up. Every tree seemed to be full of them all trying to out sing each other, what a row. Between them, the frogs for the first house and the nightingales for the midnight matinee we got but little sleep. Then there were the grasshoppers. These were about six inches long, and, with the aid of membranous wings could jump over six feet. That was in order but when they jumped and landed on your face every few steps it got annoying.[44] (Sapper Thomas Rowatt)

As the summer passed and the war began to tighten its grip on the surrounding countryside, the glory of Helles began to fade. Each successive battle hastened the natural process of the changing of the seasons, imbuing it with a grim symbolism and degrading the landscape just as it degraded and corrupted many of its participants.

When we first landed the country was absolutely beautiful, all shades of green, the silver olives and a great variety of flowers. But that was soon changed. I expect it would have parched fairly rapidly anyway but what between shells, wheel tracks, men tramping about and above, and enveloping all the dust, the whole landscape took on a uniform dust colour. And not only the landscape but us and all our belongings. Dust was all pervading.[45] (Sapper Thomas Rowatt)

The contrast between the early beauty and the slow corruption of the fighting became pronounced. Douglas Talbot, who had been promoted to captain since the landings, commented to a friend in England, 'You say Gallipoli sounds a bloody place; in many ways certainly. The whole place reeks of dead; and yet it is a mass of flowers and would be quite divine without the war.'[46] The more squalid side of life at Helles which characterized the front line formed a closer parallel with conditions at Anzac. Where the two armies met, the battlefield was confused but not as complex. The trenches, thrown randomly across the ground which lay inland from the beaches, reflected the ebbing tide of the fighting. Without organization or planning they did not run in straight lines and sometimes even failed to connect places of tactical importance. Like ley lines of death they had been scraped out, or captured, at the very limits of human endurance. If the men could have gone on further they would have done so. But where they had been driven to ground, the positions became fixed.

The longer period of fighting at Helles which lasted almost continuously up to 8 May and the greater depth of the position prevented the early development of deep trenches like those on Russell's Top and 400 Plateau; instead the British line was more haphazard, as Guy Nightingale, also now a captain, explained:

> The trenches are awful – very badly made – narrow, not bullet proof and smell absolutely revolting from dead bodies. We are occupying Turkish trenches which we captured, but there is an absolute maze of trenches. We are all round the Turk and they are all round us too. The Dublins' trenches have their back to Achi Baba and face our Base, the Turks being between them and us! We share several trenches with the Turks, with a barricade between and throw bombs at each other over the top! The whole place is up and down *hill* not in the slightest bit like the trenches in France. To get to our trenches we go four miles up a deep nullah with sides 200 feet high. There is a great barricade up right across the nullah at the furthest point we hold. To get into our trenches we go up a zig zag track and enter a hole in the cliff which leads into our support trenches and from them there are innumerable communication trenches leading into the firing line. Of course you can't show your head above the trench for a second, but have to look through periscopes or through peep holes. Between the trenches are any amount of dead and decomposing bodies of our own men and Turks lying on the heather. The smell is awful, though we throw down quantities of Chloride of Lime and creosote. We are always sapping and digging day and night, and so are the Turks, who in places are about 30 yards away and in others 100, and where we share trenches only the other side of the barricade.[47] (Captain Guy Nightingale)

The presence of so many decaying bodies was extremely unpleasant. But it also represented a potentially greater threat to the long-term health of the troops.

This place is nothing but a mass of dead KOSBs and Turks which fell on the 25th and are still unburied yet and the sun makes them very unbearable; I should think we shall have disease shortly as the flies are getting awful. You say, why not bury the bodies? They are on the enemy's side of the parapet and if you put up a stick it is hit at once even, so it is impossible. . . . Two of our men did go out to bury one fellow who was more objectionable in his talk than the rest, and in spite of several issues of rum they have been sick ever since.[48] (Captain Douglas Talbot)

As the trench system developed so the siege techniques of sapping were introduced. Skilled engineers or miners, sometimes – like Joe Murray – recruited from infantry units, would dig saps to create first outposts and then, as they were joined together, a new front line.

A sap is a short trench towards the enemy. We start digging underneath the parapet. We go through there and we've got a hole. We'd come up just in front of the parapet. We dig and dig and dig. There was two men, I was digging and my mate was dragging away, then he was digging. Only picks and shovels, lying down. About two to three foot deep, that's all. Every time your shovel went up a bullet would hit it. We were comparatively safe – you have to keep your head down in the mines you know – you get used to it. We used to fill the bags and the Manchester chappies used to drag them away. When we'd gone three or four yards the infantrymen themselves used to start digging. The soil they got out they used to chuck it over the sides. They made the trench deeper. We went forward about twelve yards; a trench about five foot deep and two feet wide. When we got as far as we wanted we kept the sandbags and made a sort of barricade, a proper bombing post. All away the front line there was these saps. Eventually we would get the infantry to start digging a trench from one sap to the next sap, probably ten to fifteen yards away. It was under cover. The Turks used to do the same so you would get the trenches right together without anybody going over the top. When I talk about the trenches being ten yards apart, you probably say, 'Oh well that's a lot of bloody nonsense, how the

hell do you get the trenches ten yards apart?' Well that's how.[49]
(Ordinary Seaman Joe Murray)

On 11 May the 29th Division were able to rest for the first time since the landing and the position that the left flank of the division had occupied on Gully Spur was taken over by the 29th Indian Brigade. On the cliffs above Y Beach the machine-gun post which had proved so devastating throughout the Second Battle of Krithia remained in place. But once in the line Cox put forward a scheme to use the 1/6th Gurkhas to outflank and capture it under cover of darkness. On the night of 12 May a strong party of Gurkhas moved quietly along the base of the cliffs to the foot of the northernmost nullah, which climbed up from Y Beach. Moving up the cliffs, the Gurkhas reached the summit and pushed their line around the head of the nullah. A second party of equal strength then repeated the actions of the first and extended this line to the south towards the machine-gun post, which was situated above the southernmost nullah. Realizing that they would soon be surrounded the Turks withdrew from the post and the remainder of the 1/6th Gurkhas, with the 14th Sikhs on their right, then moved forward 500 yards to extend the line from the head of the nullahs to Gully Ravine. The operation was impeccably executed and the cliff beyond Y Beach became known as Gurkha Bluff. The tactics employed were intelligent and imaginative, taking full advantage of the ground and the skill of the troops, and contrasted sharply with the three days of futile, headlong assaults made a week earlier.

Preparations for a renewed attack continued throughout the rest of May. No-man's land was steadily eroded by a combination of sapping and small-scale night attacks, while communication trenches were dug behind the lines to secure the relatively safe transport of men and supplies up to the front. The Helles force was marginally strengthened by the arrival of the final 126th Brigade of the 42nd Division and the reunification of the RND on the return of the four battalions from Anzac, although the British responsibility correspondingly increased when they took over a greater share of the front line from the French. On 24 May the three divisions at Helles were formed into the VIII Corps under the command of Hunter Weston. But for all his optimism the situation remained grim. Many of the battalions were still under-strength and the men were betraying an increasing frailty of health as various diseases, dysentery in particular, got a grip on them. The extreme shortage of shells continued and on 20 May GHQ ordered normal expenditure of ammunition to be limited to just two rounds per day. The greatly reinforced Turkish forces were also quiescent, but not idle. They too were busy digging.

The security of all the positions on land was underpinned by the British naval supremacy. The presence of the fleet and its potential firepower, however unpredictable the level of accuracy, still gave the Allied troops a welcome degree of moral and material support. But this position was soon dramatically altered by a series of disasters. The first occurred when the Turks launched a daring torpedo-boat raid on the two battleships and five destroyers posted each night to guard the army's flank in the Dardanelles. At 01.17 on 13 May the *Goliath* was on station in Morto Bay when it was struck by three torpedos fired from the Turkish *Muavenet-i Millet*.

I was woken up by the explosions. The ship listed at once to an angle of 5 degrees to starboard. There was no panic as it was all too sudden for anyone to realize what had happened. I went up to the quarter deck in my pyjamas. The ship was then heeling over fast. When the starboard side of the deck was level with the sea she stopped for about 30 seconds. Then she heeled rapidly again. Then I dived over the port side. I struck the side of the ship with my face. It was a horrid feeling as I felt my nose slithering over the wet side. I suppose I dived about 30 feet as I saw a good many constellations when I struck the water. I swam about 200 yards away & then turned round to see her sink. She had heeled back to almost an even keel & was going down bows first with her stern about 40 feet up in the air. You could plainly hear all the crockery and furniture tumbling about & breaking up inside her. She then heeled completely over until her bottom was uppermost & she slid right under. You could hear the cries of drowning men all round. I swam down with the current to the *Cornwallis* which I could dimly see in the dark about 2 miles away. There was a five knot tide helping me on. When I was about a mile from the scene of the disaster I came across a big spar about 30 ft long. I hung on to it for a few minutes to get my breath & then abandoned it as I could get on quicker without. I was eventually picked up by the *Lord Nelson*'s cutter & taken to a trawler.[50] (Midshipman Wolstan Forester RN)

Forester had been fortunate, as only 183 of the ship's complement of 750 survived. Although this attack was a serious setback, tightened precautions greatly reduced the chance of a repeat performance.

A far more serious threat lay in the German submarines which had been dispatched to the eastern Mediterranean. Of these the most effective was the *U21*, under the command of Lieutenant Commander Otto Hershing, which had set off from the German naval port of Wilhelmshaven on 25 April. *En route* she was spotted many times and in anticipation of her arrival off the Gallipoli beaches anti-submarine precautions were adopted. On 17 May the number of battleships lying off Helles was reduced from seven to four and at Anzac the number was halved to only two. In the remaining ships a diligent anti-submarine watch was kept, anti-torpedo nets were hung out and escorting destroyers tried to keep the U-boats away from their prey.

The *U21* reached Gallipoli on 25 May and went straight into action. At first the anti-submarine defences seemed to work. Destroyers spotted her periscope and prevented an attack on the *Swiftsure* off Helles, while a torpedo fired at the *Vengeance* was spotted and successful avoiding action taken. Moving north a new target in the form of the *Triumph* was stalked off Anzac. At 12.25 *U21* struck and although the torpedo was spotted it was too late.

I was range finder up in the aloft position. One day midday I came down to get my ration of rum. I'd just drunk it when I heard a lot of commotion, guns firing, so I immediately returned to my position. On my way up a torpedo struck us. Then when I did get up I saw one of our boys aiming his rifle at a torpedo coming through the water. Unfortunately he missed but he stuck to his post firing at this torpedo trying to divert it. No luck so it came through and hit us. We didn't know that the Germans had invented a net cutter on the front of the torpedo. We were protected by huge steel nets pushed out on booms to try and stop the torpedos. But they just passed straight through and hit us. I could feel the ship listing over. Remembering I had a brand new pair of boots on which I'd bought the previous day I took them off and hung them on the rigging thinking to myself that if nothing happened they'd still be there and I came down the rigging. By this time the ship was heeled pretty bad and the majority of the ratings were catching hold of the nets, the leeside, the side in the water. I didn't like the idea, I don't know why, and I jumped off and got in the water. Shortly after the destroyer *Chelmer* came up and started picking us out. Then she put her bows on the stern of the ship which by now had heeled almost on one side. A lot of the men got on board of her that way.[51] (Ordinary Seaman W. G. Northcott)

As a result of England's skilful handling of the *Chelmer* only seventy-five men from the *Triumph* were lost.

The arrival of the German submarines changed the whole situation for the British supporting fleet. The loss of the *Triumph* caused the emergency withdrawal of all the remaining battleships to the protected anchorage of Imbros. The next day De Robeck decided that, despite the risk, two were always to remain available for supporting bombardments at Helles, one in the Aegean and one in the Dardanelles facing the Asiatic batteries. In accordance with this arrangement the *Majestic* was stationed off W Beach. Her presence was meant to improve morale ashore and reassure the infantry that the Royal Navy had not deserted them. But many saw her as a tethered goat and the end proved swift. Rowatt was sea-bathing off W Beach when she was hit.

Suddenly her siren began to blast and to our amazement she began to roll over, with men jumping into the water. We grasped that she had been torpedoed and was sinking so we hurriedly pushed off one of these [derelict] boats wading out as far as we could, pushed her off and jumped in to discover that we had no oars, so we had to meekly swim ashore again whilst the battleship turned completely bottom up.[52] (Sapper Thomas Rowatt)

Once again casualties were mercifully slight and only forty-three were killed.

It was to prove the high-water mark of the German submarine

campaign against the British capital ships. Although more and more U-boats arrived, they never again equalled these early triumphs. The navy ceased to expose battleships and cruisers off the peninsula, keeping them instead at Imbros in Kephalos Bay unless the army specifically requested their heavy guns in support. Day-to-day support was provided by destroyers and later on by shallow-draught monitors or ships fitted with anti-torpedo bulges around the water line. But the U-boats were successful in posing a perpetual threat to the British lines of communication, which stretched back across the Mediterranean. Transports and shipping were sunk and administrative arrangements were rendered even more complicated. The disappearance of the larger ships also had a distinct effect on the morale of the British troops. Their presence had been deeply reassuring and indicative of a joint effort being made by the two services. To the soldiers, as they faced the renewal of an offensive that had been undertaken only because the navy had failed to pull off the campaign on its own, the withdrawal of the ships was seen as a desertion.

6

Trench Warfare
at Helles

Despite the failure of the Second Battle of Krithia, Hunter Weston retained his belief that the capture of Achi Baba was feasible. The largely defensive posture of the Turkish garrison at Helles coupled with the imminent arrival of reinforcement drafts and the 52nd Division was significant in maintaining this. He recognized that the Turkish defences were becoming more formidable as each day went by and he saw it as imperative that a further assault should be launched before their defences became impregnable. General Gouraud had relieved d'Amade in command at the CEO on 15 May, and he shared Hunter Weston's optimism. Hamilton would have preferred to wait for more men and munitions but he bowed to their judgement and at a GHQ conference on 31 May plans were finalized.

In planning for what was to be the Third Battle of Krithia, GHQ and VIII Corps Headquarters had to take into consideration the fact that, by then, most of the characteristics of trench warfare were firmly in place at Helles. Both sides had continuous lines of trenches right across the peninsula which allowed no scope for manoeuvre; barbed-wire defences were starting to proliferate; in front-line areas the machine-gun and snipers made it certain death to linger in the open; and artillery on both sides restricted the movement of reserves to the 'decisive' points during battle. These restrictive factors were recognized in the detailed set of operational orders issued by the VIII Corps on 1 June in which, although the British and French were to attack right across Helles, the objectives they sought were to be strictly limited so that land occupied could be retained in the face of the inevitable Turkish counter-attacks.

The attack was to be preceded by a meticulous and concentrated four-hour bombardment incorporating a short break, as a simple ruse, to tempt the Turks into the trenches before shelling was reopened. The British and French field batteries were assigned to destroy barbed-wire defences in no-man's land, smash the Turkish front-line trenches and close off the Turkish communications trenches to disrupt, or prevent, the arrival of reinforcements. Meanwhile the Royal Navy was to destroy or keep quiet the Turkish batteries. At the appointed time the troops would advance in two waves, the first to capture the Turkish front line, the second to leap-frog them and take the second and third lines to a maximum depth of 800 yards. Special digging parties were to concentrate on consolidating the captured trenches, while mopping-up parties eradicated any snipers. To allow the artillery to monitor the troops' progress red screens would be carried forward by the advancing troops and placed above captured trenches. In addition the armoured cars of the Royal Naval Division were to join the attack.

On the far left, between the Aegean Sea and Krithia Nullah, was the sadly depleted 29th Division, but the orders still assigned them a tough task in capturing a series of Turkish trenches on either side of Gully Ravine. Next in line between Krithia Nullah and Achi Baba Nullah was the 42nd Division attacking on a front of some 1,200 yards. To their right the RND was attacking on a front of less than 1,000 yards between Achi Baba Nullah and Kereves Dere. Finally, on the far right, the French 1st and 2nd Divisions were to attack the formidable Haricot Redoubt at Kereves Dere. A major unresolved problem was that the whole British and French reserves combined consisted of only eighteen miscellaneous battalions, widely scattered and with no idea of their probable role in the approaching battle.

In the final days the practice of sapping forward to reduce the distance they would have to charge across during the attack was continued. This eminently sensible measure threw up an example of Hunter Weston's continued intransigence and lack of adaptability to the necessities of circumstance. Brigadier General Marshall had been attached to the 42nd Division to provide assistance to the inexperienced staff of the 127th Manchester Brigade when he learnt of this proposal.

A night advance was to be made on the night of 2nd June and all the troops destined to carry out the attack were to dig themselves in within 200 yards of the enemy trenches. In front of the Manchester Brigade the line of the enemy trenches formed a re-entrant, and, with an almost full moon, I would have preferred not to advance into this re-entrant, so I ventured to point out that the resulting casualties might be very heavy. However the orders were very explicit and had to be carried out. The result was the brigade made the advance successfully, and dug itself in all along the line within the stipulated two hundred yards. Luckily the enemy fired high and the resulting casualties only amounted to fifty or sixty, nearly all being wounded cases. Hunter Weston came down on the 3rd personally to congratulate Lee's Brigade on their successful effort; to me he said: 'There you are! You see the thing has been done with no casualties.' I gently murmured 'Fifty' to which he retorted: 'Well, that's nothing, it would have been worth doing if you had five hundred.'[1] (Brigadier General William Marshall)

Major Norman Burge, of the RND's Cyclist Coy, was not aware of the imminent attack until late on 3 June and his account, although intended to be humorous, nevertheless neatly illustrates the mood during the night before an attack:

You always know when there's going to be a battle, because people come & tell you to get up, & bally well be smart about it too, at 2am. So up you spring with a pleased smile & wring him warmly by the hand ... & put on everything you can find, prattling merrily all the time such as 'What a delightful morning,' 'How nice you look, old dear.' Then someone strikes a match, 'cos he can't find his best girl's lock of hair to wear next to his heart (messy habit I call it) & he is gently reproved by those in authority with a smiling 'Nay brother, nay, lest the light attract the attention of the enemy, so please blow out that light.' At least, it's something like that, only generally longer & a little louder. And then the men fall in with a certain amount of scuffling. It appeared in the early stages that everyone desired to be an even number when they numbered off. This was because the odd numbers carried a pick or shovel as well as the ordinary gear. Now they know the value of these tools and the scuffle is to get them. Then everyone moves off & presently you get to a maze of trenches. When you get to the middle, you find a Staff Officer

189

who says you're all wrong & you'd better go back. You argue with him, but more out of convention than anything else, 'cos he always wins. Well, you try to please him & go back, but you can't because another battalion is coming up & the trench is very narrow. Eventually a compromise is reached. One lot (the one who lost the toss) scrabble as close to the side of the trench as they can & the others squeeze past, scraping grooves in the stomachs of the scrabblers with stray bits of equipment which may and do happen to stick out. As soon as the General has had two bits of bacon, the battle begins.[2] (Major Norman Burge)

Friday, 4 June was a hot summer's day. The bombardment of identified Turkish strongpoints opened at 08.00 and at 11.05 the concentrated barrage of the whole Turkish front line began. Once again only the French 75s, some of which had been loaned to the British sector, were well supplied with high-explosive shells and by far the great preponderance of shells fired by British guns were ineffectual shrapnel. Probably as a result of this imbalance, reactions to the bombardment varied widely among the troops, depending on the amount of destruction in front of them. Some were mightily impressed.

It was such an inferno of noise, that I was stone deaf for a fortnight afterwards; and there was a tornado of hellish fire, so fierce and terrible, that spread death and destruction all around. Any orders that were given had to be passed down the Trenches from man to man, by his yelling in to the ears of his mate as loudly as he possibly could. The bombardment consisted of shrapnel and lyddite; and shells in thousands were dropped, blowing parts of the Turkish Trenches to atoms, and completely carrying away the barbed wire entanglements which the enemy had erected. Every shell that dropped seemed to tell; for we saw, hurled up into the air, Legs, Arms, Heads, Bodies, parts of limbs and every imaginable thing. It was an awful and fearful sight, most gruesome in the extreme, and blood curdling.[3] (Private R. Sheldon)

But in other areas it was a sad disappointment to those who knew that their lives might depend on the efficacy of the bombardment.

We were told that we were to have an intense bombardment. But when it got nearer to 12 o'clock, we said: 'When are we going to have the intense bombardment?', and we were told we'd had that! Well now, whilst I don't know the numbers of shells fired I wouldn't have thought it was more than five or six thousand. Our General of artillery was affectionately known as 'Monsieur la general un coup par piece'. They knew we were short of shells.[4] (Sub-Lieutenant Arthur Watts)

For the ordinary soldiers waiting in the trenches all along the line the period before going over the top was a nightmare.

In the firing line it was packed. We were standing there, couldn't sit down, couldn't lie down, just standing there. The fellow next to me was messing about with his ammunition, fiddling about, cleaning his rifle, looking in the magazine. Another fellow was sort of staring. The blinking maggots from the dead bodies in the firing line were crawling round right under our noses. Every now and again if a bullet hit the parapet there was a Psssst, wind, gas – it smelt like hell. The sun was boiling hot. The maggots, the flies – the stench was horrible.[5] (Ordinary Seaman Joe Murray)

As arranged, the bombardment stopped for ten minutes at 11.20 to try and trick the Turks into thinking that the attack was being launched. As the troops made their feint attack by showing their bayonets and cheering the Turks responded with an absolute torrent of fire, and machine-gun bullets lacerated the parapet sandbags. When the bombardment resumed the assault troops in the front line had no illusions as to what was waiting for them.

Honestly and truly the next half an hour was like an age. The bullets were hitting the parapet – Bang, Bang, Bang – actually coming through the parapet, disturbing the dead bodies, the stench. . . . Ooooh dear me! It was horrible. . . . Between you and I, I said my prayers. . . . 'Please God, not only for myself but for my parents may I survive.' I remember Lieutenant Commander Parsons standing on the ladder, he called out: 'Five minutes to go men. . . .Four minutes to go.' At that moment young Corbie, he'd be annoyed if I called him that, a young sub-lieutenant, only a youngster, he walked past me and said something to Parsons, so

191

he missed number two or three. The next time: 'One minute to go men. . . . Now men.' He blew a whistle and off we go. The moment we started to leave this particular traverse where we were – it was ten or twelve feet long – men were getting out by the ladders but falling back into the trench. I should imagine most of the men who attempted to attack on that particular order fell back either into the trench or on to the parapet. There was dead all over the place.[6] (Ordinary Seaman Joe Murray)

As the infantry attacked all along the line at 12.00 the artillery switched their fire to the trenches immediately in the rear of the Turkish front line.

On the 29th Division front the 29th Indian Brigade suffered severely as they tried to advance.

On the extreme left the 6th Gurkhas moved forward under cover of the cliffs and reached the end of the first enemy trench almost unobserved. The attached Lancashire Fusilier Battalion attacking the centre were mown down almost to a man before they had got many yards from their own parapet. The 14th Sikhs, on the right of the Brigade, started with the advantage of some dead ground, and made some progress, but when they emerged into view they were practically annihilated, and though some of the survivors got as far as the Turkish wire, they were there killed. The 14th Sikhs, as a fighting unit, had ceased to exist. The 6th Gurkhas were therefore left in the air and, most of their British officers having been shot, they retired, losing heavily in doing so.[7] (Brigadier General William Marshall)

The main reason for their failure seems to have been the failure of the artillery bombardment in the Gully Spur area between Gully Ravine and the sea. No howitzers with their more lethal plunging fire had been assigned to the sector, and to make matters worse a number of the guns initially assigned there had been diverted on to other targets.

To the right of Gully Ravine, on Fir Tree Spur, 2nd Lieutenant Richard Reeves of the 1st KOSB was in the second wave as they launched themselves over the parapet and he captures the frenzy of that moment:

> At 12 punctually the intense bombardment ceased – it was an infernal noise – no words can describe the hideous din – the earth simply shook & parts of the support trench in which I was, fell in from the reverberation. A and B Coys attacked and lost very heavily. . . . C & D Companies followed 50 paces behind, and we had to get up a very high parapet in the face of a perfect hail of shrapnel and machine-gun and rifle fire – I ran on blindly shouting to my men – we lost heaps – men falling all around me and with such terrible wounds. . . . My men were splendid – nothing stopped them – we dashed into the 1st Turkish trench (H9) and all the enemy were standing there with white flags, their hands up – some had their hats hoisted on their rifles: we took the lot – and I at once detailed an escort for them – we dashed on to the next trench (H10), the same thing happened there – all told about 56 prisoners – I collected some men, Worcesters and KOSB mixed by this time and we rushed on to H11: about 10 yards from this, I turned to shout to them to come on, when I fell with a twisted ankle into an awful barbed wire entanglement. All this time shrapnel whizzing all around and men falling – it was too awful – I had no wire cutters – my coat was torn in numbers of places – my puttees to ribbons and my breeches too – I tried everything to get out of it – and simply could not do so – I saw 4 Turks coming towards me – I fired my revolver 4 times at them 2 fell and I don't know what happened to the others – I lay in that tornado for about ¾ hour – our men in the meantime had got to H11 the third trench and a stiff bayonet fight went on – we eventually got possession of it and after that I saw them press on to the next one. I lay in the barbed wire expecting to be hit every moment – By the mercy of God I wasn't although a sharpnel bullet struck me on the heel of the boot – quite suddenly I felt myself free of the wire, how I don't know, but I couldn't get up as my ankle was too painful. A wounded officer from the Worcesters near couldn't move either – he was hit in the leg and I gave him my water bottle – numbers of men all around very badly wounded – I gave morphia tablets to several – at last the shrapnel ceased slightly and the Worcester man and I crawled

back together very slowly – we passed through H10 and H9 and at last got back to our original trench – we took ages doing it, and he poor chap was awfully weak – he died.[8] (2nd Lieutenant Richard Reeves)

The 1st KOSB and the 4th Worcesters had made a considerable advance and actually reached the last Turkish line. But they were not supported and eventually were forced to fall back as the Turkish reserves arrived.

In the centre of the line the 42nd Division's assaulting battalions of the Manchester Territorial 127th Brigade made an impressive start as they surged forward between Krithia Nullah and Achi Baba Nullah. Despite heavy casualties, within five minutes they had captured the front-line Turkish trenches and half an hour later the second line was overrun. During the afternoon the Mancunians penetrated as far as the Turkish fourth line and found there was no serious fortification between them and Achi Baba. It seemed as if the elusive 'breakthrough' had been attained, even though the objectives of the attack had been limited.

Less success crowned the efforts of the armoured cars as they rolled into action up the Krithia Road. G. V. Sharkey was in the *Fox*:

What a cheer we got from the troops as we dashed along the Krithia Road passing one line of trench after the other. The boys inside the cars were shouting their old war cry 'Belt it in' & the Tommies were shouting 'Come on the Navy' etc etc. . . . The cars got a certain distance & then got stuck between the two firing lines. The noise inside the cars caused by the bullets hitting against the armoured plate was deafening & then after a bit they started pitching H.E.s at us. But lucky for us the Turks' shooting was bad & not a car got seriously damaged. About 12.30 I sent a car to base with its gun damaged & completely out of action. Lieutenant Holden's car was sent back with its turret off, Holden himself being badly wounded inside. . . . Rummings had half his head blown off so they told us & the driver of their car (Scott) practically went mad inside. Nobody was hurt inside the *Fox*, we had the best of luck. Our tyres were blown to pieces, also our wheels but we managed to return.[9] (G. V. Sharkey)

The potential of primitive armoured fighting vehicles in frontal attacks across broken ground was as yet purely theoretical and awaited the application of caterpillar tracks and a more robust construction.

On the Royal Naval Division front, between Achi Baba Nullah and Kereves Dere, the Howe, Hood and Anson Battalions advanced under heavy fire suffering severe casualties as they crossed no-man's land. On reaching the Turkish front line they found it unoccupied, save only the dead and wounded Turks. Their initial objectives had been achieved but they had to hold the ground they had gained with only some 20 officers and approximately 300 men remaining.

To their right the French had met with stiff opposition in their attack on the Turkish strongholds in the Kereves Dere sector. Although they made some progress in the face of terrible casualties, the position taken could not be maintained. They were forced to withdraw, and this was to prove fatal to the whole attack. The domino effect once again came into play, and as the French fell back the British flank was exposed to enfilade fire.

The Collingwood Battalion had begun to move forward at 12.15, as planned, to carry forward the assault of the RND. As it did so the effects of the French failure became cruelly apparent. It came under a vicious cross-fire not only from the slopes of Achi Baba directly ahead but also in enfilade from the right on Kereves Spur above Kereves Dere. From his viewpoint in the recently captured Turkish trenches Murray saw the result of this concentrated fire:

I looked back and I could see the Collingwoods coming up in fairly good line. They hadn't reached our first line, they were coming up in reserve. They were lying down and getting up again and they would seem to be getting quite a bashing. When they laid down, whether they were frightened, injured or killed I don't know but there didn't appear to be many getting up.[10] (Ordinary Seaman Joe Murray)

Only around 300 out of the Collingwoods reached the positions held by the assaulting battalions. The situation was plainly deteriorating and the Howe Battalion on the right of the RND front, next to the French, were beginning to come under extreme pressure. Despite this the remnants of the Anson, Hood and Collingwood Battalions attempted a further advance at 12.30 and a few stragglers even reached the Turks' third line. This only served to weaken further their exposed position. Sub-Lieutenant Arthur Watts of 'B' Company, Collingwood Battalion attempted to help:

> They were short of ammunition and we were asked to take some up. I started off with a party of four chaps. None of those survived. We got hardly anywhere. The Turks spotted us immediately we went over the top. I was hit and the leg went numb – I had no feeling in it at all. I had to scramble back into our trench. They were all 'standing to' wondering whether the Turks might counter-attack. What happened then I really don't know because the leg had made me groggy.[11] (Sub-Lieutenant Arthur Watts)

He was to have his leg amputated a few days later.

By now only three officers remained unwounded with the troops in the Turkish third line. At 12.45 these remnants were forced out by the encircling Turks and withdrew, suffering further casualties, to the British front line they had left only three-quarters of an hour before. It was a charnel house: 'What a sight, three or four men deep dead on the floor, that had been killed at the outset of the attack and fallen back into the trench. Never even got out of the trench, never even saw a Turk.'[12] The situation was so dire that the Drake Battalion, the only reserves left under the control of the RND, was ordered up – not to continue the attack but to guard against an all too likely Turkish counter-attack.

Unfortunately the withdrawal of the RND to the original British front line at 12.45 had in turn exposed the open right flank of the 42nd Division. The Turks showed an ominous understanding of the domino theory and sent in their bombing parties covered by enfilade rifle and machine-gun fire to attack the increasingly isolated 127th Brigade. By 13.30, the overall situation was one of failure on the flanks but the centre of the Turkish defences had been overcome by the 42nd Division, although its own flanks were endangered. The question now was where to deploy the reserves. In making their decision Generals Hunter Weston and Gouraud had the benefit of accurate situation reports. The choice was between reinforcing success or failure; there were just not enough reserves to do both. In making their decision it had to be borne in mind that the MEF had no more reserves at all, and in view of the prevailing ignorance as to the forces available to the Turks some sort of reserve had to be kept to meet eventualities. After deliberation it was decided to use the reserves where the first assault had failed on the RND and French sectors in a renewed attack at 16.00. At around 15.00 the French confessed that they could not be ready in time and two hours later Gouraud told Hunter Weston that the French could take no further offensive action that day. The idea of a renewed assault by the RND alone was patently ludicrous and the attack was cancelled.

In essence nothing had been done to relieve the pressure on the flanks of the 42nd Division and their situation continued to deteriorate throughout the afternoon, until at 18.30 the order was given to withdraw the whole of the 127th Brigade from their hard-won advanced positions to the original Turkish front line. Even then a gap remained on the right, and a link had to be forged with the remnants of the RND further back in the original British front line. As the remaining reserve battalions moved up, they faced a barrage of fire.

> Maintaining a steady double, we soon reached Achi Baba Nullah again. Here the scene beggared description. The Turks did not seem to be taking any notice of our battery on the Nullah's edge. They knew that our reinforcements would pass that way and they blasted the place with high explosive shells. We were now part of a long line which kept running on. As we ran, man after man was brought to the ground and we had to jump over their bodies. On each flank streams of our wounded were making for the rear in a pitiable plight. Some were falling exhausted and there was none to help.[13] (Able Seaman Thomas Macmillan)

The Turkish artillery was not their only problem during the move up. At the best of times trenches are congested thoroughfares, but in the middle of a fully fledged battle, they were almost impassable.

When everything seemed set fair we were brought up with a jolt at a trench junction and further progress became impossible. Our Chief Petty Officer investigated the cause of the block and I understood him to say when passing that the trench was full of stretcher cases ahead and that it was an utter impossibility to get through. The column was reversed but on retracing our steps another jam occurred.[14] (Able Seaman Thomas Macmillan)

The Nelson Battalion was given the task of constructing a number of separate posts across no-man's land to link the RND to the Manchesters. By nightfall this had been achieved but the battlefield was by no means quiet, as both sides jockeyed for position.

On 4 June the Turks provided a dynamic opposition which shattered the fleeting hopes offered by the initial successes in the centre of the line. Furthermore the practical difficulties encountered in moving reserve units about a battlefield are often forgotten in retrospect by armchair generals. Perhaps Hunter Weston missed an opportunity and if he had reinforced success they might indeed have advanced up the slopes of Achi Baba beyond Krithia or, by using the same techniques as the Turks, attempted to roll up the Turkish front line. However the Allied reserves were minuscule and the over-stretched troops, with no more available reserves, might well in turn have been caught by the inevitable Turkish counter-attacks with fresh troops a day or so later. Success on 4 June could well have been the prelude to a real disaster on 6 June. Even as it was the Turks were not disposed to allow the British to retain their limited gains and for the next few days they counter-attacked viciously in an effort to regain their losses.

The confused fighting that followed in the gullies on the 42nd Division front was vividly recalled by Private George Peake of the 1/8th Lancashire Fusiliers:

All of a sudden we got the order to move up the communication trench. 'A' Company went forward, I think we were the first. One fellow, he got a spent shell, only a small one about two inch, it came through and hit him in the head and stuck there, it never went off. He just dropped down on his hands and knees his head touching the floor. I was just behind him and I had to jump over him to get along. Another fellow near me got a bullet through his wrist and his rifle flew up out of his hand. The next minute we were in the firing line. The back seemed to have been blown away. A bigger shell hit on the corner of the firing line and the communication trench and it blew me on me back and me rifle out of me hands. Just at that time there were two Turks jumping at me with their hands out, one was to grab me by the throat if he could. I was too quick, I rolled over and I rolled right on me rifle. I got it and found that there was no bayonet fixed on it, it had been blown off. I rushed at him without the bayonet but before I could dig him Lieutenant Wilds came up with his revolver and they both put their hands up. The gully was quite near, we were on the right hand side. We lined the trench with our rifles. I got me bayonet fixed on and got my rifle pulled through and cleaned up and we jumped up on the firing step waiting for them coming over. All of a sudden we saw them coming, not towards us but towards the left hand side of the gully. We could fire at them without being fired at and we were all up firing like anything and dropping them. I was only about four or five men from the gully. Our officer shouted, 'Cease Fire!' Well what were we ceasing fire for? We were all dumbfounded. So we stopped firing. Our troops had left their trench and gone for the Turks with the bayonet. Well, My God! Just fancy doing that! There was such a lot of Turks; there must have been a thousand or more charging over. Then the officer said, 'Come on, in the gully. They're coming down the gully.' They must have turned round from there and come down the gully towards us. It wasn't very deep. We met them in the gully. We started firing, stood up firing. My lieutenant was next to me with his revolver in one hand, sword in the other. He just dropped dead. We fired as much as we could and eventually drove them back up on to the right into trenches on their own side. There was only six of us left. Billy Cotton was with us. Just then all the remainder of our company and the battalion must have gone over, we could hear them going over cheering.[15] (Private George Peake)

Many of the units involved in the battle were seriously affected by their failure on 4 June, during which the Allies had suffered 6,500 casualties of which 4,500 were British. Although they had done their best it was apparent that further frontal attacks would lead to heavy losses in the face of determined Turkish opposition.

> I met our Brigade Major who told me the KOSB had done magnificently . . . but oh! we paid the price – I feel all on edge and very jumpy – what a miracle I wasn't hit – but oh! I don't want any more fighting or bayonet charges – I never saw in France or Belgium such a tremendous bombardment or such a hail of shrapnel &c which greeted us.[16] (2nd Lieutenant Richard Reeves)

After the severe losses suffered at Helles the focus of GHQ attention swung away from the idea of further bludgeoning attacks at Helles. They recognized that even if Krithia was captured the Turks had extensive fortifications right up the slopes of Achi Baba and that operations against them would continue to be extremely costly. Hamilton and GHQ were beginning to look elsewhere for the chance of a real breakthrough. This view was not however shared at VIII Corps Headquarters, who still believed that with reasonable reinforcements they could achieve a decisive breakthrough. They therefore continued to prepare for further attacks at Helles. Hamilton allowed them to do so mainly because he recognized that even if they failed they would distract attention from any other operations that were being considered.

The arrival of the 52nd Lowland Scottish Division on 6 June allowed the weary troops of the original divisions to spend a few days in shifts on the island of Imbros. Throughout the rest of June the fighting never actually stopped at Helles as there were constant small-scale attacks designed to improve the tactical position of the British front line, which invariably provoked a Turkish response with the end result an enlarged casualty list for a very small territorial gain. Any tactical advantages were eroded by a surge of compensatory Turkish digging.

*

Hunter Weston and Gouraud's primary objective was to remove the Turks from their entrenchments across Gully Spur and Kereves Spur. It was the failure to capture these two flanking positions on 4 June that had led to the failure of the attack in the centre. Before there could be any general advance these positions had to be captured. The potential offered by concentrated howitzer fire employing high explosives was now clearly recognized. Shortages of ammunition precluded the necessary density of fire for a simultaneous assault on both flanks and so two entirely separate operations were planned.

The French, who had ample HE ammunition, fixed the date for the first assault on Kereves Dere as 21 June. After detailed planning and preparation the massed artillery opened fire.

This morning the French, about a mile to our right, attacked. First there was a terrific bombardment, the dust and shindy kicked up was something fearsome, I was mighty glad I wasn't nearer than a mile! I managed to find a bit of high ground where I saw the whole thing beautifully with my glasses. The French gunners had the range to a nicety and fairly pounded the Turk's firing line. One could see the beggars running for shelter and occasionally a direct hit would throw up a lot of black specks which were bits of men, equipment etc., I suppose. By the time the French charged the dust and smoke pretty well obscured things but I managed to make out lines of figures running across the open.[17] (Lieutenant Leslie Grant)

The crushing bombardment ensured almost complete success as the Turkish front lines and even the Haricot Redoubt were overrun. The next few days were filled with bitter fighting as the Turks counter-attacked repeatedly. Despite the destruction wrought by their own artillery, which rendered the captured Turkish trenches difficult to consolidate, most of the gains were retained and the power of concentrated artillery was confirmed.

The next stage was the capture of Gully Spur, which was assigned to Major General Beauvoir de Lisle, who had taken over the command of the 29th Division. For the first time, the British attack scheduled for 28 June was to be strictly limited in its objectives, not only in the depth of intended penetration desired but also in the width of the frontage attacked. The 29th Division was to capture a heavily wired series of trenches known as the 'Js', which crisscrossed Gully Spur. These were strongly built with dugouts which had proved capable of resisting medium artillery fire. To the right of the Gully Ravine, de Lisle was given the use of the 156th Brigade from the newly arrived 52nd Division to seize the first two 'H' trench lines on Fir Tree Spur.

It was accepted that the key to success lay in a heavy artillery bombardment and considerable attention was devoted to this, with co-operation being sought from both the navy and the French to counter-balance the chronic British shortages of both howitzers and shells. Brigadier General Marshall had specially requested French assistance to eradicate a Turkish redoubt positioned on the right of Gully Ravine which threatened the 87th Brigade's advance along Gully Spur.

> The Divisional orders for the attack reached me on the 26th and, curiously enough, omitted all mention of the Boomerang redoubt which would enfilade our projected attack at close range. I represented this, but was told that, if my Brigade were successful in taking the trenches the Boomerang would ipso facto fall; to this I replied, that that would no doubt be the case but that a great many of my own men would also fall. Eventually it was arranged that we should take the Boomerang five minutes before zero hour. A trench mortar (nicknamed La Demoiselle) was lent to us by General Gouraud and this, under charge of a French sous officier, duly arrived and was dug in such a position that it could pump its death dealing bombs (100lb melinite) bang into the dangerous Boomerang redoubt. The sous officier was most particular about the emplacement for La Demoiselle, and about arrangements for his own protection; as he very wisely said 'Elle est bonne, mais très, très dangereuse.'[18] (Brigadier General William Marshall)

For the attack the troops were issued with a strange new piece of equipment, large pieces of tin cut in the shape of an equilateral triangle with sides about twelve inches long. Marshall had been responsible for this innovation after a conversation with the Commander of the 29th Division artillery.

One day I was down talking to General Breeks (CRA 29th Division) at his observation post, when a discussion arose as to the best means of distinguishing the trenches occupied by our men, when we had made an advance and taken trenches from the enemy. The system of the infantry carrying forward screens, khaki on the side towards the enemy and red on the side towards our guns, had been a failure, because in many cases the Turks had recaptured trenches by counter-attack; the men in charge of the screens had been killed and the screens left in position or otherwise utilized by the enemy. Looking from Breeks's observation post our trenches were well defined by a line of shimmering empty ration tins at the back of them, I therefore suggested that, instead of carrying screens or flags, each man should carry a piece of tin in his haversack, and these tin discs could be flashed from newly won trenches. The idea was taken up and improved on. In future each man in the attacking line carried a triangular piece of tin on his back. This method proved of immense value to our gunners during all our further attacks; the flashing line of tin being perfectly visible at ranges when the men themselves were indistinguishable.[19] (Brigadier General William Marshall)

When the bombardment opened the French trench mortars certainly made their mark on the Boomerang Redoubt.

The first of these torpedoes was fired at 6 am. Its flight was easy to follow & was wonderfully fascinating. Reaching a height of, perhaps, two hundred feet and appearing to be directly overhead, it slowly turned over & still more slowly (it seemed) began to descend. It almost imperceptibly drew away from us and landed with a dull thud on the outer works of the Boomerang. A remarkable silence followed & then tons of earth, sections of entanglements, bodies, clothes and limbs were sent into the sky. A terrific explosion of unparalleled violence, causing the earth upon which we stood to tremble & spreading its pungent fumes, like a mist over everything & everybody, was the result. Its terrifying roar re-echoed along the ravine until drowned by the ships' guns at sea. Before the air was clear another torpedo was fired.[20] (Petty Officer F. W. Johnston)

By dint of allocating a third of all the shells available at Helles a decent bombardment had also finally been secured on the Turkish lines on Gully Spur when the conventional artillery opened a little later.

> For an hour & a half they sent 'death itself' into the enemy positions. Parapet after parapet went into the air accompanied by bodies and rags. The air became so thick that at the close of the bombardment, to see a yard in any direction was impossible – it reminded me of a London fog – green in places, to a shade of brown.[21] (Petty Officer F. W. Johnston)

The concentration of such resources as were available on to such tightly controlled targets led to success. The bombardment lifted at 10.45 and, as Marshall had planned, the Boomerang Redoubt was rushed by the 1st Border Regiment.

> At 10.40 am we are ordered to fix bayonets and the artillery resorts to 'rapid fire' thus redoubling the fury of the bombardment. High explosive and shrapnel shell is now falling in a veritable hail on to the enemy trenches and it seems impossible that any of them can live through it. One more minute and the word 'Ready' is passed along. In that one minute we unconsciously take one look at the sun and the sea and involuntarily commend our bodies and souls to our Maker and then before we realize it a hoarse shout of 'Over' and we are up the ladders and racing like the wind for the redoubt about 800 yards distant. No sooner are we over then a tremendous burst of rifle and machine-gun fire meets us. Here and there a man stumbles and falls by the way but we race on and are soon on the trench. The enemy however did not wait and we find our entry unopposed. . . . Hastily we set to work to reconstruct the shattered parapet of the trench as far as possible in anticipation of a counter-attack.[22] (Private Sydney Evans)

The evacuating Turks ran straight into a trap. Petty Officer Johnston and his RNAS machine-gun team were ready for them:

> My gun, trained on the main Boomerang sap, now found a target – dozens after dozens of Turks in their endeavours to get away rushed from the redoubt to the cliff side & incidentally into the fire from my gun. Three belts were hurriedly got through before

the khaki of our own troops came in pursuit showing that the Boomerang was in our hands.[23] (Petty Officer F. W. Johnston)

The overture had been a success. At 11.00 the rest of the 87th Brigade advanced along Gully Spur freed from the threat of enfilade fire from their right flank. The surviving Turks were in no fit state for prolonged resistance and their first two lines of trenches were captured relatively easily. The 86th Brigade then leap-frogged them and, although the Turks counter-attacked with considerable vigour behind a hail of bombs, they were held off and the captured lines secured.

Hamilton watched the show from his observation post much further back and was entranced by the success of the tin triangles:

The spectacle was extraordinary. From my post I could follow the movements of every man. One moment after 11am the smoke pall lifted and moved slowly on with a thousand sparkles of light in its wake: as if someone had quite suddenly flung a big handful of diamonds on to the landscape.[24] (Sir Ian Hamilton)

On Fir Tree Spur the Scottish Territorials of the 156th Brigade went over the top for the first time.

Bob yelled: 'Come on boys!' I gave him a leg up and Jimmy Fleck shoved me up just at his heels. . . . When we got up over the parapet my platoon were practically enfiladed, the air seemed thick with bullets, I remember thinking the puffs of sand all around were awfully funny; the platoon started going too much to the left, I yelled to them to keep to the right but I hardly heard my own voice for the row. The gap between my platoon and 'D' Coy on the right got rapidly wider. I dashed off to the right thinking they would follow, I crossed an old trench and then saw the Turkish trench perhaps twenty yards further on, looked around . . . and suddenly realized I was all alone! 'C' and 'D' Coys were perhaps 150 yards apart and I was about mid-way between. I think perhaps some cells of one's brain must be numb because I don't seem to have had the slightest sense of danger at any time, it reminded me of nothing so much as a football match, the thrill of a good dribble up field. . . . I reached the Turkish trench and found it almost battered to pieces, further along on either side it wasn't so bad and there were a lot of Turks about putting up a good fight. By the mercy of Providence I had struck a bit which was almost obliterated. I sank in almost to my knees in the soft earth, the place was in a fearful mess, blood everywhere, arms, legs, entrails lying around. There was only one man who tried to put up a fight, although what looked like an officer badly wounded tried to get me with his revolver. It sounds horrible in cold blood . . . but at this time all that is savage in one seemed to be on top. I remember two things distinctly, one was wanting to cut off a man's ears and keep them as a trophy, the other was jumping on the dead, hacking their faces with my feet or crashing my rifle into them. . . . Looking along to my left I saw dozens of our men, they came on to within a yard or two of the trench, seemed to hesitate, then dashed into it. . . . Men fought with their rifles, their feet, their bare fists, a pick, a shovel, anything. But the orders had been 'Go for the 2nd trench, never mind the 1st.' So it was on again. I scrambled out, something seemed to force me on, and started running again.[25] (Lieutenant Leslie Grant)

On Fir Tree Spur the artillery preparation had not been anywhere near as devastating as on Gully Spur, and the 156th Brigade met with considerable opposition. Although the 1/4th and 1/7th Royal Scots managed to reach the Turks' second line, to their right the 1/8th Scottish Rifles were ripped to shreds by heavy machine-gun fire. The brigade reserve, the 1/7th Scottish Rifles, fared little better and only a few reached the Turkish front line before, inevitably, being driven back. Further efforts were made throughout the day, but even with the assistance of the 88th Brigade nothing else was achieved and eventually they settled for consolidating what gains had been made in the face of increasing Turkish counter-attacks.

For the generals the action on 28 June had reinforced their earlier mechanistic beliefs – without heavy artillery bombardments from high-explosive shells, preferably fired by howitzers, success was unlikely against strongly defended Turkish positions, whereas with such a bombardment a limited advance was possible. Hunter Weston summed it up in his report:

It was unavoidable, owing to the shortage of howitzers and ammunition, that the trenches east of the ravine were insufficiently bombarded by howitzer high-explosive shell. This was the cause of the failure and the heavy casualties at this point. A complete success yesterday would have required another 8 howitzers and 600 more rounds of ammunition.[26] (Lieutenant General Aylmer Hunter Weston)

While Hamilton wrote: 'Hunter Weston, Gouraud and Braithwaite agree that: – had we only shell to repeat our bombardment of this morning, now, we could go on another 1000 yards before dark – result Achi Baba to-morrow or, at the latest, the day after.'[27]

The Turks were extremely worried by the threat posed by the advance made along Gully Spur, and a whole series of counter-attacks were launched over the next few days to little effect. The culmination of these efforts was a simultaneous attack all along the line on 5 July. The preliminary bombardment was ineffective and the Turks advanced into the jubilant sights of the British. Among them was Guy Geddes, who had recovered from his shoulder wound suffered during the V Beach landing, and was in command of the Munster Fusiliers, holding the trenches known as Worcester Flat:

The men appeared in particularly good form & the companies in reserve came rushing up to participate, & started squabbling with each other to get a shot in, it was really ridiculous & the trenches of course far too congested. The attack fizzled out at 06.00, a hopeless failure. . . . One peculiar incident was that of a Turk who caught fire & was a living torch lighting up in the dim light his comrades near by. A good many Turks unable to get back to their trenches lay in the scrub between our lines but with some judicious shrapnel . . . were flushed like birds to be brought down by our snipers.[28] (Lieutenant Colonel Guy Geddes)

For the battered survivors of the 156th Brigade it was a much appreciated chance to get their revenge: 'We had a great day shooting Turks with machine-gun and rifle, and got some of our own back. The same made me feel more hopeful than I had felt since I landed here.'[29] The Turks suffered heavy casualties right along the line and after this salutary experience accepted the new status quo in the Gully Ravine area.

Hunter Weston and Gouraud had seen the successful advances on the left and right flanks as merely the first stage before a joint attack by the British and French to bring the lagging centre into line. Although Gouraud had been wounded by shrapnel while visiting a French hospital on V Beach on 30 June, his successor, General Bailloud, was in agreement. The importance of the superior French artillery was now clear and as it would not be ready until 12 July this was the date adopted for the attack. Meanwhile it had belatedly dawned on Hunter Weston that all three of the original British divisions were now suited only to fairly passive line-holding duties until they had had a chance to rest and assimilate their reinforcement drafts. Therefore the task was allotted to the newly arrived, but already blooded, 52nd Division. Hamilton had hoped to use this division at Anzac but his scepticism about Helles frontal attacks was overcome by his desire to capitalize on any Turkish weakness following their crippling losses on 5 July, and he approved the plans put forward by Hunter Weston. Yet the delay before the attack could be organized inevitably gave the Turks a vital breathing space in which to recover and reorganize their defences.

The attack on 12 July was again planned to take place in two halves to allow the artillery to concentrate on each in turn. In the morning the 155th Brigade on the extreme right of the British lines were to advance in conjunction with yet another assault by the French on the banks of Kereves Dere. To the left of the 155th Brigade, the 157th Brigade were to remain in their trenches while the guns swung round and bombarded their objectives on either side of Achi Baba Nullah. Unless a real opportunity presented itself they were not to advance until late afternoon. The already battered 156th Brigade was to be the divisional reserve. All the troops in the initial attack were to advance in four waves starting at the same time, one from each of the British trench lines. The objectives were strictly limited to the first three Turkish lines, although this was to cause considerable confusion as in many areas only two Turkish lines had been completed.

The bombardment duly opened up at 04.30, with the French 75s as usual causing devastation in the Turkish trenches. At 07.30 the gunners lengthened their range to put a ring of scything steel around the area which it was hoped would prove impenetrable to the Turkish reinforcements inevitably rushing to the scene. The leading waves of troops set off across no-man's land while the 157th Brigade tried to keep the Turks' heads down with the rattle of small-arms fire. The Scottish troops reached the Turkish trenches with relatively few losses but then became bogged down in the labyrinth of smashed trenches.

> Unless one has seen it there is no imagination that can picture a belt of land some 400 yards wide converted into a seething hell of destruction. Rifle and machine-gun bullets rip up the earth, ping past the ear, or whing off the loose stones; shrapnel bursts overhead and the leaden bullets strike the ground with a vicious thud; the earth is rent into yawning chasms, while planks, sandbags, clods of earth, and rugged great chunks of steel hurtle through the air. The noise is an indescribable, nerve-racking, continuous, deafening roar, while drifting clouds of smoke only allow an intermittent view of the damnable inferno.[30] (Major D. Yuille)

Under these circumstances efforts to locate and capture the largely non-existent third line of trenches caused many unnecessary casualties. In the confusion many of the soldiers were isolated in the 'third line'.

> I managed to get to the furthest point, that was the third Turkish trench or dummy trench. It was about one foot deep, and we had to set-to and fill sandbags. We were packed together and enfiladed from the left. Our fire rapidly diminished, till there was no one left to fire. Then I was knocked out. When I came to, our little trench was occupied by a Turk to every two yards. Four or five of our men were lying across me, and I could not get up. I was bayoneted six times in the back whilst lying there. A Turk officer, at the point of his revolver, ordered the Turks to release me.[31] (Private Nixon)

The French had advanced in similar fashion and reached the Turkish second line. This time they maintained a link with the British right and avoided the domino collapse which had so plagued the Allies. This left the attack balanced between success and failure and the generals faced a difficult decision as to whether to continue with the afternoon attack. Valour once more prevailed as Hunter Weston agreed to the 157th Brigade attacking in conjunction with a renewed assault by the French and 'tactical advances' where possible by the 155th Brigade. The second bombardment opened up on the Achi Baba Nullah sector and at 16.50 the 157th Brigade went forward to a repeat performance: initial success, confusion caused by the absence of the third trench and eventual consolidation in the Turkish second line in touch with the 155th Brigade on their right. The outcome was still in the balance. No breakthrough had occurred and although Turkish trenches had been captured they were extremely vulnerable to counter-attack. The Royal Marine Brigade of the RND was moved up as an immediate reserve in any such emergency.

> The Battalion moved from our rest area in the afternoon. As we approached the 52nd Divisional Headquarters which was in the position normally used by our own Brigade Headquarters when we were in the line, the CO said: 'I do not want to have to halt the Battalion here, so run on and find out where they want us to go.' I reached the Headquarters dug-out, saluted, and asked for orders. A voice from the depths said: 'Don't stand up there my lad, you may get shot. Come down here and sit down.' To my surprise I found myself being addressed by the Divisional General. His next remark was: 'I have been up since four this morning, and feel so tired.' I suppose that for years past, the old man had had an afternoon nap. Without it he was defeated. He was quite unfit to command in battle.[32] (Lieutenant Arthur Chater)

Overnight the troops in the newly captured Turkish trenches faced the hard graft of consolidation. Trenches had to be turned round, old communication trenches barricaded off, new communication trenches dug back to the old British front line, the wounded had to be evacuated and supplies brought up. All this against a backdrop of chattering machine-gun fire, flares and shrapnel bursts.

That night Petty Officer Johnston was sent up to find a position for his RNAS machine-gun team. When he reached the new front line he could see the scale of the problems faced:

> What a state it was in! Long stretches of parapet had been blown away leaving deep and dangerous holes, the floor was strewn with many dead. . . . The trench had been hewn out of an extremely rocky substance & was not more than three feet deep. Where our shells had wrecked it, or blown the parapet in, it became as shallow as one foot. The 4th Royal Scots who manned the part wherein my gun was to be placed were in a thoroughly exhausted state. They had been without water all day.[33] (Petty Officer F. W. Johnston)

While Johnston was awaiting the arrival of his machine-gun the Turks attacked:

> I was terrorized by the shout 'Here they come.' The counter-attack! I looked into the darkness & there sure enough were the black shapes of men. I had often wondered whether I would experience this present sensation, but never expected it to happen at a time when I would be without my gun. All along our line the exhausted troops – now superhuman – blazed away into the dark line.[34] (Petty Officer F. W. Johnston)

Armed only with a revolver Johnston decided to keep his head down:

> I heard the Turkish priests calling to God – Allah! Allah! Allah! & then a scuffle in the traverse to my left, told me that at least some of the enemy had forced an entry. I waited a moment or two, my heart thumping & eyes wide open trying to pierce the awful darkness. Nothing happened, no huge figure jumped upon me & no rifle blazed point blank. I could see to my right a mass of struggling men – What was happening? Rifles were going off in all directions; the dull red flash increased in brightness by the intense darkness. Yells & screams interrupting the weird chanting of the priests. Terribly excited I crouched against the wall – figures passed, some dropped & I could make nothing of it. It seemed much longer but after ten minutes or so the figures of reinforcements could be discerned on the other side of the trench.

Scrambling down, they threw themselves into the fray, but all I could see was a mass of indistinct figures struggling among themselves. Still crouching I moved from off the body I had been all the while sitting upon & laid myself full length beside it. Suddenly from out of the darkness a figure rushed down on me – at once I knew I was hit, but the figure above me had ceased to move & easing myself I saw that the body was that of a British officer. His rifle laid across my hand; its bayonet had pricked my arm as it fell. Along the trench I saw dark figures upon the parapet & others scrambling up its side. The Turks in retreat! A sheet of flame was poured into the thin line & very few ever regained their own trench.[35] (Petty Officer F. W. Johnston)

The troops were now almost finished. 'Very few were keeping a look out – the majority, dead beat, were fast alseep.'[36] At dawn confusion was still rampant in the new front line and the 7th Highland Light Infantry suffered a panic attack when attempting to reorganize their front line while under pressure from the Turks. An order was garbled as it passed down the line and before the officers and NCOs could act the men were streaming back. The situation was quickly stabilized by local officers but reports of the incident made grim reading at VIII Corps Headquarters. In an attempt to forestall a major Turkish counter-attack Hunter Weston decided to use his last meaningful reserves in an effort to achieve the original objectives, which would at least mean that any counter-attack would have to be launched from 500 yards further away, greatly increasing the security of the new front line. Although he himself had reported that the RND was unfit for offensive action they were the only feasible option. The Royal Marine Brigade was therefore ordered to attack at 16.30 on 13 July, in conjunction with the French, to try to secure the original objectives. In circumstances of dreadful confusion the orders were late in reaching the battalions and the Chatham Battalion failed to attack, leaving only the Portsmouth and Nelson Battalions to attack alone. To make matters worse they attacked from the original British front line across 400 yards of open ground, where perfectly good communication trenches now existed. The remnants reached the lines already held by the 157th Brigade, who were frankly flabbergasted at such a method of approach. In the Horseshoe trench beside the Achi Baba Nullah, Lieutenant W. Millar of the 5th Argyll and Sutherland Highlanders greeted them with 'What the ————do you want?'[37] Many of the Marines attempted to push on, but to no avail, as the misunderstanding over the non-existent Turkish third line was replayed and they were caught in the open. All they achieved for the loss of over 500 casualties was a modest reinforcement of the front line. On the right the French had however managed to make a little more progress in the Kereves Dere sector but it was no real compensation for the overall losses.

The battle was over and the exhausted Allies continued their consolidation, while the Turks, as predicted, merely dug another set of trench lines further up the slopes of Achi Baba. With strong reinforcements and an adequate supply of HE ammunition more might have been achieved if further attacks had been launched, but Hamilton had had enough of the Helles butcher's bill. In all, the piecemeal operations of 21 June, 28 June and 12 July had cost approximately 12,300 Allied casualties, of which 7,700 were British. Their lives had bought improvements to the overall Helles position and they and their comrades had levied severe casualties among the Turks, particularly during their massed counter-attacks. But was it really worth it? 'We were all boys together at school, we'd started jobs as apprentices, we'd formed relationships. . . . And there they were a line of them all killed at one time, none of them over seventeen.'[38]

7

New Hope at Anzac

The men at Gallipoli had spent June and July fighting and dying in a series of battles at Helles which a prompt, firm strategic decision would have rendered unnecessary. In London the High Command struggled to make up their minds as to their response to Hamilton's request for reinforcements made on 17 May, but they were distracted by the replacement of the ruling Liberal administration with a coalition government. As a result the War Council was retitled the Dardanelles Committee, and this new body only met for the first time on 7 June. Their discussions were influenced by two papers which had been written over the past ten days. The first, written by Kitchener on 28 May, outlined the situation that had been recognized by the old War Council on 14 May. While stressing that nothing should be done to jeopardize the security of the British Isles, he admitted that operations outside the Western Front could be pursued if the armies there remained on the defensive. In examining the options at Gallipoli he again outlined the three options that had previously been discussed. Evacuation was still unacceptable and might be militarily disastrous; he did not believe that large resources were available for an immediate major attack. His preference was the third, compromise option of a slow progress carried out with the troops already assigned; a conclusion that showed his continued perception of the campaign as a cheap option.

The second paper was written, on 1 June, by Churchill who, although no longer First Lord of the Admiralty, remained a member of the new committee. As it had been earlier in the year, his opinion was less cautious and more energetic than Kitchener's. Believing the Western Front to be deadlocked and Britain to be safe from the threat of direct attack, Churchill argued that the strategic gains from a well-supported and successful attack both on the Gallipoli Peninsula and the Dardanelles far outweighed any other possible gains at that time. By concluding the campaign as quickly as possible, this would achieve all the original aims and then allow the undiverted resources of the Entente to be directed against the Germans on the Western Front. At the meeting on 7 June, Kitchener, again echoing the events of February and March, revealed he had undergone another change of mind and announced that he was, after all, in favour of a full-scale renewal of the campaign at Gallipoli. Combined with Churchill's paper, this decided the committee. They agreed that Hamilton's request for four divisions should be met in full. Because the 52nd Division had already been sent out to him as agreed on 10 May, the three remaining divisions of the first New Army not yet detailed for use on the Western Front, consisting of the 10th, 11th and 13th Divisions, would now also be sent to Gallipoli. This decision was forwarded to Hamilton on 8 June. Unfortunately by then the strength of his force had been considerably eroded both by the fighting which had taken place in an effort to advance the British line and by the sick list caused by the appalling conditions of service which confronted the troops on the peninsula. Once again the putative strength of the force was already less than would be required to carry out the intended operations.

Following the first meeting of the Dardanelles Committee opinion within the British Government slowly moved towards even stronger support for the campaign. This was a result of the relentless activity of Churchill, who, now that he was no longer responsible for the Admiralty, was able to turn more of his energy towards the Dardanelles, which had lain at the root of his demotion. Churchill was aware of the weakened state of the divisions already at Gallipoli and in a letter on 11 June he urged the Dardanelles Committee to add two more territorial divisions, the 53rd (Welsh) and 54th (East Anglian) Divisions, to the strength of the MEF, as well as any troops which could be spared either from Egypt or from Britain. Four days later he wrote to Kitchener stressing that these two divisions should follow on the original three immediately, in case they were needed to carry forward an attack if it was held up. He then sent another memorandum to the government relating Gallipoli to the Western Front and reiterating the importance of the original strategic aims of the campaign. By 17 June these arguments had achieved their effect and at a meeting of the Dardanelles Committee on that day only the question of transportation prevented more troops from being sent.

A shortage of transports meant that the last of the three New Army divisions would not arrive in the eastern Mediterranean until after the middle of August, a month later than the date soon after which the Dardanelles Committee itself had hoped the renewed offensive would begin. Despite the scale of the loss that would result if they were sunk by submarines, three of the biggest passenger liners were chartered to speed up the transportation of these divisions, and any decision regarding the additional troops was postponed until the new estimated date of arrival was known. When this was shown on 21 June to be 28 July, much closer to the desired starting date of an offensive in early August, Kitchener asked Hamilton if he would like one more division. Not surprisingly, Hamilton accepted. Recent events in France had also suggested to Kitchener that any offensive there in the immediate future 'would only result in heavy casualties and the capture of another turnip field',[1] and on 28 June he felt able to offer Hamilton a fifth division which again he accepted. But each new division offered in this way in successive stages entailed a rethinking of the logistics of where the troops were to be stationed until they were needed and a revision of the planned offensive to incorporate them. It was a frustrating means of providing reinforcements and, despite the clearly increased level of commitment shown by the government, a formal decision had still not been reached over the relative merits of Gallipoli and the Western Front.

This strategic impasse was only really resolved when the interests of the Gallipoli campaign briefly came to coincide with the interests of the Western Front. The huge initial successes of the Austro-German offensive which was launched against Russia on 13 July seemed to threaten Russia's very ability to stay in the war. The Gallipoli expedition remained the only feasible method of directly assisting Russia by means of opening up the Dardanelles. If Russia was not assisted and did cease to play an effective role in the war, many of the German divisions then fighting on the Eastern Front could be freed for a huge German offensive on the Western Front.

Gallipoli was seen as having a vital role if Russia was to be kept in the war and it was also seen as essential for Hamilton to finish the campaign as quickly as possible so that his divisions could be brought back to reinforce the Western Front. This dual interest was enough to persuade the remaining waverers on the Dardanelles Committee and finally on 28 July the British government at last demonstrated a whole-hearted commitment to the campaign. Kitchener telegraphed to Hamilton: 'We should like to hear from you after considering your plans whether there is anything further in the way of personnel, guns or ammunition we can send you, as we are most anxious to give you everything you can possibly require and use.'[2] By then it was too late, for the August offensive was almost under way.

During the summer months most of the fighting had taken place at Helles, but from an early stage Hamilton was aware of the chance that existed of a significant success at Anzac. Although the Anzac Corps had been largely passive since early May, Birdwood and his staff had not been idle. The physical realities of the Anzac position meant that a frontal attack offered no chance of success, but on the northern flank the Turkish positions were by no means continuous and often poorly manned. On 13 May Birdwood wrote to Hamilton pointing out the possibilities that this presented. His suggestions were to bear fruit in the August offensive, but at this stage he merely asked for the use of the 29th Indian Brigade to break out to the north of Anzac and sweep through to capture Koja Chemen Tepe, the highest peak of the Sari Bair range, by surprise. With the British line lying along this range the Turkish positions at Anzac would be untenable and their communications with the Helles garrison severely impeded. Hamilton saw that this outflanking manoeuvre offered a stark contrast to further bludgeoning frontal attacks at Helles after the failure of the Second Battle of Krithia on 8 May. After further discussion Birdwood was empowered to develop his scheme as part of a full assessment of the situation at Anzac.

Birdwood recognized that detailed reconnaissance was a prerequisite of success if troops were to advance across the tortured terrain that would be encountered north of Anzac. Patrols were therefore sent out by the New Zealand Mounted Rifles to explore the Sazli Beit and Chailak Dere valleys, which seemed to offer the best prospect of a route up to the Sari Bair peaks. Unsurprisingly this patrolling activity, although carried out as discreetly as possible, was noticed by the Turks, who began to build more defensive outposts in the area from the end of May. Nevertheless they do not seem to have been excessively alarmed and no network of trench lines appeared to crisscross the northern hills and valleys.

Although naturally distracted by the Turkish attack on 19 May and its aftermath, Birdwood completed his scheme, which he forwarded to Hamilton at GHQ on 30 May. He suggested a surprise night advance from Anzac to capture Hill Q and Chunuk Bair followed by the seizure of Battleship Hill, Baby 700 and 400 Plateau next day. At this stage Koja Chemen Tepe was excluded from the plan. To achieve this he requested that the Anzac Corps be reinforced by the 29th Indian Brigade for the breakout and then a further whole division for the subsequent drive to cut the peninsula in two.

While this plan was being considered Hamilton's whole mental frame of reference was changed by two events: the dreadful failure at Helles on 4 June, and the long-awaited news on 8 June from Kitchener that three more divisions were on their way to Gallipoli. Hamilton had four options for the deployment of these fresh troops, which broadly matched the strategic conundrum he had faced at the inception of the military campaign. They could try again at Helles, where, as we have seen, the optimism still displayed by the VIII Corps Headquarters was not echoed by Hamilton and his GHQ staff. A new landing could be made north of Bulair, although the original disadvantages of a Bulair landing had been exacerbated by the submarine threat. An Asiatic landing could be tried but, in view of the fact that the Allies were already on the peninsula, this could only really be a diversion which would stretch even the reinforced army to breaking point while offering only minor improvements to the Helles position. The last option was an adaptation of Birdwood's scheme at Anzac, and in the circumstances Hamilton and his staff seized on the imaginative opportunities that it offered.

The major concern in pursuing Birdwood's scheme was the difficulty in launching a major offensive from the very limited space that the Anzac beachhead allowed for the secret concentration of the necessary troops. The solution which presented itself was a further landing to either the south or north of Anzac. In view of the strong defences identified around Gaba Tepe and the corresponding weaknesses apparent in the Suvla Bay area, the latter was soon regarded as a more favourable potential site. Hamilton and his staff began seriously planning this Suvla landing throughout June and naturally brought in Admiral De Robeck and his staff to consider the feasibility of landing a division in the bay simultaneously with the breakout planned from Anzac. De Robeck was able to offer the use of specially designed motor lighters for landing troops. These had been originally designed for Fisher's proposed Baltic expedition. Although his scheme was an unrealistic and slightly ludicrous phantasm the lighters that resulted were of great potential value. Capable of carrying 500 men, they had armoured sides, drew only seven feet of water and had a ramp to allow a quick, dry exit under enemy fire. As such they offered a solution to many of the problems experienced on 25 April. On the negative side the naval staff vetoed any landing actually in Suvla Bay itself as it was not effectively charted and they feared uncharted rocks and shallows. They recommended that the troops be put ashore on the beach stretching a mile south of Suvla Bay.

Hamilton's confidence in the scheme was gradually increasing and he telegraphed to Kitchener: 'I think I have reasonable prospects of eventual success with three divisions; with four the risk of miscalculation would be minimized; and with five, even if the fifth had little or no gun ammunition ... success could be generally assured.'[3]

For the type of operations that GHQ were planning a special calibre of leader was required. Later, when the August offensive had actually started, Hunter Weston wrote to Hamilton offering his timeless advice as to the qualities that the field commander needed:

I pray to God that the new leaders of these new formations may know how to get hold of their men and lead them, and yet on occasion drive them unceasingly without any regard to losses or fatigue, without any regard to the yelping of subordinate com-

manders for reinforcements or to their cry that their men are dead with fatigue. In the enterprise in which you are engaged push unrelenting, push without ceasing, push without mercy by a commander in whom the men have confidence is all important.[4]
(Lieutenant General Aylmer Hunter Weston)

Hamilton fully recognized the importance of having the right men in command but Kitchener was not about to allow such considerations to deflect him from proper respect for seniority according to the Army List. On 9 June he proposed that Lieutenant General Sir Bryan Mahon, who was bringing out his 10th Irish Division, should be made commander of the new IX Corps. But Hamilton was opposed to Mahon, whom he considered 'Good up to a point and brave, but not up to running a corps out here.'[5] Instead he asked for the services of Lieutenant General Sir Julian Byng or Lieutenant General Sir Henry Rawlinson, both serving with considerable distinction on the Western Front. Kitchener refused point blank. He was determined that Mahon should be allowed to command the division he had raised from scratch in Ireland, and therefore whoever was to command IX Corps must be senior to Mahon. This ludicrous stipulation meant that the only serious candidates were Lieutenant General Sir John Ewart, who was in command of Scottish Command and was felt to be physically unsuited to the rigours of Gallipoli, and Lieutenant General Sir Frederick Stopford, who in 1915 had been in retirement for five years and was acting as Governor of the Tower of London. This 'dynamic' figure was perforce selected. Stopford had many qualities as a human being which had won him the respect and comradeship of his fellow officers throughout a long career. Unfortunately he had never commanded large bodies of troops in the field, most of his experience was theoretical, he could never be called decisive and his personal health was poor and declining. This choice of Stopford was to prove fatal to Hamilton's plans.

In all, five divisions had now been promised to Gallipoli but, in view of the already lengthy gestation period, Hamilton decided to launch the offensive on the arrival of the first three divisions to avoid the inevitable further delays caused by the difficulties of transporting out such a large body of troops. Moonless nights were a prerequisite for the build-up of forces at Anzac, while the landings at Suvla required first darkness as the troops approached the shore, with the moon rising later to illuminate the proceedings once the troops were safely ashore. So the opening of the offensive was fixed on the night of 6/7 August, because such conditions would not recur until September. At this stage in the planning process two divisions were to be used in the breakout from Anzac, while the third landed at Suvla. Hamilton had also planned to use the 52nd Division to reinforce the new division at Suvla but, after the failed attack on 12 July, this unit was no longer fit for offensive action and was left at Helles. The other two promised divisions, once they had arrived, were to be used if necessary as reinforcements, but otherwise were to be landed on the Asiatic shore.

Birdwood was in ignorance of these putative plans for a Suvla landing and on 1 July he provided an update to his plan, taking into account the extra two divisions that were the maximum he felt could be contained and concealed at Anzac. By now he had decided to expand his objectives to include the whole of the Sari Bair range as far north as Koja Chemen Tepe. Significantly he identified Turkish artillery units apparently situated on the Chocolate and W Hills as a possible serious interference and included in his plans provision to land a brigade inside Suvla Bay to overrun them. This was obviously not necessary if the capture of this area was added to the objectives of the division that Hamilton was already planning to land at Suvla. With this exception Birdwood's general scheme for the breakout from Anzac was accepted at a GHQ conference he attended on 2 July and he was told to get on with his detailed plans for Anzac alone. Another addition to the ever expanding plans commissioned by GHQ was the idea of a holding operation at Helles – a minor diversionary attack, although the ever sanguine, and sanguinary, VIII Corps Headquarters still hoped that progress could be made towards Achi Baba.

Towards the end of July Birdwood produced his final plans for the Anzac offensive. The first element was a strong diversionary attack on 6 August on the Turkish fortifications at Lone Pine, which was on the southern half of 400 Plateau on the Anzac right flank. The breakout to the left would begin with the capture of all identified Turkish outposts covering the deep-water courses or 'deres' leading up to the Sari Bair Ridge. The assaulting columns would then drive up these gullies and capture the key heights of Koja Chemen Tepe, Hill Q and Chunuk Bair before moving south down the ridge to clear Battleship Hill and Baby 700 in conjunction with another attack from Russell's Top across the Nek. These plans were accepted by Hamilton.

At Suvla the original GHQ plan was to land the 11th Division south of Nibrunesi Point on to beaches designated by the letters C and B, on the night of 6 August to surprise and overwhelm any local Turkish troops on Lala Baba immediately north of the beaches. They were to seize the commanding heights all around Suvla Bay, namely Karakol Dagh and Kiretch Tepe Ridge to the north, with the Tekke Tepe Ridge, Chocolate Hill and W Hills to the east. It was throught by GHQ that Turkish defence works of indeterminate strength on the southern slopes of Chocolate and W Hills could prevent a direct approach to these last objectives, so the assault troops were to skirt the Salt Lake, which lay behind Suvla Bay, and approach them from the apparently unguarded north to secure them by 'a "coup de main" before daylight in order to prevent the guns which they contain being used against our troops'.[6] It was these guns which had been regarded as a threat by Birdwood. After daybreak on 7 August this covering force was to be strongly reinforced by the 10th Division and the whole force was to assist the Anzac forces, if necessary, in the battle for Koja Chemen Tepe. The plan was built round an appreciation that speed was to be of the essence if it was to succeed. Every minute wasted after landing would allow the Turks time to move up their reserves and organize a counter-stroke.

These plans were explained to Stopford on 22 July. His initial reaction to the staff officer, Lieutenant Colonel Aspinall, who briefed him, was strongly favourable: 'Tell Sir Ian that I have been studying the situation from available information ever since I left England and this is the plan which I have always hoped he would adopt. It is a good plan. I am sure it will succeed, and I congratulate whoever has been responsible for framing it.'[7] However, he soon wavered after discussions with his own senior staff officer, Brigadier General Hamilton Reed VC, a man who had been strongly influenced by his experiences earlier in the war on the Western

Front and by his contacts with the Turkish army, to which he had been attached as a liaison officer during the Balkan Wars. The essence of Reed's objections was that 'The whole teaching of the campaign in France proves that troops cannot be expected to attack an organized system of trenches without the assistance of a large number of howitzers.'[8] As a result of these doubts and Stopford's own second thoughts they made a request on 26 July to revise the scheme. Their main objection was that, as howitzers could not be landed till the morning of 7 August, the Chocolate and W Hills could not be captured before dawn as envisaged. Furthermore the troops would, in their opinion, be physically unable to get as far as the Tekke Tepe Ridge by this time. Finally, as they were advised to attack Chocolate Hill from the north, could not a landing be made actually inside Suvla Bay to reduce the length of the long march round the Salt Lake?

These were not negligible objections and it should be recalled that Reed's dictum was the very message that frontal attacks had driven home at Helles. The irony was that at Suvla there were only three Turkish battalions and their defences were either illusory or, even when well dug in, lacking in barbed wire or machine-guns. Reed's error lay, not in his grasp of a basic principle of war, but in applying it to a situation where it was irrelevant. Furthermore in doing so he ignored other more pressing principles of war, including the importance of surprise and seizing the high ground.

The GHQ staff failed to recognize the timidity and lack of resolve which marked the IX Corps reservations and they co-operated by making amendments on 29 July to the original plan which freed Stopford from the original commitments to capture the high ground before dawn. A key sentence in the orders summarizes the backtracking: 'Owing to the difficult nature of the terrain, it is possible that the attainment of this objective will, in the first instance, require the use of the whole of the troops at your disposal.'[9] The 'primary objective' was now to secure Suvla Bay as a base for the new northern zone. The troops were to secure Chocolate and W Hills and henceforth support the Anzac operations only if it did not prejudice this priority, and all reference to this being a *coup de main* of the first importance had been expunged. The navy was also persuaded against its better judgement to land one brigade of the division inside the bay on what was to be known as A Beach. The other two brigades were to land as before at C and B Beaches. As with the Anzac advance, tactical details were left to Stopford.

Unfortunately, although a letter written by Stopford to Hamilton on 31 July showed that he still appreciated the basic intentions of the scheme, the actual orders he issued reveal the effects of the dilution that GHQ had endorsed. These stated, as had been agreed, that the primary objective was to secure Suvla Bay as a supply base and that afterwards the troops would endeavour to assist the Anzac operations. Yet although precise in such mundanities as 'Camp kettles will be handed to the Ordnance Officer of the camp at which units concentrate before embarkation. They will be forwarded at first opportunity,'[10] there was no mention of the all-important necessity of speed in securing the hills as soon as possible before the Turkish reinforcements arrived. The 10th Division, which was meant to exploit success, was not given any task in the orders. This watering-down process continued in Major General Frederick Hammersley's orders which he issued to his 11th Division on 5 August. By now the capture of W Hills was only to be attempted if possible. One of the original purposes of the Suvla landing, as envisaged by Birdwood, had been to clear by dawn the guns believed to be dug in on W Hills and capable of interfering with the Anzac flanking movements. But things were now so blurred that Hammersley believed that one of the reasons for the Anzac operations was to 'distract attention from our landing'.[11] By the time brigade and battalion orders were issued within his division the process of dilution was complete and no one was left responsible for the original concept of a *coup de main* and the capture of the hills before dawn.

A clear and common sense of purpose is necessary from all participants in a military endeavour. This was already conspicuous by its absence among the British command.

The first arrival of Hamilton's new divisions was the 13th Division, which landed in early July. Although it had been decided to deploy it at Anzac, it was sent to gain some experience of battle conditions at Helles. This was to prove invaluable and it is no coincidence that this division performed better in August than the other two divisions of New Army troops. One young officer, 2nd

Lieutenant Joseph Napier, felt that 'At least we'd had a fortnight to know what trenches meant; what fighting meant; what the sound of a rifle or gun meant. But those poor blighters, simple people like all our men were, were put ashore and told to attack.'[12]

The 10th Division arrived next in mid-July and suffered the fate of being dispersed between Lemnos and Mitylene, which in fact anticipated its fate in action as it was to be used to reinforce both the Anzac and Suvla assaults. The 11th Division, which was to lead the Suvla landing, arrived last, reaching Imbros in late July. One brigade was diverted to Helles for a short period, while the other two remained at Imbros until the attack. The battalions engaged in landing exercises, but it remained unclear exactly what their role would be. At both Helles and Imbros the troops became all too familiar with dysentery. The 53rd Welsh Division and the 54th East Anglian Division, which made up the rest of the five divisions promised to Hamilton, were still *en route* to Gallipoli when the battle commenced. The 2nd Mounted Division, which had been earmarked as possible reserves, were retained by Lieutenant General Maxwell as part of his Egyptian garrison until their despatch to Gallipoli became absolutely necessary.

Hamilton had considered that it might be wise to use the experienced 29th Division for the landing at Suvla, but the idea was rejected owing to the division's weakened state, despite the arrival of reinforcement drafts from the UK. It was also felt that no one could realistically expect the unit to make another landing after its ordeal on 25 April.

Although Hamilton was happy with the number of divisions that had been given to him, one problem still haunted him – the question of high-explosive ammunition supply and the 4.5-inch howitzer batteries to fire it. The 53rd and 54th Divisions had not got their complement of artillery and despite Hamilton's increasingly desperate pleading Kitchener had refused to allot any more howitzer batteries to Gallipoli and only grudgingly supplied the necessary shells for the pitifully few batteries that Hamilton had.

At Anzac the preparatory effort was incredibly intense. Some 25,000 men with their full equipment had to be got ashore and concealed without alerting the Turks, who were only 1,000 yards from the beach. It was a huge administrative effort to prepare hundreds more dugouts in terraces on the steep slopes not under direct observation, while adequate water supplies and rations had to be secured.

Secrecy had to be maintained but it is generally felt that the GHQ staff went too far. One example of the secrecy and the problems it caused can be seen in the deception practised over the maps issued to the divisions. They were being prepared by the Survey of Egypt under a then unknown British intelligence officer, one T. E. Lawrence.

> In the very early days of the fighting we had the great fortune to capture a Turkish officer who had on his person a complete set of a new set of maps, the survey of which had just been completed. Small sheets covering the whole Gallipoli peninsula and a large part of the Asiatic shore. We were suddenly presented with this extremely good map. Of course the thing was to get it reproduced as quickly as possible by the Survey of Egypt. The General Staff were so anxious that it shouldn't give away any of their plans that I was instructed to order the same number of copies of every single sheet although many of the sheets were of the Asiatic shore and even inland towards Mount Ida. Of course all this took a long time to carry out. When the Suvla operation was being planned the staff were very anxious to get maps as soon as possible. Each consignment of maps arrived by ship, slowly one or two at a time. Lawrence evidently made up his mind that the right tactics should be a landing on the Asiatic shore and all the maps that arrived were all maps of Asiatic shore. The staff were getting more and more touchy about whether the right maps had arrived and I was summoned to appear to know when the damned maps were going to come. I said nothing at all as it was entirely in Lawrence's hands. Eventually they arrived only a week or two before the actual Suvla offensive.[13] (Captain Tressilian Nicholas)

The maps were actually issued to the divisional commands as they arrived and as a deception it worked, for most of the troops believed they were to be landed on the Asiatic shore. Unfortunately it also restricted the time available for officers to plan their movements or gain familiarity with the battle areas.

The curse of excessive secrecy also meant that on 6 August many of the battalions of the 11th Division, instead of being fully briefed and practised in their complicated roles, were in ignorance of any details as to their role *that same night* as assault battalions in an invasion force. As a result instead of enjoying a day's rest, many of them had engaged in a full day's training.

The Turks were also preparing, although naturally hampered by their ignorance of where the next blow would fall. The combination of the drying up of the Salt Lake and the patrolling activity of the New Zealanders to the north of Anzac had aroused the attention of Marshal Liman von Sanders as to the vulnerability of his right flank at Anzac. But he believed it more likely that the attack would take the form of a new landing at Gaba Tepe coupled with a right hook from Anzac, so the 9th Division under the German Colonel Hans Kannengiesser was sent to organize the thorough defence of the coastline there. As a result the whole of the defence of the Suvla Bay area was left to one small force known as the Anafarta Detachment commanded by the German Major Willmer. It consisted of only four battalions (he was to lose another one when it was diverted to Sari Bair on the opening of the Anzac attack), a pioneer company, a squadron of cavalry and nineteen guns. In view of this paucity of resources Willmer saw his role as to delay any British attack, and his success or failure would depend on whether the attackers could secure and consolidate their hold on the high ground which surrounded Suvla Bay before the arrival of the Turkish reserves. His troops were therefore ordered not to risk being cut off but to retire whenever necessary to the next line of defence, ready to fight again. With considerable imagination he had sited his forward positions at Kiretch Tepe, Hill 10 and Lala Baba, but they were weakened by a lack of barbed wire.

For both sides the long months of planning and preparations were over at last and the offensive was about to begin. The first act of the August offensive took place at Helles on the 6th, with the aim of preventing the Turks from directing reinforcements to Anzac while the Sari Bair operations were under way. The attack was to take place on either side of Krithia Nullah and was again planned in two parts to make the most of what little artillery and naval suppport could be amassed. However, although it was only intended as a diversion, the acting commander of VIII Corps, Major General Douglas, and his staff, with little reason, were so optimistic of success that they planned further attacks and even predicted the capture of Krithia and Achi Baba.

The first attack was to be made by the 88th Brigade of the 29th Division. They were to attack the frontage between Gully Ravine and Krithia Nullah. The bombardment opened at 14.20 but the Turkish artillery retaliated in kind, causing many casualties in the packed British trenches. At 15.50 the infantry attacked and succeeded in reaching the Turkish front line. But the counter-attacks were ruthlessly efficient and numerically overwhelming. The few survivors were knocked back to their starting positions within an hour, having suffered nearly 2,000 casualties. The 29th Division Headquarters did not appreciate what had happened and in the belief that the attack had been at least partially successful the divisional commander, Major General de Lisle, ordered a night attack by the 86th Brigade to 'complete' the task. Lieutenant Colonel Guy Geddes commanded the 1st Munster Fusiliers, which had been moved up into the line as one of the battalions ordered to attack at 22.30. But the chaotic circumstances in the front line were such that Geddes was prepared to risk his whole career to try and stop what he rightly judged to be a futile gesture. At 22.00 he sent a message to brigade headquarters:

> The chaos is indescribable. I have only 50 men of my battalion with me. I cannot state when I shall be ready to attack. The firing line is subjected to heavy rifle and machine-gun fire. The left of the Worcestershires is uncertain. I have informed the Dublins I am not ready to attack, and not to do so till I inform him that I am.[14] (Lieutenant Colonel Guy Geddes)

The attack was cancelled and Geddes had saved his battalion to fight again.

The overall sacrifice of the men of the 88th Brigade was wasted, because Liman von Sanders had not in any way been distracted by the assault, which by its very failure had demonstrated that the Helles front was secure from British assaults. He therefore overruled his local commander, who naturally remained concerned, and ordered the Helles reserve division north to Anzac.

The strength of the Turkish response did not deter VIII Corps Headquarters from their planned second attack using the 42nd Division between Krithia Nullah and Achi Baba Nullah. The attack was launched at 09.40 on the following morning. Once again the results were dismal, with the 127th Brigade being reduced to below battalion strength, though the 125th Brigade made some small gains in the area known as the Vineyard only to suffer the usual round of Turkish counter-attacks. The fighting smouldered on for several days until both sides considered honour satisfied and their respective positions were finally consolidated. The casualty rate for these operations had been totally unacceptable and Hamilton ordered an end to all further so-called diversionary operations at Helles as they were actually jeopardizing the security of the British lines.

Hamilton had also agreed to launch a series of diversionary attacks designed to misdirect the attention of Turkish reserves in the immediate vicinity of Anzac. They sought to deflect attention from the main Sari Bair assault breaking out to the north of Anzac, by a strong attack on key Turkish positions within the southern sector of the Anzac perimeter. The 1st Australian Division was to attack first at Lone Pine, then at German Officer's Trench and finally, if all went well, at Johnston's Jolly.

The Turkish trenches at Lone Pine on 400 Plateau were extremely formidable as the Turks had greatly strengthened their original positions and roofed them over with solid timber. The Australians intended to use the underground trench system which their miners had laboured to construct under no-man's land during the summer. Linked tunnels ran to within thirty yards of the Turkish front line from which the troops would be able to break out and launch a surprise attack. The actual assault was assigned to the 1st Australian Brigade and was timed for the afternoon of 6 August.

At 4.30 every gun that could do so opened fire on the Pine, probably about 20 5″ howitzers. The enemy replied like hell with all their guns, bombs, mortars so that for a solid hour the noise was deafening, with the slither through the air of our howitzer

shells (which could be clearly seen in flight) and the crash of Turkish shells. At 5.30 pm our shelling ceased and punctually to time the 1st, 2nd and 3rd Battalions dashed out. . . . Our first line dashed over the front line of enemy trench while the second line engaged front trench, third line reinforcing. Overhead cover was very little hurt so that men were hopping about on top trying to pull the logs off to get into the Turks, poking their rifles into the loopholes and firing, the whole under shrapnel and rifle fire from the north. Once they got in the slaughter was tremendous.[15]
(Major Carl Jess)

The struggle in the trenches and tunnels of Lone Pine that ensued was one of incomparable savagery as the two sides battled continuously for two whole days before the Australians finally controlled the position. The courage demonstrated by the soldiers of both sides can be indicated by the seven VCs that were awarded for various heroic actions by Australians during the fray.

At midnight it was the turn of the 2nd Australian Brigade to assault German Officer's Trench, emerging from pre-prepared tunnels in front of Steele's Post. The initial attack was a terrible failure despite the painstaking preparations and further attempts achieved nothing, other than more casualties. In view of this the proposed attack on Johnston's Jolly was cancelled.

The Anzac diversionary attacks were more successful than those at Helles in drawing in the Turkish reserves, mainly because of the success of the Lone Pine assault. Yet this success was subsequently to prove counter-productive as the Turkish troops which were moved north towards 400 Plateau from their bases south of Anzac were also marching towards Chunuk Bair. As the nature of Hamilton's left hook from Anzac became apparent to Liman von Sanders, he was able to divert these troops on to Chunuk Bair to thwart the British assaulting columns at the vital moment.

The northern breakout from Anzac was the centrepiece of the whole August offensive. Everything else was intended to be subordinate to its successful conclusion. If it succeeded, the tactical gains would be so tremendous that the whole Turkish position on the Gallipoli Peninsula would be endangered.

Major General Sir Alexander Godley, the commander of the NZ&A Division, which had been responsible for the northern sector of Anzac, was placed in command of the breakout forces, which included the 13th Division, the 29th Indian Brigade, the dismounted 3rd Australian Light Horse Brigade and the 29th Brigade detached from the 10th Irish Division. The overall plan was developed by the chief staff officer of ANZAC, Brigadier General A. Skeen, and envisaged two separate assaulting columns, each preceded by covering forces, who were to secure the flanks on the line of approach. The right column, commanded by Brigadier General Francis Johnston, was to advance up the Sazli Beit Dere and Chailak Dere valleys to seize the summit of Chunuk Bair. Meanwhile the left assaulting column, commanded by Brigadier General Cox, was to capture Koja Chemen Tepe and Hill Q via the Aghyl Dere. As dawn broke at 04.30 two converging attacks were to be launched to complete the capture of the Sari Bair Ridge: one working south from the newly captured Chunuk Bair, and the second pushing out from the existing Anzac positions on Russell's Top across the Nek on to Baby 700.

As soon as it was dark, at around 21.00 on 6 August, the Right Covering Force of the New Zealand Mounted Rifles Brigade together with the Otago Mounted Rifles began to move out of their places of concealment to begin the first stage of the complex assault. They had the vital role of seizing as quickly and as silently as possible the Turkish outposts guarding the entrances to the deres that led up to the heart of the Turkish position. The Auckland Mounted Rifles had the difficult task of capturing the strongly fortified Old No. 3 Post at the head of Sazli Beit Dere. To achieve this, a cunning ruse had been in operation for some weeks. Every evening a destroyer had taken station off the coast, switched on a searchlight and opened up a bombardment. This began promptly at 21.00 and ended at 21.10 and then opened up again for another ten minutes at 21.20. On 6 August the *Colne* opened fire as usual, but under the cover of this fire, while the Turks were sheltering in their dugouts, the New Zealanders approached the summit of the outpost. As the destroyer bombardment ended they attacked and overran the totally surprised Turks. The Wellington Mounted Rifles were also successful in capturing other Turkish outposts on Destroyer Hill and Table Top, although these operations were not completed until midnight. Meanwhile the Otago and Canterbury Mounted Rifles had marched further up the coast and turned into Chailik Dere, where they were to clear Bauchop's Hill, which lay between that valley and Aghyl Dere. Resistance here was more severe but the hill was nevertheless clear of Turks by 01.00 on 7 August. So far all was well, although the preliminary tasks had taken two-and-a-half hours longer than expected.

The Left Covering Force, which consisted of half of 40th Brigade from the 13th Division, moved out at 21.30 and marched along the coast to Aghyl Dere. It had been assigned the task of capturing the spur of a hill called Damakjelik Bair to cover the flank of the Left Assaulting Column. As it advanced up the Aghyl Dere, 2nd Lieutenant Joseph Napier was with the 1/4th South Wales Borderers:

> The instructions were that it was to be a quiet affair as far as possible: no firing of rifles – in fact no ammunition in the rifles – no shouting. We had patches on our backs, coloured ones we tied to our jackets, so that our supporting ships could see where we had got to. We lined up in a nullah called Aghyl Dere. I don't think the Turks were really expecting anybody. When we moved out to assault Damakjelik Bair, which was supposed to be held by the Turks, I don't think anybody had any idea as to what we would come up against. One knew nothing and saw nothing you might say. As far as I was concerned there was no difficulty in getting up, it was a straight run in the dark, with my troops. It wasn't particularly dark, but you couldn't see much because the country was so encrusted with nullahs, hills, steep ravines and so on. I was the left platoon of the whole of the Left Covering Force. We went up this slight rise and there were some trenches at the top. Very indifferent ones, the Turks were not there in any great force. I saw a few Turks but they gave, as far as I was concerned, no trouble. Having arrived at the point which we were due to get to I was standing there in the dark waiting to see what was going

to happen. Suddenly a bomb went off, not far from me, which lit up the whole scene around me. I was looking back towards our line and I saw one of my fellow platoon commanders, Taffy Jenkins, charging straight at me with a rifle and bayonet. I remember saying: 'Hello Taffy, what are you doing?' I happened to make this casual remark because his platoon should have been some way off. Some days later Taffy rather hesitantly said: 'You know Joe, that evening I was just going to bayonet you, if that bomb hadn't lit the atmosphere and you hadn't said, "Hello Taffy", I think you'd have been a dead man much to my regret!'[16] (2nd Lieutenant Joseph Napier)

The hill was captured by 00.30 and the troops began to dig in, in case of any threat to the flank. Although behind schedule the two covering forces had done their work well and now controlled the hills around the entrances of Sazli Beit, Chailak and Aghyl Deres, thus opening the way for the assaulting columns to pass through without hindrance on to the heights above.

The Right Assaulting Column, consisting of the New Zealand Infantry Brigade under Johnston, had been further sub-divided. The Canterbury Battalion was to move up the Sazli Beit Dere, while the Otago, Wellington and Auckland Battalions proceeded along the Chailak Dere. Once they were at the heads of their respective deres they were to combine again on the lower slopes of Rhododendron Spur, between 01.00 and 02.00, prior to the final advance before dawn on Chunuk Bair just over a mile away. Both forces started off late due to the slow progress of the covering forces on Bauchop's Hill but eventually a start was made at 23.30. The passage of Chailak Dere was difficult due to the formidable barbed-wire obstructions at the entrance and because further stoppages were necessary as isolated pockets of Turkish resistance were eliminated. Eventually the battalions reached Table Top just short of the rendezvous on Rhododendron Spur. Here Johnston and his men sat down to await the arrival of the other party. Unfortunately the Canterbury Battalion had got completely lost in Sazli Beit Dere and after marching and counter-marching up various blind gullies actually ended up back at their starting point. These hours that

Johnston spent fruitlessly waiting were to prove the hours of missed opportunity, for Chunuk Bair was empty of Turkish troops.

Brigadier General Cox's Left Assaulting Column was made up from the 29th Indian Brigade and the 4th Australian Brigade. They were to advance up the Aghyl Dere as a single body before dividing up at its head. Two Gurkha battalions were to ascend up Chamchik Punar to attack Hill Q, while the remainder of the column crossed from the head of Aghyl Dere to the head of the neighbouring valley, the Azma Dere. They were then to climb on to Abdul Rahman Spur, where they were to form up prior to launching their attack up the spur and on to Koja Chemen Tepe before dawn. This plan was sound enough as an outflanking concept, but it was extraordinarily optimistic as to what was and was not possible on a night march through unknown and tortuous terrain by men already in poor health.

Throughout the column's march it was beset by a series of delays. A late start was made at 23.00 and then a disastrous short cut actually added hours to the journey. Once finally in the Aghyl Dere the necessity of struggling through the maze of inter-cutting ravines and the light but elusive opposition from the Turks slowed progress to a crawl. In ideal country for an ambush the troops were further hampered by the fear of what the Turks might have in store for them behind every twist and turn. It became a dreadful test of endurance for the troops, and the leading 4th Australian Brigade had already been greatly weakened by its experiences over the last three months at Anzac. The column fell further and further behind the timetable and inevitably was soon lost. When the Australian battalion commanders thought they had reached Abdul Rahman Spur they were merely on a continuation of Damakjelik Bair, still a long way from their objective. The exhausted troops could march no more, forcing the abandonment of any further advance. The brigade therefore dug in along the Damakjelik Bair, in effect forming a continuation of the Left Covering Force's position. Behind the Australians the 29th Indian Brigade also got lost in Aghyl Dere. Although meeting no serious opposition from the Turks, the topography defeated them and the brigade finished the night widely scattered across the heights leading up to Hill Q and Chunuk Bair. In fact, by accident rather than design, they formed a weak link between the New Zealanders on Rhododendron Ridge and the Australians on Damakjelik Bair.

As dawn became apparent, the scheduled assault from Russell's Top across the Nek and on to Baby 700 was due to commence. As the Right Assaulting Column was known to be behind schedule and had failed to reach the summit of Chunuk Bair the question arose at ANZAC Headquarters as to whether the frontal Nek attack should be cancelled or postponed in view of the absence of the support the New Zealanders were meant to supply from behind the Turkish positions. The Nek was a narrow causeway and, as the only route from the old Anzac area to Baby 700, was well entrenched by the Turks, who had further arranged interlocking machine-gun fire from either flank. Birdwood was faced with an extremely difficult decision. There were obvious advantages in pinning down the Turkish forces at Anzac while the encircling columns struggled on to their objectives, but the cost of an unsupported frontal assault was likely to be awful at such an unfavourable point. Birdwood decided that the sacrifice was worthwhile to boost the chances of the main columns.

The attack was undertaken by the 8th and 10th Australian Light Horse Regiments. Following a short half-hour bombardment, which achieved little but to forewarn the Turks, the Australians made a valiant dash across the sixty yards of no-man's land. It was hopeless from the moment the first wave went over the top and was almost casually annihilated by the Turks. Yet a combination of mistakes and circumstance sent three more waves to their deaths. Nothing was achieved and in 'popular history' the episode has come to epitomize the whole conduct of the campaign, in which an incompetent British command is regarded as having wasted Australian lives to no good purpose.

On Rhododendron Spur Johnston decided that he could wait no longer for the Canterbury Battalion, which had still not emerged from Sazli Beit Dere. At last at 07.00 his troops set off up the spur to Chunuk Bair, leaving one of his three remaining battalions behind as a reserve, which was a clear illustration of the futility of his long wait. As they moved off, Colonel Hans Kannengiesser arrived on the summit to carry out a reconnaissance prior to the arrival of his Turkish regiments. These units had been moved up from Gaba Tepe in response to the Australian attack on Lone Pine and had been diverted to Chunuk Bair to counter the threat which Liman von Sanders had discerned to his northern flank. As the New Zealand column reached a feature known as the Apex they came under fire.

> Suddenly the enemy infantry actually appeared in front of us at about 500 yards range. The English approached slowly, in single file, splendidly equipped and with white bands on their left arms, apparently very tired, and were crossing a hill-side to our flank, emerging in continually increasing numbers from the valley below. I immediately sent an order to my infantry – this was the twenty strong artillery-covering platoon – instantly to open fire. I received this answer: 'We can only commence to fire when we receive the order of our battalion commander.' This was too much for me altogether. I ran to the spot and threw myself among the troops who were lying in a small trench. What I said I cannot recollect, but they began to open fire and almost immediately the English laid down without answering our fire or apparently moving in any other way. They gave me the impression that they were glad to be spared further climbing.[17] (Colonel Hans Kannengiesser)

The attacking column halted. After further delay and a reconnaissance, Johnston came to the remarkable conclusion that no further progress could be made before dark owing to the growing opposition and the exhausted state of his troops. At 08.00 he reported as much to NZ&A Division Headquarters. His actions were in direct contravention of Birdwood's original orders, which had sought to impress on all senior commanders the pressing need to push on. At divisional headquarters Godley therefore rejected Johnston's excuses and insisted that an attack must be carried out that morning at 10.30. Johnston remained unconvinced and further undermined whatever meagre hopes of success remained at this late stage by assigning only a small proportion of his available force to the attack: just three companies of the Auckland Battalion and two companies of the 2/10th Gurkhas, which had joined them at the Apex from the Left Assaulting Column. It was too little too late, for by then Kannengiesser's small party had been reinforced in sufficient strength to establish a firing line barring the way to the summit and they easily repulsed the half-hearted attack. No further effort was made by Johnston's column that day.

To the north even less was achieved by the Left Assaulting Column. Despite reinforcements, the 4th Australian Brigade was unable to recover from the night's efforts and the 29th Indian Brigade was scattered ineffectually among the hills and valleys above Aghyl Dere. The 39th Brigade was released from the 13th Division reserve and sent up to join them. But even in daylight they managed to get totally confused and wasted the day marching and counter-marching to no effect.

By nightfall on 7 August it was obvious that the initial plan for seizing the Sari Bair Ridge had failed, as none of the objectives had been gained. The expansion of the scheme to take the whole of the ridge had fatally compromised the plan, since the consequent marching schedule and objectives assigned to the tired men of the Left Assaulting Column had been unrealistic. It is however possible that if these units been added to the Right Assaulting Column advancing up Chailak Dere then a decisive number of troops could have arrived at Chunuk Bair at daybreak before the Turks could assemble any real opposition. If Chunuk Bair had been secured, then Battleship Hill might well have been taken as originally intended by a two-pronged assault and the Turkish stranglehold on the old Anzac positions could have been broken. Nevertheless there remained limited grounds for optimism. Not many casualties had been suffered by the columns and the Turks had not had time to get on to the ridges in any real strength, although their main reserves were marching up from Bulair. If a new attack could be quickly organized then the heights might still be secured, but speed was of the essence.

Cox faced terrible problems overnight in trying to organize a renewed attack with the exhausted and scattered Left Assaulting Column. Although he intended that four *ad hoc* columns should assault the main ridge on the morning of 8 August, the commanders of No. 1 and No. 3 Columns were unable even to find the respective constituent units of their columns in the maze of gullies and precipices and consequently achieved nothing. The 4th Australian Brigade made up No. 4 Column and they were to try once again to traverse Abdul Rahman Spur on to Koja Chemen Tepe. Even without opposition this would have been a near impossible task in the time allowed, but the reinforced Turks had little difficulty in driving them back to their starting positions. The No. 2 Column made up of the 7th North Staffords and 9th Worcesters was to move forward up the Aghyl Dere and join the 1/6th Gurkhas in their advanced position up in the hills at around 04.15. The two battalions had spent the night lost in the Aghyl Dere nightmare and at 08.00 Major Cecil Allanson, in command of the Gurkhas, used his initiative and moved up on to Hill Q without waiting for the rest of the column. They had made promising progress before the Turks opened fire and Allanson himself dashed back to try and secure reinforcements, but he could find little more than a company. This was not sufficient and soon his force became pinned down in positions immediately below the summit.

> Further movement was impossible; it was now 9.30 am, and blazing hot; I lay there without moving till 6 pm with every conceivable shot flying in the air above one, shrapnel, our own maxims, rifles, and our own high explosive bursting extremely close, which told me how near I was to the top. I lay between two British soldiers; the man on my left had a Bible, and read it the whole day; the man on my right I found was a corpse. I wondered if I ought to make good resolutions for the future, and did not. The sun on one's back was most trying.[18] (Major Cecil Allanson)

After dark Allanson gradually moved his mixed party closer and closer to the peak of Hill Q until they were dug in just 100 feet away. Unfortunately, because of the chaotic circumstances in the Aghyl Dere sector, Cox and Godley remained unaware of this considerable achievement and at 14.00 had suspended operations in the sector to allow preparations for another attack on the following day. The chance to capture Hill Q thus hung in the balance.

To the south Johnston had arranged for his reinforced forces to assault Chunuk Bair. At 03.00 on 8 August the Wellington Battalion moved forward followed by the 7th Gloucesters and 8th Welch Regiments from the 13th Division. The divisional commander was watching the attack.

> There is an observation post here . . . and from it one can see a large portion of the country over which we are operating. To that post about 4.15 went a procession of sleepy Generals and staff carrying glasses, telescopes and anxiously awaiting the dawn, to show the success or otherwise of the troops. It began to get gradually lighter and all glasses were turned on the summit of Chunuk Bair, which was the only point of attack which could matter. Still it got lighter, and then someone said: 'I see men on Chunuk Bair.' 'They are our men,' said another, and then: 'By Jove! They are our men,' and so they were. We reached the summit, should we hold it and should we progress?[19] (Major General Frederick Shaw)

To everyone's surprise the Turks were found to have abandoned the hill and the Wellington Battalion's advance was unopposed. Before dawn the New Zealanders had the crucial summit and had begun digging in on both the forward and rear slopes of Chunuk Bair.

Chunuk Bair was enfiladed by the Turkish positions on Battleship Hill, as expected, but also from Hill Q, which by the time dawn broke should have been under attack from Cox's columns. The collapse of Cox's plans meant that the Turks were free as the light improved to open a devastating fire, which caught the 7th Gloucesters and 8th Welch Regiment in the open as they toiled up the hill behind the Wellingtons. Only a few succeeded in reaching the crest and even then there was little respite from the constant enfilade fire, which gradually whittled away at what remained. It also ensured that no significant reinforcements could be got forward to assist the Wellingtons. During the day the Turks counterattacked but a determined resistance kept them at bay until night fell and the Otago Battalion and Wellington Mounted Rifles moved forward to join them under the cover of darkness.

*

Another day had thus passed and although some success had been achieved it was extremely precarious. The Turks were gradually building up their forces on Sari Bair and the initial trickle of reinforcements from the immediate vicinity of Anzac was about to become a flood-tide as the reserve divisions began to arrive from Bulair. Units of the 7th and 12th Divisions from XVI Corps commanded by Feizi Bey had begun to arrive late on 8 August after their forced march from Bulair. Liman von Sanders had intended them to attack at once but the troops were exhausted after their long march. Their divisional commanders begged Feizi Bey for a rest before they were thrown into action, a request to which he acceded, postponing their attack until dawn on 9 August. He had not, however, consulted Liman von Sanders, who was furious and pre-emptorily replaced him with the hard-driving Mustapha Kemal Bey. By the time Mustapha Kemal reached his new headquarters it was too late to do anything but ensure that there were no more delays in launching the attack on 9 August.

It was by now apparent that something fairly dramatic was required from the British generals and their exhausted troops if they were to prevail. Yet in essence all that was proposed for 9 August was a reduced version of the original plan, now lacking any element of surprise and facing strongly held positions.

The battalions remaining in a fit state for battle were to concentrate on the capture of the main ridge from Chunuk Bair to Hill Q, which was simply bowing to the inevitable as there was now no chance of the enfeebled 4th Australian Brigade advancing against stiff opposition all the way round to Koja Chemen Tepe. A three-pronged attack was envisaged: to the north the remnants of Cox's force consisting of miscellaneous elements of the British 39th Brigade and the 29th Indian Brigade were to renew their stalled attack on Hill Q; the main thrust in the centre, on the northern shoulder of Chunuk Bair, was to be from an *ad hoc* brigade of four battalions under Brigadier General Baldwin; while Johnston's men attacked the southern shoulder of Chunuk Bair and then on towards Battleship Hill. If these attacks were not to be defeated in isolation it was vital that Baldwin's force arrive promptly in the centre. A short bombardment would commence at 04.30 to be followed by a joint attack at 05.15.

Unfortunately such hopes were ruined by the choice of route. Johnston had advised Baldwin that the relatively direct route up Chailak Dere via Rhododendron Spur on to Chunuk Bair was unwise due to the enfilade fire which swept the approaches during the day. In fact as the approach was to take place at night this would not have been a serious problem. Nevertheless, not unreasonably, Baldwin took Johnston's advice and planned a tortuous route which began in Chailak Dere, crossed Cheshire Ridge, moved along Aghyl Dere and then up via the Farm Plateau on to Chunuk Bair. As might have been expected everything went wrong as Baldwin's men replayed the night marches of 6 August with the additional hindrance of the wounded who now choked the valleys as they tried to get back to safety. At dawn his column was still straggling through the Aghyl Dere a significant distance from where they were to attack at 05.15. On the right, on Chunuk Bair, Johnston's exhausted New Zealanders were already under heavy fire from the Turkish positions, and in the absence of Baldwin's force in support, an attack was clearly not viable. Only the intrepid detachments led by Allanson perched just below the crest of Hill Q were ready.

> The roar of the artillery preparation was enormous; the hill was almost leaping underneath one. I recognized that if we flew up the hill the moment it stopped we ought to get to the top. . . . The moment they saw me go forward carrying a red flag everyone was to start. . . . Then off we dashed all hand in hand, a most perfect advance and a wonderful sight.[20] (Major Cecil Allanson)

The mixed force of Gurkhas and British troops reached the top of Hill Q in a triumph of persistence and determination.

> I flew up the ridge and felt a very proud man as I put my foot on it and had not lost a man practically. Below were bolting the Turks at whom our fellows fired standing up and a wonderful view which seemed to me the key to the whole peninsula: below were the Straits, Kila Nahr, the rear of Achi Baba and the communications to their army there. And then followed disaster which may cost us thousands and thousands and was the most appalling sight I ever saw. I saw a flash in the Bay. Suddenly 3 or 4 or 5 high explosive shells burst among us. The first hit a Gurkha in the face: the place was a mass of blood and limbs and screams

though the casualties were not really very heavy. The whole force flew in a panic down the hill. . . . There were left on the crest Le Marchand, myself, two officers of the South Lancs and about ten men. . . . but the Turks saw what had happened and began to come up the hill; we fired a few shots into them but they were about 250 yards away and it was useless to stay. So I shouted 'the Retire'.[21] (Major Cecil Allanson)

Even back at their battalion headquarters below the crest the effect of the blast was felt by the Medical Officer, Major Selby Phipson: 'The blast was so tremendous that, although protected by the ridge, I was blown backwards heels over head out of the fox-hole, but I was not hurt.'[22] The immediate effect of the shells was catastrophic as the survivors tumbled back into their line just below the crest.

Meanwhile, Baldwin's force had only emerged from the Aghyl Dere at 06.00 to begin their advance across the Farm Plateau below Chunuk Bair. It was too late: the Turks were there in strength and their fire was overwhelming.

I've never heard, or imagined it was possible to hear such an inferno – I can't describe it nor yet compare it to anything. You've heard the expression a sea of lead – well I realized then what it meant. We had about 400 yards open flat to cross before getting under cover of the hill and it was broad daylight. I for one did not get across it and I am afraid only comparatively few did out of our battalion.[23] (Lieutenant Thomas Watson)

All they could do was dig in on the lower edge of the plateau and attempt to consolidate the fragile links with the New Zealanders on the Apex.

The first counter-attack by Kemal's new command took place at 04.30 that morning when the Turkish 7th Division unsuccessfully advanced against Damakjelik Bair, guarded by the 1/4th South Wales Borderers and the 4th Australian Brigade. All along the putative British line the Turkish pressure was building up as their reinforcements were moved into the line.

On Hill Q the Gurkhas and British detachments still clung to their positions but casualties mounted throughout the day. Allanson himself was wounded and soon the only British officer left of 1/6th Gurkhas was their Medical Officer.

> That afternoon the Turks attacked five times, and we should have fared badly if it had not been for our three machine-guns, which, with the greatest of difficulty, had been brought up from 1000 feet below. That same evening Allanson, whose wound by then was very painful, was ordered down by Bde HQ and, before leaving, to hand over the command to Geoffrey Tomes (53rd Sikhs) who had been sent up for the purpose. But Tomes was killed a very short time after he had taken over, and I was able, at least, to soothe his last moments. When I told Allanson of his death, he thought for a minute and said, 'A splendid fellow, Tomes. Well Phippy, there's no one left to hand over to but you. Do all you can to help Gambirsing Pun (the Sergeant Major) he'll never let you down.' . . . Left to myself and feeling rather lonely, I started to take stock of the situation. My first thought, oddly enough, was that I must cease to claim the protection (if any) of the Geneva Convention, and so I removed my Red Cross brassard, and put it in my haversack. I might, I thought, have to deal with combatant officers of other units, and although I held no combatant commission myself, I thought it was, perhaps, just as well to look as if I did.[24] (Major Selby Phipson)

Having taken command, Phipson sent written messages to try and secure some reinforcements:

> The troops on our flanks . . . the South Wales Borderers, the 9th Worcesters and the South Lancs – replied that they had either retired, or expected to retire, and themselves needed reinforcements or were momentarily expecting an attack, so it was evident that we were out on a limb and in no shape to hold a determined Turkish counter-attack, which, indeed, seemed imminent. . . . The night of August 9/10th was harassed by constant sniping apparently from our flanks, and desultory rifle fire along the whole of our diminished front, but the Turks never approached nearer than 20–30 yards. I borrowed a rifle and took my place in the firing line and dealt with a Turk who had wriggled up un-noticed to about 15 yards from our line.[25] (Major Selby Phipson)

By the end of 9 August the question was no longer whether the British could seize control of Sari Bair but whether they could hold on to the gains they had made. During the day Hamilton had rushed across for a conference with Birdwood and his divisional commanders. Hamilton was impressed by the continued fighting spirit of the Anzac commanders, and offered them his last available army reserve, the 54th Division, which had finally arrived, for use in one more attempt on the peaks. Birdwood rejected the offer, pointing out that the already stretched Anzac base could not cope with feeding and, more crucially, watering such an even larger force. He felt that the relative openness and ease of communication at the huge natural harbour of Suvla meant that the division could be more effectively deployed there. After all, the IX Corps having secured its landing at Suvla was meant to be assisting ANZAC in capturing the Sari Bair range. As reinforcements could not then be accommodated at Anzac, all attention focused on the importance of retaining the lodgement on Chunuk Bair which might still eventually compromise the entire Turkish position at Anzac.

Overnight attempts were made to relieve those troops who had been in action longest. The New Zealanders on Chunuk Bair and the Pinnacle were replaced by the 6th Loyal North Lancashires. The 5th Wiltshires were also supposed to move into the front line, but they had got lost on the way up and in exhaustion had misguidedly taken shelter in Sazli Beit Dere. In the whole tortuously complicated area between Rhododendron Spur and Chunuk Bair there was now an equally complicated mixture of units totalling only about 2,000 men. Similar situations existed all along the front line which had developed north of Anzac. The men were badly entrenched, exhausted, hungry, thirsty and lacking in local leadership as a result of the high casualties among their officers and NCOs. Above all the divisions and brigades had become totally intermixed, with no clearly defined command structure and they were bereft of orders to tell them what they were meant to be trying to do. It was a potentially disastrous situation.

Just before dawn at 04.45 on 10 August the Turks launched a massive counter-attack against this fragile line with murderous efficiency. Six battalions surged over the top of Chunuk Bair completely overwhelming the outpost and main line of the 6th

Loyal North Lancashires, before tearing down into the hapless 5th Wiltshires.

> As daybreak dawned at 4am everyone thought themselves safe, and we were just beginning to dig ourselves in again, when our covering party scouts came in and said the Turks were coming up on all sides in thousands and before we had time to prepare to meet them we were under heavy fire with shrapnel and machine-guns and the men began to fall. . . . 'A' and 'C' companies was nearly all done for in no time . . . caught in the open and killed before we had time to get our rifles even, but 'B' and 'D' were more fortunate, as they were in a small trench, and they made a good fight for it. . . . I think I must have been dazed by a shell exploding, as I can't remember anything after till I found myself in the Gully with a lot more, some wounded, some not![26] (Corporal A. G. Scott)

The Pinnacle was captured but the scattered British and New Zealand units managed to cling on to the Apex back towards Rhododendron Spur. To the north the Turks swept down from Chunuk Bair on to the Farm Plateau like Assyrians on the fold, and Baldwin's exhausted collection of battalions had fallen back on to Cheshire Ridge after a fierce but unavailing struggle by around 10.00. Further north the line was forced by this exposure of their right flank, allied to continued frontal Turkish pressure, to fall back as part of a general withdrawal into Aghyl Dere. Even the valiant few, under Phipson, still clinging on just below the summit of Hill Q were forced to release their grip on receipt of a direct order at 12.00.

> I sent another salaam to the Sergeant Major, read the order to him and asked him how the retirement should be carried out. Fortunately we could both converse in Hindustani of a sort, and it soon became apparent, to my relief, that he knew the drill from A to Z, and I marvelled at the precision with which he described the different phases of the retirement and the proper precautions to be taken, such as the removal and disposal of the bolts of rifles which could not be taken; the disposal of surplus ammunition, collection of stores, destruction of equipment which could not be carried, and the timing of the movement itself – and what a

movement. To retire 900 feet down a rocky declivity, intersected by deep and narrow gullies, many of them choked with corpses, and the infinitely difficult job of carrying down the wounded – all these problems, insoluble to me, presented little difficulty to Gambirsing Pun, whose knowledge and competence seemed complete and indefeasible. I recalled Allanson's words, 'He'll never let you down.'[27] (Major Selby Phipson)

The British came tumbling back from the hills sometimes in good order, sometimes not. The Turkish assault had been devastatingly successful but mutual exhaustion now took hold from the continuous fighting in such dreadful terrain. The attempt to seize the Sari Bair Ridge had thus ended, as it had begun, in failure. The British forces had fought hard and had significantly increased the original Anzac position, but although the ground captured was to prove valuable in practice it was poor compensation for the glittering prizes that had eluded them.

Over the next few days the dying echoes of the battle reverberated around the hills as positions were established and local confrontations resolved. On a military level they were irrelevant. The strategic questions, as opposed to the tactical niceties, had been answered. The Anzac offensive had really failed by dawn on 7 August, when the assaulting columns were not entrenched up on the heights. After that failure success was never particularly likely as more and more Turks arrived to oppose further assaults which were essentially rehashes of the original, failed plan. In the end the capture of Chunuk Bair came to be seen as the crux of the operation but it was fatally compromised by the attempt to include the whole Sari Bair range. Yet it must be remembered that the capture of Koja Chemen Tepe to the north was supposed to have been carried out in conjunction with assistance from the IX Corps at Suvla Bay on the night of 6 August.

8

The Landing
at Suvla

The plans for the landing at Suvla had been considerably complicated at an early stage by the GHQ decision to avoid the direct
route straight across from C and B Beaches to the Chocolate and
Green Hills because of the existence of Turkish defences on the
western and southern slopes. The necessity of circling right round
the Salt Lake to approach from the north had led directly to the
decision to shorten the march by landing actually inside Suvla Bay
at A Beach, despite the warnings from the navy about uncharted
shoaling waters. It was therefore ironic that aerial reports received
in the last days before the landing indicated that the Turks had not
only recently dug trenches on the northern slopes of the Chocolate
and Green Hills, but also prepared a redoubt at Hill 10 directly
inland from A Beach. Aerial reports also suggested that the Salt
Lake would no longer be an obstacle to troops taking a more direct
route as it was almost completely dried out. This intelligence
however arrived far too late to affect the planning of the landing.

The invading force was organized into three echelons to land
on the beaches. The first echelon, consisting of 10,300 troops of
the 11th Division under the command of Major General Hammersley, was to begin its final approach to the beaches at 21.45 on 6
August. There were to be 500 troops aboard each of ten destroyers
and ten new motor landing craft. The destroyers were to approach
their designated beaches in line abreast, each towing a picket boat
and one of the landing craft. Having got as close as possible to the
shore the destroyers were to cast off their tows before anchoring.
The landing craft would then run into the beach and land the 500
troops they were carrying before returning to the destroyer to pick
up another 500, to be landed in the same way. Meanwhile the
picket boats under the control of midshipmen were to assist the

landing craft and to provide covering fire if necessary from machine-guns mounted in the bows.

The 34th Brigade, commanded by Brigadier General William Sitwell, was to land from three destroyers and accompanying landing craft at A Beach to the north of the Cut, a drainage channel from the Salt Lake to the sea. The brigade's first objective was to secure both the immediate landing area around the beach and the northern hills surrounding the Suvla Plain. One of the leading battalions was to move directly forward to capture the Hill 10 redoubt while another turned left along the beach, overran the Turkish positions at Ghazi Baba and advanced up the Kiretch Tepe Ridge as far as Point 156, where the ridge met the Tekke Tepe Ridge. Once the beach was secure the second-wave battalions were to link up with the battalion on Hill 10 and launch an attack around the northern border of the Salt Lake to take the Turkish positions on the Chocolate and Green Hills. This was not to start later than 01.30 on 7 August.

The main landing was to be made from seven destroyers and their accompanying landing craft at B Beach. The first two battalions of the 32nd Brigade, commanded by Brigadier General Henry Haggard, were to land at the northern end of B Beach and capture Lala Baba, thus securing the southern 'horn' of Suvla Bay. They were then to proceed across the Cut to Hill 10, where they would await the rest of the brigade and join the 34th Brigade attack on the Chocolate and Green Hills under Sitwell's overall command. Meanwhile the 33rd Brigade, commanded by Brigadier General Robert Maxwell, would land on B Beach slightly further to the south, charged with covering the right flank of the whole Suvla landing. The first two battalions were to entrench from the beach across to the Salt Lake, while the rest of the brigade were to follow 32nd Brigade to Hill 10, where they would form the divisional reserve.

The second echelon was to arrive at B and C Beaches at 22.45 and consisted of 3,000 troops including engineers, signallers, two 10-pounder mountain batteries and one 18-pounder field battery. The third echelon was to be made up of transport horses, carts and waggons, and it was hoped that this would be ashore on C Beach by about 03.00 on the morning of 7 August. Once the 11th

Division was safely ashore the landing craft were to be used to disembark six battalions of the 10th Irish Division at around dawn. By then it was to be a matter of getting as many troops, artillery and supplies of all kinds ashore as quickly as possible.

Special attention had been paid to one absolute essential, the question of ensuring water supplies over the first few days. Four water lighters were to be towed in to the beaches by the large water tank steamer *Krini*. The landing craft also carried water tins, from which the assaulting troops could refill their water bottles, while two of the transports carried a mass of water-holding receptacles to get the water from the beach to the front line.

Sir Ian Hamilton, remembering his sense of isolation from events during the landings on 25 April, had urged Stopford to remain at Imbros and to land at dawn at Suvla. From Imbros all the necessary wireless and cable links could easily be maintained with Hammersley at 11th Division Headquarters until IX Corps Headquarters went ashore as planned at dawn on 7 August. However, Stopford wanted to maintain a physical closeness to his men and he and his executive staff were put aboard the sloop *Jonquil*, which unfortunately lacked any of the sophisticated signalling facilities that a mobile headquarters required.

As planned, at 21.45 on 6 August the first echelon approached the shore in total darkness. Midshipman Bush, a veteran from the earlier landing at Anzac, was in command of one of the picket boats operating off B Beach:

> At 9.50 the seven destroyers slipped their tows, which was the signal for all motor lighters to go full speed ahead for the beach with picket boats following. The run-in took less than ten minutes. But how different from Anzac! The landing was a complete surprise. There was no opposition and not a single casualty. A few rockets were fired, and one or two rifle shots rang out in the darkness, but that was all. Our motor lighter grounded rather far out, making it necessary for the men to wade in about three feet of water. They made a poor showing – no dash and a certain amount of talking. Indeed a handful, who obviously had

had the wind up, looked as if they were afraid to land. Petty Officer Main sang out and told them to get a move on. They went ashore after that.[1] (Midshipman Eric Bush RN)

B Beach was undefended and many of the landing craft, with the assistance of the picket boats to keep them straight, dropped their ramps actually on to the beach so that the troops did not even get their boots wet. By 22.00 the first four battalions were safe ashore without casualties.

The 7th South Staffordshires and the 9th Sherwood Foresters of the 33rd Brigade moved off and were able to dig the right-flank defensive lines undisturbed, thus securing the right flank of the invading force. To their left the 6th Yorkshire Regiment of the 32nd Brigade overran the Turkish positions at Lala Baba and Nibrunesi Point by midnight but suffered considerable casualties, especially among their officers. This relatively small-scale attack was the first made by any unit of Kitchener's New Army. Behind them the other three battalions of the 32nd Brigade were converging on Lala Baba with the divisional reserve battalions of the 33rd Brigade behind them. At this time all was going reasonably well, although many of the troops were already betraying signs of fatigue.

Unfortunately the 34th Brigade's landing on A Beach was a disaster, with the Royal Navy's fears about the shoaling waters fully justified. In an echo of the landing at Anzac, the navy made things worse by anchoring the destroyers, not only in the wrong order, thus landing the troops in the wrong position relative to each other, but also in the wrong place. As a result the three destroyers anchored some 1,000 yards south of their intended stations – right in the middle of the worst shoals. The Turks by then were more alert and opened fire almost as soon as the landing craft set off for the beach at 22.30. Midshipman Henry Denham RN was aboard an accompanying picket boat: 'Suddenly, I distinctly heard a sharp click ashore, which must have been the cocking of rifles, for only a few seconds later there was one shot followed by hundreds, rapid independent.'[2]

The landing craft from HMS *Grampus* carrying three companies of the 11th Manchesters got through the shallows unscathed but were far too far to the south and landed them on the wrong side of the Cut, not far from Lala Baba. After some initial confusion, during which one company was detached to guard the Lala Baba flank, the Manchesters determinedly moved off to the north, where their objectives lay. Despite their bad start, they cleared the isolated Turkish posts at Ghazi Baba, thus securing the left horn of Suvla Bay, and then moved on to the Kiretch Tepe Ridge. This battalion showed what could be achieved with determined leadership, for despite Turkish opposition by 03.00 they had got two miles along the ridge.

Meanwhile the landing craft from HMS *Beagle* and HMS *Bulldog*, which were carrying the 9th Lancashire Fusiliers and the fourth company of the Manchesters, were not so lucky with the shoals and ran aground about fifty yards from the beach. The men struggled to the beach through deepish water weighed down with equipment. 'The soldiers were naturally not too keen to get ashore and, especially at the end, it took quite a lot of persuasion from the sergeants to clear the lighter. Then the ammunition had to be carried ashore, so by the time the lighter was cleared it must have been well past midnight.'[3] Although they were intended to attack Hill 10, which lay directly in front of A Beach, the Lancashire Fusiliers found themselves to the south of the Cut facing across the eerie wastes of the Salt Lake, with no sign of their objective in the pitch dark. The battalion vainly searched for Hill 10 but never got further than dispersed positions in the Cut area, where they were plagued by elusive Turkish snipers who targeted officers and NCOs mercilessly. The battalion was isolated, as the Manchesters had by now moved off to the north and the other two battalions of the 34th Brigade had not yet got ashore. Just a mile away to the south, the 32nd Brigade and half the 33rd Brigade from B Beach were concentrating at Lala Baba and should have moved off towards Hill 10 to join them in an assault on the Chocolate and Green Hills. The confused situation in front of them made the senior officer present on Lala Baba decide that rather than add to the confusion they should stay put. The absence of clear orders from Stopford and Hammersley insisting on the vital importance of haste and determination in the face of obstacles had taken effect. Local commanders lacked the flexibility of purpose and mind to take over the role of capturing Hill 10 from the 34th Brigade before thrusting inland as planned.

By 03.00 the rest of the 34th Brigade had still not been able to get ashore as the shoaling Suvla Bay waters trapped the landing craft one by one. After being refloated, the *Bulldog*'s landing craft picked up the second wave of troops but ran aground again, this time 100 yards off shore. On its second trip the *Grampus*'s landing craft also ran aground, marooning most of the 8th Northumberland Fusiliers for hours.

> The lighters seemed a long time in getting back, and the Turks began to shell us with shrapnel, and that was the worst I thought when we were all crowded together in the TBDs [Torpedo Boat Destroyers] and the first time most of us had ever been under fire. Luckily they never hit us, the shots going right over us. Then the lighter came back and we got on board. . . . When we got about 150 yards from the shore the lighter ran aground and we were stuck. We could not get out and walk ashore as it was too deep and of course impossible to swim with all our equipment on, rifles, etc. . . . Eventually we got help from a beach party about 2.30, and they took us in small rowing boats to within 40 yards of the shore, where we got out and walked ashore. Then it was quite a job collecting the company.[4] (Captain Montie Carlisle)

Further along, the *Beagle*'s lighter could not be refloated at all after the first grounding and the delays in fetching a replacement from B Beach meant that those troops were not all ashore until after dawn.

With the exception of the 11th Manchesters, Sitwell's 34th Brigade was hours behind schedule, while Haggard, now in overall command of the 32nd and 33rd Brigades on Lala Baba, waited for the situation to be resolved. At last at 03.00, Haggard finally sent troops forward but, despite having several untouched battalions available, a mere four companies moved off to join the 34th Brigade. Inevitably these were sucked in isolation into the chaos around the Cut. Instead of taking decisive action Haggard waited for certainty as to the course of events – and so the course of events passed him by. The detailed timetable, so dependent on punctuality, was off the rails. This left a vacuum at the centre of the British line and at about 03.30 the Turks had the temerity to launch a minor counter-attack which exposed the weakness of the bridgehead covering the beach. 'I thought the whole show might be over and we would have to retire into the sea, the unfortunate fact was that there was nobody there to command, the Brigadier was held up in landing and we had no orders at all.'[5]

The attack was beaten back. When Sitwell got ashore he realized that the situation was dire and sent a message to Lala Baba to request urgent assistance. In the meantime he was determined to try and capture Hill 10 and ordered the 9th Lancashire Fusiliers to attack as dawn was breaking. Understandably, in all the confusion, the assault was misdirected on to a nearby sand dune and broken up by enfilade fire from the Turkish positions on the real Hill 10, which lay 400 yards to the north. At daybreak at 04.30 the 11th Division should have established positions in the hills around the Suvla Plain but Hill 10 had not even been captured.

Hammersley eventually began to grasp the situation his division was facing as the disparate reports from his subordinates were received at his headquarters established behind Lala Baba. At 05.20 the 32nd Brigade was at last ordered forward to assist the 34th Brigade. The remaining battalions moved off at around 05.30 and reached the Cut at 06.00; the Turkish sniper fire was by then dying down and Hill 10 had now been located. On their arrival a combined attack was finally directed at the Turkish trenches on Hill 10. Only around 100 Turks were holding the hill and with no chance of successful resistance they followed Willmer's standing orders to retire to the next line of defence before the British overran the position.

The next phase of the plan called for a concerted attack round the northern border of the Salt Lake on to Chocolate and Green Hills. Although the plan was behind schedule it could yet be salvaged. But most of the battalions in the area had lost sight of their objectives and moved off in the wrong direction on to the lower slopes of Kiretch Tepe to the northeast, which reflected on the lack of briefing and ignorance of the geography of the area common among the battalion commanders.

At around 04.30 the transports carrying the 31st Brigade and half of the 30th Brigade, part of the 10th Irish Division, arrived from Mitylene, as planned, to be landed ready to continue the push inland. The consequences of the excessive secrecy now became terribly apparent as the senior officer, Brigadier General Felix Hill, had not the slightest clue what was going on ashore or what he and his troops were supposed to do. Hill therefore went across to the *Jonquil* to receive his orders direct from Stopford. The corps commander had intended them to go ashore at A Beach and to complete the capture of Kiretch Tepe but the débâcle suffered by the 34th Brigade in the shoaling waters inside Suvla Bay meant that he decided to switch the landing place to C Beach, immediately north of B Beach. On landing, Hill's force was to operate under Hammersley's orders, but as C Beach was south of the bay and their objectives were to the north, this decision was unfortunate and risked further confusion ashore. Ironically even as Hill was returning to his transports, Commodore Roger Keyes arrived on the *Jonquil* with the news that the navy had located an acceptable landing place on the northern side of the bay, which would have been perfect for Hill's purposes. Unfortunately Stopford refused to change Hill's orders, believing it would lead to delay and confusion. So for the sake of a change of orders half of the 10th Division was landed on the wrong side of the bay. At 07.30 another three battalions of the division arrived from Mudros with their divisional commander Lieutenant General Sir Bryan Mahon. They were therefore directed to the new landing beach and told to push along the Kiretch Tepe in support of the 11th Manchesters. As a result of these actions the 10th Division, which had already lost the 29th Brigade to the Anzac force, was to remain split for several days with a consequent disruption in staff work and supporting services.

The first artillery units arrived shortly after dawn, and Bombardier George Dale was with 'A' Battery, 59th Brigade, RFA, as they landed at C Beach:

> In brilliant sun the tug's bow squelches into sand and we jump ashore with only wet feet, and stare about. To the right, a sobering picture, khaki forms with blood-stained bandages lie in rows on the beach, and bearers are coming over the dunes with another burden. . . . A large Red Cross flag is being hoisted. On a sand dune fifty yards inland a group of staff officers study a map and point. Now all becomes orders and bustle. Drivers are getting

the horses ashore. Ankle deep in the fine sand, we gunners know we've got a real job on our hands getting guns and limbers with narrow iron-shod wheels up that steep beach of powdery sand. And the CO is calling for speed. Now for one of those brief, foolish incidents which somehow stick in the mind. Bombardier Bodkins, who never loses a chance to show himself, bustles up to me: 'Here – hold my rifle while I go in the water to help.' . . . *What!* And me a bombardier too! I start to redden and swell like a turkey cock. 'Hold your own (something) rifle,' I shout. 'I'm coming in too.' We exchange baleful stares; then lay our rifles above the beach and wade in together. One must stand on one's dignity sometimes. With horses pulling, gunners straining on drag ropes the first gun is on the move, when inland someone slams a big door. Comes a queer whining note, increasing to a harsh shriek as our first round of shrapnel bursts out to sea with a vicious clang. Somebody hit in a lighter? It's Dan Gray? Well, well, first casualty the sanitary orderly. Shells whine over at irregular intervals, many falling short or over; but we know they'll have the range soon. With wheels nearly axle deep it takes all we've got to get those guns etc on to firmer ground. . . . More shells drop on the beach. 'Dirty dogs, firing on the Red Cross' somebody shouts, ignoring our own landing against it. As Major Cowell, mounted and stern faced, rides past I hear him mutter: 'Let me get my battery into action!'[6] (Bombardier George Dale)

At last everything was ashore and off the beach and the battery moved to a position behind Lala Baba, a gun at a time with two of the gunners following on foot while the rest went under cover. Dale did not enjoy the experience:

As we wheel right from the beach a shell thuds into the hillside above, and the drivers whip up their horses. Away they go, leaving Hubert and I alone – orphans of the storm. We grab hands and break into a trot. 'Faster – faster!' I seem to hear my guardian angel say as another shell lands short. Now we're in top gear with rifle, bandolier with fifty rounds, haversacks askew, water bottles and mess tins clanking, stumbling like stampeding cattle over sait bushes, puffing hard and mucksweat streaming. (No, no, it wasn't funny chums!) BANG – scream – ker-*ack*!

Down now on our bellies while pellets thud into the ground.
I'm hit in the head! No, it's the darn rifle. Damn near, that one.
'Y-you all right, George?' 'Ye-es, are you Hubert?' Up again and
scuttle on – it's our first Gallipoli Gallop. (Oh, if Mother could
see me now!) We've got it all to ourselves on that unforgettable
half mile. 'Mean to say you were *afraid*?' somebody might say.
'Very much so, chum.' Hair standing up straight; eyes protruding
like the white balls on chapel hatpegs. 'Show me the hero who
stayed calm under his first shellfire and I'll show you a liar!'[7]
(Bombardier George Dale)

By mid-morning a constant stream of contradictory orders and
reports was being passed between the various divisional and brigade
headquarters as Hammersley strove to organize the much delayed
attack by his troops on Chocolate Hill. Sitwell, the senior brigadier
in the Hill 10 sector, felt that the 32nd and 34th Brigades could
not join in such an advance as the troops were tired and thirsty, had
suffered heavy casualties and were anyway fully engaged in the
operations to the northeast of Hill 10. This assessment was overly
pessimistic and in fact most of his battalions were relatively intact
and were then still physically capable of a further advance. When
Hill's troops finally reached the Cut area late that morning he in
turn was worried about attacking without support. Time and time
again orders were issued for the attack and then cancelled as the
responsible brigadiers lost their nerve and sought to defer to higher
authority. This only added to the confusion, as Stopford had
injured his knee and decided not to come ashore, but remained on
board the *Jonquil*, almost completely out of touch with what was
going on. It was at this time that the earlier insistence that
Chocolate and Green Hills should not be attacked by the obvious
direct route from the 33rd Brigade flank guard positions south of
the Salt Lake became a crucial complicating factor. But the existing
Turkish defences were inconsequential in the face of the kind of
force that had been landed by the late morning of 7 August, but no
one was prepared to take any risks, and so, while the generals
prevaricated, vital hours slipped away.

At last, after extensive consultation, Hill ordered an attack by three of his battalions round the north of the Salt Lake on Chocolate Hill, but not until shortly after 12.00, and he still received no support from any of the other brigades. Even while the battalions were advancing round the Salt Lake the plan was changed again and the attack was suspended. A larger attack following essentially the same route was to be launched at 17.30 with the participation of all the available battalions of the 11th Division, with a supporting artillery and naval bombardment.

The attack developed slowly and it was dark, around 19.00, before the Irish battalions, who had by now reached the lower slopes of Chocolate and Green Hills, were boosted by the arrival of the 6th Lincolnshire Regiment and 6th Border Regiment, the 33rd Brigade divisional reserve, who had gone directly across the Salt Lake to save time – an option that had always been available as it was dry. With their help the Irish surged up the hill slopes and at last Chocolate Hill was captured – not before daybreak as planned but after nightfall. To make matters worse the night was then spent, not in pushing further on, but in reorganization and consolidation. Indeed, the almost untouched battalions of the 32nd and 34th Brigades, which had finally caught up, were recalled to the beach instead of looking to make essential progress. The importance of W Hills, lying not far to the east, was forgotten by the British local commanders. But Willmer recognized their crucial importance and had conserved his limited manpower to defend them by ordering his troops to fall back when seriously attacked on the relatively irrelevant Chocolate and Green Hills.

To the north the operations directed on Kiretch Tepe had also floundered despite the encouraging start made by the 11th Manchesters. The three battalions of the 10th Division, which were now all that Mahon had under his control, were due to land at the newly located A Beach on the northern horn of Suvla Bay at around 08.00, but they too were badly delayed by confusion in their orders. They eventually commenced landing at around 11.30 and continued throughout the day. When they did get ashore the troops had to face primitive landmines laid by the Turks, and to 2nd Lieutenant Ivone Kirkpatrick, with the 5th Inniskillings, they came as a rude awakening. 'I felt strangely exalted and told my sergeant that I was enjoying myself. Not long after someone trod on a land mine a few yards away. I felt less exalted and rather frightened.'[8]

The first two battalions moved up on to Kiretch Tepe at 14.30. On reaching the 11th Manchesters' positions, they stopped and made no effort to advance further. They also failed to establish any link with the 34th Brigade to the south on the lower slopes. Instead the 5th Inniskilling Fusiliers, who had relieved the exhausted Manchesters, began to dig in.

> There was no one in front of us but the enemy, of whose whereabouts or number we had no knowledge, and we must try to dig in, as the staff were of the opinion that we should be shelled in the morning. That night was one of the most arduous and uncomfortable I have ever spent. The soil was hard and rocky; our only digging implements were entrenching tools. We dug all night and when dawn broke had little to show for our labours. Most of the men had succeeded in digging shallow graves with a parapet of loose earth and flints, but some who had struck rocks had not even that.[9] (2nd Lieutenant Ivone Kirkpatrick)

Instead of digging in they should have been on a forced march to complete the seizure of Kiretch Tepe to the point where it joined the Tekke Tepe Ridge that bounded the plain to the east. It would have been no less tiring, but a lot more productive.

Overall the British troops, once ashore, had behaved like lost sheep, mainly because no one knew where they were or what was happening. Yet it remained true that very few of the battalions had actually been in action other than from harassing artillery fire and the ever present sniping. This last was to prove a real problem.

> In their retirement the Turks had artfully concealed a whole army of snipers in a thousand and one different places. . . . What an effect these pests had on our progress is best described in the casualties which were mostly the victims of some fiendish snipers. Already we had lost the majority of our commissioned officers, to say nothing of a good few NCOs and men. Parties would go out – voluntary – in search of these fiends, but all to no good, for

generally they would return with the majority of them missing –
victims to the snipers.[10] (Private G. A. Handford)

There were not that many snipers in numerical terms but in
operating against inexperienced, tired British troops blundering
across a strange landscape they had a disproportionate effect.

Another problem affecting the fighting ability of the troops was
the shortage of water. The navy had been unable to get ashore all
of the artillery, transport, food and water supplies which formed
part of the second and third echelons. The carefully planned landing
arrangements were disrupted by the stranded lighters, altered
landing places, the failure of the troops ashore to seize the heights
and the consequent continuation of disruptive artillery fire on the
beaches, which delayed the building of essential piers and jetties.
The immediate result of this was the breakdown of water supplies,
and it was too hot to be without water.

A great brass sun beats relentlessly down from a clear sky, and we
soon learn what the term 'thirst' really means. Lips crack and
heads go dizzy in the stifling heat. Infantrymen come begging for
water but our bottles are empty. . . . I notice that it's not tea, beer
or champagne I long for, but just that stuff which the lions
drink.[11] (Bombardier George Dale)

When some water did get ashore there was a breakdown in order
as the thirsty men took matters into their own hands.

Further along the beach we came to a long hosepipe to water in a
boat. Right Ho! Here's a place to get water. But it had been cut
all around so that it was impossible to get anything. Some of the
lads who could swim stripped off and went out to the boat. It
was ruptured just as though it had been pricked all over with a
bayonet. It was letting water out all roads.[12] (Sergeant William
Kirk)

A combination of irresolute leadership, sudden death from an
unseen enemy and thirst conspired to paralyse initiative among the
British battalions, despite the minimal nature of the Turkish
opposition. This was a serious situation but, although detailed
arrangements had been made to ensure communications between

Suvla and Hamilton's GHQ on Imbros, no adequate reports were sent in by Stopford and his divisional commanders. Even the first news that the troops were ashore was passed to Hamilton in somewhat farcical circumstances.

> The Imbros end of the cable was connected to a clock faced dial in the signals tent at GHQ, and from 10PM onwards the face of that dial had been watched with tense anxiety. The first movement of its needle would show that the troops were ashore. Hour after hour the needle remained motionless. Hour after hour no message came from the *Jonquil*; and the Commander-in-Chief, restlessly pacing backwards and forwards from his own tent in search of news, could only be told that none had yet arrived. Suddenly, about two o'clock, the needle began to swing, and, amidst almost unbearable excitement, the telegraphist spelt out its first message from the shore: 'A little shelling at "A" has now ceased. All quite at "B".' That was all. It was not an official report, but a private message from the Suvla operator to his mate. But the tension was broken. The landing had been made good![13] (Lieutenant Colonel Cecil Aspinall)

In the disgraceful absence of any reports from his commanders in the field Hamilton had to make do for the whole of the first night with vague information supplied by this telegraphist. On the morning of 7 August reports at last began to come in describing the successful landing and indicating that the troops were pushing inland. The first report from Stopford himself was received at 12.00 and detailed the position five hours before; it included the pregnant phrase: 'We have been able to advance little beyond the edge of the beach.'[14] As it had been so much delayed in transmission this message was largely ignored and reports from Hammersley's headquarters seemed to indicate that the Turkish opposition was weakening. On 7 August Hamilton and GHQ were the control centre for three simultaneous attacks – the diversion at Helles, the main thrust at Anzac and the Suvla landing. Given the known weakness of the Turkish forces at Suvla, once the 11th and 10th Divisions were safely ashore, 'No one anticipated that the IX Corps would experience any further trouble in pushing forward to its objectives.'[15]

In fact as night fell on 7 August the objectives of the 11th Division had not been attained because they had not been seriously attempted. Willmer and his three heroic Turkish battalions had been successful in holding Suvla Bay against all the hordes of troops that Hamilton had marshalled against them. At the end of the day the Turks were left in command of all the tactically important high ground, and all the British had achieved was the capture of some minor outposts. From this point onwards, as in the battle for Sari Bair, the situation became a race as the British sought to land and deploy their troops faster than the Turks could call up their reserves from Bulair. Already another three Turkish battalions had been ordered up during the actual night of the landing, but at 07.00 on 7 August Marshal Liman von Sanders had accurately assessed the situation and ordered up the 7th and 12th Divisions. Once actually on the road the expected marching time they would require to get from Bulair to Suvla was approximately thirty hours, which meant they would arrive some time late on 8 August or early on the 9th. Everything therefore depended on speed of thought and action by Stopford and his commanders. In these circumstances the pendulum was already swinging against IX Corps.

At daybreak on 8 August the scene was peaceful with only the occasional crack of rifles. Hammersley had consulted his brigadiers early but found them desirous of more rest and reorganization for their troops. Influenced by their views and the lack of any pressure from Stopford, who was still aboard the *Jonquil*, he decided to accede to their requests and issued orders which were essentially defensive in character. Thus at 06.10 he told Sitwell to move some of the battalions still clustered near the Cut area forward towards Sulajik, which lay inland in the centre of the plain, in an attempt to link Kiretch Tepe with Chocolate Hill. This was not the rush to the hills that was needed. On Kiretch Tepe, Mahon was just as cautious as Hammersley, reporting that opposition was stronger than expected and that he needed artillery to make further progress. After receiving the reports of his divisional generals and worried by the lack of artillery and stores which had been landed, Stopford decided that no advance could be made until that evening at the earliest. In his mind the defence of the landing place remained all-important and the attitude which underlay his changes to Hamilton's original instructions was becoming clear.

On Imbros Hamilton, although distracted by the assault on Sari Bair, had begun to recognize that with Stopford no news was not good news. At daybreak Aspinall, now one of his most senior staff officers, was sent post-haste to Suvla to report directly to Hamilton on what exactly was going on. Unfortunately the destroyer specially put aside for such a contingency developed a boiler problem and Aspinall had to endure a slow trawler trip before arriving at 11.30.

Back at Suvla, after the usual delays, the 32nd Brigade began to move forward towards Sulajik. They encountered no opposition, but the troops were dead beat and the sheer length of the line they were trying to establish across the plain caused terrible disruption. Inevitably the brigade fragmented as the battalions were pulled to the left and right. Its one success was that the attached divisional pioneer battalion, the 6th East Yorkshires, in their efforts to link up with Chocolate Hill succeeded in taking up a position on the unoccupied but tactically important Scimitar Hill, to the immediate northeast of Chocolate Hill. There they entrenched as they came under fire from W Hills at about 11.00. The other three battalions of the brigade were widely separated and straggled back across the plain through Sulajik towards Hill 10.

At 11.00 Stopford was reminded by an increasingly frantic GHQ as to the importance of grasping a firm foothold on Tekke Tepe, but the orders he issued in response at 11.30 were pathetically inadequate. True, they pointed out the importance of seizing the high ground, but then he undermined the resolution of his junior commanders by defining their excuses in advance. 'If you find the ground lightly held by the enemy push on. But in view of want of adequate artillery support I do not want you to attack an entrenched position held in strength.'[16] This was despite the fact that by now he had been repeatedly told of the weak state of the local Turkish defences and was aware that, although reserves would be on their way from Bulair, air reconnaissance indicated that the plain behind Tekke Tepe remained empty and hence that they had not yet arrived. He informed GHQ of this order shortly afterwards at 12.00.

When Hamilton received this message he saw that the writing was on the wall and, to his credit, the devoted non-interventionist was shaken into action, perhaps remembering the missed opportunities at Y Beach on 25 April. But his destroyer was still out of action and only after a five-hour wait could he get transport aboard HMS *Triad*; he did not reach Suvla until after 18.00. In the meantime Stopford's order had the obvious effect as all his divisional and brigade officers not unnaturally decided that *they* could not possibly advance. This included the 32nd Brigade, who stopped in their tracks for the night. Trepidation breeds trepidation, and by now the whole Suvla plan was stillborn.

From the crest of Kiretch Tepe the results of this inactivity could be clearly seen as the men looked down on Suvla Plain.

On Sunday everything was absolute peace and quiet, the Turks had in fact withdrawn all their guns, there was no shelling and very little rifle fire to be heard. Looking down you could only see a mob of our chaps all round the beaches trying to get water. We were fortunate in our position because the destroyer *Grampus* cut one of its own water tanks loose and floated it ashore and supplied us from that. Of course the quantity of water was very little, you got about a pint a day which with the temperatures verging on a hundred isn't very much. . . . We all knew that something very wrong was happening, that we ought to be advancing not just sitting there.[17] (2nd Lieutenant Terence Verschoyle)

Aspinall finally reached Suvla at around 12.00, and his initial impression was reassuring: 'Convinced by the holiday appearance of the place that the hills had at last been captured. The whole bay was at peace, and its shores fringed with bathers.'[18] He was accompanied by Lieutenant Colonel Maurice Hankey, now the Secretary of the Dardanelles Committee, who had been sent out from London to report on the build-up at Gallipoli:

A peaceful scene greeted us. Hardly any shells. No Turks. Very occasional musketry. Bathing parties round the shore. An entire absence of the expected bustle of a great disembarkation. There seemed to be no realization of the overwhelming necessity for a rapid offensive, or the tremendous issues depending on the next few hours.[19] (Lieutenant Colonel Maurice Hankey)

As Aspinall and Hankey walked inland, their initial optimism at the casual nature of the scene by the beaches was soon tempered by the realization that the troops had not reached the heights. After a pessimistic briefing from Hammersley, Aspinall rushed off to the *Jonquil* to meet Stopford, who still had not come ashore due to the injury to his knee that was paining him considerably. Their conversation was barbed. '"Well Aspinall", he said, "the men have done splendidly and have been magnificent." "But they haven't reached the hills, Sir", said Aspinall. "No," replied the General, "but they are ashore."'[20] Aspinall pleaded with Stopford for an immediate advance before the Turkish reinforcements arrived from Bulair. But Stopford, an old man trapped by his age, infirmity, inexperience and dulled perspicacity, only repeated in essence his 12.00 report to GHQ. Aspinall by now was desperate and he moved to the naval flagship to send an explicit message to Hamilton that their dream was fading. 'Just been ashore, where I found all quiet. No rifle fire, no artillery fire, and apparently no Turks. IX Corps resting. Feel confident that golden opportunities are being lost and look upon the situation as serious.'[21] By this time Hamilton was already on his way.

Perhaps prompted by Aspinall's obvious desperation, Stopford now at last came ashore and visited the 11th Division Headquarters, where he was briefed as to the state of his available troops. This was an opportunity for Stopford to offer the decisive leadership that was required.

About 4 p.m. General Stopford arrived at DHQ. I was called to him, and I gave him the same account . . . marking the positions of the various battalions on his map, and telling him that the various commanders I had seen were confident that an attack was feasible. He seemed very pleased and said that we must attack at once, lest the Turks forestalled us. The words he finished up with I remember; he said, 'It may cause us casualties, but not one tenth of those we shall suffer if we delay.' He seemed perfectly confident, and said General Hammersley was to go and see him on the *Jonquil* directly he returned to camp.[22] (Captain J. F. S. D. Coleridge)

Hammersley was actually absent, arranging the assault of W Hills by the 33rd Brigade for the morning of 9 August, and when he learned of this Stopford gave his divisional commander a free hand as to the time of launching the assault. He then returned to the *Jonquil*, where he received a message which Hamilton had despatched before leaving Imbros. This informed him that all available intelligence, mainly from air reconnaissance, was that the Turks were still conspicuous by their absence on the Tekke Tepe Ridge and promising him further reinforcements from the 53rd Division under Major General the Hon. John Lindley. At last, at 17.30, Stopford therefore ordered a simultaneous advance to seize the heights all around Suvla Bay, but he delegated the time of attack to Hammersley, who, by now, had arranged for the 33rd Brigade to attack W Hills on the morning of 9 August. Hammersley issued an additional order so that while the 33rd Brigade was to attack W Hills, the 32nd Brigade was to advance against the Anafarta Spur of the Tekke Tepe Ridge, and the village of Anafarta Sagir, which lay beyond it. Meanwhile Mahon, who by now had five battalions under his control, was to capture all of Kiretch Tepe and the Tekke Tepe Ridge. But the time of the attack was not brought forward and so no major attack was to be attempted on 8 August despite all the troops available.

At 18.00 Hamilton arrived and held a conference with Stopford and Aspinall at 18.30 aboard the *Jonquil*. To him the Tekke Tepe heights were now the absolute priority as they would be the first point of contact with the Turkish reserves marching from Bulair. If the British could just establish and secure a hold on these heights before the Turks arrived then the Anafarta Spur and W Hills could be enfiladed and rolled up. Stopford told Hamilton that after another night's rest the 11th Division would be ready to attack at dawn on 9 April, but Hamilton was beside himself with impatience and frustration and explained that 'Next day might be too late.'[23] In despair he effectively took over local command and he rushed ashore aboard a picket boat to see if Hammersley could not bring forward the time of the attack, leaving Stopford behind complaining of his bad knee.

On Hamilton's arrival at Hammersley's headquarters a sharp exchange of views ensued as Hammersley insisted that his troops could not advance before 08.00 on 9 August and his superior told him that it was not optional – Tekke Tepe at least must be captured before daylight. Still the excuses came: all the battalions were scattered; no reconnaissance had been made; difficult terrain; lack of time to get the orders distributed. Hamilton remained adamant – at least one battalion had to be got to the top of Tekke Tepe and no excuses would be accepted. At last Hammersley conceded that the 32nd Brigade, which he believed to be concentrated in the Sulajik area after their advance earlier that day, might be able to advance that night. Hamilton leapt at the chance and verbal orders were sent to extend their objectives from the Anafarta Spur to as far north as Kavak Tepe on the Tekke Tepe hills. More importantly they were no longer to wait until 9 August but were to attack during the night to ensure the presence of at least one battalion on the ridge at dawn. A much relieved but still tense Hamilton then returned to De Robeck's flagship.

Despite Hamilton's best intentions the chain of events that ensued from his intervention was catastrophic. The 32nd Brigade was not, in fact, concentrated at Sulajik, but spread out right across the Suvla Plain. The 9th West Yorks were actually 1,000 yards in front of Sulajik, while the 6th East Yorks were holding vital positions on Scimitar Hill. Patrols from the latter battalion had actually reported that the Tekke Tepe hills were held only by sentries and if these battalions had just moved forward the hills perhaps could have been secured. The vision of success is clear with hindsight, but on the night in question all was confusion. At 32nd Brigade Headquarters nobody knew where the battalions were, and none of the patrol reports had been received. As a result an order was issued to concentrate the brigade at Sulajik by 22.30 prior to the attack. For the two rear battalions this was of little consequence – one was there already, the other merely moved forwards from the Hill 10 area. Unfortunately the acting brigadier, Lieutenant Colonel J. O'B. Minogue, decided to wait until the whole brigade was concentrated before anyone moved off. Hours were spent by the messengers tracking down the two battalions and once located more valuable time was wasted as they withdrew from their valuable forward positions to march *back* to Sulajik. It was not until 02.00 on 9 August that the 6th East Yorks arrived at the Sulajik rendezvous. Still the brigade waited for 9th West Yorkshires, until their absence was finally accepted. After five-and-a-half hours of utterly futile waiting, at 03.30 the order to advance was finally given.

By now the hapless 6th East Yorkshires were exhausted by their efforts and in no fit state to do anything other than sleep. Eventually at around 04.00 just one company set off; the rest were to follow as soon as possible. Not for the first time it was too little too late.

> The rampart of hills to the east of us was black against the chill, pale sky as we moved out across the grey flats that led to the foot of Tekke Tepe, towering up to nearly 1,000 feet ahead of us. And we came under fire from our right flank almost from the very start. The foot-hills of the range were rough with boulders, and deep cut by rocky ravines. As we moved on and on, up and up, men got lost in the prickly scrub oak, holly they called it, and it became increasingly difficult to maintain any sort of formation. But the enemy's fire grew in volume as we mounted, poured into us at ever decreasing range from the right and from the front. . . . Those who were hit stayed where they fell, and those who were whole climbed on. The only complaint heard upon that hillside was that no enemy could be seen to fire upon. . . . About thirty of us reached the top of the hill, perhaps a few more. And when there were about twenty left we turned and went down again. We had reached the highest point and the furthest point that British forces from Suvla Bay were destined to reach. But we naturally knew nothing of that.[24] (Lieutenant John Still)

It was now well after dawn and suddenly the Turkish reserves came crashing over the hill. The small party fell back under fire but were cut off and the few survivors were taken prisoner.

The Turks were the men of the 12th Division, who with the 7th Division had arrived from Bulair late on 8 August. Significantly Liman von Sanders had faced the same sort of vacillation from his divisional commanders as Hamilton, but as we have seen he showed a different kind of determination by immediately sacking the man responsible. While the 7th Division marched on to Sari Bair to counter the breakout from Anzac, the 12th Division arrived on the Suvla front just in time. Yet although the race for the top of Tekke Tepe had been lost by only half an hour this was illusory as the few disordered battalions of the 32nd Brigade would have been no match for the Turks on their arrival in strength early on 9 August. The hills should have been occupied before noon on the 8th to allow time for proper defensive positions to be established and held by at least one brigade with whatever artillery support could be arranged. Hammersley should have let his troops rest on the hills, not on the plains.

As the other battalions of the 32nd Brigade tried to move forward they came under heavy fire and when the Turks pressed home their attack actually surrendered ground. The emergency caused a rude awakening for 'A' Battery, 59th Brigade, RFA, who were by then in position on the back slopes of Chocolate Hill.

> Right at dawn the Sergeant Major's cattle calling bellow drowns the echoes of our last combined snore. '"A" Battery – Action!' (Here where am I? What goes on?) As we stumble to our 18 pounder, enthusiasm at a low ebb, mutterings predictable. Sgt Styles takes up the theme. '*Move*, you there!' (Gosh, isn't this our third night with little or even no sleep?) Aiming point, angles, range and fuse are coming along, and Hubert and I get busy on the gun seats. . . . As Hubert slams the breach on a round the order comes for '*Gunfire*' (As fast as possible with due regard for accuracy.) Never before can the rural ambience of that leafy nullah have known such a din as breaks out now. BANG! BANG! Often a double or treble blast. Sleep forgotten now the sweating gunners are happy. We're doing our stuff – the end result of all that gun drill! This lasts for maybe two hours – time just stood still. The end comes when each No 1 reports: 'No more ammo, Sir.'[25] (Bombardier George Dale)

And so their guns fell silent until more ammunition limbers could be brought across from the landing beaches.

The Turkish advance opened up a gap in the British line north of Sulajik which was precipitately filled by a combination of battalions from the 34th Brigade and the 159th Brigade of the 53rd Welsh Division, which had landed overnight. The 1/4th Cheshires were one of the battalions that set off on the march across the open Salt Lake plain towards Anafarta Sagir, though they themselves had no idea where they were heading.

> We set off in artillery formation in echelon but eventually we had to go in extended order, one long line. Across Salt Lake an arid terrible place. We'd gone about four hundred yards when we heard a yell – 'So and so's been hit.' 'Is he alright?' 'Yes they've got him, sent him down.' He was a tram conductor. 'Next stop, Tranmere Rovers!' . . . It was sandy, very rough sand, not easy to march on, horrible, about three or four inches deep. . . . We were very tired because we hadn't had much sleep in the last forty eight hours. We had a very heavy pack, it was dreadfully heavy with the ammunition, too heavy altogether. It was a hundred and two in the shade, the beating sun it was terrible.[26] (Corporal Ernest Haire)

As the reinforcements arrived, the Turkish attack subsided – they had gained their prime objective of the Tekke Tepe heights and were content to look down on the British line as it evolved below them on the plain.

The endless delays that had afflicted the 32nd Brigade in their attack planned for the evening of 8 August meant that they were not much further ahead in their attack than the 33rd Brigade, who were to attack W Hills and Anafarta Spur at dawn on 9 August in accordance with Hammersley's original plan. At 02.00 the troops moved off from their positions in reserve at Lala Baba, but as they neared Scimitar Hill so recently vacated by the ill-fated 6th East Yorks they came under heavy fire. The Turks had reoccupied the hill and their reserves were seen streaming up across Anafarta Spur. They were determined to secure their possession of Scimitar Hill and it became the focus of a chaotic battle which raged to and fro as both sides exchanged local superiority. At around 05.00 two of the 10th Division's battalions were called forward but still the Turks pressed hard. Eventually at 09.00 two battalions of the 160th Brigade, 53rd Division were sent in. Corporal Arthur

Hemsley was with the 2/4th Queen's Royal West Surreys as they moved off towards Chocolate Hill, where they were ordered to assault Scimitar Hill:

> When the daylight came we fell in and were ordered to pick up picks and shovels and one small man found himself with a five foot crow bar to carry. We'd only gone a short distance, starting on our journey across the Salt Lake, when a staff officer dashed up and said, 'You can drop those. You're here to fight not to dig.' So we all put the stuff down and carried on marching. We formed clear long lines, ten feet apart crossing the Salt Lake with our Colonel in the front line. It was a large plain of sand, nothing more, the other side of which the land rose, Chocolate Hill. On our way across I saw the Colonel was halted by a messenger running across with a message to him, he handed it over and fell flat on his face, dead on the ground, which was our first casualty. The whole of the time while we were going across there, not noticing anything wrong, there was a hissing sound of the bullets from the Turkish side falling amongst us, without us even knowing what the noise meant. Then we arrived at the first trench that had been already captured by the troops before us. I had my first sight of dead bodies lying around. We followed them up through the hill and we were getting fewer and fewer in numbers and those in front were beginning to drop back. Fortunately our second in command came with his revolver in his hand and said: 'Make a halt here, dig in wherever you are.' Despite digging down we were losing men and they were all being shot in the head and it dawned upon me that this fire was coming from above. So I told my machine-gunner, Private Rabitts, to turn his gun on to the trees. He swept the trees all round us with machine-gun fire and the Turkish snipers fell down from the trees almost like ripe fruit. From then on we had less trouble with this sniping. Unfortunately Rabitts having done this good work set his gun up, stood up for a moment and was shot through the head. That was the end of him, pity about that.[27]
> (Corporal Arthur Hemsley)

As the day wore on the Turkish shelling increased and the tinder-dry scrub on top of Scimitar Hill caught fire under the bursting shells. Gradually the British troops were forced back and the hill was lost at around noon.

To the south the 9th Sherwood Foresters had advanced into the Azmak Dere, which ran parallel to W Hills, in an attempt to link the new position at Suvla to the enlarged Anzac area, which now reached as far as Damakjelik Bair. The battalion ran into heavy opposition in an area which had been empty of Turks the day before. Eventually a line was established from Azmak Dere to the area round Kazlar Chair, but contact was not made with the British troops on Damakjelik Bair. The 1/1st Herefords of the 158th Brigade, 53rd Division were sent forward to assist. For newly landed officers straight off the boats it was a nightmare. Their colonel left the divisional headquarters in a state of total bemusement.

> I do not know whether I was singularly stupid or most unfortu-
> nate, but I had never been told anything about the Anzac position,
> and troops on the left of that position. This was most regrettable,
> as I know now that the Herefords were the extreme right of the
> IX Corps, and should have been in touch, if possible, with Anzac.
> I can say with certainty that, bar the vague position of the
> Sherwood Foresters, no information as to operations and plan of
> action was mentioned, and no information was given as to what
> our side was trying to do.[28] (Lieutenant Colonel A. Drage)

The battalion moved off into the chaos of battle.

> It became increasingly difficult, owing to the dust raised by the
> shrapnel (enemy shrapnel) and the nature of the terrain, to see
> anything to the flank, as we approached the Azmak Dere . . . a
> dried up watercourse with steep little banks about two foot
> high. . . . We pushed on and eventually reached a low hill covered
> with scrub to our immediate front. . . . The left flank company
> commanders (Rogers and Capel) came to me for orders. I was in
> a quandary and confess I did not know what to do. I had lost
> touch with my two leading companies. In front was a jungle with,
> according to the map, an extremely difficult line of country at the
> back of it. No knowledge of the enemy's position and with a very
> vague idea of our troops on the left. It also seemed to me that I
> was over 1,000 yards in front of where I was told I might get in

touch with our own side. . . . I decided to withdraw the supports to the Azmak Dere, whose left bank provided two feet of cover, in places, and a fairly open field of fire.[29] (Lieutenant Colonel A. Drage)

The difficulties of exercising command without information on which to base a rational decision are manifest in this account. Before his decision could be acted upon, a shell burst over the battalion headquarters, and Drage and several others were wounded. He struggled on, but as they reached the Azmak Dere a staff officer arrived and ordered the battalion back all the way to Lala Baba. Their foray had achieved nothing – except casualties and the loss of an apparently intelligent and perceptive commanding officer. Next morning they were ordered back to join the 9th Sherwood Foresters. Useless marching and counter-marching all under the fire of Turkish guns.

Over on Kiretch Tepe the 10th Division attacked at 07.30, supported by naval gunnery from HMS *Foxhound* and then HMS *Grampus*. The initially slight resistance began to stiffen as they approached the highest point on the ridge. But the total opposition still consisted of only three companies of Turkish Gendarmerie – about 350 men, who had been there since the original landing. At 13.30 what was to become Jephson's Post was captured by the 6th Royal Munster Fusiliers but the combined effects of heat, thirst and exhaustion meant that they got no further. On the lower southern slopes of Kiretch Tepe two battalions reached as far as Kidney Hill, but again the identical afflictions led to a loss of resolve and they fell back to their original positions.

By nightfall on 9 August almost nothing had been achieved and most of the IX Corps was in serious disarray. Since 6 August the 10th and 11th Divisions had suffered severe casualties and had become hopelessly intermingled. The newly landed 53rd Division had been thrown into battle piecemeal all along the British line. The chaos and confusion of orders and counter-orders, lack of maps or briefing and the linked curses of heat, thirst and exhaustion had visibly reduced morale throughout all three divisions. Private Ernest Lye rejoined the 8th Duke of Wellingtons after missing the landing through illness and was shocked at the change in the men.

We could see them in the distance, skirting the Salt Lake and, even though we were so far away, they appeared to be almost too tired to drag one foot after another. It was when we came up with them and could see their faces that we got the biggest shock of our lives. What terrible thing had put that indescribable look of horror in their eyes? They looked haunted with a memory of the sight of hell! With their faces dirty and unkempt, and with their clothes torn and ragged, I thought of them four days ago as they passed me as I stood by the doctor's tent, with their laughing faces and tin triangles. I looked for some of the familiar faces – Ernie Shaw, yes! He's there. Tommy Knott, no. 'Where's Tommy Knott?' 'Killed.' 'Herbert Butterworth, and his pal Frank Boyes; have you seen them?' 'Frank was wounded and Butterworth went back to help him, and we haven't seen them since.' 'Where's Paddy Whitehouse?' 'Oh! Over there with Lance Corporal Hullah' and so on. There were twenty left of our platoon of sixty-one. Only two officers left in the whole battalion. . . . We had a roll call on the slope of York Hill and the sight will be pictured forever in my mind. I thought of a picture I had once seen, giving a similar incident in the Crimean War. The picture was good, but the artist couldn't put into the picture the wild haunted look I saw in the eyes of my comrades as they answered their names, nor could he put on canvas the heart broken sobs as some man's name was called and not answered.[30] (Private Ernest Lye)

The ninth of August marked the end of any real chance of success at Suvla. Any further attacks can be seen as futile, as the pattern of events was by then fully established. After spending the night aboard the *Triad* Hamilton watched the course of the day's events in despair. He was now quickly losing patience with Stopford, whom he found ashore, having finally landed his IX Corps Headquarters.

[Stopford was] busy with part of a Field Company of Engineers supervising the building of some splinter-proof Headquarters huts for himself and Staff. He was absorbed in the work and said that it would be well to make a thorough good job of the dugouts as we should probably be here for a very long time. I retorted, 'Devil a bit; within a day or two you will be picking the best of the Anafarta houses for your billet.'[31] (General Sir Ian Hamilton)

Yet still Hamilton did not grasp the nettle, as Liman von Sanders had done, and dismiss him or even take over command himself. Instead he meekly acquiesced in Stopford's continued paralysis over operations and, thoroughly depressed, rushed off at 12.00 for a conference that afternoon with his Anzac commanders, who were also staring defeat in the face on Sari Bair.

Now that the advantage of surprise had been thrown away the imperative for the IX Corps was a thorough reorganization to disentangle the battalions, brigades and divisions from each other. This would enable staff to issue orders with some idea of where the units actually were on the ground. The supply systems also needed to be given some chance of getting food and water up to the troops. In this sort of situation Stopford was in his element and he fully intended to spend 10 August on such matters prior to any further offensive action. However, at 17.00 on 9 August he received a further prodding from Major General Braithwaite at GHQ on Imbros to launch a further attack with six to eight battalions on W Hills and Anafarta Spur next day. This he took as an order and entrusted the task to Lindley and his 53rd Division.

Lindley had little idea of exactly where his troops were located but issued orders for the attack to commence at 06.00 on 10 August led by what could be found of the 159th Brigade in an assault on Scimitar Hill, while the 158th Brigade was to follow through on to Anafarta Spur. The attack was a terrible failure. The experiences of the men of the 1/4th Cheshires were fairly typical.

> My company commander said: 'Alright Boys we'd better go' and we made a bee-line. It was heavy going and with the rifle and bayonet fixed you were sort of half plunging and stumbling along. We couldn't run, we were too handicapped, the ground wasn't good and we were very, very tired. Only walking, just walking trying to get further on. We had no cover we just had to face the enemy. We could see the flashes of the rifles and the machine-guns. They opened several machine-guns on us and that did the damage. We lay down we were too physically tired to go any

further. We finally slid back – we went back where we started from.[32] (Corporal Ernest Haire)

Just three hours later the battalion was ordered to renew the attack.
We thought it was ridiculous to try again. One fellow said, 'I'm too bloody tired to go.' We had to try to struggle. It was a fruitless thing. We were obeying orders – we had to. I was no more frightened than any others, we were all afraid. You must be when you're facing machine-guns. We did try and make the attack not because we wanted to but because it was our job as soldiers. We were met by withering machine-gun fire. I was hit and fell. They had to retire again and I was there between the lines in the blazing sun, I was hit at midday. I put my field dressing on, I knew it hadn't hit the artery or otherwise I would have died – blood would have been pumping out – and it missed the bone. I cut the khaki drill off and my knee was exposed and it went black with the sun. What I was afraid of was that the Turks had a habit of bayoneting the wounded and I was scared stiff. One of my old Sunday School friends, Ernest Galloway, spotted me. He'd been searching the place. I was very weak, I'd been out eight hours. I said: 'It's through here.' He said: 'I'll stand you up.' Then I fainted and he carried me three hundred yards, and I was ten to eleven stone, until he found a stretcher. He put me on it and said: 'Bye Bye lad. I'll see you again sometime.' He was killed.[33] (Corporal Ernest Haire)

Captain Kenneth Taylor was with the 1/5th Royal Welch Fusiliers of the 158th Brigade as they pushed through the remnants of the 159th Brigade to try and take Scimitar Hill:
The first 50 yards was a hell for leather race, no cover, and every chance of striking eternity. We were getting a bit tired by now, and the Turk was having the best shooting he could wish for, unworried by fire from us as we could see nothing to shoot at. . . .
That 50 yards accounted for a good many, and my only recollection of it was the splendid way the men behaved. And so we arrived at the bank, and had another breather. Evidently there had been some dirty work here, as there were some ghastly sights

of charred bodies. It looked as though they had been wounded and overtaken by a scrub fire. I was out of touch now with anyone on my left, although I tried hard to find them. Shortly the order came down to fix bayonets, and get ready. . . . Soon the order came to charge. The density of the oak scrub absolutely ruined all chance of a decent charge, as we had to follow goat tracks and watercourses in single file to get through. Either the Turk could not see us or he was preparing to retire, as few bullets came over and we had little difficulty in getting to the top, and to my immediate front everything was quiet. But being split up into small parties by the scrub caused more confusion because so many parts of line were out of touch and it was impossible to tell how things were going on in other spots.[34] (Captain Kenneth Taylor)

The position proved untenable and the attacks were eventually abandoned, having achieved nothing but a hefty casualty list, and another division had been ruined during its first two days of action.

As the 53rd Division fought and died at Suvla on 10 August, the 54th Division were just landing. It represented the last immediately available reserve and GHQ had intended to deploy it as a complete division for a decisive blow in an effort to capture Tekke Tepe. Unfortunately despite these good intentions the first six battalions to land were used by Stopford to plug the gap which had opened between units of the 10th Division on Kiretch Tepe Ridge and the various units spread across the plain. The process of piecemeal deployment was soon once again under way as the newly landed battalions found themselves wandering about the plain to no obvious purpose. Among them was John Harding, a future Field Marshal, but then just a 2nd Lieutenant machine-gun officer with the 1/11th London Regiment:

We were told that we were going to do a night attack. We set off in the dark and we marched in column halting at frequent intervals. Whenever we halted we were ordered to put out a sentry on each flank. We seemed to go about a 100 yards at a time and then halt – my recollection is that it was a very, very slow process. We were being guided, so we had no idea where we were going. We went on, I don't know how long and then we were told to halt and lie down. So I, with my platoon, lay down in a little dip in the ground amongst the hills, and there was an awful stench and we'd no idea where it came from. However we got to sleep but when we woke up in the morning at daylight we saw that we'd been lying alongside four or five dead Turks. Well then we were told to go back to the beach.[35] (2nd Lieutenant John Harding)

All told, 10 August was a disaster at Suvla. The General Staff at GHQ was unaware of the scale of the defeat and considered that, although the Turks had a firm grip on Tekke Tepe, it was not as yet unshakeable as their reserves must have been stretched by the full-scale assaults and diversions launched along the Gallipoli Peninsula. This was an extremely sanguine view, as the Turks really did possess all the battle advantages they could wish for. As a result of this misplaced optimism GHQ issued an order early on 11 August urging Stopford to use the 54th Division in another attempt on Tekke Tepe at dawn on 12 August with the 10th, 11th and 53rd Divisions relegated to a purely supporting role. Stopford basically ignored this order and continued his reorganization of his scattered, demoralized units throughout 11 August, and once more Hamilton made the journey to Suvla to put heart into Stopford.

Recriminations over the failure of the Suvla plan had by now fully overtaken Stopford as he sought to blame everyone and everything but his own lack of resolve. His basic premise was that the troops he had been given to carry out the plan were no good and had been ill suited for the task in hand. He put this to Hamilton at their interview on 11 August.

He tells me straight and without any beating about the bush: 'I am sure they' (the Territorials) 'would not secure the hills with any amount of guns, water and ammunition assuming ordinary opposition, as the attacking spirit was absent; chiefly owing to the want of leadership by the Officers.' . . . He goes on then to ask me in so many words, not to try any attack with the 54th Division but to stick them into trenches.[36] (General Sir Ian Hamilton)

Hamilton could not accept this assessment, but, as no preparations for an attack had been made, he was forced to accept another day's delay – he now insisted that 54th Division must assault Tekke Tepe at dawn on 13 August. In fact the poles of generalship had now been reversed. Stopford was now almost certainly right in his view that such an assault could not and would not succeed. But, because he had cried wolf too often, he had lost Hamilton's confidence and his opinion was no longer respected or heeded.

Next day, on 12 August, the situation was still chaotic. The Turks were not much in evidence except for continuous sniping, which drained lives and morale from the battalions as a dripping tap empties a cistern. As usual officers and NCOs were the most prized targets and many units had begun to take precautions.

> We found that our officers were being shot off too quickly as against the men. The first thing we did was everybody dropped all badges of rank, stripes were taken off your arms and so on. With indelible pencil on your shoulder you had sergeants stripes, officers diamonds. They could be seen only when you were a few feet away. That was all that was allowed.[37] (Corporal Arthur Hemsley)

To prepare the way for the main attack by the 54th Division on 13 August, it was decided, at a IX Corps conference on the morning of 12 August, that the 163rd Brigade should push forward that same afternoon to the foothills of Tekke Tepe, clearing away pockets of snipers, to establish a secure line from which the main assault could be launched next day. If, however, this advance brigade met strong opposition, the whole idea of a dawn attack on 13 August would be abandoned.

The attack began at 16.45 on 12 August with, from left to right, the 1/5th Suffolks, 1/8th Hampshires and 1/5th Norfolks advancing in line, while the 1/4th Norfolks moved forward in support on the left. They advanced across rough ground which had not been reconnoitred, with no maps, no clear idea of the objectives or where the Turks were hidden. Private Claude Dawson, who was with the 1/5th Suffolk Regiment, summed up the situation: 'Then we had orders about four o'clock of the afternoon on the 12th of August. It's very appropriate because on the 12th August the grouse shooting begins and we were the grouse.'[38] Sergeant Tom Williamson described his advance with the 1/5th Norfolks:

We all had the orders sent to march to this particular area of plain. Open, rough, undulating country. We all extended across our particular front, our 1,000 strong Norfolks. The only instructions I remember were to advance to the enemy line and dig in for the night. The enemy line wasn't really known, they just pointed forward. If your fellow comrade fell wounded you were not to stop to assist him as you'd disrupt the line of attack. Those who were wounded had to rely on their own abilities. My duty was to just keep in order with my section and my platoon officer, advancing in sectional rushes with the others. We were annihilated, there's no doubt. . . . We lost our leaders early on. I can see them now walking, commanding the approach, smoking, so brave – a fallacy – they were hallmarked by the snipers, we lost our leaders, it demoralised the whole battalion. . . . We were ordered to fix bayonets, another fallacy because the sun glittering exposed our position immediately. It literally became a hell, fire from all angles, as we moved nearer the Turkish positions the big guns were firing from the hills. We arrived at a place where we could see the Turks. My officer went over this ridge, he fell down wounded. We had been told not to look after anybody but I rushed to his side. I took off my field dressing and his, put one on the front, one on the back. He had a wound an inch and a half wide. He said: 'Never mind Tom' he called me by my Christian name, 'You take the platoon over, what remains, never mind about me.' I could have stayed with him I think, I could have got a VC if I'd rescued him. But I had to do what he told me.[39]
(Sergeant Tom Williamson)

These men from the East Anglian battalions were under fire for the first time and their inexperience showed.

We endeavoured to advance in extended order. As we advanced I could hear what I thought were birds whistling overhead and I soon found out they were bullets. The Turks were ready for us. We just knew that we had to get on the best way we could. I don't think you had any time for nervousness. You knew there was a job to be done and you'd just got to make the best of it.[40]
(Private Reginald Johnson)

Casualties grew, and in the thick scrub units began to fall apart as they lost all cohesion. One part of the 1/5th Norfolks rushed on only to be cut off.

> I went on till we found ourselves through the Turkish lines, only just through, but behind the Turkish lines. I fired at Turks, I saw some drop, I did really. . . . But the scrub was on fire, only small fires but you couldn't lie down in the heat. Then I was shot through the right arm. I was firing and it came into the muscle just below the shoulder. I knew I had to get back. I had a section of men but they all lay still, killed. They had surrounded us. Most of the battalion went through the Turkish lines unknowingly. We were intermixed with the Turks, they were scattered around us. My only hope was to get back, I was finished as far as Gallipoli was concerned. It was then that I noticed the Sandringham Platoon, part of E Company, about 40 men, under Sergeant Aymers sheltering in a barn. The scrub was on fire, the snipers, more or less surrounded by the Turks, a hopeless position for them to be in. They were undoubtedly killed or wounded where they were. I can picture him now rallying his men.[41] (Sergeant Tom Williamson)

They had gone forward as a brigade and come back as a crippled unit with nothing achieved. Even before the attack had failed Hamilton had changed his mind and accepted Stopford's opinion that the chances of taking Tekke Tepe were remote in the extreme. The dawn attack for 13 August was cancelled and further attacks were to be launched only after more reorganization.

During 12 August the rest of the IX Corps continued its long process of reassembling its constituent parts into some semblance of military order. Nevertheless the reports reaching Hamilton from Suvla got worse and worse. The failure of the 163rd Brigade would delay the concentration of the 54th Division for any further attack until 15 August. Of even more concern were reports from Lindley asserting that his 53rd Division was no longer in a fit state to stay in the line after its horrific experience on 10 August. Hamilton was forced once more back to IX Corps Headquarters from Imbros to see exactly what was going on. Stopford was convinced that the 53rd Division was finished as a fighting unit and that the 54th

Division was incapable of attacking. In fact from a review of the available evidence it appears that the units were perfectly capable of further fighting if properly led and briefed. Liman von Sanders had acted at once when similar timidity was shown among his generals. But, once again, Hamilton acquiesced, and at 24.00 on 13 August he ordered Stopford to continue the reorganization and to consolidate his current line in positions as far forward as possible.

Perversely Stopford reacted to this essentially defensive order by at last ordering Mahon and the now reunited elements of the 10th Division to attack along Kiretch Tepe, with the aim of capturing the summit and the adjacent Kidney Hill spur. Perhaps Hamilton should have ordered Stopford to retreat on 7 August! More characteristically these orders were only issued a day later, at 08.40 on 15 August, for an attack that same afternoon. The plan was for the 30th and 31st Brigades to advance along the ridge with a supporting attack by the 162nd Brigade of the 54th Division on Kidney Hill. The attack commenced at 13.00. On the left the 7th Munsters moved forward, slowly at first as they attempted to avoid casualties, but after 18.00 they made a bayonet charge which swept the Turks back. At the same time the 6th Munsters and 6th Dublin Fusiliers charged along the crest of Kiretch Tepe until the highest point was captured. On the right 2nd Lieutenant Terence Verschoyle was advancing with the 5th Inniskillings towards a small knoll on the southern slope of the ridge just 400 yards short of Kidney Hill.

> The brigadier knew nothing about it until about half an hour beforehand and the CO and company commanders had about quarter of an hours notice. We told the chaps nothing, 'Come on chaps we've got to go.' The only plan was that two companies went forward and two companies came up behind in support. We started off. There were no tactics other than advancing straight ahead. The thick scrub absolutely prohibited any sort of supporting fire because nobody could see what was happening on each side. It was a sort of individual action. Before very long I saw my company commander sitting on a rock shot through the chest being dressed by his groom, waving us on. We went on. An absolute hail of bullets going on all the time, not shelling. . . . Our second in command was a marvellous old dugout and at the beginning of the action he was espied standing up, every button

281

polished and bright, all his leather work gleaming, looking out towards the front and saying: 'Turks, Turks I don't see any Turks,' bullets falling all about him all the time. . . . There was a lot of scrub about but there was a large bare patch which we had to cross. There was no avoiding it. Bullets all striking down and setting up little spurts of sand; it wasn't very encouraging. Still, some of us got through. The whole action was over in little more than an hour, by which time we'd had nearly 400 casualties. We realized fairly soon from the few people left that it was not a success. We did get the Turks to clear out of the trenches we were supposed to be attacking – I remember having a pot shot at one or two Turks myself – but we were about finished then. We just got stuck there. You couldn't see anybody else, that was the trouble, the tall thick scrub, you didn't know where anybody was. It was left to the individual to decide what he could do. All the officers practically had been hit and a lot of the NCOs too. I got hit by a genuine shrapnel bullet in the backside whilst lying behind a bush, not a very noble portion of the body to be hit in but there you were. When it got dark I went back to report what was happening, doling out morphia to one or two people who were *in extremis*. Got back eventually to the starting line where I reported to the brigadier. Our sister battalion had by then come up in support and they spent the whole night with their stretcher-bearers out getting all the wounded. My feeling was we wasted a damned good battalion.[42] (2nd Lieutenant Terence Verschoyle)

Another young officer with the same battalion described his inner feelings during the charge.

My body and soul seemed to be entirely divorced, even to the extent that I felt that I no longer inhabited my body. My shell at the bidding of purely automatic forces, over which I had no control, ran hither and thither collecting men, hacked its way through the scrub with a rifle, directed the fire of my platoon and in short struggled with all the duties which I had been taught to perform. But my mind was a distinct and separate entity. I seemed to hover at some height above my own body and observe its doings and the doings of others with a sort of detached interest. I speculated idly on the possibility of my body being hit and thought it probably would be. I wondered if it would be in the head, round which so many bullets seemed to be flying; I felt no fear, only a mild sense of curiosity. Meanwhile my body strove and swore and sweated.[43] (2nd Lieutenant Ivone Kirkpatrick)

In fact he was badly wounded in the left shoulder and stomach.

The 162nd Brigade advanced at the same time, acting both as a flank guard to the 10th Division and to capture Kidney Hill to the immediate south of Kiretch Tepe. Before the attack one doomed young man, Lieutenant Warren Hertslet of the 1/10th London Regiment, was putting the finishing touches to a diary letter home:

> I hope my regiment will make a good show. Of course it is a tremendous moment in the minds of us all. None of us know how we shall stand shell and other fire in the attack. I personally feel very doubtful about my prowess in the bayonet charge. Well, by this time tomorrow I shall know all about it or shall be unconscious of that or anything else.[44] (Lieutenant Warren Hertslet)

When the brigade began to advance it was forced to cross very difficult ground without prior reconnaissance. Private Horace Manton was with the 1/5th Bedfordshires, who were leading the advance:

> We'd got no cover at all. One of the lieutenants was going aside of me. We were in open formation. He got shot while we were going up the hill, I said: 'Do you want any help Sir?' He said: 'No. Carry on, don't break the line.' Our commanding officer, Colonel Brighten, got through alright. He gave us the name of the Yellow Devils. We got to the top and then we got blasted by shrapnel. I saw my cousin get killed in front of me. He was crying when he got shot. It killed him anyhow, he was only sixteen. How I missed it I don't know, shrapnel was flying all the time.[45] (Private Horace Manton)

Harding was initially in reserve with the 1/11th London Regiment. His company was ordered to carry forward the firing line and attack Kidney Hill.

I hoped I felt very brave and warlike. I had an alpine stick in one hand and a revolver in the other and on I went with my platoon. We went on some way and then dipped down into a small low valley where there were a whole lot of troops standing around really under cover. I said to one officer: 'Are you the firing line?' He said: 'Well, I suppose we are.' 'Well, you've got to come with me. My orders are to go forward to capture the hill, and to carry you with me.' I took my platoon on, we went over the slope and rifle fire started to knock around us. But there was no sign of the others following at all. They stayed in the valley. I was out on my own with my platoon deployed and my chaps started getting hit. I thought: 'Well, I don't know about this, it's not much cop!' I halted and thought I'd better try and get a message back to my company commander to say that I'd halted, to say what the position was. I got my orderly, wrote out the message on a field service message pad and told him to go back and find company headquarters. He didn't get more than about ten or fifteen yards and he was shot down. I thought: 'Well, that's not much good, I shall lose the lot if I go on like this.' So I decided to stay where I was. When darkness came we decided to go back as there was nobody on our flank at all. We started to withdraw carrying our wounded and left two or three dead on the floor. We came to a line of troops who said they were the front line, they were all mixed up together and we joined forces with them. It was a mixture, a muddle, a mixture.[46] (2nd Lieutenant John Harding)

Despite all their brave efforts the territorials could not maintain their hold on Kidney Hill and were forced to retire that night, finishing up level with the 31st Brigade's original positions. Only the 30th Brigade had made any progress. That night the aftermath of battle was terrible.

I remember the tremendous crash of rifle and machine-gun fire close to and the 'thump' 'thump' of bullets and sparks flying from the stones while an officer, sergeant and six of us pushed through the scrub towards the curve of a hill which showed up darkly against the night sky. Between the bursts of fire the silence was broken by agonizing cries which will always haunt me: seemingly from all about that hill there were voices crying 'Ambulance'

'Stretcher-bearers' 'Ambulance' 'Oh damn you my leg's broken' and then again 'Stretcher-bearers.' It was horrible, we would start for a voice and it would cease and another far away would begin. That hillside was a shambles: evidently there had been a fierce hand to hand fighting there a few hours ago, rifles, kits, water-bottles, khaki, Turkish tunics and headgear were strewn everywhere among the scrub. While we were following a phantom-like voice we came suddenly on a half dug trench which an RAMC officer had made into a combined mortuary and first aid station; there we set furiously to work sorting out the dead from the living; there reeled among us out of the darkness an officer raving, 'My men have taken that bloody hill but they're dying of thirst.' He passed on and we continued our ghastly work.[47] (Private Harold Thomas)

The 10th Division and the 162nd Brigade were exhausted by their efforts and all they could hope to do was consolidate their gains on the top of Kiretch Tepe. The reinforced Turks had other ideas and from 04.00 on 16 August they began a vicious series of bombing and bayonet attacks. The attacks were unrelenting; without fresh troops and plentiful bombs the battalions just could not hold out any longer and overnight reluctantly withdrew to their original positions. Appeals for reinforcements went unheeded.

The beleaguered troops had no chance of attracting the full attention of their higher commanders on 16 August because the simmering row between Hamilton and Stopford with their various acolytes had finally blown up the day before. In his cables to Kitchener, Hamilton had originally offered up fairly gentle hints as to his dissatisfaction, exemplified by his cable of 9 August: 'No man putteth new wine into old bottles so the combination between new troops and old generals seems to be proving unsuitable.'[48] But after being forced to accept Stopford's *fait accompli* on 13 August he was more forthright in a telegram sent next day: 'There is nothing for it but to allow time to rest and reorganize unless I force Stopford and his divisional generals to undertake a general action for which, in their present frame of mind, they have no heart. In fact, they are not fit for it.'[49] Kitchener recognized that this was not a tenable relationship between a commander-in-chief and his subordinate generals and telegraphed back on 15 August: 'If you deem it necessary to replace Stopford, Mahon and Hammersley, have you any competent generals to take their places? From your report I think Stopford should come home. This is a young man's war, and we must have commanding officers who will take full advantage of opportunities which occur but seldom. If, therefore, any generals fail, do not hesitate to act promptly. . . . Any generals I have available I will send to you.'[50] The hypocrisy implicit in Kitchener's statement was quite astounding. By his own intransigence over seniority, which cannot usually be separated from age, he had forced Hamilton to accept Stopford in the first place. More was to follow: 'Close on top of this tardy appreciation of youth, comes another cable from him saying he has asked French to let me have Byng, Horne and Kavanagh. "I hope", he says, "Stopford has been relieved by you already?"'[51]

Hamilton needed no second bidding. 'Between them, these two messages have cleared the air. Mahon's seniority has been at the root of this evil. K's conscience tells him so and, therefore, he pricks his name now upon the fatal list. But he did not know, when he cabled, that Mahon had done well.'[52] Stopford was removed from his command that same day and Hamilton replaced him temporarily with Major General Beauvoir de Lisle from the 29th Division, pending the arrival of Lieutenant General Sir Julian Byng, who was released from his duties on the Western Front to command the IX Corps – the very man whose services Kitchener had categorically refused Hamilton in the first place.

The changeover did not go entirely smoothly, as Mahon took offence at being asked to serve under the relatively junior de Lisle and asked to be relieved of his command. Hamilton packed him off to Mudros to cool his heels and Hill took over temporary command of the 10th Division. Stopford's departure was only the first of many as the key players in the Suvla disaster left the scene. Within a few days Hammersley, Sitwell and Lindley all departed, but it was too late. Younger, more thrusting generals who might have driven their men across the empty ground could do nothing against the firmly entrenched Turks, who dominated nearly all the available high ground.

On 15 August de Lisle arrived at Suvla to take over temporary command, with a set of briefing instructions prepared by Braith-waite. These set out the basic situation and made clear the objective of a strike, as quickly and strongly as possible against W Hills and Anafarta Spur. These features were still of crucial importance, not by then to support the failed Sari Bair operations, but to help protect the poor British positions scattered across the plain from Turkish shellfire. In addition to having the troops already at Suvla and the assistance of an Anzac brigade on the right flank, de Lisle was informed of the imminent arrival of the 2nd Mounted Division, which had been made available from the Egypt garrison forces after Kitchener had reminded Hamilton on 9 August that he could call on them if necessary. Within this framework the exact troops employed, date and method of the next assault were all left to de Lisle to determine. The initial report he prepared in response to Braithwaite's briefing on 16 August made depressing reading at GHQ. He estimated that, even after the 2nd Mounted Division had been included in the calculations, he would still have only 10,000 men free for an attack on W Hills. He also pointed out that it would be difficult to capture and retain the Anafarta Spur without Tekke Tepe. Grim reading like this from a general he trusted brought home to Hamilton the utter failure of his August offensive. In the whole of the Gallipoli Peninsula he now had an army of only 95,000 troops against a Turkish strength of some 110,000 in tactically superior positions. At Suvla itself a frontage of 20,000 yards was being held by only 50,000 troops when really 80,000 were required, at the accepted defence ratio of four men per yard. To make matters worse they were facing up to 75,000 Turks with reinforcements still arriving on a daily basis. Literally defeated, he reported his failure to Kitchener in a telegram on 17 August in which, having set out an account of the operations so far and the overall situation, he once again asked for a huge reinforcement:

My British Divisions are at present 45,000 under establishment, exclusive of about 9,000 promised or on the way. If this deficit were made up, and new formations totalling 50,000 rifles sent out as well, these, with the 60,000 rifles which I estimate I shall have at the time of their arrival, should give me the necessary superiority, unless the absence of other enemies allows the Turks to bring up large additional reinforcements.[53] (General Sir Ian Hamilton)

In the meantime he sent de Lisle a reinforcement in the shape of the veteran 87th Brigade from the 29th Division at Helles, which arrived on 17 August closely followed by the dismounted yeomanry of the inaptly named 2nd Mounted Division on 18 August. At IX Corps Headquarters morale was, almost perversely, slowly improving. After a further reconnaissance de Lisle decided that the Turkish entrenchments were not yet impregnable, while a series of minor operations right along the line on 18 August had resulted in several small-scale tactical improvements. A IX Corps staff conference the same day, attended by Hamilton, therefore planned a limited attack on W Hills on 21 August. That evening Hamilton decided in an attempt to guarantee success to send the rest of the 29th Division over to Suvla. He also intervened on 19 August to ensure that the objectives of the planned attack remained strictly limited to avoid any more general advance dissipating what little strength was available.

In fact any optimism was misplaced, for after their ordeals the Suvla troops needed more than a few days to recover their effectiveness. They needed time to dig wells to tap water which was almost everywhere across the plain – if only they had had the experience to dig down a few feet. They needed time to reorganize, they needed time to rest. Unfortunately Stopford, who was ideally qualified to preside over rest periods, was no longer there and the preparations for one last attack continued.

The final orders for the attack were issued by de Lisle at 15.00 on 20 August. The 29th Division was to be responsible for attacking 112 Metre Hill and Scimitar Hill from Chocolate Hill; the 11th Division was to capture W Hills from the Azmak Dere sector; while a composite Anzac brigade was to seize the small but tactically significant Hill 60, which dominated the link between Anzac and Suvla. The reserves of the 2nd Mounted Division and the 30th Brigade of the 10th Division were to be concentrated out of sight and hence artillery harassment behind Lala Baba. The attack was to be preceded by an artillery bombardment commencing at 14.30.

Many of the war-weary battalions of the 29th Division barely had time to get ashore before they were expected to attack. Nothing it seemed had been learnt in the previous two weeks about the necessity of assault troops being properly briefed, well rested, fresh and ready for the fray. With no warning, the 1st Munster Fusiliers were told to be ready to embark from their positions at Helles on 19 August.

> We spent that day fixing up everything – an awful lot of work, and at 11pm marched off to V Beach, and got on to the transport called the *Osmanieh* at 3am. No sleep till 4.30am and at 7am we arrived at Suvla Bay and started disembarking. We got on shore by 11am and spent the day being shelled in an open camp near the beach and at 7pm marched off to a hill called the Chocolate Hill 5 miles away. We didn't get there till midnight and then had to relieve other troops. There was another hill 1,000 yards in front, which was our firing line, and we were in a hollow between the 2 hills. We lost 14 men hit in the dark getting there, and it was a nasty job finding our way in the dark. I managed to get a little sleep from 3am to 5am. Spent the morning preparing for an attack.[54] (Captain Guy Nightingale)

The arrival of the famous 29th Division was witnessed by some of Kitchener's Army men of the 11th Division.

> From early morning, troops were to be seen going towards Chocolate Hill in batches of threes and fours. We were told they were men of the 29th Division who made the landing at Cape Helles. We looked at them with something akin to awe, as they were 'old sweats', while we were just 'rookies' and we had read about their deeds before leaving England.[55] (Private Ernest Lye)

Most of the men who landed on 25 April were long gone, and many of their replacements had little more experience than Lye. The mood among the surviving veterans, such as Captain Nightingale, was not optimistic. 'There was going to be a general advance and the 29th Division had been specially brought up to assist. Our Battalion was the assaulting one of the Brigade, and we had to take a hill about half a mile ahead. I never thought it would come off. Everyone was cooked with the heat, and almost too weary to stand, with no sleep for 3 nights.'[56] Lieutenant Colonel Guy Geddes, who remained in command of the 1st Munsters despite his refusal to attack on 6 August at Helles, commented despairingly, 'All of us dead beat.'[57]

The artillery bombardment opened up at 14.30 but was almost totally ineffective – there were too few guns and far too few shells of the right type. Now the Turks were properly dug in, the dictum about the necessity of intensive bombardment by heavy guns reasserted itself. The Turkish counter bombardment was probably more effective. When the attack commenced the 87th Brigade was to capture Scimitar Hill – which had been so tragically abandoned only a few days before. At first all went well and the 1st Inniskillings captured the crest of the hill. Unfortunately they found themselves exposed to enfilade artillery and machine-gun fire and soon were forced to withdraw. With the support of the 1st Border Regiment, they once more charged up the hill. Casualties were awful, but they could not secure a hold on the crest.

Immediately to the south the 86th Brigade was trying to capture 112 Metre Hill, a prominent offshoot of the Anafarta Spur; the attack was led by the 1st Munsters.

At 3pm the Battalion shoved off 700 strong. The furthest any got was 500 yards and none came back from there. They all got mown down by machine-gun fire. We lost 9 officers and nearly 400 men. The Turks shelled us very heavily and the whole country, which is covered with gorse, caught fire. This split up the attack and parties got cut up. Many of our wounded were burnt alive and it was as nasty a sight as I ever want to see. . . . Our Headquarters was very heavily shelled and then the fire surrounded the place and we all thought we were going to be burnt alive. Where the telephone was, the heat was appalling. The roar of the flames drowned the noise of the shrapnel, and we had to lie flat at the bottom of the trench while the flames swept over the top. Luckily both sides didn't catch simultaneously, or I don't know what would have happened. After the gorse was all burnt, the smoke nearly asphyxiated us! All this time our Battalion was being cut up in the open and it really was very unpleasant trying to send down calm messages to the Brigade Headquarters, while you were lying at the bottom of the trench like an oven, expecting to be burnt every minute, and knowing your Battalion was getting hell a hundred yards away. The telephone wires finally fused from the heat.[58] (Captain Guy Nightingale)

It was obvious that the 29th Division had shot its bolt and de Lisle ordered forward his reserves. Instead of exploiting success, they were faced with capturing the original objectives. Hamilton, who was with de Lisle, described him during the operations. 'He was smoking a pipe – quite calm. There is usually nothing to be said or to be done once our war dogs have been slipped. A soldier might as well try to correct the aim of his bullet after he has pulled the trigger!'[59] At 15.30 the five brigades of the 2nd Mounted Division moved off in successive lines across the Salt Lake, sur-rounded by the smoke puffs of Turkish shells.

You can't hide a division of troops advancing in broad daylight and they gave us a terrific welcome, as many as fifteen and sixteen shrapnel shells were bursting over our heads at once. I soon gulped down the lump in my throat, jammed my helmet on tighter and prepared to go through with it.[60] (Sergeant Colin Millis)

The advance of the Yeoman of England is a famous, almost peaceful scene as commemorated in watercolours by the painter Norman Wilkinson. He depicts the seemingly harmless puffs of smoke from the bursting shells hanging in the air over the advancing lines, but for Trooper Arthur Bull of the 1/1st Gloucestershire Hussars it was a nightmare. 'It was salt, pretty firm. God it was slaughter, terrible. I was stretcher-bearing and I was covered in other men's blood. I always remember one officer, he was a gentleman. He was wounded in his thigh. He said, "Don't worry, I'm all right, there's others worse than me."'[61] Despite the shelling their discipline held up. 'No confusion or shouting, just a grim determination on everyone's face, dripping with sweat and not a few with streams of blood.'[62] Halfway across, the order came to advance at the double.

Running with our pack was difficult. Across ploughed fields we went, jumping over ditches and trenches, almost falling. . . . The shells and bullets were still raining fast. . . . Presently another horror, a long belt of gorse and scrub had caught alight with the shells and which very quickly spread, there was no help for it but to rush through and chance to luck, which I did, but came out the other side . . . almost choking with the smoke. . . . An awful death trap this was and it claimed many victims, the poor devils simply dropped in dozens and were speedily burnt with the flames, a sight I shan't forget. Two hundred yards more and we had reached the base of Chocolate Hill and in comparative safety.[63] (Sergeant Colin Millis)

On reaching Chocolate Hill the division was split up. One brigade was sent to assist the 87th Brigade, two joined the 86th Brigade, while the remaining two were held in support and reserve. Another new division had been offered up on the altar of expediency. With no battle acclimatization, no briefing, no maps, no idea what was happening, they were sent on into the burning scrub on the hills. Shortly after 18.00 the 2nd (South Midland) Brigade together with the 2nd SWB hurled themselves up Scimitar Hill, only to be swept off the peak by the overwhelming fire from the flanks. They managed to establish a line on the lower slopes, but the crest remained in Turkish hands. Courage was no proof against bullets and, hopelessly enfiladed from W Hills, they bowed to the inevitable; they were evacuated before dawn on 22 August. The other two brigades of Yeomanry, who were meant to assault 112 Metre Hill, had quite simply, and unsurprisingly, got lost. Isolated detachments blundered around under heavy fire across the whole battle area from Scimitar Hill to Hetman Chair, suffering casualties but achieving nothing.

All night long, wounded men came straggling back, all with tales of our men, still lying out there. How any of us escaped I don't know. . . . The whole attack was a ghastly failure. They generally are now.[64] (Captain Guy Nightingale)

Meanwhile on the 11th Division front to the south, the 32nd Brigade had attacked towards the foot of W Hills across land covered with scrub and crisscrossed with hedges and drainage ditches. It was land ideally suited to defence and the Turks used it well. The first two battalions were cut to ribbons, and the 8th Duke of Wellingtons were hurried up ready to be thrown into the attack. 'Whilst we are still waiting the Roman Catholic Padre comes round with the most comforting news that we are about to meet our God so if we have anything to confess we should do it at once. Very cheerful sort of fellow I thought.'[65] After receiving this double-edged pastoral comfort they attacked.

3.00pm, and we lined up on the top of the trench, numbered off, formed fours and the officer gave the order: 'Quick March.' One man next to me said: 'They'll just be kicking off at Elland Road!' But football and Leeds seemed very remote to me just then. We kept to our column until bullets began to fall uncomfortably close, when the officer gave the order to 'Deploy to the right and left.' This we did, as we had done many times before in Belton Park, Grantham, during our training. Looking back I can't but marvel at the way they conducted themselves. Keeping in a line, each man two yards from his neighbour, with the officer shouting: 'Keep back No 21, get in line No 10,' while the bullets began to whistle all around us. I remember at the time my one thought was, 'How are they missing us?' . . . I suppose our discipline and formation saved us many casualties on that march forward, for we had got to within a few yards of our front line trench before our first man went down. . . . Then the man on the left went down with hardly a sound. Killed instantly. The next – the one on my right. . . . Jumping and scrambling over the front line, we continued our way, then men began to fall like flies. The Turks' line was about 800 yards from ours, away up the hillside, and at the bottom of the hill there was a line of trees and bushes running at an angle to our line, and towards these we made our way. We could see in front of Chocolate Hill that the 29th Division, who were on our left, had reached the Turks' trench but there seemed to be very few of them. Bodies were dotted all over the hillside and on the plain. I reached the trees and, pushing my way through one of the bushes (something seemed to tell me to keep away from the gaps and I'm glad I did, for I saw three men go down at one) I found myself in a dry water-way, about four feet deep, that was screened on each side by foliage. I also found the place was full of dead and wounded, and I seemed to be the only whole man for ten or twelve yards . . . on each side. I looked through the bushes in front and could see none but dead, and it would have been madness to have gone on alone. I did what I could for the men in the ditch, taking care to keep as low as possible, for machine-guns were raking the trench every few moments. Shells were bombarding us.[66] (Private Ernest Lye)

Sergeant Edward Miles was alongside him:

It seemed impossible for a worm to live under such an onslaught. I'm sure I must have had a charmed life, for several times I found myself on my own owing to my immediate neighbours being knocked over. Eventually we reached the first line of Turkish trenches but don't stop there as the trench is full of dead and wounded Turks. As I was jumping over the trench I felt a sudden pain in my knee and glancing down I saw a Turk in the act of stabbing at me again. He had caught me with his bayonet. After dispatching him I hurried on not thinking any more of it but my leg was going weak, so bending down I hastily put my field dressing round it and hurry on. It was then dusk and we were still hurrying forward. My word! but that was some scrap whilst it lasted. I'm sure I went mad, for the next thing I remember was that I was lying with about four other men in the corner of a field behind a bit of a hedge and in a small ditch about 200 yards (I discovered afterwards) in front of our own men and about 20 yards from Mr Turk. Of course we were a bit scared, after so many hair raisers who cannot wonder at it, eh? So we beat a hasty retreat, I am following behind as my leg is beginning to get stiff, back to our lines. Phew! that was a near shave.[67] (Sergeant Edward Miles)

In confusion the troops were forced to fall back to their starting positions.

Next in line to the south the 34th Brigade had been intended to capture the Turkish line running from Azmak Dere to Hetman's Chair. The troops went forward under heavy fire but managed to take their objective despite heavy casualties. It was to prove a poisoned chalice, for they were overlooked and enfiladed from the southern slopes of Azmak Dere. The 33rd Brigade was moved up to support the assault but could make little extra impact as two of its battalions repeated the failure of the 32nd Brigade, while the other two joined the 34th Brigade in defending the newly won trench.

The composite brigade drawn from the Anzac Corps was placed under the command of Brigadier General Cox. Its main objective was to support the more important attacks undertaken by the IX Corps, but it was also intended to capture Hill 60. This relatively minor hillock was located between the Azmak Dere and Kaiajik Dere valleys, both draining into the Azmak Dere plain. By geographical coincidence it was of key tactical significance as not only would it secure the junction between Anzac and IX Corps but it would also offer a view up the Azmak Dere valley deep into the Turkish lines. The *ad hoc* brigade assembled for the task was, however, in a terrible state, still reeling from the crippling casualties suffered in the assault on Sari Bair, which had been compounded by the effects of disease.

The attack began at 15.30 after another token bombardment which served only to alert the Turks and when the troops attacked they met with the usual storm of fire. Three battalions of Gurkhas made slow progress in their advance across the Azmak Dere plain and failed to cement the link with 11th Division. Acting alongside them was Captain Bryan Cooper, who was with the 5th Connaught Rangers as they prepared to attack the Turkish outpost at Kabak Kuyu:

> Here and there a man murmured a prayer or put up a hand to grasp his rosary, but for the most part they waited silent till the order to advance was given. At last, at 3.40, the bombardment ceased, the word came, and the leading platoon dashed forward with a yell like hounds breaking covert. They were met with a roar of rifle fire, coming not only from the trench attacked, but also from Hill 60, and from snipers concealed in the scattered bushes. Not a man stopped to return it; all dashed on with levelled bayonets across the four hundred yards of open country, each man striving to be the first into the enemy's trench. That honour fell to the platoon commander, Second-Lieutenant T. W. G. Johnson, who had gained Amateur International Colours for Ireland at Association Football, and was a bad man to beat across country.[68] (Captain Bryan Cooper)

The attack was a success and the Turkish position was overrun. After the capture of Kabak Kuyu the battalion had been ordered to assist in the attack on Hill 60.

> By this time companies had become very mixed, and the charge was composed of a crowd of men belonging to all the companies, mad with the lust of battle. Their officers did little to restrain them, for their Irish blood was aflame, and they were as eager as the men. The line surged up the bare exposed glacis, only to encounter tremendously heavy rifle and machine-gun fire from the crest. At the same moment the enemy's guns opened, displaying marvellous accuracy in ranging, and the attack was annihilated. In spite of this the men went on as long as they were able to stand, and fell still facing the foe. From the wells below their bodies could be seen, lying in ordered ranks on the hillside, with their bayonets pointing to the front.[69] (Captain Bryan Cooper)

After this failure the remnants concentrated on consolidating the Kabak Kuyu position and also expanded a communication trench to join with the New Zealanders of the Otago and Canterbury Mounted Rifles, who had managed to secure just a toe-hold on the southern slope of Hill 60. The attack made on the far right of the line by 500 miscellaneous Australians was totally enfiladed down the Kaiajik Dere valley and they were slaughtered.

By nightfall, despite all the blood and sweat, the Turks were still secure in all their key positions and what little advances had been made were of negligible importance without a further push. The situation of the isolated group of New Zealanders and Irishmen at the bottom of Hill 60 was extremely precarious. All night the Turks lobbed bombs down the hill followed by intermittent bayonet charges. The position was untenable and one of the precious reserve battalions had to be released to try again. On 22 August the 18th Australian Battalion launched a bayonet attack on Hill 60; this expanded the area which had been captured but still left the summit to the Turks. The position was of such tactical significance that yet another attack was ordered, but the Anzac Corps was now in such an advanced state of debilitation that to get a battalion of 1,000 fit men they had to draw from no less than nine battalions.

As a coda to the August offensive this composite battalion

296

attacked once more up the slopes of Hill 60 on 27 August. On the right were 350 Australians, 400 New Zealanders in the middle and 250 of the Connaught Rangers on the left.

At four the bombardment began. Ships, howitzers, mountain-guns, all combined to create a babble which, if less intense than that of the previous week, was nevertheless sufficiently formidable. The trenches were so close to one another that our troops waiting to advance were covered with dust from the high explosives, but no injury was done. At last, at five, the bombardment ceased and the stormers, led by Lieutenant S. H. Lewis, went over the top. They went into the Turkish trenches almost before the enemy were aware of their coming and forced their way along them with bayonet and bomb. The supporting parties, however, were not so fortunate. The range to the parapet from whence they started was accurately known to the enemy, and from every part of the trench which was not actually under assault violent machine-gun and rifle fire opened. Man after man as he climbed over the parapet fell back into the trench dead, yet the next calmly stepped forward to take his place. . . . Now, too, the enemy's artillery opened, and as, unmenaced elsewhere, they were able to concentrate all their forces on the defence of Hill 60, their fire was terrific. Incessant salvoes of shrapnel burst overhead, while the parapet of the trench from which the advance was taking place was blown in by high explosive. Yet, still, the men went on over the parapet and gradually a few succeeded in struggling through the barrage, and in reinforcing their comrades in the captured trench.[70] (Captain Bryan Cooper)

After a desperately close-fought conflict they secured a solid base on the southern slopes of the hill. The reserves were sent in from 9th and 10th Australian Light Horse and the vicious fighting continued all night.

Again and again, the Turks attacked, mad with fanaticism, shrieking at the top of their voices and calling on Allah. . . . The merciless bombing continued and the trenches slowly became encumbered with dead. . . . At last about 10.30pm, after the fight had lasted five hours, a crowd of Turks succeeded in entering the Rangers' trench near its northern extremity. This northern end was held by a small party of men who died where they stood. The remainder of the trench was, however, blocked and further progress by the enemy arrested. Still the fight raged and bombs and ammunition were running short, while the losses became so heavy. . . . Fresh Turkish attacks kept coming on, and for every assailant that was struck down, two more sprang up in his place. It was clear that soon the defenders would be swept away by force of numbers, and they were compelled at midnight to fall back to the southern end of the captured trench. This point they blocked with a sandbag barricade.[71] (Captain Bryan Cooper)

At last almost the whole Turkish network of trenches had been captured. But it was found that the Turks had sited their defences on the forward slopes, not as was then believed around the summit. When the forward slopes were captured the Turks simply converted their communication trenches, which led back across the summit to the rear, into yet another heavily fortified position. The two sides were now both exhausted and had literally fought each other to a standstill. The Turks were denied an observation point over the Azmak Dere plain but the British lost the opportunity for an observation point looking behind the Turkish lines.

Despite all the intensive effort and thousands of casualties the great August offensive had achieved nothing of real importance. The real objective – the capture of Sari Bair – had been denied Hamilton, and the IX Corps had succeeded only in establishing a base for itself. This was all that Stopford ever thought possible but, by his pusillanimity, he had ensured that the brief golden opportunities were wasted. The total failure of the gambler's last throw on 21 August marked the end of offensive operations of any size at Gallipoli. The August offensive effectively ended the career of Hamilton and many of his generals, and it ended the lives of thousands of men on both sides. Large numbers of the men who had volunteered with enthusiasm in the golden summer of 1914 had had their illusions shattered.

I had seen what war really means, with its blood, death and destruction. To hear the cries of the wounded and see the still huddled forms laid in all kinds of grotesque attitudes, boys and men who that morning had marched forward so bravely and full of life, and were even now rotting in the glare of the Sun, whilst swarms of flies were feasting on their blood and wounds, was to me a terrible nightmare that I shall remember as long as I live.[72] (Private Ernest Lye)

9

Conditions at Gallipoli

By the time the August offensive had failed it was some four months since the initial landings had occurred and the pattern of daily life had been firmly established. To the men who fought there, Gallipoli was their home from the moment they arrived until they left or died. A few survived the whole nine-month campaign, while others were evacuated after only a few hours. To grasp the unique nature of the Gallipoli campaign it is necessary to understand what life was like for the men who were there; that experience is not just a perfunctory adjunct to battle description, but its essential complement.

On landing at Gallipoli new arrivals were usually ignorant of the true horror of the conditions they were to face. The harsh realities came as a rude awakening.

> On one occasion I went down to the beach to lead three officers, who had just landed, up to the trench. When we got there they thought we were Turkish prisoners and were very shocked to find we were the guides to take them up. When we did eventually take them up to the trenches the first thing they asked for was water to have a wash and clean their teeth. We said, 'You'll be lucky to get any bloody water to drink never mind clean your teeth!'[1] (Private Harold Boughton)

One mollycoddled young officer summed up the trauma of it all in just a few words.

> We were just outside Gully Ravine, on this hard rocky soil when we were told to doss down for the night. I must say that looking back on it that it was rather a shock to me. I thought, 'Well I haven't got my pyjamas. Where's my batman? What's going to happen to me?'[2] (2nd Lieutenant Joseph Napier)

The physical conditions that had developed on the peninsula were particularly severe and the British troops lived in circumstances of utter squalor which resulted in a sick list that more than matched the casualty list in actual battle. The remoteness of the peninsula from the main British bases meant that there were great difficulties in even supplying the troops with the basic necessities of life. The beaches took the place of the railhead stores depots on the Western Front, and all the services of supply had to be carried out not only under artillery fire but also while subject to the vagaries of the weather. Between the beaches and the main base 800 miles away at Alexandria there were only two harbours that could be used, Kephalos Bay and Mudros Bay, but neither had had any piers, breakwaters, wharves or store houses before the campaign started. Ultimately, everything that the army needed had to be transported in small boats and landed at the makeshift piers on the peninsula's beaches. Here the beach personnel were assisted by working parties from the local units, and not unnaturally they were keen to supplement their meagre rations.

> The trawlers used to come to a sort of half made rickety pier. We used to carry a box from the boat, pushed it on the beach and carried a lump of rock from the cliff side and chucked it into the pier as we went along. Quite a lot of boxes of condensed milk were broken. You put them on your shoulder and a couple of tins fall in the water. Well you didn't mind that, 'That's mine later on!'[3] (Ordinary Seaman Joe Murray)

Murray even developed a code of what was and wasn't ethical. 'If we were detailed to take rations up we never touched any of it. We were really thirsting for a drink but we wouldn't take the water and we wouldn't take the food. But if there was any broken stuff on the beach well we had most of that good and proper.'[4] Once the food had been landed safely, and had escaped the attentions of such as Murray and his friends, it would pass into the hands of the divisional supply depots located near to the beach. At Suvla Bay, Lieutenant Frank Howitt was an Army Service Corps officer at one of the 11th Divisional depots in charge of a team of specialists:

> In the dusk over there is Corporal Ince, his axe glistening in the moonlight as he swirls it round and round to descend upon the

carcass of a frozen ox. With the lifelong experience of a Wigan butchery he delivers the exact amount to each zealous quartermaster as he comes along, although his calculations must all be by guess-work, the scales being useless to him. Beyond him is England with the bully and biscuits, which are simple as the boxes all contain the same number. Here is Griffiths with his great casks of tea, dealing it out with his scoop. . . . Hutchings has the charitable job; he gives out the changeable luxuries such as rum, lime juice, cigarettes and tobacco. Hutchings is a teetotaller and non-smoker, and impervious to the overtures of quartermasters of the most persuasive character, which is a worthier trait than either. . . . Over the whole Sergeant Claret in the guise of general overseer keeps his kindly eye. His is the duty of calculating the total for each unit.[5] (Lieutenant Frank Howitt)

The stores were taken up to the line by mule transport, a dangerous task exposed as they were to shellfire. The Turks knew supplies had to come up and the routes they could use were limited in number. The muleteers handed over the supplies to the regimental quartermaster's staff.

We dug two large ten foot holes under a hedge and covered them over with blankets so they were hidden from sight. In the day we slept, me and my guard of three or four men. As soon as it was dark we could hear the jingle of the Indian muleteers bringing the food in their carts. They would deliver this stuff in a great heap and depart. Then before daylight the regiment would send down twenty men to carry it up to the actual line. Everything depended on complete secrecy, nothing could happen in the daylight. This went successfully for three or four weeks. Then one night they didn't collect and we thought, 'Too bad you'll have to have a double lot next time.' So we went to sleep. Daylight came, we lifted the edge of our blanket and looked out. To our horror there stood thirty men, standing and sitting and waiting to take their rations. We shouted at once: 'Make for cover,' but too late, shellfire started and they pounded us. A number were wounded and carried away and even I got a small wound in the leg – not bad enough to matter. Of course we had to cancel the whole thing, the Turks had found out. Just an error, some NCO had not ordered the troops out in the night to go and collect the food. If they'd started an hour before they would have been there and gone back again.[6] (Corporal Arthur Hemsley)

In consequence of these problems the front-line troops did not always receive the rations to which they were in theory entitled. In particular, supplies were eroded by pilfering at every stage in the process which gradually removed the more attractive items. 'Sometimes we'd get three loaves for six of us. The sergeant would keep one himself and first time he said it we were surprised because we knew it should be half a loaf each. You couldn't protest – who could you protest to? You couldn't protest to an officer because you can't approach one without an NCO and he was the only NCO we had.'[7] This, coupled with the difficulties of establishing a cook house near enough to the line for the supply of hot meals to the front-line troops, meant that the actual rations issued in the front line were usually reduced to bully beef, biscuits, bread, jam, bacon, cheese, tea and sugar.

Tinned bully beef, the British Army staple diet whatever the climate, is now more usually known as corned beef. This was not the most suitable type of food in the hot sun. 'Most unappetizing. If you ever tried to eat Bully at over 90 in the shade where it melts as soon as you pour it out of the tin you would find it equally unappetizing.'[8] The biscuits were mainly square Huntley and Palmers that looked just like dog biscuits, and this was not the only characteristic they had in common. 'Very hard biscuits – I broke seven teeth there.'[9] They were almost universally disliked, but if anything the troops seem to have hated the jam ration even more. 'We had tins of jam, always apricot until we were sick and tired of the thing. We used to use the unopened tins to make doorsteps into the trench.'[10] Brewing up to make tea in the trenches was a complicated affair.

You had the tea and sugar mixed up in a sack, we had tins but we didn't have any field kitchens and we had to make our own tea. You put the tea and sugar in a billy can but then you had to make a fire. The only way was to burn the scrub. You had a lighter and blow, blow, blow, you'd get it to smoulder, blow, blow, blow and you'd put whatever you'd got on, blow, blow, blow – you'd spend the next half hour blowing your blinking guts out trying to get it alight. We only once made a real cup of tea in the first month.[11] (Ordinary Seaman Joe Murray)

The main problem with the rations was the monotony, 'The test of a good cook was whether they could produce bully beef so that you didn't know what it was.'[12] A certain amount of imagination was required to make these basic ingredients into new and exciting culinary experiences.

Gallipoli Pudding was created as a diversion from the hard biscuits. We used to take two or three of these, lay them on a flat stone and bash them with our entrenching tool handles into a sort of meal or flour. If we were lucky enough to have any water, we would mix it up with the flour and make a ball about the size of a cricket ball. We rolled the ball in our khaki handkerchiefs, used or unused, and put them in our mess tins with some water. We built enough fuel to make a little fire, put the tin on that and boiled them in there. Of course the khaki used to come out of the handkerchief and that was good because it used to give a Christmassy look to the pudding. When we thought they were done we used to turn this horrible mess out and eat it! But it made a change.[13] (Private Harold Boughton)

One rather more simple but much appreciated recipe was the humble pancake, which took on a new and unexpected role as a luxury food.

A little flour, a little water, made into a paste and fixed in the bottom of a mess tin lid previously smeared with bacon fat and that was the precious commodity! Reader, if you have lived for weeks without anything softer than an Army biscuit passing your lips you will appreciate what those pancakes meant to us. The smell of their cooking was ambrosia.[14] (Private Harold Thomas)

Everyone was desperate for more food and a little variety. No source of food was omitted.

A favourite occupation when off duty was to go down to the pier off Gully Beach and throw bread into the sea. Fish of the whiting type came after the bread, and then a Mill's grenade was thrown in. The fish were stunned by the explosion, and two or three men, with the help of a net, were sure of getting a good haul. The fish seemed to recover after a few minutes, unless they had been actually hit by a piece of the bomb.[15] (Captain F. W. Walker)

The wealthier officers could secure a little extra by clubbing together and sending an order home for extra luxury provisions.

One outstanding feature was the arrival of the officers' mess parcel from Fortnum and Mason which arrived fortuitously the day before we did our attack and caused great delight. I still remember a lovely large tin of asparagus. Not the asparagus itself but the juice which was carefully spooned out to each member. It was absolute wine of heaven.[16] (2nd Lieutenant Terence Verschoyle)

Another officer showed what could be done with these few extra ingredients and some culinary *savoir faire*.

We have a fine menu and a guest tonight. Tinned salmon, pineapple, blancmange, coffee and rum. They all like these blancmanges but they cause infinite amusement. I secured two tins of cornflour in Mudros at two shilling a tin and they have done wonderful work. The last we had I made from condensed snow and milk and Bourneville Cocoa. It was a chocolate one – as the condensed snow was mud coloured to start with it gave the idea of putting cocoa in to conceal its dirty appearance and really it was most wonderful good eating. The cook has made this one for tonight and it's a rum flavoured one. See what luxury we live in.[17] (Lieutenant Thomas Watson)

The ordinary soldier also received parcels from home, although it almost entirely depended on his personal circumstances, the success or otherwise of German submarines in disrupting communications and the inevitable delays, which could add up to months before they arrived. They were eagerly awaited.

Parcels! What a word of wonder, what a word to conjure with, what a word of joyous memories! Think what it meant for us who had been fed on bully beef, cold and stewed, Army biscuits, apricot jam, and tea, day in day out to receive a parcel containing such things as Cake! chocolate! mixed biscuits! Café au lait!

305

tinned tongue or tinned fruits! The ecstasy of reception, contemplation, mastication of such things is indescribable to any who have not known really straitened circumstances.[18] (Private Harold Thomas)

Yet parcels could also bring disappointment in various ways.

At first we did not get what we chiefly needed: our first scrappy notes home had been concerned with the heat and our thirst and our dirtiness and shortage of socks, shirts, etc. As a result the contents of our first parcels were disappointing in the extreme. As the weather was now becoming quite cool the appearance of lemonade power and thirst quenching tablets failed to raise enthusiasm. Socks, handerchiefs and shirts were received with unconcealed disgust and the remarks which were addressed to various brands of soap from the simple yellow to the fastidious Pears would have caused immediate liquefaction had the article in question been gifted with the power of hearing or feelings of shame![19] (Private Harold Thomas)

An otherwise reasonable selection could be ruined by one blunder.

I once saw a parcel consisting of cigarettes, cake, socks and soap into the midst of which a bunch of a dozen bananas had been inserted some six weeks earlier when the consignment had been proudly despatched from an enthusiastic but woefully ignorant English homestead. That parcel would have been a good illustration for the phrase 'the bondage of corruption' – even the socks seemed to have surrendered to the general dissolution.[20] (Private Harold Thomas)

Even if the contents of parcels had been selected with care and discretion all was not necessarily well.

Some unfortunate beings after weeks of anxious looking forward would receive a label and a piece of string and a medley of broken crumbs and broken fragments in the bottom of a mail bag. All that was left to speak of maternal or sisterly benevolence so sadly nullified by incompetence in packing.[21] (Private Harold Thomas)

One other peril aroused the troops' disgust.

There were more tragical cases still when parcels were found to have been opened en route and the major portion of them stolen, or, descending to still lower depths of blackness, it was by no means rare to discover that in addition to pilfering the contents some super-Hun had added insult to injury by filling the empty space with tins of bully beef. You can imagine the enraged feelings of a man (who had waited long weeks for the moment when he might feel the solid bulk of a home parcel) when he discovered nothing more appetizing than Fray Bentos or some other brand of the commodity which lay in mountains around us and which our digestive organs had already begun to reject through sheer nausea.[22] (Private Harold Thomas)

Enterprising Greek civilians sought to capitalize on a definite gap in the market. 'Greek fishermen used to come in and they sold us a small tin of condensed milk for a ten shilling note and we were glad to get it!'[23] Not everyone appreciated the profit margins required by the Greeks for risking the intermittent but deadly shellfire on the beaches. They also faced many of the problems of the Army Service Corps – insatiable demand, limited stock and a long journey to secure replenishments: 'Towards the end of May a Greek opened a canteen which was most useful, though a den of thieves, for a few days, but after that his stock was reduced to indelible pencils and braces. Then he would get another stock which lasted a few hours. Finally he disappeared, rumour had it that he was shot as a spy; he deserved shooting as a robber.'[24]

The very restricted diet caused medical problems. 'For want of vegetable food the skin on our hands and arms became pasty, and every sore turned septic.'[25] The treatment for this sort of complaint was basic.

I had a boil on my arm and I had a bandage on. The officer came round and said: 'Oh what's the matter with you?' 'I've got a boil.' He said: 'You'd better get down to the base and have it lanced.' 'No it'll be alright.' 'You go on!' I had to tramp three miles down to the base and I reported to the RAMC orderly, 'Hello what's the matter with you, alright come on.' I went in the tent where they were just attending to a man's leg on a stretcher. The doctor says: 'Alright come on role your sleeve up.' Oh my Goodness, no anaesthetic, no nothing, he just stuck a knife in and that was that.[26] (Private Cecil Meager)

Throughout the campaign the supply of water was a problem at Gallipoli. The local wells were adequate for the normal population of the peninsula, but the addition of tens of thousands of thirsty men and animals, all broiling under a hot sun, meant that further measures had to be found urgently. The local supplies captured and utilized in the early days had their own problems. Having been under the control of the Turks and often literally fought over there was an awful risk of poisoning or pollution. This preyed on the minds of the troops.

We had to go down with bottles. You took a puttee off, put a clove hitch round the handle of your canteen, gently lowered it down the well then filled your water bottles. But we always used to say there was a queer taste in that water. We'd been up the lines two or three times when the engineers finally put hooks down and up came a body. How it had got there no one knew. How long it had been in we didn't know.[27] (Ordinary Seaman Steve Moyle)

Such stories were widespread: 'The only thing there is to drink is water that comes from a nasty well, which tastes as if it had a dead mule in it (it probably has). However, we are given purifying tablets, which are very good and make the water taste as if it had two dead mules in it.'[28] Arrangements were also made to supplement the water supply by condensing sea-water. Even this had a macabre side off V Beach in April. 'We used a sea-water condenser. But when the stories got around that the sea had been red with blood it didn't make you feel too good drinking that. We made tea and I remember it was black – not very appetising.'[29] Even at a later date condensed water was not popular: 'This blessed condensed sea-water was always warm and tasted a little salt and oily. You imagine drinking that in a sun-baked place like that.'[30] The Royal Engineers set to work to try and develop any viable local supplies.

There were big high cliffs and you could see water trickling down, absolutely pure drinking water and very cool. So we sank these Norton tubes down, driving them down. These pipes were about six foot lengths and you could screw them into each other. We got the pumps on at various stages until we discovered we could get a good supply of water coming through. We pumped it up into big troughs we built there. Eventually we had to build a reservoir just above Lancashire Landing on the high ground there. It was our job to quarry all the stone out of the cliffs. Then we used to pump the water into the reservoir until it was full. The front line troops used to send their water carts down, fill them up and away they go.[31] (Sapper Leslie Matthews)

Local sources of water were supplemented by water brought in barges from Egypt and, despite the efforts of the engineers and their auxiliaries, the problems were such that the expeditionary force was to rely on Egyptian water until the evacuation. The problem was how to carry it once it was ashore. Colonel Patterson of the Zion Mule Corps recalled the preparations.

As one of our duties in Gallipoli would be to supply the troops in the trenches with water, an Alexandrian firm had been ordered to make some thousands of kerosine oil tins, the manufacture of which is a local industry. Wooden frames had also been ordered to fit on to the pack saddle, so as to enable the mules to carry the tins. Each mule was to carry four of these full of water, equal to sixteen gallons.[32] (Lieutenant Colonel John Patterson)

Although the mules and their drivers carried up vast amounts of water the most ubiquitous beast of burden was as ever the ordinary soldier on water-ration parties.

In the front line they tried to find their own water with makeshift wells.

We get liquid of sorts by digging a hole in the trench and letting it silt up. Of course it has to be boiled but even then it is the colour of milk and as gritty as a grindstone. Tea takes the taste away a bit, but the men say they can tell by the taste whether a Tommy or a Turk is buried beside their particular well![33] (Lieutenant Leslie Grant)

The obvious risks of pollution from many of these sources meant that the troops were supposed to chlorinate the water before use.

Our doctor thought he was a great expert on chlorinating the water which had to be done before it was safe to be drunk. He used to drink his water with the four of us in the mess. He'd say: 'I do know something about this chlorinating, you can't taste it at all and I can assure you it's absolutely safe.' I omitted to tell him that we had taken the water out of the cans before he had chlorinated it, nobody suffered at all. I don't think he ever knew.[34] (2nd Lieutenant John Chitty)

Despite all this effort, not enough water got to the troops in the front line: 'We are supposed to get a gallon a day; if we did, we could manage comfortably, but it doesn't seem we shall, and any well water is as good as drinking disease – always thought I was like a camel and could do without it – but this is too hot here.'[35] In such circumstances washing was very much a secondary consideration. Consequently the corpses were not the only bodies to smell at Gallipoli. 'I got my boots off for the first time since Saturday week. By judicious pinching of the nostrils I managed to extricate myself from the had been socks and heave them on to the parapet to air.'[36] The men were expected to shave where at all possible, and it must have been a difficult and painful business with blunt razors. They tried their best but nothing seemed easy at Gallipoli: 'I spared some of my water to go in a little tin I had, a Nestlés milk tin cleaned out. I'd get my shaving kit, heat the water with a candle underneath it and with a mirror I could shave.'[37] Most seemed to have adopted as a haircut the very, very short back and sides. 'Irvine cut my hair with clippers and has left me *none*. Suppose it will grow by the time the war is over! Hope so or I'll have to go into a monastery! It is very pleasant and cool tho' and much cleaner when one gets so dusty and can't wash thoroughly always.'[38]

Given these difficulties in keeping clean another common irritant for the long-suffering troops was lice. This came as a shock to some of the less experienced soldiers. 'We were sat down and my mate pulled his shirt off and started killing lice. He said: "Just look at them, they're like elephants!" I said: "You dirty devil you must be filthy." He said: "Have a look at your shirt!" so I had a look at my shirt and it was the same!'[39] Many different methods were tried to get rid of lice. 'Oooh dear me, we used to nip them and squeeze them. They used to get in the seams of your trousers and ooh dear me. We used to take our trousers off, sit naked, lift the seam up and go down there with a hot ember, we used to burn ourselves sometimes, you couldn't get rid of them. You got used to them.'[40] It was a never-ending battle against an enemy that seemed as implacable as the Turks. 'We used to have a louse parade every day – go down the seams of your trousers and shirt if you had a candle. Sometimes the blankets got lousy and you couldn't do anything about it. We used to get Keatings flea powder but I think they like that! You'd wriggle and squirm, some would curse and they'd get scabies and scratch their legs till blood came.'[41] Considerable doubt was thrown upon the efficacy of various household preparations sent out in parcels. 'Our relatives sent us tins of anti lice ointment and I think the swines used to feed on that because they seemed more active after we rubbed it on ourselves.'[42] For most of the men nothing seemed to work: 'Camphor was issued in small bags with tape attachment for suspension around the neck. One humorist was heard to enquire "How will this keep 'em out the seat of my trousers?" The futility of the camphor bags was admitted when one day a nest of vermin was found inside one of them.'[43] However, one unsolicited testimony was received from Private Thomas Northcote: 'I had a cake of Lifebuoy soap and I washed all over and I never got any lice. I swear by Lifebuoy soap now!'[44] Slightly more extreme was a cure recommended by Denis Buxton: 'Creosol seems to be the only remedy for lice. I soaked my clothes in a weak solution a fortnight ago and have had none since.'[45] But one cure stands out on its own as a case of out of the frying pan into the fire.

> Providentially ant colonies abounded and it was discovered later that lice were one of their pet aversions. Our shirts were therefore placed over the ants' castles with marvellous results, but we had to be careful to see that all ants had been removed before dressing again, as we found to our cost that no flea could nibble like an outraged ant.[46] (Able Seaman Thomas Macmillan)

The troops wore khaki drill uniforms which stood up to the conditions as well as could be expected. They were usually filthy dirty and ragged, for any concept of 'spit and polish' had had to be abandoned. A lot of them wore abbreviated forms of their uniform. Joe Murray and many of the Hood Battalion had cut down their trousers to shorts even before they left Egypt.

> It was getting hot so they decided that with our thick uniforms they'd let us cut the trousers down a bit and make them knee length. You ought to have seen the fun. We had a jackknife, no scissors and we had to cut them off. Well you'd cut one trouser leg off, you'd try the trouser – ooh that's fine. But when you got to the other leg it would be too short, then too long and we'd be cutting – at the finish you had very little trouser left! Cutting and carving and of course we were all half naked on the sand with our trousers spread out. People were walking about laughing their eyes out. Ooh dear me! They thought we were praying to Allah I think![47] (Ordinary Seaman Joe Murray)

Everything they wore and possessed was covered in a layer of muck, as Gallipoli had become a dust-bowl by mid-summer.

> The dust in camp was most trying. It gets into all one's belongings and irritates eyes, nose and throat. I bathed twice, but the dust follows you out to sea, and coats your wet skin as you come out. Also your tea and jam at mealtimes. It is the high wind that is partly responsible, and the fact that we have worn all the scrub and vegetation off the earth around W Beach.[48] (Private Denis Buxton)

As one soldier sarcastically asked: 'Is that sediment at the bottom of your mug the sugar, sweet delicious sugar? No – it is grit and sand blown down from the parapet overhead. Pour in a little water, swish it round and chuck the contents out. Some of the matter ejected from the mug quite possibly covered bones a month or two ago.'[49]

The lice and general filth faded into insignificance compared to the omnipresent flies.

> One of the biggest curses was the flies. There was millions and millions of flies. The whole of the side of the trench used to be

one black swarming mass. Anything you opened, a tin of bully, it would be swarming with flies. If you were lucky enough to have a tin of jam and opened that swarms of flies went into it. They were all around your mouth and on any cuts or sores that you'd got, which all turned septic through it. Immediately you bared any part of the body you were smothered. It was a curse, it really was.[50] (Private Harold Boughton)

In letters they tried to explain just how bad it was.

Think of Gulliver bound and enslaved by the mischievous Lilliputians: I feel as helpless as Gulliver. These imps of darkness settle upon one, and all belongings, in black clouds and drive one crazy. Our nights are not given over to sleep. I think I've forgotten how to sleep. If one tries to in the day-time down comes the pestilent black cloud with buzzing wings, glutinous feet and filth covered proboscis to harass one to the verge of insanity.[51] (Major Claude Foster)

The cynical mused on the inherent possibilities of the situation. 'No wind and 30 billion more flies than yesterday. I suppose there must be a maximum number allowed otherwise I don't know what will happen if each one is capable of laying so many thousand eggs per minute or whatever it is!'[52] During the summer there was never any real respite. For although things were better at night the flies were still a brooding presence. 'We made ourselves a shallow dugout with a roof of a blanket over the top. The blanket at night was solid with flies and it was a great point that if anyone came to visit you, you had to say: "For heaven's sake don't bang your head or you'll bring them all down." If you did touch it the whole mass of black flies would come on to you.'[53]

The juxtaposition between corruption and the flies was obvious. 'There was a group of Turkish dead in front of my fire step, and I observed that in almost every case the head was thrown back and the mouths wide open. Into the gaping mouths the flies poured and out of the gaping mouths on to us they came.'[54] It was not only the corpses that the flies frequented prior to the troops' food. The latrines were an obvious attraction to the discerning fly. 'Myriad flies made the place their happy hunting ground, and myriad paid dearly for it since it gave us no end of satisfaction to bury them when covering our outpourings with sand.'[55] To eat food contaminated by flies was to risk dysentery or other debilitating diseases, but the only alternative was not to eat. 'If you were having jam and bread you'd have them on your bread right up to your mouth. You didn't throw it away you know, if you did that you wouldn't have any, you had to eat it.'[56] The troops tried to protect themselves from the flies but with little success. 'You had one hand slapping flies all the time and trying to eat with the other one.'[57] The trouble was that with so many flies and so few hands the battle was hopeless. 'Bang, you'd squash them. But you see that made dampness and within seconds there was twice as many as what there was originally. You couldn't get rid of them.'[58] Some tried for mass killings: 'I used to cover the top of a box with sugar and kill flies en masse with a sort of home made ping pong racquet, but although I often went on killing till I was tired, it never seemed to make any difference.'[59] Other solutions were sought. 'We were given fly bags to put over our heads. Into that you would put your biscuit and jam and close it up underneath. Then eat with a buzzing all round you so that you couldn't even see through it for the flies outside.'[60] Diversionary tactics were tried: 'What we used to do was stick a pot of jam in front of us to draw them away, they'd flock down there.'[61] One gifted young man strove manfully to prove that his pen was indeed mightier than the cursed fly.

> There once was a man who said: 'Why,
> Should I suffer the bites of this fly?
> I'm prepared to concede,
> That it must have a feed,
> But let it be Jerrold, not I.'[62]
>
> (Sub Lieutenant A. P. Herbert)

His hoped-for victim was Lieutenant Douglas Jerrold of the Hawke Battalion, who was to survive to write a history of the RND. The flies were to persist until the great blizzard in late November.

*

314

The latrine arrangements available to the troops were uniformly primitive at Gallipoli, and the traditional latrine story has a long-standing appeal to the British sense of humour. 'We had pails. The sanitary squad used to empty them anywhere. One chap emptied it over the trench but the other side of the trench was another trench where an officer slept and it went all over him. It was a great joke amongst the regiment.'[63] Other misfortunes awaited the unlucky.

> The latrines were a trench roughly six feet deep and a yard wide.
> Roughly about ten feet long. The seating was two posts driven
> into the ground at each end forming an 'X' and then a pole was
> lodged along on the cross piece. You sat on that in full view of
> everybody. Of course it didn't matter a damn because there was
> nobody around, no women or anything like that. On one occasion
> I heard a terrific shout and the pole had snapped and the four
> men sitting on the pole fell into the muck. To get them out they
> had to put rifles down for them to hang onto. They came out like
> slimy rabbits. The sergeant who was near said: 'Clear off down to
> the beach and get into the sea.' They had to because no one
> wanted to get near them.[64] (Private Harry Baker)

The combination of a totally unsuitable diet, flies, putrid corpses and latrines resulted in the terrible debilitating disease of dysentery, which afflicted almost everyone who set foot on the peninsula. 'House flies are much the most important means of spreading dysentery. Their two favourite articles of diet are faeces and jam.'[65] A fly generally defecates while eating and so the infection went round in the most vicious of circles. It was this disease, above all, that caused the rapid disillusionment which afflicted those who landed at Gallipoli. Thousands of men suffered agonies as they lived with a hole in the ground as a toilet, no paper and no way of washing the muck away.

> With dysentery you keep on trying to discharge something but
> there's nothing to discharge, it's only slime, just slime, no solids
> at all. Then of course we didn't have any toilet paper and you had
> to wipe yourself with your hand, there's nothing else. Then you'd
> wipe your hand – originally on the grass, but grass was getting a
> bit short – rub your hands on the sand and your trousers.[66]
> (Ordinary Seaman Joe Murray)

The result was that 'You felt so weak with dysentery, you'd got no strength, you were as weak as a kitten. The doctor asked me one night how many times I went to the latrines, I said sixteen times. You rush out there and when you get there you couldn't do anything.'[67] Once the disease took hold the deterioration in a soldier's physical condition was rapid. 'Very often you had to run out in the open and not trouble about latrines, you couldn't help it. You had to drop your trousers on the ground anywhere. You felt terrible in yourself generally, you lost a lot of weight.'[68] Troops in this state were not militarily efficient. 'You're not able to do anything. Not when it gets you as bad as that. You don't feel like doing anything. You just say, "Och, let me die, I don't care."'[69] Self-preservation ceased to have any meaning. 'If you saw a man with dysentery if he was able to sit up he was lucky, he'd generally lie down wherever he was, exposed, it didn't matter at all, just dead to the world.'[70] Gradually the victims lost all control of their bodies. 'You had to keep running to the toilet, you had your trousers soaked through. You had blood through your trousers.'[71] In time the latrines became places of horror.

> If you'd looked in there you'd have been sickened. You'd think they'd parted with their stomachs or their insides. It was awful. You had to cover it and dig another. It hadn't to be so high or else you could fall down. There were no supports or anything, it was just an open trench but it was fairly deep.[72] (Private Harold Pilling)

Eventually men in the final stages of the disease had neither the strength nor the inclination to drag themselves away from these cess-pits of despair. 'You had perpetual diarrhoea, when you were very bad you had to sleep at the latrines – you'd see men taking their blankets to the latrines, terribly weakening.'[73] If they reported to the Medical Officer there was little he could do.

> You looked ill, you had no energy. I was in a bad way. I went to see the MO and said: 'I think you'll have to send me away now.' He said: 'Stop another few days, we've got no sergeants left, we've nobody left hardly. We're short of officers, NCOs and everything. Stay another couple of days.' 'Oh,' I said, 'alright.' So I went back to my wet trench.[74] (Sergeant William Davies)

Under the active-service conditions, which caused endless reinfection, there was no cure, and eventually those with serious dysentery either left Gallipoli or died.

> I saw the MO and said: 'I'm going now.' He said: 'Alright lad.' I left them and walked down towards the beach. I fell. I couldn't do any more. I'd got my rifle and my equipment. I couldn't get up. A fellow came along. He said: 'What's up sergeant?' He picked me up and we walked down to the beach. He laid me down on the beach. I didn't remember anything more until I was on the French Hospital Ship *Garçon*.[75] (Sergeant William Davies)

Dysentery was a truly awful disease that could rob a man of the last vestiges of human dignity before it killed him.

> My old pal, a couple of weeks ago he was as smart and upright as a guardsman. After about ten days to see him crawling about, his trousers round his feet, his backside hanging out, all soiled, his shirt – everything was soiled. He couldn't walk. My pal got a hold of him by one arm, I got a hold him by the other. Neither he nor I were very good but we weren't like that. It's degrading, dragging him to the latrine, when you remember how you saw him just a little while ago. We lower him down next to the latrine. We're trying to keep the flies off him. We were trying to turn him round, put his backside in towards the trench. I don't know what happened but he simply rolled into this foot-wide trench, half sideways, head first into this slime. We couldn't pull him out, we didn't have any strength and he couldn't help himself at all. We did eventually get him out but he was dead, he'd drowned in his own excrement.[76] (Ordinary Seaman Joe Murray)

There were other prevalent diseases which capitalized on the weak state of the troops until often one man would have a combination of distressing ailments, all spread by the flies and insanitary conditions. For Major Claude Foster the disease was jaundice. 'It puts one into a rotten condition. The liver gets congested as well, so that walking becomes a horrible thing and one suffers constant pain and uneasiness.'[77] He agonized over his predicament:

I'm torn between a feeling that I ought to stay here as long as I'm fit to crawl about, and a common sense prompting to go away, and seek conditions most suitable for recovery, strength and health, and the latter has triumphed. . . . But jaundice! To think of me being put out of business by jaundice, after having dodged shells and bullets and dysentery all these months! Well it makes one feel sore.[78] (Major Claude Foster)

Jaundice was not usually regarded as very serious but it was often part of a cocktail of ailments. Another sufferer recalled the sick parade he attended while at Lemnos:

We paraded for a sick parade. Well I had my eyes all bitten with flies, my hair cropped. A couple of the doctors came along. One said to me: 'Any Chinese in your family?' I said: 'No.' He said: 'You sure?' The other one said: 'What do you think?' 'Well, he looks like it, I think his mother must have been chased by a Chinaman!' Anyhow they marked me down for evacuation. I'd got dysentery and yellow jaundice.[79] (Private Arthur Bonney)

Another common component of the Gallipoli cocktail was paratyphoid or enteric fever. This was spread by an existing sufferer from the disease, because the infecting organism could still be present in his excreta up to a year after he had had the illness. From there it was a short step with the flies to the food and water of others, and so the infection spread until there were about 5,700 cases at Gallipoli in all. The symptoms included headaches, stomach pains, diarrhoea, a bronchial cough, large irregular spots and a high temperature with the associated sweating. Although not often fatal it was a debilitating condition. Prevention once the disease was established proved impossible, as mild cases were not often correctly diagnosed and thus continued to spread the infection. Inoculation was partially effective but offered its own perils. 'It was decided that we should be re-inoculated against fever and the doctor came along puncturing each of us with his needle. Unfortunately the needle broke and he said: "Well I haven't got another one," so the rest of the men had to have the needle banged into them.'[80]

Even malaria was a problem, particularly to those soldiers of the 29th Division, such as Captain Nightingale, who had served in

India and contracted the disease there. Attacks were recurrent. 'I had a slight touch of malaria yesterday when I woke up but by taking a large quantity of aspirin I managed to sweat it out before the evening and am alright today, though feeling a bit weak.'[81] This relief was only temporary though, for soon he was writing from a convalescent ship: 'I indulged in 6 days malaria and was finally sent on board here last night to recover, as there seems to be no chance whatever of my getting rid of it where we were.'[82]

A further effect of the conditions was the collection of symptoms known as disordered action of the heart or 'soldier's heart'. This is the generic name for a variety of cardiac disorders suffered by soldiers, usually due to a combination of over-exertion, mental strain and lack of sleep acting on a constitution weakened by some form of toxaemia or disease. As can be imagined, this disorder was very prevalent at Gallipoli, where these conditions were the typical lot of the average soldier.

Another trial which could greatly add to the misery of the troops was toothache. This could be a relatively trivial discomfort, but if dental treatment became necessary it was very primitive. 'I had a toothache and, resting on that fire step, every time a bomb went off, the vibration went through the earth and up through into my jaw. I could feel it more with the tooth. A chap who was supposed to be a dentist pulled a couple of my teeth out with a pair of signalling pliers.'[83]

The overall effect of all this sickness among the troops was the dreadful appearance which caused a shock to new arrivals.

> We walked around after a time like skeletons, finding it difficult even to move at times. If we were out of the line on fatigues like water carrying or helping to dig roads and so on it was as much as we could do to lift the tools or whatever we were carrying. There was a time when down on the beach some reinforcements arrived and looking at them it was quite clear the contrast between what would be normal and after life on Gallipoli after a few months. These young fellows had come out from home and we were quite struck with their fresh rosy complexions, we almost thought they were from another world. They too I suppose would

look at us and see these sallow lean skeletons and regard us too as from another world.[84] (Signaller R. J. Carless)

For most of these new arrivals Gallipoli was their first time under fire and, though they may have had their heroic fantasies, most just wanted to control their fears.

When they started shelling that scared me stiff. The shrapnel came over, it was like hailstones. I only got the wind up once and it lasted for the rest of the war. We had to go immediately up the front line and bullets started flying about. Really and truly the man who says that he wasn't scared is a liar! George Washington said he liked the sound of bullets whizzing over his head – but he wasn't in my war![85] (Ordinary Seaman Joe Murray)

Gradually they settled down: 'One gains courage for the first week as a rolling stone gains impetus; after that one's courage gradually oozes away again.'[86]

The daily routine of trench life to which they were introduced was one of a sordid, filthy monotony slashed by sudden death. The men slept in what dugouts they had managed to hollow out in the side of the trench or more usually just on the fire step or bottom of the trench.

There is so little room for the men to sleep in the firing line that they *have* to sleep on the firing step many of them, and some actually prefer to lie at full length on the floor and put up with the kicks of the patrolling officer. They never wake. I suppose a really tired man seldom does.[87] (Lieutenant George Hughes)

Morning brought 'stand to'. This was, as it suggests, when the whole of the battalion would stand to to repel any Turkish attack – a period of heightened readiness administered in different ways in different units but usually taking place at the hour of dawn.

All the men are supposed to be standing on the firing step for an hour before dawn, the reported hour when all armies attack one another because man's vitality is at its lowest ebb then. Certainly after an hour of waiting about in the dark wandering up and down my precipitous section of trench, my vitality was generally at a very low ebb.[88] (Lieutenant George Hughes)

A twenty-four-hour sentry-duty rota was established to keep an eye on the Turks. With the ever-present threat of a bullet through the head from snipers, it was obviously too risky to look directly over the parapet when on daytime sentry duty. One solution was to use periscopes where available. But even such a simple device was not fool-proof.

We'd just arrived at the first trench and one of our men had been given a periscope to carry which he'd no idea what it was for. So we told him he had to look through that and he could see over the trench what was happening in front. So he stood there looking through this with care. He said: 'I can see water.' 'Oh good.' 'I can see a big ship . . .' 'Oh you silly . . . you're the wrong way round.' So we turned him round and of course all he could show us then was bushes and trees![89] (Corporal Arthur Hemsley)

The average sentry would not look over the top all the time even with a periscope but would glance for a moment or two just to check all was well while listening for signs of increased Turkish activity. Even at night he had to be careful of Turkish snipers, fixed-line rifles or casually firing machine-guns.

One night I was sat down at the bottom of the trench and my rifle and bayonet were gleaming in the moonlight. I felt reassured when I saw that rifle gleaming and a fellow was watching out. He'd just got his head over, you daren't put your head over too much. There was a way you had to put your head over. You didn't look quick and down again, you put it up slow so they wouldn't notice and down again.[90] (Private George Peake)

An older, experienced soldier would often try to reassure his comrades.

Some of them were quite nervous. They wanted you to be awake to give them a bit of confidence. One or two, youngsters, would look at the wire and the post. All of a sudden their eye would water and they would swear blind that there was somebody coming: 'Stand by, stand by,' and there was nobody at all there. You had to put up a Verey light then to see if there was anybody about. I never felt there was any danger, you were just unlucky if you got shot.[91] (Lance Corporal Alexander Burnett)

The junior subaltern's role was to patrol the front lines checking the sentries were alert. Their advice was not always appreciated. 'The officer, he'd come round when it was dark and tell you you had to look over the top. Which I thought was daft you know. Of course you had to turn and face front when he was talking but when he'd gone you didn't do with it. Because you couldn't see and if there'd been any bullets you could have been killed.'[92] It was not an easy task for the officers as they made their rounds along the crowded trenches filled with sleeping soldiers. They were only too aware of the consequences if they found a sleeping sentry.

As an officer I knew what a serious matter it was to be court martialled for being asleep on sentry duty. Also it was a serious matter if, as an officer, you found somebody asleep and you didn't report the matter. So what we used to do was to go down the trenches and if we thought a chap was asleep we'd knock his legs from under him and then go on twenty yards, then turn back and come and talk to him. He was invariably awake by then![93] (2nd Lieutenant George Horridge)

In fact of course the poor sentry was only too aware of his peril, but exhaustion, coupled with ill-health, often meant that it was a near physical impossibility to guarantee not to go to sleep: 'I was on watch and I don't remember anything until suddenly I fell down with a blooming crash at the bottom of the trench. Rifle and bayonet – it was a wonder I didn't kill myself. But I never thought about being hurt. I scrambled back as quick as I could because I'd be for a court martial.'[94] The men would help each other as much as they were physically able, given their own exhaustion: 'There was lots of cases where men fell asleep but his chum would wake him. I remember lots of times I shut my eyes and then all of a sudden I was awake, somebody had given me a kick. We were so exhausted. You had to stand on the fire step and you used to slide down the wall eventually finishing on your backside at the bottom of the trench. No idea, no warning.'[95]

One other duty of sentries was guarding against any form of infiltration by the Turks, who had gained a great reputation for this kind of thing among the British troops.

> Turkish officers had been getting into our communication trench, saying is Mr So and So there and as soon as ever the officer went down they'd shoot him and back in to the Turkish lines in no time. They warned us about this and asked us to keep guard on that. We were in a little bit of a corner in the trench, me and another chap. We waited and we heard two coming up talking. So we jumped out quick and I got my bayonet under one's chin and I said: 'Who are you?' 'I'm Brigadier Frith.' It was the general. He had his chin in the air with my bayonet underneath it![96] (Private George Peake)

Another form of sentry duty was that of listening posts actually out in no-man's land. 'Listening was not a nice job by any means. A small party of picked men, who can be trusted not to sleep and not to get nervous, are sent out in reliefs, two men for each relief which lasts an hour. They go along a sap, crawl out into the open in front of our lines and take a half hour turn each listening through an instrument.'[97] Harry Baker was obviously one of those who could be trusted not to get nervous:

> Between stand to at night and stand down in the morning men had to go and lie between the two trenches. They were unarmed and their business was to report any movements from the Turks. All you had was a knife and a piece of string which you pulled if there was any sign of movement. But the Turks used to come out sometimes and rob the boots of the dead men and empty their packs. You laid there for one hour. One night I was out there and I'd got shorts – I'd cut off my trousers and made them into shorts – and suddenly I felt something on the back of my right thigh. At that very moment a Verey light went up and lit up the whole area. I stealthily looked round and there was a big mouse sitting on the back of my thigh, which I was very glad to see instead of a Turk.[98] (Private Harry Baker)

323

While the sentries were on duty other men would be engaged in the repair and improvement of the trenches. Although some of this could be attempted during the day most of it was carried out at night. Another task that certainly could only be attempted at night was erecting, consolidating and repairing the barbed wire in front of the trenches.

> One can't of course go putting up elaborate entanglements driving stakes in, and all that, but we build up lengths in the trench, shove 'em over and then go out and roll them quietly out about 15 or 20 yards. . . . A wooden framework – 14 feet long and looped round with barbed wire. But the difficult part is that just in front of our trench there are old loose ends and bits of Turkish wire. I and another fellow were shoving one of these things out the other night and I got into a network of stuff and was thoroughly hung up for about 10 (years it seemed) minutes I suppose. I could have sworn the wire was human. Lying absolutely flat you'd get one leg clear and without moving it an inch you'd find wire wrapped all around it while you were freeing the other leg. But the worst part is that the men *will* chuck empty bully beef tins over the parapet and it's very difficult to move about sounding like a milk cart.[99] (Major Norman Burge)

With the lines often so close together, patrols in no-man's land were not a major feature of Gallipoli trench life, but nevertheless they were carried out in some areas. 'You had to be careful in getting out of our trench to patrol at night because there were two places where you could get out of the trench fairly easily and the Turks had machine-guns aligned on them. I think we lost about half of our officers from blind shooting at night.'[100] In many units patrolling was a voluntary activity and some officers resisted all blandishments to do so.

> Patrolling is a game of hide and seek in the dark, generally with no particular object except to come across an enemy patrol, in which event, both sides run. . . . This adds to the interest of the game . . . but it's a risky game if you are to do any good, and the result generally nil. I decided early that I would not risk my neck voluntarily.[101] (Lieutenant George Hughes)

Sergeant Edward Miles of the 8th Duke of Wellingtons took out a fairly typical reconnaissance patrol.

> I proceeded out from Jefferson's Post, through our wire and continued crawling out until we reach the Turkish wire. This was a dangerous job as you will see. We creep along this wire looking for any gaps (which we have to report, as it may be an indication that the enemy is going to make a raid), and we have to fall flat on our stomachs as one or other of the Turkish sentries spots us and fire. After getting wet through and covered with mud, we make our way back into the lines down by Green Knoll. The sentries there were told to expect us just before daybreak, so we manage to crawl in without being fired on. Tired and weary, I make my way to the Company Officer's Dugout to report.[102] (Sergeant Edward Miles)

Miles would perhaps have been outraged if he knew what some officers thought men like himself had been doing.

> The men drop over the top of the parapet, creep through the wires, not a difficult thing in front of our lines, past the listening posts, which are blissfully unconscious of their presence, and so on wherever the fancy leads them. The only essential is to invent a story by 4 o'clock next morning when they return, to conceal the fact they have been quietly sleeping in some hollow. . . . The sergeant major and I always faked the patrol's report, and generally invented something original to please the CO such as Turkish working party heard in the deserted trench at midnight.[103] (Lieutenant George Hughes)

2nd Lieutenant Reginald Rathbone was sent on a fighting patrol in December:

> I took out a good bomber and a couple of riflemen. I said: 'We're going to get as close to the Turkish trenches as we can and I want you to throw as many bombs as you can into them, then we get back.' Well we got fairly near and I said: 'Carry on now with the bombs.' There were loud crashes, it was too dark to see if they'd actually got into the Turkish trench but I hope they did. They promptly opened fire and I said: 'Righto that's enough, we'll get

back.' We didn't run but we lost no time in getting back to the trench.[104] (2nd Lieutenant Reginald Rathbone)

When the troops were out of the line they were based in rest camps nearer the beaches. 'I've been puzzling why it's called a rest camp. The only solution I can think of is that some bullets hit the trenches and the rest come over to us!'[105] The dugouts the troops used there were of a simple nature. 'We dug a grave-like hole about six feet long, two feet wide and as deep as we could get according to the nature of ground, sometimes only two feet, sometimes we'd go down four feet – quite nice. We put a waterproof sheet over the top and lumps of stone on each corner, protection not from shrapnel but from the sun.'[106] From such simple beginnings the troops tried to protect themselves as best they could from the shells, which could rain down without warning at any time of the day or night. Everyone tried to 'win' materials to strengthen their dugouts.

Robson and I made a very fine dugout. It was in an old Turkish trench. We dug the head in under the solid earth and lined it with biscuit tins filled with earth. Then for a roof we first 'won' some wood and corrugated iron from a RE dump. When we had it finished one of the officers from the dump came and examined it and said: 'That is a nice roof.' 'Yes Sir.' 'When you have finished it just put the wood and iron back on my dump.' 'Yes Sir' said we despondently and proceeded to remove our roof back where it belonged.[107] (Sapper Thomas Rowatt)

Periods in the rest camps were not even necessarily times of relaxation for the troops.

Of working parties there seemed no end. Our Division was kept on the trot so constantly that they came to be known as 'The White Slaves of Gallipoli'. As a result of overwork, tempers went from bad to worse. On being detailed for fatigues, groups would sing aloud, even in the presence of the officers:

> Working, Working, Working
> Always bloody well working

> Working in the morning
> And working all day long.
>
> And this would be followed by muttered curses, coarse and gross. To demonstrations of this kind our tolerant Company Commander turned a deaf ear.[108] (Able Seaman Thomas Macmillan)

All this activity both in and out of the line left only limited opportunities for recreation, and the easiest form of entertainment available was conversation. 'Sometimes in the evenings the Doc and I have little sorts of competitions. One will ask the other "Describe all the carpets you can remember," or a discussion on the size and price of sheets. But talk like that is invariably only the curtain raiser to the tragedy: "What would you be having for dinner and what show would you go to after – if you were in London tonight?"[109] A sense of humour was a great asset under such conditions.

> When Pincher had no real news to impart he never failed to be diverting. In a loud voice he would put the question: 'Have you heard the news?' To this we would reply automatically in full voice: 'No, what's the news this morning?' 'The Swiss Navy has put to sea' was one of his hardy annuals. Among others more subtle were: 'Mr Asquith is now a cabinet maker and Lloyd George is learning his trade' and 'Lloyd George is getting more shells from the sea shore.' When his invention failed, he trotted out the old favourite about the squire's daughter being foully murdered. It was an ill day when Pincher could not be funny in the morning.[110] (Able Seaman Thomas Macmillan)

Amusing incidents were treasured by all ranks for the release of tension that they offered. Thus one group of officers demonstrated that they were more than a match for the Turkish mouse. 'We killed a mouse today, Staveley having 5 shots at it with a revolver. The excitement was something frightful. If my British warm doesn't come, I had better keep the skin.'[111] The local wildlife also offered the chance of amusement in pursuing a primitive form of propaganda warfare.

> There were tons of tortoises and sometimes we used to get them, make a little hole in the shell on their back, stick a piece of wood

into it, cut a niche in the wood and put a piece of card in it with a rude message to Johnny Turk. We steered them off towards the Turkish trenches, I don't suppose they could read it but anyway it occupied some time.[112] (Private Harold Boughton)

Rumour was a way of life, which the *Peninsula Press*, a single-sheet newspaper distributed for the troops, merely fanned into greater life. 'Rather a disturbing message today. Reported arrival in Constantinople of German chemists and the belief is that they are there to make asphyxiating gas. Very disagreeable! Shells are bad enough already, but we have our precautions. It's a depraved and devilish idea.'[113] A good idea of the range and nature of rumours concerning the progress of the war is given by an RND surgeon's diary: 'Yesterday was the most prolific day in buzzes we have ever had. They included the following: 1. Naval battle off Calais, 12 German and 5 English ships sunk. 2. Crown Prince's Army smashed or surrendered and captured. 3. Great Russian victory near Riga. 4. Romania and Bulgaria both joined in with us.'[114] Two days later he wrote: 'News today good: 1. Russians retaken Warsaw. 2. French advance 4kms with gas. 3. We've captured 3 submarines out here in nets, drowned the crews and are now using the submarines ourselves.'[115]

Letters from home were keenly awaited. Unfortunately a combination of the distance to be travelled, submarine sinkings, pilfering and plain inefficiency meant that letters were few and far between, arriving months out of date. 'Not a line from anyone yet. It's getting too much. If no news is good news then I've had enough good news!'[116] The letters would usually arrive six weeks or so after posting and then often in batches. This was not necessarily a disadvantage.

> Yesterday evening I got no less than 6 letters from you all in one bundle, the last dated Aug 7. That is the way to get letters. It takes something more than the usual line or two to break the potent and malignant spell of the war bound soldier. But when he has six letters then he is led away to heaven and kept there for so long

he has almost forgotten the abominations of life in the trenches and the sorrows of exile.[117] (Major Claude Foster)

Depending on the soldier's character they would write on a regular basis to their immediate family, sweethearts, wives and close friends. These letters were often fairly mundane, restricted as they were by the knowledge that the censor would be reading them before their correspondent. Yet it is strangely touching to read the outpourings of a man who survived Gallipoli only to die on the Somme in 1916.

> Always you are both in my thoughts, I think of you both in that little kitchen by yourselves, I know that you are thinking of me and wondering perhaps if you will ever see me come back again. Every night at 9 oclock out here which is seven o clock in England, I think that it is the Boy's bedtime and I always can picture him kneeling in his cot saying his prayers after his Mummy. But 'Cheer Up' My Scrumps, this will all end soon and we shall be together again and carry on the Old Life once more, but we *must* have patience and not worry.[118] (Corporal Bert Fielder)

Writing materials were scarce and this could impede even the most devoted of correspondents. 'Excuse this paper, it is out of my note book. I am trusting to finding some kind person with an envelope; don't forget to put one in your letters when you write if you want an answer. . . . Oh this is an awful pencil and my fountain pen is dry.'[119]

The censoring was carried out by an officer or padre and it was generally regarded as a fairly tedious task, leavened only by moments of often unintentional humour. 'Censored letters again, a job which seldom repays doing more than once or twice. For one gem you wade through pages about foodstuffs and parcels!! One fellow after two pages of talk about tinned foods declared that this place made you forget all your finer feelings.'[120] Some even forgot the glazed eye of the censor. 'Another villain declares: "I'm afraid I shan't get home yet, my health is too good."'[121] Others used it as an excuse: 'One man writing was very brief, he said: "Dear Aunt,

This war is a fair b—. I cannot say more, the censor won't let me. Your loving Nephew Jack."'[122] Often the letters were written to a formula: 'He was a sprightly fellow, who always started his letters to his girl: "Things are still just the same out here, as black as they could be," a sentence which I equally regularly crossed out.'[123]

For those who were religious the imminence of corporal dissolution made it crucial to attempt to organize some religious services. Harold Thomas was a Church of England curate who had enlisted as a stretcher-bearer with the 1/3rd East Anglian Field Ambulance. After the Church of England padre had been sent home sick:

> The Methodist decided to hold a Communion Service and issued an invitation to all who cared to come. I went with another parson ranker and a Methodist minister who shared with two others my sand hole. The Service was held in a hollow among the sand hills, the 'elements' consisted of pieces of army biscuit on a paten which half an hour earlier had been the bottom of a tobacco tin; the wine was water seasoned with a lemonade cube – the reason for the insertion of the lemonade cube was I remember a mystery to me at the time – perhaps it was intended to make a difference from ordinary water. Anyway no better substitutes could be devised and we received the distribution in faith and were not a little comforted. In the evening a few of us gathered together and with the help of two prayer books managed to sing a few well known hymns. I gave the Absolution and the Blessing while the Methodist Chaplain led in extempore prayer. There was no feeling of constraint in either Service; there was need of God to the few of us who believed in Him, forms had ceased to have any meaning to us; we realized our oneness in Christ and that where 'two or three of us were gathered together there was He in the midst of us'.[124] (Private Harold Thomas)

After a while Thomas and a fellow clergyman private managed to get the necessities for celebrating Communion, but the problems they faced were typical of those faced by padres conducting services within the range of enemy guns.

> It was held in the open by the Corps flag staff wherein many bullets had embedded themselves. Our altar was made of empty

boxes and the congregation knelt on the ground. . . . I suppose nothing could have been much further from the idea of a Solemn Evensong than those strange Services of ours. To begin with our method of summoning our parishioners was one to which a missionary to the Sandwich Isles would hardly be reduced. We borrowed the cook-house gong which was an empty shell case upon which we battered furiously with the long spoon used for stirring the bully beef stew. When we gathered a sufficient number to warrant a start being made we divided our flock into groups of four or five who did their best to get a glimpse of the tattered hymn book which was all we could allot to each group. Hymns not infrequently came to extreme grief through the mistake of key at the outset: the first line would go alright and then often enough we would find ourselves reaching up to notes rarely touched by prima donnas in their prime or scraping down to depths untouched by Santley. The Sermon was nearly always dogged by misfortune. Generally as soon as one had given one's text 'whoosh', 'whoosh' would sound above us and crump crash on the sand dunes by the sea and half your congregation would turn round to see the column of black or yellow smoke spout up fountain like from the ground. That was bad but worse was to follow as the preacher of experience well knew; we had five 60 pounders down there and almost immediately after the explosion of the Turkish shells there would shoot out five wicked looking tongues of flame and the splitting crashes. . . . And yet in old days we had heard of clergy being annoyed and put off by some old lady coughing in the body of the church!! Well, well to have stopped speaking on account of noise at Gallipoli would have been to condemn oneself to perpetual silence. Guns or no guns the service would go on and often the last lingering touch of rose on the peaks of Imbros would fade away as one gave the Blessing of 'the peace of God that passeth all understanding'.[125] (Private Harold Thomas)

Devout souls like Thomas were often lonely voices crying in a literal and metaphorical wilderness. The cult of tobacco seems to have had a far greater grip on the imaginations of the ordinary soldiers. Those who smoked could smoke – but only if they had the wherewithal. In the absence of tobacco, desperate measures were taken. 'The inveterate smokers would be smoking dried tea leaves and things like that, the paper would be coarse, well if you inhaled it was like fish hooks.'[126] Many of the men smoked pipes: 'My mother bought me a lovely present. She went to the little village shop and bought a pound's worth of dark shag tobacco. Packed in this tobacco in a tin were six clay pipes. These were very useful because we could pick up cigarette ends and smoke those.'[127]

Gambling and cards have long been associated with the British soldier under whatever circumstances. 'There was a card party, 7th Platoon I think. The *Goeben* let go with one of her guns and the shell landed right in front of this party and covered them in soil and what have you. I was one that dashed up to give them a hand. We were scratching away like mad and I said: "Who's buried?" "Oh, it's the bloody cards we're looking for," they said!'[128] A similar devotion to gambling was evinced by two men of the 2/4th Cheshires after landing at Suvla. 'We had a couple of lads, one was a bugler and both were underage, there they were on a foreign shore playing brag, that vulgar form of poker, and they quarrelled. A war, enemy soil and they are quarrelling over cards.'[129]

Another rarer form of 'entertainment' was the camp concert, a proceeding which could be enlivened by the occasional shell. The quality of some of the performers seems to have varied:

There was a sing song in the next camp t'other night. In the dark of course, which was lucky for some of the singers who'd have met a dreadful fate if they could have been recognized. There was the usual harrowing song, sung by a gentleman in high pleasure at hearing his own voice and never left go of a note till forced to by lack of breath. He sang 'Darling I'm growing Oh-Oh-Old-*de*, Golden turns to whi-hi*te*', and so on. As there was no accompanist he was able to see that no mistake occurred over the encore by commencing his 2nd song (5 verses long) immediately he'd finished the first. All I remember of it was 'Light of my Life (cough), Child of my Dream*ss*' etc. Awful. Then there was the usual gentleman who started much too high, and the also usual gentleman who forgetting a line in the 3rd verse promptly started off again with the 1st verse to give himself a good start to get over the obstacle. But what was *really* good, was a sort of Irish comic song – you know the sort I mean – absolutely full of words. Only instead of Irish – it was a Tyneside song, full of allusions to Jarrow etc and with a real Noocassel accent. I haven't laughed so much for years, it was awfully clever. A Sub Lt with a good voice sang a topping sort of 'Follies' song, 'Agatha and her Aeroplane' or something like that – with a splendid swing in the chorus.[130] (Major Norman Burge)

Football was not a common recreation for obvious reasons, but some was played.

There was a piece of land where the troops used to play football and I think the Turks used to watch with their field glasses. That was before football was very well known in Turkey. There was not one shell hole on that piece of ground, not one, it was absolutely flat. It was hard and sandy and you could play good football on it. There was the Dardanelles Cup to be fought for by the different regiments. I played left back for the battalion, the ruins of the battalion I should say. We played the Hood Battalion in the Dardanelles Cup and we drew one each. They'd got goal posts made up of trees, they looked a bit raw. They marked out along the side by marking in the sand the lines, no whitewash or anything like that. We stripped right down, our side wore shirts and the other side didn't so it was no trouble for the referee to sort them out. It was quite good, we'd got two professionals in our team.[131] (Private Harry Baker)

Sea bathing is not usually a recreation associated with a fighting front but Gallipoli offered the opportunity to swim under fire. 'We were able to go down and bathe. We used to go down during the day time. Occasionally the Turks would have a snipe at us but there may have been one or two people hit but there certainly weren't more than that.'[132] The Turks certainly caused maximum discomfort for Harold Barrow and his mates, who took shelter without due care and consideration when the Turks opened fire. 'It was very near to Morto Bay and we could bathe there. They put a shot or two over from the Turks' side at Chanak. We were all in our birthday suits taking cover in prickly gorse! We were pulling thorns out of ourselves from all over the place! It was very funny in a way.

About 130 of us squatting out in our birthday suits!'[133] Another problem was the sea itself as the currents were strong and life-threatening. 'We were having a rest when I heard shouts of alarm and looked out. There we could see a lad, we called him Farmer Bell, he was in trouble. Lots of fellows went out and tried to get him but he was lost.'[134] Even the cautious bather could have his enjoyment shattered as the water in the tideless Mediterranean became awfully polluted. 'I flung off my clothes and swam out and sat stride legs on the *Majestic* for a bit. The water reminded me of Leith docks, every kind of filth seemed to be present and swimming back I very nearly ran full tilt into a dead horse. I would have if the smell hadn't warned me in time.'[135]

Gallipoli was unique in that there was no safe rear area – whether the soldier was in the front line, the rest camp dugout or swimming at sea there was always a chance that he could be killed or maimed by enemy fire. Nevertheless, although this strain was continuous, the level of routine day-to-day fighting was less intense than that generally experienced on the Western Front. The main difference lay in the artillery situation, for at Gallipoli both sides were inadequately provided for in terms of both guns and ammunition. 'Fortunately Mr Turk does not seem very well supplied with shell, at all events very little HE shell, otherwise he could make it very uncomfortable for us, indeed it would be a matter of donning our Gieves waistcoats and taking to the water.'[136] The British were in an even worse state and had no HE shells at all at one stage in June.

The total number of shells fired may not have been large but being in the close vicinity of bursting shells was a horrible experience for an individual soldier, whether it was just a couple of strays or part of a rare concentrated bombardment.

> You crouched as low down in the trench as you could, right flat down in the trench and as near to the parapet as you could because you hoped that any explosion would be behind. The ground used to rock and chunks of HE used to fly just like cats miaowing. So long as you heard the explosion you were alright. If you didn't hear the explosion you were not here anymore![137]
> (Private Harry Baker)

The troops gradually learnt to distinguish between the different sorts of artillery fire.

> Shrapnel . . . just whistles through the air like a very big bullet and bursts (there's one just gone) with a puff of smoke which usually has the distinction of being the only thing that can be seen with any resemblance to a cloud. This shell should burst about 20 yards in the air and scatters bullets forward about 200 yards, with a lateral effect of 25 yards. Then there are the other shells, their strident notes varying in shrillness according to their weight. The heavy 60lb shell goes with a tearing grunt that makes your guts ache till you're used to it.[138] (Lieutenant Thomas Watson)

In such a bombardment there was nothing to do except make the best of whatever cover was available – no matter how illusory it was. Wherever the troops were on the peninsula, they were well within the range of Turkish guns and therefore at risk. Unlike the Western Front, where a battalion would serve its period in the line and then retire on rest out of shellfire range, at Gallipoli the mental strain of possible imminent death or maiming was unremitting. Even when communing with nature at the latrines one was at risk: 'Then this morning I *did* hear one coming and couldn't bolt because I was literally caught with my trousers down. Didn't waste any time buttoning up though.'[139] After a few weeks most could say that 'I've had a good many narrow squeaks – not any more than anybody else of course – but somehow they interest me more.'[140] After a while those who survived gained practical experience which reduced the mental and physical torment by enabling them to judge when they were under immediate danger.

> Most shells are gentlemen. To begin with – the vast majority of 'em you hear coming and a very little practice enables you to tell the probable size of it (as if it mattered), its direction, (more important) and probable place of explosion (*most* important). So that newcomers duck and dive and assume most comic attitudes over noises which do not in the least disturb the equanimity of the Cook.[141] (Major Norman Burge)

They also began to realize that most shells missed any meaningful target. The trouble was of course that, even when an individual had accustomed himself to shellfire, pride could come before a fall, as can be seen from Private Harold Medcalf's last remark before being wounded by a shell. 'I'd just come off patrol and the Turks were firing little shells over. I said to my mate, the sergeant, 'They couldn't hit pussy!'[142]

The most famous Turkish batteries were the guns firing from the Asiatic shore and collectively known as 'Asiatic Annie'. These concentrated their fire on the beaches, where they knew that all the British stores, equipment and men had to land. The fire was of an intermittent nature rather than a fierce bombardment. 'From this platform above W Beach we could see the flash of the gun as it went off, then the damn thing would drop – Hell of a Row! You could hear it coming like a train after the damned thing had dropped!'[143] It sounded bad but its bark was worse than its bite. The saving grace for the beach personnel was that 'Eight times out of ten they never exploded, dud shells. But it was frightening for all that.'[144]

Another constant threat to the British troops was the Turkish sniper. As we have seen, in the confusion of the early days they inspired both grudging admiration and undying hatred as a result of their activities behind British lines. When the trench lines were properly established they remained a mortal threat to the unwary. Under the circumstances which prevailed at Gallipoli the Turks were almost always on the higher ground, with a consequently enhanced view into the British trenches. An unnoticed gap in the parapet of just a few inches could spell sudden death. 'One morning in the trench just behind our dugout a couple of people were talking. The Company Sergeant Major was standing next to me more or less touching when he suddenly put his hand up and fell down. A bullet enfilading us had taken him straight through the head.'[145] Obviously the men were careful, but vigilance against exposure to the Turkish sniper had to be continuous and some amount of risk was inevitable. 'I'd been working building sandbags up on the edge of the trench chucking them up. Another chap said: "All right Boughton I'll relieve you now." I stepped down and the first sandbag he put up a sniper got him, that would have been

Photographs of the 1/7th
Manchester Regiment,
42nd Division, at Helles
during the later months
of the campaign.

Officers and men in Gully
Ravine.

A rifle inspection.

Photographs taken by Captain Guy Nightingale, 1st Royal Munster Fusiliers, 29th Division.

The 1st RMF at Helles eighteen days after the landing: 5 officers and 372 Other Ranks.

Scaling ladders used in the recent assault being brought down from the fire trenches at Helles, July.

Captain Guy Nightingale (left), Adjutant, Captain Charles Williams (centre), 2nd in Command, and Lieutenant Colonel Guy Geddes DSO (right), Commanding Officer, outside Battalion HQ Mess at Helles, July.

Men of the 1st RMF bombing a Turkish sap from the position known as Viper's Fang at Sulajik on the inland edge of the Suvla Plain, October.

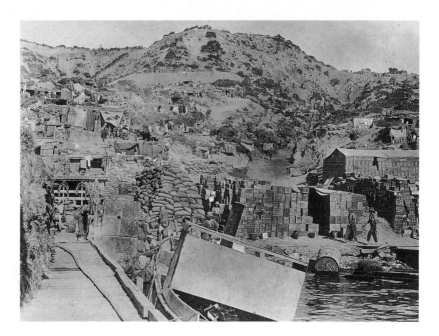

Plugge's Plateau, the first position stormed by the Australians on 25 April, seen from a pier leading off Anzac Cove later in the campaign.

Dead Turks being removed for burial during the armistice at Anzac on 24 May.

Men of the medical service filtering water at Suvla before its issue.

The 5th Royal Irish Fusiliers, 10th Division, holding the British front line at Suvla.

Lieutenant Colonel Guy Geddes DSO, 1st Royal Munster Fusiliers, 29th Division.

Ordinary Seaman Joe Murray, Hood Battalion, RND.

2nd Lieutenant (later
Lieutenant Colonel)
Malcolm Hancock MC,
1/4th Northamptons,
54th Division, re-visiting
C Beach, Suvla Bay, in
1983.

Private Harry Baker,
Chatham Battalion
RMLI, RND, at the
Cenotaph in London on
25 April 1991.

Stores burning at Suvla, 05.00 on 20 December 1915, shortly after the first successful evacuation, seen from HMS *Cornwallis*.

W Beach, looking across the shoreline towards Cape Helles, cluttered with wood and stores, on 8 January 1916, shortly before the final evacuation.

me.'[146] There were many intimidating reminders of these unseen enemies that lurked, not in the imagination, but all too close to hand. 'We had periscopes to look over to the Turkish lines. I had one and a Turkish sniper broke the glass on it. It splintered and it cut my thumb and nose.'[147]

Such accuracy was intimidating and the average soldier did not usually indulge in sniping himself as it was too dangerous, although the basic method was simple. 'You watch all likely places till you see some sign of movement then you lay down the periscope and get on to the parapet, take a quick aim, loose off a round then duck down again. You don't want to overdo the aiming bit of it!'[148] What they were looking for was the careless or over-confident Turkish soldier.

> One day there was a head kept bobbing along, walking down the trench, he must have been about seven feet high. As he walked along his head came up two or three inches. I had a couple of shots at him through the steel plate and he didn't appear any more. I expect I got him. He didn't know he was on show, but he was, and he was on show to the wrong man![149] (Private Harry Baker)

This was a far cry from actually taking on a Turkish sniper, which was nerve-racking in the extreme.

> One morning there was a Turk who they said was picking off our men and would I have a go at him. It was just 'stand to' and he was supposed to be on top of the trench. You could just see his head above the top of the trench. I lined up and fired. Just at that moment one whistled past my ear like that, Wheeeee. . . . I reckon we both fired together and we never had any more bother from him but I reckon he missed by about that much. . . . 'Cor that was close,' I said to Sergeant Hook.[150] (Private Harry Baker)

Even with protective sniper plates you were not safe.

> We had an iron plate with an aperture big enough to get a rifle through. One day I was sniping. About 300 yards away the Turkish trench was. I got a jam on my rifle and I withdrew the rifle and was trying to get the cartridge out when the sniper put a bullet through the aperture, it was only about four inches square.

So I said: 'Righto Boy you're a better shot than I am!'[151] (Private Steve Moyle)

One alternative was to use the periscope rifle, which meant that snipers could fire without exposing themselves to the Turks.

I got a lot of fun with the periscope rifle really. It was pushed up over the top of the trench and it had a reflector fitted on so you could see from down below up along the barrel of the rifle. On one occasion by systematically aiming at the top of the sandbag it made a little jag in it. You then went down two or three inches and gradually split the sandbag down. We were able to completely disrupt one of those sandbagged areas and you could see the part built to hold a machine-gun start to slip. We were rather pleased with it. Of course they built it up at night and next day it was back. That was the kind of thing we were engaged in – just being a damn nuisance as far as we could.[152] (2nd Lieutenant Malcolm Hancock)

Most soldiers seemed only to have fired their rifle in an unaimed fashion, either in response to an urge to hit back without taking risks or out of panic while on sentry duty.

On almost our first night in the trenches some of my men got rather jittery, I don't know why, and started firing at the Turks. Began raising their rifles without aiming them over the trenches and just loosing them off. This encouraged others to join in and we were getting a responding fire from the Turks. This went on till the company commander came along with orders from the CO to stop it which we did. Next day we had a count of the ammunition on each man and it was my platoon in particular. I got a hell of a ticking off![153] (2nd Lieutenant Joseph Napier)

The machine-gun's main role was in defence, where the extra concentrated firepower it offered to supplement rifles and artillery meant that frontal attacks from both sides were costly, if not doomed to failure. Machine-gun posts were established in the line itself.

I was put to help build a machine-gun emplacement. You dug a small excavation out the bottom of your trench to beyond the parapet, broke up through and then you had to cover the excavation with timber and earth. The machine-gun was put in that little pocket.[154] (Sapper Frederick Sanders)

Different methods were used, depending on the circumstance. 'We took a part of the parapet out and put a steel plate which had an opening so that you could traverse. Not much up and down but sideways. Then packed that round with sandbags for frontal protection.'[155] Once in place the machine-gun team would try to identify a point of weakness in the Turkish defences.

> You always had it trained on a certain spot. If you could see the intersection of where the Turks' communication trench came down to join the front line. Usually they had it covered overhead but they'd got to get through that first each way. We'd get lined up on that and every so often we'd give them a burst. We may not have hit anything but we made them keep their heads down at any rate. Of course they did the same to us.[156] (Private Joseph Clements)

Just as the development of trenches recalled the siege warfare of an earlier age, so troops of both sides turned to an old weapon in the hand grenade, or 'bomb' as it was then known. Where the trench lines were close together bombs were a vital tool of offensive and defensive warfare. The British were not initially supplied with hand grenades and the first ones used were improvisations. 2nd Lieutenant Malcolm Hancock was the bombing officer of the 1/4th Northamptons while on Hill 60 at Suvla:

> One was what we called a jam tin into which was put a charge of explosive. It was filled with all kinds of odds and ends; bits of stone, flint, empty cartridges; bits of iron, nails. . . . Then a fuse was inserted into a detonator. The neck of the detonator was crimped together to hold the fuse into the detonator. It was put in through the top of the lid down into the explosive and then you've probably got four or five inches of fuse exposed. In order to use it you would hold it in one's left hand and the thing was that to light the fuse you had to be darn careful not to show a light at night. I often would use the end of my cigarette – we were always smoking – that was very effective. Then as soon as you heard it begin to fizz you kept it for two or three seconds –

not too long but not too soon either – you tried to get it to explode on landing. It wouldn't be in the air very long and you had to try to get your timing right. You hoped it dropped into the Turkish trench.[157] (2nd Lieutenant Malcolm Hancock)

Bomb-throwing was nerve-racking and there were many accidents in the trenches. 'It was the easiest thing in the world to hit the parapet and down it falls back on top of you. You are anxious to get it out and at the same time if the trajectory is not just right it'll fall in.'[158] With the primitive technology employed it was no wonder that many of the bombs used by both sides failed to explode on landing.

One source of bombs was Turkish jam tin bombs. They were the same as ours. They had a fuse into a detonator, pushed it inside, lit it and threw it over. I should think 30% of them failed to go off. We heard them fall and if they didn't go off we marked them down, 'There's a dud there,' and at night I used to go out crawling about in no-man's land collecting these damned things. We were damned short of bombs. All we had to do was to take the fuse out that hadn't burnt through, take that out, re-fuse it with a detonator on the end and chuck it back! They always went off, a highly satisfactory sound.[159] (2nd Lieutenant Malcolm Hancock)

Some did not wait to see if they would explode but tried to throw them back before detonation.

They have great long fuses on theirs, and several times I counted to 10 after a bomb had dropped before it went off. If you have the presence of mind you can hurl them back before they burst. Personally, when one came just a foot off me, I couldn't muster the presence of mind to catch hold of it. . . . All you do is to run behind a traverse of sandbags.[160] (Lieutenant Thomas Watson)

Even when they did explode these primitive bombs were often more sound and fury than devastation. The Turkish bombs were no better, as was shown in a sharp bombing exchange on Hill 60.

We thought we might have a bit of fun, chuck a few bombs over. The Turks started throwing the stuff over and we got quite a lot of aggro going. I was in a little bomb bay right up underneath our front line. Without my knowing a Turkish bomb came in right beside me and the bloody thing went off. It knocked me flat and just for a moment I wondered what the Hell's happened. But why I wasn't killed I can't imagine. It was one of their jam tins and it exploded into no end of tiny fragments of tin. It made a bit of a mess of my face but it was only skin deep. It was frightening more than anything, the terrific noise of the thing going off that's enough to make you think that something frightful had happened.[161] (2nd Lieutenant Malcolm Hancock)

One precaution adopted by British troops confirms the lack of real explosive power. 'We used to have an old blanket or greatcoat and if a bomb dropped in your bay you flung one of these things over it and when it exploded it collected enough of the bits to save you any great damage.'[162] But bombs could, and did, kill and wound many men unlucky enough to catch the full blast of an explosion or just a stray piece of metal in a vital spot.

Another contrivance from the Middle Ages also made its appearance to mixed feelings. To some like Hancock, when he was appointed bombing officer of the whole of the 162nd Brigade, it was a new and exciting toy:

It was a wooden contraption meant to work on the principle of a catapult. There was a hollow wooden cylinder on a framework which on either side had a strong elastic tape. You primed and cocked the thing by winding a handle. You pulled back the cylinder until there was a pretty good tension on the rubber and then fixed a catch. You got the bomb, lit the end of it, dropped it in the cylinder and then released the catch and up she went. Well it was literally cock-shy because there was no question of seeing where it went, you just guessed at what angle you set the thing, high or low and you had to work the tension of the rubber so it didn't go too far. It was a very hit or miss affair. It was quite fun really.[163] (2nd Lieutenant Malcolm Hancock)

The troops in front of these unreliable contraptions had a more jaundiced view.

The operators were brigade people and as soon as we heard they were coming everybody would say: 'Those bastards have come, take cover.' They'd set themselves up and start firing. Not scientific – so amateur – the bombs would go anywhere, to the right, to the left, you never knew where it was going. Instead of facing the enemy everybody in the front line and supports would be looking backwards to see the bomb wasn't going near them. And laugh!!! When you saw a bomb going right smack in the middle of another company. Laugh!!! They'd rush left and right to get out of the way of this awful bomb. Sometimes they would fall out of the sling and burst in the trench. Arrgh!! If you weren't concerned it made you laugh.[164] (2nd Lieutenant Eric Wolton)

In the circumstances of stalemate prevailing at Gallipoli it was inevitable that mining operations would be seen as a possible way forward. The initiators were the Turks at Anzac, where the possibilities of literally blasting key Australian positions off the side of the hills were obvious. Their underground offensive was begun by an explosion on 29 May under a platoon of the 13th Battalion at Quinn's Post. The Turks rushed forward and occupied the immediate area of the crater before counter-attacks threw them back to their own lines. The Australians immediately organized their own mining and had soon established underground galleries which duplicated their front lines.

At Helles mining began slowly but after the line settled down the underground war began in earnest in August. The Royal Engineers could not supply the manpower necessary for the increased efforts demanded and ex-coalminers were recruited from the infantry. One such was Ordinary Seaman Joe Murray, who in July had been attached as a sapper to the VIII Corps Mining Company organized by Captain H. W. Laws with their headquarters at Pink Farm. The miners worked in teams on a shift system. The shafts were dug down from the British lines and then out under no-man's land. To keep them straight, 'You've got two plumb lines hanging down. After you've gone say ten feet you want to make sure you're going straight. So you line it up with your candle by moving it to the left or right, as soon as you get it dead in line you make a sooty mark on the timber and that's dead centre.'[165] To see they used candles. 'We used to make like a notch and put the candle in there. They were tallow candles about three inches long and about as thick as your middle finger. But they were good. There wasn't much light but that didn't matter.'[166] Dress underground was relaxed: 'Sweat like a pig, no shirt on, only a pair of trousers.'[167] As old coalminers they worked quickly and effectively. 'We used to take the bottom out, about a foot and then you could bring the top down, down she came. It's a work of art but it's the only way to do it. You've got to have a loose end always it's no good just banging away.'[168] The local infantry would supply working parties to drag out the loose soil.

> The work below was not pleasant. You had to move on your hands and knees. The colliers used to load the soil into sandbags. We had a sandbag with a large loop at the end. We used to pass this loop from under us over our necks and crawl like a cart-horse with a collar round his neck to the foot of the shaft. There were always two men at the top of the shaft who would hoist up the sandbag, empty it and throw it back. . . . I was on three of these mining parties. In favour of mining was that you were out of the terribly hot sun in the trench but the air down below was very foul. We were digging by candlelight and the candles were burning oxygen, we had no ventilation. We were not allowed to smoke because the tobacco fumes would have meant that the men on the face would have been almost choked. It was a little cooler. If there was any shelling we couldn't hear them coming over we just felt the dull thump as they arrived.[169] (Private N. W. Prophet)

As at Anzac the idea was to create an underground system of galleries almost duplicating the trenches above ground but under the Turkish lines or as near to them as it was possible to get. The Turks were not idle, attempting to create exactly the same sort of system under the British lines. The two systems interconnected in a bewildering underground war. As the galleries converged the British miners could hear the Turks getting closer.

> They would call the Royal Engineer officer who would come down with a stethoscope with a large mouth piece. There was absolute silence and this would be put against the wall and he could hear if the enemy were approaching. If they were he would

order everybody out, they would fill the head of the tunnel with explosive and blow it. That would cause the enemy mine to collapse and bury their mining party.[170] (Private N. W. Prophet)

This was the dangerous period for the miners. 'We all realized it was a risky job, it was touch and go. Whilst you could hear him digging you were perturbed but not worried. It was when he stopped digging because we never knew – is he planting a mine – or what the hell is he doing if he's not digging? So we used to stop.'[171] At this point they would prepare a camouflet mine designed to blow up the Turkish workings without harming the British galleries.

> We decided to make preparations for a blast. We had to make a recess in the side, a little bit to the left so that we didn't blow our own mineshaft. We had to stop him without stopping ourselves. Lieutenant Dean came up and he gave permission, the officer had to do that and they came up with all their paraphernalia. There were three 10lb tins of ammonal. I put two detonators in one tin of ammonal, then I wrapped the cable round the tin and then round a sand bag so that when we pulled on the cable it wouldn't displace the detonator. Then we started tamping. All the sandbags were already filled and we packed them up to a barrier of about five feet, really tight. The point is that you have to make the place of least resistance upwards not along the tunnel or it would blow out your tunnel. The cable had to go right to the surface to the firing line. There the officer had the detonator box with batteries, two wires that he fixes and a plunger. The moment he pulls that plunger up he warns the officer in the line that: 'Oh well, I'm going to do a bit of blasting, mind your heads.' All the troops in the line stand to on the firing step with their rifle ready because we don't know what's going to happen. 'Stand to, men.' Down goes the plunger. As soon as the plunger goes down the lot goes up. I thought that's fine, thank the Lord for that. There was this terrific noise, mass of dust and great big chunks of clay falling everywhere.[172] (Ordinary Seaman Joe Murray)

If they misjudged the moment, the Turks could either blow up the British workings or attempt to explode a mine under the British front line. Casualties among the infantry holding the front line above them was the mark that a tunnelling squad had failed.

I was in the front line, it was just dusk when the Turks blew a mine. The distance between the trenches was 25 yards. The Turks must have been unprepared because it went off in the middle of no-man's land. One lip of their crater carried away all of our barbed wire and all our parapet causing a lot of casualties. Out of a section of ten in one fire bay there was only myself and one other fellow left – the others were all killed or wounded. We expected the Turks to make their attack but nothing developed so after the end of two minutes we made the attack. We went in, manned the crater and Colin Wray and myself, the two survivors, lay amongst the rubble, by this time it was dark, giving covering fire against anything we could see against the false skyline you can see if you lie flat on the ground. We consolidated the crater, we were only three yards away so we could dominate his front line. We made it so that there was two hundred yards of his front line that he couldn't use. On this particular occasion we lost our company commander, Captain Crawley MP. Ever after that it was known as Crawley's Crater because he was buried in it.[173] (Private N. W. Prophet)

The miners fought their own private underground war right through to the end of the campaign.

One entirely new weapon was the aeroplane and the various opportunities that it offered of dealing death from the air. The most obvious was the bomb.

I've quite decided (since this morning) that the worst one of all is the sinister swish of an aeroplane bomb coming down. You feel such a 'fearful ass' (in every sense of the word). You can't *do* anything and there's nowhere to go and no time to get there if there was. Everyone shouts 'Bomb Coming' which is a peculiarly fatuous remark.[174] (Major Norman Burge)

Lieutenant Frank Howitt had a glimpse into the future. 'The effect of these aerial bombs is much more stupefying than an ordinary shell, as you can see them coming, without the slightest chance of getting out of their way. I cannot imagine why every nation does not possess hundreds of them.'[175] Ironically the Turkish aircraft also used one of the oldest weapons of war.

> There was an aircraft came over and dropped two boxes of aerial darts rather like crossbow arrows, steel, about a foot long. It pinned through men on the floor, pinned through horses, screams of agony, some were killed, some weren't.[176] (Private Edward Robinson)

They were also used to strike at Hamilton's headquarters at Imbros.

> One morning at shaving time a Boche aeroplane came over and we didn't take all that much notice of him. Suddenly our sergeant major ran out of his tent shouting: 'Bombs, spears, darts, arrows.' True enough this chap had thrown over steel arrows that were falling all over the place and also a bomb. Nowadays it would be laughed at but in those days it appeared to be an enormous bomb and it had landed reasonably close to Sir Ian Hamilton's tent.[177] (Corporal Robert Cook)

The Britsh air presence at Gallipoli was initially provided by No. 3 Squadron (later Wing) of the Royal Naval Air Service, which had arrived at Tenedos at the end of March under Wing Commander Charles Samson. During the early days of the campaign they had a reconnaissance role as they plotted, photographed and mapped the Turkish defence works while dropping bombs as appropriate. During the naval campaign and actual landings they flew as spotting planes for the Royal Navy to locate targets and correct long-range gunnery. Samson himself was an irascible character although, as his temper blew over fairly quickly, he was popular among his men.

> We were being attacked by Turkish aircraft and he'd got a Nieuport Scout. I was the mechanic on it. He came out whilst the bombs were dropping swinging his goggles to get in the machine and go after them. But when I got there I hadn't got my dope can – that's a little can of petrol you had to put under the valves of about three cylinders then she'll go. I swung it and hoped it would go. No. Swung it three times. He said: 'Have you

doped it?', I said: 'No sir.' Ooh you ought to have heard his language. I had to go a hundred yards to get that dope can and he swore at me all the way there and all the way back. He never said the same word twice. He stood the machine on its tail to get up after these Turkish. He came back grinning, 'I nearly got them' he said. Not worried, no recrimination at all.[178] (Leading Mechanic Arthur Beeton)

The RNAS had a landing strip constructed at Helles in May so that observers could land to report urgent information to VIII Corps Headquarters direct. As it was under close observation from Achi Baba this facility was not often used due to the risk of heavy shelling. However, the flimsy nature of the planes meant that it was sometimes essential for them to force-land there until a mechanic could arrive to fix it. This was not a popular duty.

The news came that one of the BE2c's had come down with the engine seized up. The machine wasn't damaged. The job was to get a fresh engine out to it. My mate was a devil, go anywhere anytime, he says we'll go. The navy sent this little Greek steamer. They picked up the engine, George Lacey and I and our tools. The Aegean Sea that day was a bit nasty, rolling and pitching, and I didn't feel too good so I laid down on the deck. I must have napped off because when I woke up we were passing through the fleet all firing at Achi Baba. I went up to the front and I said: 'Whereabouts is the aerodrome?' 'Aerodrome,' he said. 'What's that?' 'Where the machines land.' 'Oh,' he said, 'that's just over . . .' and he pointed with his finger. Just as he pointed a great cloud of red fire and smoke went up. He said: 'Do you see where that shell just burst, that must be right on it.' Oh it was awful![179] (Leading Mechanic Arthur Beeton)

The RNAS strength gradually increased until No. 2 and No. 3 Wings were moved to Imbros in August, where they were under the overall command of Colonel F. H. Sykes. He also had at his disposal two kite balloon ships for observation and two early aircraft carriers. The reconnaissance role of the RNAS was invaluable to GHQ. One example was the intelligence provided by Flight Commander Reginald Marix of the arrival of another Turkish division at the port of Ak Bashi Liman on 17 May. This was confirmed by Samson, who also bombed the port that day, causing considerable panic among the troops. As a result of these reports GHQ realized an attack was planned at Anzac, warnings were issued on 18 May and the 'surprise' Turkish night attack of 19 May was repulsed where it might have succeeded. Air reconnaissance had also provided the largely accurate reports of the Turkish forces and dispositions at Suvla before the landing and had also, in the days that followed, monitored the movement of the reserves. Unfortunately intelligence is of no value if it is not used.

Bombing operations were also undertaken and by 23 November Samson could report that '179 bombs of 100lb weight and 507 bombs of 20lb weight have been dropped.'[180] Targets were numerous: Turkish troop concentrations and gun positions; crucial communications facilities such as railway junctions, bridges, port installations and troop transport ships. One more milestone of war was passed on 12 August when Flight Commander Charles Edmonds, flying a Short seaplane over the Sea of Marmara, sighted a Turkish steamer amid a group of sailing ships and a tug:

> I glided down and fired my torpedo at the steamer from a height of about 14 feet and range of some 300 yards, with the sun astern of me. I noticed some flashes from the tug . . . so presumed she was firing at me and therefore kept on a westerly course, climbing rapidly. Looking back, I observed the track of the torpedo, which struck the ship abreast the mainmast, the starboard side. The explosion sent a column of water and large fragments of the ship almost as high as her masthead. The ship was about 5,000 tons displacement, painted black, with one funnel and four masts. She was lying close to the land, so cannot sink very far, but the force of the explosion was such that it is impossible for her to be of further use to the enemy.[181] (Flight Commander Charles Edmonds)

Given the state of signalling technology in 1915, the other main task of the planes, spotting for the long-range guns of the Royal Navy, was a thankless one.

Captain Collett he was going round and round in circles over the top there. He didn't dare go too high or he'd have got in the way of the shells. He was firing Verey lights to indicate where the shells were going. Green was right on target, red was too far and so on. After about two hours he came down. He said, 'The Navy don't like us, they're not taking a damn bit of notice of me at all.'[182] (Leading Mechanic Arthur Beeton)

The infantry for whom all this effort was being expended were in themselves a danger to their pilots.

We did once see an aircraft and I think everybody fired at it. I don't think anybody knew whether it was Turkish or English. It was such an extraordinary sight that people seemed to think it was the thing to shoot at it, I think they treated it as a joke![183] (2nd Lieutenant Malcolm Hancock)

For the pilots flying in their flimsy machines with no parachute a flying accident was often fatal. Flight Commander Charles Collett was killed on 19 August.

He picked up George Lacey and took off over the cliffs. There was always an undercurrent on the cliffs you had to watch. He hit this undercurrent and instead of going forward he turned and came back, lost flying speed and crashed. George saw it coming and he was in the seat under the engine. On these BE2c if they hit the ground the engine dropped on top of you. When he saw they were crashing he got half way out and it threw him, ooh fifty yards away – compound fractures of both legs but he got no burns. There was Collett trapped in this damned machine. In between where he came down and where we were there was a ravine about 70 feet deep. We had to go down it and up the side, a difficult thing to do. When we got to the other side we saw it was on fire and there was Collett trapped in this damned machine. We tried to get him out but we couldn't; we got our hands and faces scarred. This chap Mick Keogh saw what had happened and he had picked up a big black tarpaulin and he wrapped that round himself and went in and pulled him out. He got the George Medal for that. But Collett was so badly burned when you'd catch hold of him, you got handfuls of flesh. He was still alive, he said to the doctor: 'Put me out, put me out.' We buried him and put his propeller up on the hill there.[184] (Leading Mechanic Arthur Beeton)

Whether they were hit by shrapnel, blasted by high explosive, sniped, blown up by mines from below or bombs from above – the wounded were denied the instant relief from suffering that death provided. They would usually be collected from the regimental first-aid posts by the stretcher-bearers of the Royal Army Medical Corps. This was hard and dangerous work.

We would take a stretcher, two men to a stretcher, fill it up with stores, medical whatever and go up to near Krithia. Four miles. When you got there you'd hear some voice saying: 'Come on you chaps where the hell have you been.' Put your stores down. Get one of the wounded especially if he's got a red border on his label, pick him up and take him back down to the base where he'd be treated. When we got back we had to do it again. On and on and on till we dropped.[185] (Private Harry Robinson)

One of them recorded their work in song:

> Tramping up the gully,
> Tramping up the gully,
> With your stretcher every day and night,
> While the shrapnel overhead is zipping,
> And the bullets all around are pipping,
> When your feet are weary,
> And you're far from cheery,
> And you seem to know quite well,
> You're going, you're going,
> Tramping up the gully,
> Tramping up the gully,
> That will lead you to the gates of hell.[186]
>
> (Private Richard Yorston)

As the situation stabilized and if circumstance allowed, ambulances would come as far as they could to collect the wounded.

Yorston was a driver of an ambulance working in Gully Ravine at Helles.

There was one ambulance to each section. We would go about a mile up the gully and the local unit stretcher-bearers would bring the wounded down to us. They'd been at their local regimental first-aid posts. We had two stretcher places on each side and we'd strap them in. We weren't supposed to carry any others but we'd always take a few if there was any there. We could get about half a dozen on the floor. Once they were loaded on board we got ahead as fast as we could go. We used to take it very softly, very gently. The medical orderly would be on the box and he'd keep an eye on them. The ambulances were square, with canvas tops, an open back and solid rubber tyres. They were driven by four mules with two drivers and the waggon orderly he looked after the patients. I was the wheel driver. It was a bit rough going up, just enough room for one waggon but you got used to it. We took them right to the dressing station. The nursing orderlies would unload them.[187] (Private Richard Yorston)

Not everyone could get taken to the beach and in a big attack what was defined as walking wounded could be hard on suffering individuals.

Then began one of the most awful and trying walks I have ever had to face in my life. Just think of it! Five miles to face, in full marching order, with my rifle and all my equipment . . . all the way from the firing line down to the base; however I did it, I do not know, for my rifle weighed nine pounds five ounces. I walked, I crawled; I dragged myself along as best I could, resting every few minutes; and I never knew there were so many Field Telephone Wires before, for I was continually stumbling over them. But somehow or other I kept pressing on; and the fact that I was going further and further away from the firing line, each step I took, gave me courage to plod on – nay, it was nothing less than an inspiration.[188] (Private R. Sheldon)

Once, by whatever means, the wounded had reached the beach they had to wait for an opportunity to get away on a hospital ship. This was a nerve-racking time – so near to a safe evacuation, but still under shellfire.

> I was more scared in the hospital than I'd ever been at Hill 60. I could hear shells coming. There I was lying on a bed, couldn't move. . . . In a trench you can get down and hope for the best. . . . I felt helpless, shells going over the top – there might be a short one. The hospital was just a big canvas tent, in a bed – no protection from side, top, bottom or anywhere.[189] (2nd Lieutenant Eric Wolton)

Although the Turks did not seem to fire deliberately at the Red Cross tents, accidents could and did happen:

> I was three days on a stretcher on the beach. Some fool brought an ammunition waggon through the dressing station and the Turks fired on it. They killed two doctors and I got a dose of shrapnel in the back. Not much – you could pick it out with forceps.[190] (Corporal Ernest Haire)

At the beach dressing station they could expect only minimal treatment unless they were in danger of expiring. 'The field dressing had stuck so the doctor said: "We're going to leave this lad – you're alive and your pulse is good."'[191] Not all of the doctors, especially those from territorial units, had much experience of military wounds. 'They were learning their trade these suburban doctors from Manchester. They'd probably never had anybody who'd been shot in the guts or with brain damage; real gunshot wounds; hit with shell fragments – they were more like ordinary doctors.'[192] At Gallipoli they soon had the practical experience. Even the men of religion also usually in attendance did not always bring comfort. Some saw them as the harbingers of death. 'The padre asked me what my religion was and I remember saying: "Ooh is it as bad as all that?" He said: "No, but we have to ask these questions."'[193] The actual loading of the wounded on to the hospital ship could be terrifying, as it was for one soldier who was paralysed below the waist after being shot in the hip and the groin.

> I was put on the hospital ship at about 12 noon on the Monday. I was taken out there by lighter and then you're winched up by crane. When I was getting near the top of the boat the stretcher

sort of slipped and I thought I was going to slip off back into the water about fifty feet below. Fortunately I managed to hang on with my hands, I couldn't do anything with my feet. I hung on till they got me to the top of the boat.[194] (Private Frederick Coakes)

Once on board ship they were safe from everything but torpedoes, the possible fatal effects of their wounds and the dreaded gangrene. They were taken to Lemnos, Alexandria, Malta or, if extremely lucky, straight back to the United Kingdom.

Those who died were buried on the peninsula.

While I was there, two lieutenants of the 5th Essex came, and I found they had come down to the burial of their friend Lieutenant Marshall. So I went back and arranged things for them. We walked out in the darkness to the little cemetery on the beach below and I performed the last rites. No light, of course, or book. So by heart I used what prayers seemed most suitable, ending with that one which unites the whole Church in Paradise and on earth. The only thing one could think of to say to them was that Paradise must be a wonderful pleasant place with so many friends there.[195] (Reverend Charles Hood)

The sense of unfulfilled lives was almost tangible.

There were always two opened graves waiting to receive the bodies of those about to die. Often I was taken from my ordinary duties to bury some poor fellow who had been brought down from the trenches and had died on the way. There was something unutterably pathetic in those simple burials, the body laid on the stretcher, blood soaking through from the mortal wound, the dead boy still wearing his soiled and tattered khaki in which he had fought and toiled and eaten and slept and now slept the last long sleep. How smart and soldierly he must have looked at his last home parade with sun-helmet and puggaree; almost certainly a photograph . . . stood on some mantelpiece. And now! – the wreck of what once was a man, thin and wasted with exhaustion, mangled, smashed beyond recognition with battered misshapen helmet resting over crossed hands on his breast. And at that very moment some fond mother or wife or sweetheart was telling in all probability her friends how my Tom had gone to Gallipoli! Yet these received orderly Christian burial with the great words of Eternal Hope read over them; hundreds lay rotting in the burning sun where they had fallen in the cruel scrub.[196] (Private Harold Thomas)

The graves were marked where possible with a makeshift cross. On one of my inspections in the RND section of the front I found a wooden cross inscribed:

> To Harry Duge, Anson Bn, RND
> Sleep on, your duty you have done,
> Your death we nair thought soon
> But this token send with deep regret
> From all in the Third Platoon.[197]
>
> (Private Stanley Parker Bird)

Those who died on the battlefield had no such formal burial and there were a number of factors which meant that the situation at Gallipoli became almost intolerable. The areas of ground which made up the front were minuscule in size and were fought over continuously throughout the campaign. Casualties were still occurring on V Beach in January 1916, nine months after the landing. Corpses could not be evacuated to the rear as there was no rear – everywhere was under fire. Just gathering together to bury a corpse could mean more casualties and more corpses to bury. The close-fought nature of the campaign also meant that corpses had to be buried *in situ*. No-man's land was often ridiculously narrow and usually under constant and deadly observation. Men killed there had to remain in place until one side or the other advanced, which meant they could be there for months. The result was that as you approached the peninsula the ghastly smell of corruption made itself apparent. Once ashore and moving inland it got worse.

There was a terrible smell in the air and I said to somebody who was already there: 'What's that awful smell?' He said: 'That's dead men in front of our trench there, 700 of the Hants and Worcesters lying out there up in front of our trench and over to the right over 800 of the Anson Battalion.' That was over two miles away and you could smell them – the stench in the air. Well if you've ever smelt a dead mouse it was like that but hundreds and hundreds of times worse. It was a smell – the smell of death – you never got it out of your system. I've still got it, I can still remember exactly how it was.[198] (Private Harry Baker)

At Helles the climate meant that it was not very long before the body began to decompose. 'All the time there was that nasty sulphur smell. A man might be shot at twelve o'clock and at one o'clock instead of being an eight stone man he'd be a fifteen stone man, swollen right up. The bullets used to go into belly, Thttt, and deflate them, and so he'd swell up again. All over, they were everywhere.'[199] The corpses weren't just out in no-man's land. Even if the Turks' trenches were captured in an assault they were often in a terrible state. 'The Turks' trenches are simply too ghastly at present, miles of corpses in every stage of decay lining the parapet and of course heaps in between the trenches. The smell simply knocks you down and living and eating in it with black smelling creatures just over your head is jolly. We buried 54 one morning from the parapet alone – just on the front of 3 platoons.'[200] Over a period of time the troops would gradually bury those corpses they could get at, without too much danger of adding to their number, mainly on their side of the front line or built into the parapet. However, the dead were often just buried by a few inches of earth. 'We noticed that the ground we were treading on was full of maggots. It was where they had buried the dead not very deep.'[201] There is something peculiarly disgusting about maggots that can cause nausea in even the hardiest of stomachs. 'The ground was covered with maggots; great juicy ones with black heads and such intelligent looking eyes.'[202] The thought of maggots disturbed Murray's sleep.

Half the parapets were made of dead bodies and the maggots, ooh lousy things, crawling about, hundreds of the things, can't get rid of them. I think the worse thing there was the maggots. You'd lie down beside a dead Turk or Englishman and all of a sudden you'd feel yourself thinking, Oooh bloody maggots and you'd be moving round, kept on thinking you had maggots.[203] (Ordinary Seaman Joe Murray)

Even when your own trenches had been dealt with, the problem of the corpses lying out in no-man's land remained. Where it was feasible the men would be sent out or volunteer to go out at night to bury them, but some areas of no-man's land were just impossible to get to without adding to the corpses lying there. In their frustration the troops tried desperate measures.

I remember a Turkish patrol coming and we were very proud because we shot 2 or 3 of them. We were proud of seeing their bodies lying in front. Until the smell was so awful, too awful, we wished we'd taken them in straight away. We used to hope that by shooting into the bodies the smell would go but they kept swelling and swelling, getting worse and worse. However many bullets you pumped into them it didn't seem to make any difference. I thought the gases would have escaped and gone but it didn't appear to, not for a long time.[204] (2nd Lieutenant Eric Wolton)

Although they were living in charnel-house conditions, the troops soon became acclimatized. 'Just as we entered the trench going up into the system there was a body. A lot of the trench had been built up with dead bodies covered with earth. And a hand was sticking out. It was all dried probably been a fortnight, three weeks. And a New Zealander said: "Well that chap I've known him for some time. He must have been a dry old stick." Well the first time we saw that it wasn't awfully funny. But you'd hardly credit this, we got so callous that every man as he went past used to shake hands with it.'[205] Finally the dead could become the macabre props of the battalion humorists. 'I found myself gazing at the legs and arms and the crown of a head sticking out of the earth at the top of a communication trench. The sun had burned away all the hair from the head and had left a plain shiny surface on which the letters "R.I.P." had been printed in indelible ink.'[206]

*

Many soldiers seemed to have a strange fatalistic optimism which boded ill for their comrades and was possessed of no logic. 'I don't think it really had occurred to us that anything might happen to each of us individually, generally we thought the other fellow would get it.'[207] Some even congratulated themselves on their avoidance of superstition, while quite firm in their own ability to survive. 'I never thought that I'd be killed. The rumour came round that thirteen was an unlucky number. Now we had to make our wills out and I'd made mine out on page thirteen, lots of them had. So they all started changing their wills from thirteen to fourteen. I left mine where it was!'[208]

Every soldier had to find his own motivation for maintaining morale under fire. 'The thing I was most afraid of myself was that I would show that I was afraid. I don't suppose there was anybody who wasn't a bit afraid when they found they were being shot at. I wasn't very happy about it but I was always rather afraid of showing I was scared.'[209] Most of the soldiers knew that their comrades were as scared as they were, but the point was not to allow these fears to affect their performance in action. Major Norman Burge, whose letters were normally witty evocations of Gallipoli life designed as much to amuse as to inform, wrote one passage, pregnant with significance, where his inner feelings escaped, just for a few lines, before his sense of humour reasserted itself:

> I've been rather trying to analyse one's feelings at different times and find it very difficult. Mostly, I think, one doesn't have any feelings to speak of and yet at other times you sort of look at things in a light you'd be rather ashamed of, that is if you didn't happen to know that all the other fellows are feeling just the same. I know they do, 'cos I asked them and they said they did. So each of us was quite happy to find the others had nervousy moments. For instance on a Monday – down here in the rest camp. You hear that there's going to be a night advance of 100 yards . . . on Tuesday. On Tuesday morning a sinister message all about stretchers and where the 'dressing station' will be at comes in etc and also what part of the line we'll be in and so on. I don't mind confessing that for a moment one feels as if you hadn't had your breakfast. . . . Sudden flashes of awful horrors one can

picture only too easily, intrude themselves on one's mind in a most insistent way. . . . The uncomfortable feeling generally comes on when you know you've got to do something at a certain hour and you are just sitting down waiting for the clock to strike as it were. That feeling again stops with a click directly you begin doing it, whatever it may be, and from then on you cease thinking how absurdly inadequate Government pensions for widows are and mild wonders as to how the world can possibly get along without you – and all that sort of morbid nonsense.[210] (Major Norman Burge)

The stress of combat was the supreme test for thousands of young men who felt that their whole lives had been a preparation for such a moment. For 2nd Lieutenant Horridge the test came as he was part of the front-line garrison during the British attack at Helles on 4 June:

I looked over the top and saw one of these Manchester fellows evidently wounded lying on his tummy about thirty yards in front of the trench holding up his hand. What came into my mind was what would happen when I actually got out there with metal flying all about the place. When I saw this chap, it struck me that this was the moment I'd been waiting for – what was I going to do – and if you don't go now and do something you'd remember all your life that you failed at that moment. Nobody else would know you failed – you would know. I was forced by these feelings to go and try and get this chap in. I went to one of my platoon, Parkes, and I said, 'Look Parkes, let's go out and see if we can get this chap in.' So Parkes jumped out of the trench and I followed him. I hadn't got more than six yards before I felt as though I'd been hit by a sledge hammer in the ribs and I knew I'd been hit. Well as soon as I'd been hit all ideas of bringing the Manchester man in disappeared – all I was concerned about was getting back into the trench. So I turned and ran, jumped into our trench which was about seven feet deep and sprained my ankle which lasted longer than the wound I'd got. Parkes brought the Manchester in but he died in the afternoon.[211] (2nd Lieutenant George Horridge)

There were many different sources of inner strength. Some found motivation in their belief in the justness of 'the cause'.

The work to be done before a soldier can see his home is great, in fact the task seems only just to have been begun. And it has got to be done cost what it may. Justice must triumph. England, the British Empire, must under Providence free itself from the mortal danger that threatens it. Humanity, civilization must be rescued from the foul dragon seeking to destroy it. 'It's a long long way' said that prophetic little song, and now it looks as if it were going to be longer than we ever thought in our most pessimistic thoughts. But our endurance must be equal to the utmost demand upon it. God help us that it may be so![212] (Major Claude Foster)

Others clung to the fading belief that they were fighting in a war to end war and thus save future generations from the sort of horrific experiences which assailed them from all sides. 'I have seen some terrible sights but am getting hardened to them now. Perhaps me going through it now is saving our little Rex having to go through it in years to come.'[213] Unfortunately it did not.

Humour and comradeship could be important, as 2nd Lieutenant Rupert Westmacott found when he overheard two regular veterans of the landings and the First Battle of Krithia discussing their situation. 'I got in this shell hole and I heard these two men talking and one of them said: "I don't know what's the matter with me," and the other said: "I know, it's what the newspapers call demoralized, fucking well demoralized!"'[214]

A refusal to accept that it was all happening at all was another refuge for those near the edge.

I can't bring myself to believe in the reality of things here, it is as if you were watching a cinema show or children playing at soldiers. I feel inclined to treat the whole thing as a big joke. Even when you see men you have known knocked flying or blown into smithereens you only say 'Poor chap' and think no more about it. I suppose it is a mercy one *doesn't* realize it or you would be in such a mortal funk you would be paralysed.[215] (Lieutenant Leslie Grant)

So, as the strain told, many men became more and more impervious to the sufferings and death that surrounded them.

> One gets, or always has been (the same in the end) very callous indeed to other folks' suffering. You say 'poor old So and So' and soon forget all about him and when you *do* remember you sort of mechanically say to yourself 'Poor old chap' as if it were a necessary formula that you ought to have repeated more frequently.[216] (Major Norman Burge)

Some even came to see the death of others as a personal inconvenience, as when a newly arrived officer aroused Nightingale's wrath by his poor behaviour in the mess: 'One was hit last night during dinner and fell into the soup, upsetting the whole table, and bled into the tea-pot making an awful mess of everything, and we finally didn't get dinner till after dark.'[217] Joseph Napier's reaction to an awful personal tragedy is equally revealing:

> We'd just pushed the Turks out of a line of trenches which were not very deep and I should think at about six o'clock that morning some soldier came down the line to my platoon and said: 'Your father's been hit, better come and see him.' So I went down through the trenches and when I arrived I found he was out at the back of the trench which sloped down away from the enemy being bandaged up. He had his jacket over his head, so they could get at the wound, while the sergeant major, I think it was, prepared a field dressing. There was a certain amount of blood about and I watched a few moments in some interest, not thinking it was serious probably. I finally said: 'How are you feeling?' I got no reply so I took his jacket back over his head and I saw at once that he was completely dead. No question of it. People have asked me what one felt on an occasion like that and it's very difficult to say. I don't think I had any immediate reactions of great sorrow because one had been in the midst of all this sort of thing. One had seen so many dead bodies lying around and being young one had got hardened – when I saw him dead I just accepted it as another of the facts of war. I didn't stay very long. As I walked away I just had a feeling of pride that he'd done his job. I went back to my own trench and as I've told several people my own

batman was killed next day and to be quite honest I felt really upset because he knew where all my things were and I didn't![218] (2nd Lieutenant Joseph Napier)

The unending strain under which men were placed was reflected in different ways. Nightingale noticed the change in Lieutenant Colonel Geddes: 'Geddes is a ripping commanding officer to work with, but he is frightfully worried and his hair is nearly white. I've never seen fellows get so old so quickly.'[219] Later he remarked: 'I laugh whenever I see him without his cap, as he had very red hair before.'[220] Nightingale himself put on a fine show of bravado in his letters: 'Lots of fellows are going off their head out here but personally I've never felt better in my life, I eat and sleep like a pig and feel most awfully cheery.'[221]

For some the pressures of modern warfare were unbearable and they turned their minds to escape.

This fellow tried to work his ticket with his eyesight. He said to the doctor: 'I don't know doctor, it's my eyes.' The doctor said: 'What's wrong with your eyes?' He said: 'Every now and then they start up and down like that.' The doctor said: 'Get it out of your head, you're not going on it!' The hospital ship in the bay goes up and down![222] (Lance Corporal Alexander Burnett)

The temptation to go sick was always there – in Boughton's case, 'I only had one pair of glasses and without them I was pretty blind but I never broke them. On several occasions I was tempted to because I should have been blind and I should have got sent off. Several of my pals tried to kid me: "Go on break them and get sent off." But I didn't. I wanted to see it through.'[223]

Desertion was not a feasible option at Gallipoli, so the next option was to try and get a minor wound, not life-threatening or disabling but just enough to get evacuated to safety. 'I knew one place where the Turks had got a fixed line and we used to say, "Here you are, put your hand out there and you can get home."'[224] Some were rumoured or known to have succumbed to the temptation. 'Many were so "fed up" that they exposed themselves recklessly hoping to receive a slight wound which would send them off for a month or two. How a chap smiled when he caught a slight one, and how we envied him.'[225] Murray was witness during the attack on 4 June to a self-inflicted wound.

Tubby was in an awful mess, he was only a youngster, eighteen and a half, well damn it all so was I. He was crying his eyes out, scared stiff. I said: 'Come on Tubby, shake yourself up.' I didn't take any notice. He moved forward with his hands round his rifle, he actually put his hand on the trigger and bang. He's howling and jumping about like a cat on hot bricks, I said: 'You bloody fool.' I tried to bandage up his thumb which was on top of the muzzle. In the front of the tunic there's a little pocket where you have a field dressing, gauze and a bandage. I took it and started trying to bandage him up. The flies and the blood was squirting about all over the place. I put this gauze on, flies and all, I couldn't get rid of the flies, I tied it round the hand, I thought that'll do to get to the dressing station, no bother, but the damned thing fell off. I said: 'Look Tubby, this bit's no good is it?' He said: 'No.' So I got a hold of my knife and I start sawing away trying to cut this off. Blood all over the place. So I put his thumb on the butt of his rifle, put my knife on top and with a hefty blow I chopped the offending bit and the damned thumb fell on the floor. Now the bandaging was easy. He said: 'You won't split on me.' I said: 'Of course I won't split on you, it was an accident, as you were getting out of the trench and somebody behind us was firing and a bullet hit your hand on the rifle.'[226] (Ordinary Seaman Joe Murray)

Some poor souls broke down entirely:

One poor sergeant went demented, we had to send him down, he couldn't stand it. He was one of the worst sergeants we had on the parade ground. A disciplinarian. Now he was shattered. The men were annoyed with him, 'You're a fine sort of fellow.' I felt sorry for him because he went absolutely mental. He wouldn't move, do anything, say anything.[227] (Private Cecil Tomkinson)

Suicide, the ultimate abrogation of responsibility, was not unknown. 'One went out and he shot himself. They said it were through trouble at home.'[228] Sometimes death really did seem the easy option. 'Hear one of our men who went down to the rest camp last night feeling sick committed suicide by blowing his brains out. Have had several more men with shattered nerves.'[229]

Morale is not just a personal affair. Unofficial 'truces' with the Turks were not as uncommon as higher command might have wanted. This was not intended as a subversive gesture; it was merely a way of coexisting with your enemy when initiating a fight just added to the casualty list for no obvious purpose.

> In the hot weather in August we'd come to the point, 'Well if you don't start mate we won't.' Every now and again an officer would come up and want to make a show and we'd start bombing, Bang, bang bang, we'd lose three or four men and everyone was happy.[230] (Ordinary Seaman Joe Murray)

Although the Turks were directly or indirectly responsible for all their tribulations, they do not appear to have been individually unpopular with most of the British troops, who gave them the nickname of Johnny Turk.

> The Turk he is an honest man,
> And fights us fair and true,
> But we annoy him all we can,
> As we are paid to do.[231]

10

Admission of Defeat

With the failure of the August offensive the prospects of a decisive breakthrough on the peninsula were all but dashed, and Hamilton's telegram of 17 August requesting an extra 95,000 men was placed in front of an increasingly sceptical British government which found itself assailed on all sides by bad news. The Russians were still being hard-pressed on the Eastern Front, the Italian summer offensive against the Austrians had failed and Bulgaria was about to throw her hat into the ring on the side of the Central Powers. The very optimism of Hamilton's previous reports gave the gloomy tone of this telegram more impact.

The Gallipoli campaign remained the centre of intense debate between the 'Easterners' and 'Westerners'. In France the bitter internal political and military in-fighting had been raging all summer. The French government and many of its generals could no longer stomach General Joffre's domineering insistence on devoting irreplaceable resources and young French lives to his seemingly futile assaults on the Western Front. At first the French government seemed to have got the upper hand. After a meeting on 22 July the French Prime Minister, Raymond Poincaré, wrote: 'Our meeting today was largely concerned with the Dardanelles, and it was unanimously agreed that any success there would be of first rate importance – far more so than any of the little offensives on our own ground.'[1] But Joffre was a determined, inflexible man and this, coupled with the French government's pusillanimity in the face of the political crisis that his resignation would cause, allowed him slowly to claw back his position during the high summer. Soon the autumn offensive he desired on the Western Front was once again at the top of the agenda, and at a meeting with Lord Kitchener and Sir John French on 16 August he secured their promise of full British support by insisting that it was essential to maintain French morale. Kitchener and French announced their intention to co-operate with the French in a major autumn offensive at the meeting of the Dardanelles Committee on 20 August, which was debating the response to Hamilton's request for further reinforcements. Such an offensive could not coexist with the manpower needs of Gallipoli, but the real alternative of evacuation was held to be unthinkable because of the crippling losses it would entail and the consequent immense loss of prestige that would result throughout the East.

The committee attempted to pursue a middle course and Hamilton was cabled on 20 August with the news that he was to get just 13,000 reinforcing drafts for his threadbare units and 12,000 in new units. He was told that he 'must understand that no reinforcements of importance can be diverted from the main theatre of operations in France.'[2] In effect this signalled that the Gallipoli campaign was over and the Western Front had regained the centre stage. The absence of any prospect of a quick breakthrough at Gallipoli to help relieve the pressure on the Russians or release troops for the Western Front meant that any brief alignment of Western Front and Gallipoli interests was at an end. Hamilton seethed with impotent frustration:

> A three or four mile advance *should* be easy enough, but, in the West, that would mean just three or four miles of land; nothing more. But *here*, those three or four miles – nay, two or three miles – (so ineffective in France) are an objective in themselves; they give us the strategical hub of the universe – Constantinople! . . . Victory by killing Germans is a barbarous notion and a savage method. A thrust with small forces at a weak spot to bring the enemy to their knees by loss of provinces, resources and prestige is an artistic idea and a scientific stroke: the one stands for a cudgel blow, the other for rapier play. We take it for granted that we have to 'push' in France and Flanders; that we *have* to exhaust ourselves in forcing the invaders back over their own frontiers. Whereas, content to 'hold' there, we might push wherever else we wished.[3] (General Sir Ian Hamilton)

Hamilton could still defend the theoretical advantages of the Gallipoli campaign, but the last attack at Suvla on 21 August brought him another defeat and his resulting report included the first reference of the possible need to abandon the Suvla positions due to the lack of troops to hold the line. He was losing his grip on the situation as the chronic problems of undermanning and the indomitable Turkish opposition threatened to swamp him.

> An ugly dream came to me last night. My tent was at Imbros right enough, and I was lying in my little camp bed, and yet I was being drowned, held violently under the Hellespont. The grip of a hand was still on my throat; the waters were closing over my head as I broke away and found myself awake. I was trembling and carried back with me into the realms of consciousness an idea that some uncanny visitor had entered my tent. . . . Never had I suffered from so fearful a dream. For hours afterwards I was haunted by the thought that the Dardanelles were fatal; that something sinister was a-foot; that we, all of us, were pre-doomed.[4] (General Sir Ian Hamilton)

Then, amid the gathering gloom, on 30 August an apparent miracle manifested itself as the French government informed Kitchener that they were to send no less than four new divisions to make a new landing on the Asiatic side of the Straits with the support of the two French divisions already there who would be withdrawn from Helles. Kitchener cabled Hamilton with the news and further promised that he would replace the French pair with the British 27th and 28th Regular Divisions from the Western Front. Hamilton was ecstatic. 'From bankrupt to millionaire in 24 hours. The enormous spin of fortune's wheel makes me giddy!. . . Constantinople is doomed.'[5]

The French government had been alarmed by the news of the August offensive's failure and had promised the new divisions in support of what it considered to be a strategic priority. Their opponent Joffre, while agreeing that the troops should be sent, refused to send any until after 22 September – in other words only after his Western Front offensive. The French promise was therefore hollow, as they lacked the willpower to bring Joffre to heel and it was further undermined by critical appreciations by the French

General Staff of the Asiatic scheme which, as they were under Joffre's control, unsurprisingly condemned it as unfeasible. For the moment the government stood relatively firm and on 7 September it went so far as to order Joffre to send the requisite four divisions in early October to be ready to begin operations in November.

On 11 September Kitchener met with Sir John French, Joffre, General Maurice Sarrail, who had been appointed as the putative French expeditionary force commander, and the French Minister of War, Alexandre Millerand. They concurred with the arrangements that had already been made, but the tensions on the French side were now apparent to Kitchener and he reported them to Hamilton.

> Joffre's objections appear to be that a landing in Asia opens up a very wide field if the force be not immediately successful, and that in that case more troops, munitions and drafts would be eventually required than he could spare with due regard to the safety of France. Secondly, he is not very confident of Sarrail's leadership, particularly as the plans Sarrail has made seem to be worthless. Joffre is having careful plans worked out by his Staff for the expedition on the Asiatic shore which, he says, though unfinished, do not look promising. The same objection on his part would not, I gather, be felt if the French troops were given a definite area or objective on the Gallipoli Peninsula, where the scope of their activities, and consequently the support required from France, could be limited.[6] (Lord Kitchener)

Hamilton began to recognize the writing on the wall, and finally his previously unshaken confidence in Kitchener began to fade: 'He has lost his faculty of forcing others to act. He makes a spurt but he can't stay the distance.'[7]

By then events in the Balkans made these discussions irrelevant. On 6 September the Bulgarians had concluded an agreement with the Germans and Austrians over the invasion of Serbia. Towards the end of September the Bulgarians issued their mobilization orders and the Serbian government called on their Greek neighbours for the support of 150,000 troops in accordance with treaty agreements. Greece was unable to provide the troops herself as she needed them for the protection of her eastern borders. She therefore asked France and Britain to provide the troops and, as the Serbians were likely to be overrun quickly without such help, the two allies agreed. The obvious place from which to send the troops was Gallipoli and the ambitious French plan withered on the vine. On 25 September Kitchener ordered Hamilton to despatch one French and two British divisions to Salonika, which was to be the base for the operations designed to defend Serbia. He further suggested that Suvla might have to be evacuated.

> It is evident that under these circumstances some troops will have to be taken from the Dardanelles to go to Salonika, but it must be clearly understood that there is no intention of withdrawing from the peninsula or of giving up the Dardanelles operations until the Turks are defeated.[8] (Lord Kitchener)

Hamilton railed against the stupidity (as he saw it) of committing troops to the Salonikan wastes and mountains. He now deeply regretted ever having mentioned the possibility of withdrawing from Suvla: 'The situation has greatly changed since I first suggested the possibility of abandoning the Bay, and its abandonment at this stage would, I feel convinced, enormously accentuate the difficulties of any subsequent attempt to capture the Narrows.'[9] He proposed a compromise – to retain Suvla but to send only one British and one French division, which was accepted by Kitchener. Nevertheless the removal of these two divisions 'marked the beginning of the end of the Dardanelles campaign'.[10]

The much vaunted Loos and Champagne offensives on the Western Front, which opened up on 25 September, were successful only in very small territorial gains and killing a proportionate amount of Germans. The British and French in return suffered around 250,000 casualties – more than twice the total number of reinforcements that Hamilton had requested. It all seemed so unfair. Furthermore the Salonika campaign got off to a bad start, as the Greeks had become embroiled in a dangerous political argument. King Constantine had not been consulted by his Prime Minister, Venizelos, over the question of requesting help from the Allies and, as he felt that Germany would win the war, he was insistent on maintaining Greek neutrality. In the end Venizelos was forced to resign, and instead of a new alliance the Allies faced the prospect of traversing the sovereign territory of a neutral power that would only grudgingly allow them to use Salonika as a base.

Belatedly the government in London began to consider whether it could maintain a third European front. Recognizing perhaps that it had no war strategy it sought the combined opinion of the Admiralty War Staff and the General Staff at the War Office in an attempt to salvage something from the awful mess that faced it in early October. The combined staffs reported on 9 October with a scepticism as to the prospects of the Salonikan front, professing instead a firm belief in the value of an immediate further effort on the Western Front if Joffre, now perversely against any further offensive for at least three months, could be brought round, and recommending that, if Joffre remained adamant, the troops destined for such an offensive should be used at Gallipoli. This did nothing to clarify the situation except to mark the growing triumph of the 'Westerners'. The needs of the Western Front were now firmly in the ascendancy and Gallipoli had been marked down as an afterthought.

Now that the army had failed, the Royal Navy finally began to bestir itself, like a sleeping giant restless in his slumbers. Since its failure to force the Straits on 18 March and the withdrawal of the battleships to protected anchorages following the arrival of the German U-boats in the eastern Mediterranean, its main contribution to the campaign had been by its supporting bombardments, escorting vulnerable troop and supply transports, the operations of the Royal Naval Air Service and the exploits of its own submarines in the Sea of Marmara, which had succeeded in impeding Turkish communications.

Commodore Roger Keyes had never accepted the failure to force the Narrows and had been carefully marshalling his arguments for another attempt:

> The problem of forcing the Straits is not now so difficult as it was on the 18th March. An attack would probably surprise the enemy. It is possible that he has moved many of the small guns that make mine-sweeping so difficult. The presence of the long range monitors makes the attack on the Chanak Forts, Suan Dere Batteries and the Torpedo Tubes (if they can be located) much more deadly, as they can be shelled from the west side of the

Peninsula. The Navy now possesses an efficient air service – balloon and aeroplane – so that difficulties of spotting are much less than when the *Queen Elizabeth* used indirect fire from Gaba Tepe. Above all there is now an efficient sweeping flotilla. . . . If the attack fails the Navy will be still easily capable of carrying on its present duties – the ships that will be risked are those at present in Mudros. If three or four ships succeed in entering the Marmara with say six to eight destroyers, the Squadron will, in combination with the submarines, be sufficient to complete the domination of that sea.[11] (Commodore Roger Keyes)

The improvement to the mine-sweepers held the key to any possible success. In March they had been unsuitable trawlers with a top speed of 5 knots working against the Straits' 2–4 knot current and they were largely manned by partially trained civilians. Since then a number of destroyers had been fitted up and trained as mine-sweepers. Trials were to show that they could sweep effectively at a speed of 14 knots, which it was felt would make them a difficult target for the shore batteries. In addition eight of the Grand Fleet mine-sweepers had arrived. Like Hamilton, Keyes was a man with a vision and he could be very persuasive indeed; Rear Admiral Wemyss, for one, was convinced.

I should find it very difficult not to agree with your memo of 17th. Whilst there was any chance of the Army winning through, the argument was different, but late events have quite altered the balance of the scales. A naval attack on our objective is the only way now to avert a winter campaign, whose greatest achievement can only be stalemate at the cost of much wastage.[12] (Rear Admiral Rosslyn Wemyss)

Vice Admiral De Robeck, the man who had to bear any responsibility for failure, was not so sanguine. 'To attack Narrows now with battleships would be a grave error, as chance of getting even a small efficient squadron past Chanak very remote.'[13] Nevertheless he allowed Keyes to continue his planning.

*

On the peninsula the military situation was stalemated and neither side had any realistic prospect of making a successful attack. Small-scale operations and mining were the only offensive gestures of which the British were now capable. Although reinforcing drafts and units had begun to arrive, this was offset by the withdrawal of the 10th Division for Salonika and the forced evacuation of the 2nd Mounted Division due to poor health. In addition, the drafts that did reach the existing units were not sufficient to counter-balance the daily wastage from sickness that scourged the weakened veterans. 'By the 10th October the troops at or *en route* for Gallipoli numbered 114,087; if all units had been made up to establishment they would have mustered 200,540.'[14] These figures actually masked the true gravity of the situation; as Hamilton pointed out, 'We have 100,000 men on the peninsula, 50,000 of whom are unfit.'[15] There was also a great shortage of munitions and artillery, and the individual batteries were perforce limited to two rounds a day per gun except for emergencies and counter-battery fire. What guns they had were by now also suffering from a lack of maintenance and workshop facilities.

The seeming inevitability of a winter campaign meant that a huge effort was begun to amass all the stores and equipment that would be necessary. Proper dugouts would have to be constructed and, as building materials were not present on the peninsula, they would all have to be imported. Winter uniforms would have to be brought over and issued. All these stores would have to be landed via makeshift harbours which could not withstand any sort of bad weather; therefore huge stores depots would have to be built up so that there would always be at least one month's supply in reserve to guard against a prolonged spell of bad weather.

The British government was confronted by difficulties on all sides and as a result for the first time the previously unthinkable appeared on the agenda. On 11 October Kitchener cabled Hamilton asking him to estimate the numbers he would lose in evacuation. Hamilton was incensed: 'If they do this they make the Dardanelles into the bloodiest tragedy of the world! Even if we were to escape without a scratch, they would stamp our enterprise as the bloodiest of all tragedies!'[16] Next day he replied: 'Our losses would depend on such uncertain factors, enemy's action or inaction, weather, question whether we could rely on all troops covering embarkation to fight to the last, that impossible to give you straight answer. . . . My opinion now is that it would not be wise to reckon on getting out of Gallipoli with less loss than that of half the total force.'[17]

This uncompromising answer arrived at a time when the political and military establishment in London was beginning to lose faith in Hamilton. The crisis had reached its height and firm moves were required to identify a scapegoat. The government and its military advisers were not to be tarnished with the blame, and Hamilton was the ideal sacrifice. He had promised success again and again but always he had failed. The growing unrest against Hamilton was exacerbated by the actions of two embittered men with axes to grind in the London corridors of power.

The first was Lieutenant General Stopford, who since his return had been brandishing his own account of the Suvla operations, which was riddled with inaccuracies and, not unnaturally, harshly critical of Hamilton, who had dismissed him. Despite the fact that Hamilton was given no chance to comment on this report, it was taken seriously by Kitchener, who had it analysed by a committee of generals. Their report was fairly non-committal but included the words: 'The whole series of tasks planned for the IX Corps is open to criticism, but we do not feel justified in suggesting such criticism at this period of the war without much fuller information from those actually on the spot.'[18] This fair assessment was transmuted by Kitchener in his report to the goverment into: 'Considerable criticism of Sir Ian Hamilton's leadership'.[19]

The second was Keith Murdoch, an Australian journalist who had been shocked by what he had seen during a visit to the peninsula. In fairness there was plenty to concern any reasonable visitor, but Murdoch egregiously exaggerated many of his charges, including an allegation that British officers had been ordered to shoot any soldier who lagged behind or loitered. Hamilton had already tried to refute this calumny. But, when a contentious letter written by Murdoch to the Australian Prime Minister was circulated as a state paper by Asquith to the British Cabinet, the mud began to stick.

The 'Westerners' seized their moment at the next meeting of the Dardanelles Committee on 14 October. Hamilton's estimate of 50 per cent losses proved the final straw, and he was replaced in command of the Mediterranean Expeditionary Force on 15 October.

> The War Council held last night decided that though the Government fully appreciate your work and the gallant manner in which you personally have struggled to make the enterprise a success in face of the terrible difficulties you have had to contend against, they, all the same, wish to make a change in the command which will give them an opportunity of seeing you.[20] (Lord Kitchener)

Hamilton was informed that his replacement would be General Sir Charles Monro and, as it was decided that Monro would take out his own Chief of the General Staff, Major General Braithwaite was also recalled. Hamilton saw that the game was up. 'Had he been sent out here in the first instance he would never have touched the Dardanelles, and people who have realized so much may conclude he will now clear out.'[21] Monro indeed was a man with firm convictions who felt that every available man and gun should be deployed on the Western Front, that only there could the war be won and that all other campaigns were irrelevant distractions to the business of winning the war.

Hamilton said goodbye to the rest of his staff and left on 17 October: 'The adieu was a melancholy affair. There was no make-belief, that's a sure thing. Whatever the British Officer may be his forte has never lain in his acting.'[22] An assessment of Hamilton is difficult to reach, as his attractive personality and clear sense of strategic vision appear to obscure his considerable faults as a military commander. He delegated too much authority to his often inadequate subordinates, which led him to endorse plans which on occasions were wildly over-optimistic. This failing also rendered him almost incapable of strong intervention when something was going wrong, even when he was in a better position to judge the situation than the local commander. It could also be considered that in planning attacks his enthusiasm for diversionary actions sometimes dissipated the limited strength he had available, to no real advantage. Overall he was not alone in his initial underestimation of the fighting spirit and determined leadership of the Turkish Army, but his relationship with Kitchener, fawning and based on the past, left him unable to stand up to him properly in the battle for reinforcements and artillery which the Turks' vigorous resistance rendered absolutely essential if the British were to be successful. Hamilton's case was further weakened by his over-optimistic reports, which concealed from London the true state of affairs in the MEF throughout the summer; by the time he revealed the grim truth it was too late. London was probably right to remove him when it did.

On Hamilton's departure Lieutenant General Birdwood was left in temporary command and in his reports to Kitchener he endorsed the grim news already furnished by Hamilton. Units were under-strength and there was no prospect of a successful offensive without major reinforcements. He also reported that, now that the Turks had a sure supply of German munitions via Bulgaria, the only way of remaining on the peninsula would be to push the Turks back so that the beaches were clear of artillery fire.

The British General Staff remained opposed to deploying considerable forces in Salonika, but the French had now abandoned all thoughts of a renewed Dardanelles offensive and were totally devoted to Salonika. At a conference with Kitchener in London, on 29 October, Joffre requested at least 150,000 troops for Salonika and backed it up in his inimitable bullying style with the threat of his resignation and dark murmurings as to the future of the Entente. Kitchener gave way and on 30 October the British government agreed to co-operate.

A further complication was provided by Keyes's continued personal crusade to get a renewed naval assault. A plan had now been drawn up by him and submitted to De Robeck on 23 September. Keyes was tireless: 'I never lost an opportunity of talking to the Admiral on the subject, and urging my view, but it was quite evident that he would have nothing to do with it.'[23] In view of these tactics perhaps it was partially self-interest and a desire for a quiet life which led De Robeck to allow Keyes to accompany Hamilton home to put his ideas forward in London. He reached London on 28 October and threw himself into the task with abandon. The First Lord of the Admiralty, Arthur Balfour, was not unsympathetic, but everything was put on hold until Monro reported from his new command.

Monro, who arrived at Imbros on 28 October, had been instructed by Kitchener to report to him as quickly as possible on the military situation both at Gallipoli and in the Near East in general. He arrived against a backdrop of more bad news from the Balkans, where Serbia was crumbling before the Bulgarian onslaught. Monro and his Chief of Staff, Major General Arthur Lynden-Bell, had been charged to suggest any way in which the Gallipoli deadlock might be overcome. On 30 October Monro visited Helles, Anzac and Suvla all in the same day and spoke to the corps and divisional commanders. He asked all of them whether their men were capable of a sustained offensive and whether they would be able to resist determined Turkish efforts throughout the winter to drive them from their present positions. The consensus was that only a short offensive lasting twenty-four hours would be possible and that, while at the present their men might be able to hold the Turks, if the Turks received unlimited ammunition it would be difficult to predict the outcome. The following day Monro telegraphed Kitchener that with most of the divisions locked into unfavourable positions, unable to manoeuvre or build up sufficient artillery support prior to an attack, and incapable of sustaining prolonged effort, there existed little hope of mounting a successful offensive.

> I am therefore of opinion that another attempt to carry the Turkish lines would not offer any hope of success. The Turkish positions are being actively strengthened daily. Our information leads to the belief that heavy guns and ammunition are being sent to the Peninsula from Constantinople. Consequently, by the time fresh divisions, if available, could arrive, the task of breaking the Turkish lines would be considerably more formidable than even it is at present. On purely military grounds, therefore, in consequence of the grave daily wastage of officers and men that occurs ... I recommend the evacuation of the peninsula.[24] (General Sir Charles Monro)

Despite harsh criticism from such as Churchill, who commented: 'He came, he saw, he capitulated,'[25] this report did generally reflect the views of most of the senior commanders at Gallipoli in the absence of any news of prompt and massive reinforcements of men and material. Without such a promise of help there appeared to be no alternative to evacuation. The main dissenter was Birdwood and even he agreed with Monro about the military prognosis but felt that the political effects of withdrawal were too serious to contemplate.

Events in London were still surging along under their own momentum. Kitchener, who shared Hamilton's assessment of the likely cost of evacuation in men and Eastern prestige, was deeply concerned by Monro's report. He was also attracted by the potential of the plan proposed by Keyes, with whom he had recently had a brief meeting. In essence he saw it as a possible means of avoiding the need for evacuation and it was in this frame of mind that he approached the first meeting on 3 November of the new War Committee, the renamed Dardanelles Committee, that was now charged with the strategic conduct of the war. Influenced by Kitchener's obvious doubts, the Committee was reluctant to accept Monro's advice and decided to send Kitchener out to Gallipoli to examine the situation himself.

Before he set off he became involved in an increasingly farcical scheme for a combined assault with the navy. After a further conversation with Keyes he produced a wild plan for a new landing at Bulair while the navy rushed the Straits. In a strange episode which highlighted his capricious nature he sent a cable to Birdwood on 4 November which ordered him to assume command of the MEF and transferred Monro to the command at Salonika, while he predicted that De Robeck would be replaced by Wemyss. Birdwood was appalled at the whole idea and kept the signal secret while he tried to get Kitchener to change his mind. But the fantasy plan was already unravelling. Keyes had more sense than to back a landing at Bulair and most of the navy began to get cold feet about the fleet rushing the Dardanelles. After considerable discussion the First Sea Lord, Admiral Sir Henry Jackson, refused to countenance it on the grounds that without a joint military assault the ships would just get cut off even if they did reach the Sea of Marmara.

Kitchener set off, still in turmoil, and arrived at Mudros on 9 November, where he met Monro and Birdwood. Monro was by now aware of his replacement by Birdwood, although Birdwood had still not told anyone else out of loyalty to Monro, whom he regarded highly. The next few days were occupied in an endless round of meetings to discuss the feasibility of evacuation. The discussions were complicated by Sir John Maxwell's and Monro's almost perverse adoption of yet another scheme for a fresh landing at Ayas Bay in an attempt to cut the Turks' communication lines at Alexandretta to counter-balance the political effects in Egypt and India and the British Empire's lost prestige in general should Gallipoli be evacuated. This scheme was unsurprisingly rejected out of hand both by the General Staff in London and by the French government.

Kitchener embarked with Birdwood on a three-day inspection of the positions at Gallipoli. The reality of the situation was quickly brought home to him and on 15 November he sent back a report which fundamentally mirrored Monro's earlier conclusions. As a reflection of this belated conversion to Monro's point of view Kitchener decided to appoint him overall Commander-in-Chief of all the British forces in the Mediterranean outside Egypt, with Birdwood appointed to local command at Gallipoli and Lieutenant General Mahon at Salonika.

However, in order to help the navy and also to mitigate, however slightly, the admission of the campaign's failure that would be signalled by an evacuation, Kitchener decided to recommend only the evacuation of Anzac and Suvla, retaining Helles for the foreseeable future. This conclusion was cabled back to the War Committee on 22 November. The following day the Prime Minister replied, forwarding a general acceptance of the proposal but stating that the War Committee preferred the idea of evacuating all three areas together. However, this final decision would have to be taken by the full Cabinet at its next meeting. Believing therefore that the decision would be reached quickly, Kitchener sailed for England on 24 November. Independently the General Staff had completed a study of the evacuation question and they too decided that the nettle had to be grasped.

Yet, at its meeting on 24 November, the Cabinet failed to give its approval, demanding instead more time to consider the matter. A faction, led by the Lord Privy Seal, Lord Curzon, asked for a delay of forty-eight hours in which to prepare a case for remaining on the peninsula. Curzon's arguments, which focused on the political consequences of the decision and the extreme difficulty of carrying out the operation successfully, had such strength that the decision was delayed another week.

> A moment must come when a final *sauve qui peut* takes place, and when a disorganized crowd will press in despairing tumult on to the shore and into the boats. Shells will be falling and bullets ploughing their way into this mass of retreating humanity. . . . Conceive the crowding into the boats of thousands of half crazy men, the swamping of craft, the nocturnal panic, the agony of the wounded, the hecatombs of the slain.[26] (Lord Curzon)

While the government procrastinated another force took a hand. In November the weather had become considerably cooler but few took seriously warnings as to the real nature of Gallipoli's prevailing climate.

> About 24 November we were optimistic enough to believe we were still going to have good weather because of a small leaflet called 'The Peninsula Times' which had been issued by General Headquarters and gave a forecast of the weather implying that it would be lovely weather during November but that we could expect severe weather and a blizzard in January. Their timetable was wrong. [27] (Signaller Frederick Griffiths)

The bad weather started with an intense rainstorm on the evening of 26 November.

> We've had another kind of hell vouchsafed us lately and one infinitely worse than shot and shell. . . . Down came the most glorious thunderstorm I've ever seen and I never want to see another like it. Lightning and thunder absolutely incessant for 2 hours and rain indescribable since the Flood, it simply dropped in lumps, whole solid chunks of it which washed everything before it.[28] (Lieutenant Thomas Watson)

All over the peninsula the storm wreaked its havoc: 'The trenches were flooded, four feet of water. In the air were waterproof sheets flying about like huge bats. Bones lying about everywhere from corpses being washed up.'[29] Now the troops could see the effects of fast-flowing flood water, a geography lesson that explained all too graphically just why the peninsula was riven by deep gullies.

> The water came down a real river. It cut a ravine through what we termed our parade ground. A ravine in which you could have put a street of houses. It filled the trenches with five or six foot of water. The Turks got out on to the parapet of theirs, we got out on to the parapet of ours. You could not get into the trench for about a week. That was bad enough because we had to lie there in wet clothes and had no means of drying them.[30] (Signaller Frederick Griffiths)

An extreme case of this occurred in Gully Ravine, where Joe Murray was based immediately alongside the ravine; he saw temporary dams being formed from the debris washed down by the flood waters.

> All of a sudden the dam would break and the whole volume came down carrying everything before it. Corpses, all sorts of gear, some people drowning. On our side of the Gully the water came so much down the trench that it was cascading over the cliffs into the Gully. The Turks were standing about and so were we. There was no trench to go in, they were all full up with water. It was raining like hell. . . . They were standing there, we made no attempt to do anything – we couldn't, half of us didn't have any rifles, they'd been flooded in the trench somewhere. The Turks could have walked through as far as they liked. There was no defence at all. Not where we were. Everywhere was washed up. Fellows ill with dysentery had fallen down and drowned in their own communication trenches and of course other people were going down walking on them. It wasn't till after the storm that we realized what a lot of people were drowned.[31] (Ordinary Seaman Joe Murray)

Under conditions like these even a world war seemed irrelevant compared to the business of personal survival. 'We got washed out of the trenches. We had to dig in on the parapet. Sleeping on top of the parapet. The Turks were just the same. There was an unspoken truce.'[32] Unfortunately such informal truces were not universally respected, as some Turks discovered to their cost. 'There was one saving grace. The wretched Turks were evidently in a worse plight than we and small groups of them walked about collecting brushwood to light a fire and thaw themselves. This afforded sport to those who were warm enough to shoot and we potted several.'[33]

If the period of bad weather had restricted itself to that spell of torrential rain all might have been well. 'The morning of November 27th was sunny nor was there any particular touch of cold in the air to warn us of what was to come.'[34] But during the day the weather began to break up: 'About noon . . . the sky had become covered with low grey clouds and the wind had gone round to the North East developing a shrewd Black Sea bite as it shifted. Darker and darker grew the sky and colder and colder the breath of the wind; about 4pm the first light flakes of snow began to drift down on us.'[35] Snow or freezing rain soon set in, with awful effects. The temperature fell below zero and for those who had to remain on duty in the trenches conditions were almost unbearable.

> My pal and I, Corporal Dean, sat on two empty tin biscuit boxes up against the wall of the trench. We pulled some blankets over our heads, some ground sheets over that, put our arms around each other and sat like that all through the night with water right over our boots. There was nowhere else to go so we sat there until the morning. When we tried to move we could lift these blankets and ground sheets off us like bent sheets of corrugated iron. Our feet, well they were frozen in the water and we could hardly move to pull them out. All around us there were chaps moaning and crying. Some of the sentries standing on the fire steps had frozen stiff and when they were touched fell over. Frozen. I had frostbite in my hands and feet. Some of them were so bad that they were told get down to the beach as soon as they could. That was the only place they could be treated but there was no road and no means of taking them down there. So I saw men crawling on their hands and knees. Grown up men crying like babies − even the quarter master sergeant of the Royal Marines.[36] (Private Harold Boughton)

Come the dawn the men arose to a strange landscape.

In the morning light the whole mountain top glistened with ice. One couldn't walk; you just slid to where you wanted to be. Broken arms and legs were not uncommon and were looked upon with something like envy by those who hadn't them, for they meant a trip to Imbros, Lemnos, Malta or even Blighty itself. Greatcoats were so frozen that to bend them was like bending a board. Some of the fellows with soaked blankets threw them over the bushes, with the remark that 'they would dry some time'. In less than an hour these blankets could be reared on end, much in the same way as a large sheet of three ply wood.[37] (Private Ernest Lye)

The situation was desperate, 'Hundreds of men died of frost during the next few days. Those who survived owe it mainly to the fact that they had the good sense to walk about all night but it's a very tiring process. But we did it.'[38] They were, however, in an awful state.

We fell to a lower degree of dirt and personal uncleanliness than ever before. The water carts were frozen up and what little water there was was used for the cookhouse and the dressings for the patients. I suppose we *could* have done something to improve our conditions but everyone was so sunk in abject misery that we simply let things slide. . . . Our faces and hands were swollen, blackened and cracked, vermin multiplied hourly upon us and uniforms were caked with the mud of the deluge which had now frozen upon them.[39] (Private Harold Thomas)

The big freeze ended on 30 December. Joe Murray discovered that not even entombment in a block of ice could get rid of the lice on his shirt. 'I spread it on a stone in the trench behind me, it had been three days in a solid block of ice. And do you know, I looked at this shirt and believe it or not the blinking lice were still alive and crawling all over the shirt. They'd been three days in a block of ice, you'd have thought that would have killed the damn things – but it didn't!'[40] After the storm was over one slight advantage was gained by some of the troops. 'After the storm we had fresh meat for the first time. It was all the mules used for transport, they must have died of exposure and they used them as fresh meat. I didn't know I was eating mule or I wouldn't have enjoyed it so much. It was alright, just like stewed beef.'[41]

Thousands of men had to be evacuated with frostbite, and hundreds were drowned or frozen to death. The beaches had also suffered as the storm lashed the piers, and lighters were driven ashore. The work needed to repair the storm damage at Anzac and Suvla was irritating but not serious. However, at Helles it was much worse and was to take several weeks to put right.

11

Stealing Away

Even though the Cabinet had not yet finally made up its mind to evacuate Gallipoli, prudence dictated that the planning for such an eventuality be progressed as quickly as possible and a basic plan was produced by a local joint naval and military committee convened under Sir Charles Monro's instructions. This plan called for three distinct stages. A first, Preliminary Stage, to start immediately, would remove all the men, animals and stores not needed for defence throughout the winter. Once the Cabinet's final decision was received, a second, Intermediate Stage, to take place over ten nights, would then begin to reduce the remaining garrisons, including the guns and ammunition, to a minimum level capable of holding the existing positions for one week against sustained Turkish attacks should the weather disrupt the continuity of the evacuation. Only when this level was reached would the remaining men then be taken off in a third and Final Stage to take place at the earliest possible opportunity that the weather would allow. Monro insisted that this Final Stage should not take longer than two nights. It was also agreed that at none of these stages would lives be jeopardized to save guns, stores or animals, the priority throughout being the safe removal of as many men as possible, and if complete success was to be achieved the need for secrecy was absolute. Lieutenant General Birdwood, following his appointment to command the newly designated Dardanelles Army, began to enact the Preliminary Stage at once.

Following Lord Kitchener's return to London there was still prevarication, as he and the politicians twisted and turned in their efforts to avoid evacuation. Most of the suggestions which had already been made were revived: the Keyes plan briefly reappeared, endorsed by Rear Admiral Wemyss (who had replaced Vice Admiral De Robeck when he returned home on leave) but opposed by the Admiralty; the idea of evacuating Salonika and sending the divisions for a new thrust at Suvla was also promulgated until crushed beneath the absolute opposition of the French. Throughout this period, while others wavered, Monro remained firm and true to his single-minded belief – Gallipoli had to be evacuated. He was the man with the clearest vision and in due course he attained his aim. On 7 December the full Cabinet met and finally bowed to the inevitable. Gallipoli was to be evacuated, but only partially. Suvla and Anzac were to be abandoned, but Helles would be retained for naval and political reasons, as originally suggested by Kitchener in his report. Although the scheme prepared by the joint staff committee had envisaged a simultaneous evacuation of all three positions, the loss of a significant number of boats and lighters during the recent storm meant that it would no longer be possible to do this anyway, giving a further practical reason for delaying the evacuation of Helles.

When confirmation of the Cabinet's decision was finally received at Dardanelles Army Headquarters on 8 December, Birdwood was at last able to issue the order to begin the Intermediate Stage immediately. The Preliminary Stage had already progressed as far as it could, with a large amount of stores having been removed, and following the withdrawal of the attenuated 54th Division the combined garrisons of Suvla and Anzac were reduced to 83,000 rifles. The tactics for the Intermediate and Final Stages of the evacuation of the two areas were initially left to the respective corps commanders. At Anzac Lieutenant General Godley, now in command of the Anzac Corps, proposed to thin out gradually the number of men holding his line but to retain until the last all his present positions with these reduced numbers. By doing this he hoped to preserve an appearance of normality and to lull the Turks into believing all was proceeding as usual. However, at Suvla, Lieutenant General Byng, who had been considering the question of evacuation since his appointment to command the IX Corps in September, preferred a gradual withdrawal of the whole line to new positions around defended areas of embarkation. Perceiving the fundamental difference between these two approaches and also the immense advantages of Godley's scheme over Byng's if it could be successfully implemented, Birdwood felt compelled to order Byng to adopt the Anzac proposal at Suvla and hold his present line until the last night of the Final Stage.

As the navy could guarantee to remove only 10,000 a night from both Anzac and Suvla, the Intermediate Stage was intended to reduce each garrison gradually to a total of 20,000 in readiness for the Final Stage, which was set to take place over two nights – on 18 and 19 December. In anticipation of this gradual reduction of numbers and the increasing danger it presented in the event of an attack, Godley had instituted 'quiet periods' as early as 23 November. Instead of zealously covering no-man's land to maintain local superiority, the Australian and New Zealand soldiers were ordered not to fire at all during the period of darkness unless their lines were attacked. However, if and when this occurred, the attacks were to be fiercely repulsed. In this way the Turks gradually became accustomed to the silence that would inevitably follow the departure of the last men, without associating it with the line being undefended.

The ordinary soldiers were amazed when they eventually found out what was happening. First came the rumours.

'We're leaving this place.' 'Get away!' 'He's right.' 'You think so?' 'I'm certain!' 'Where've you got it from?' 'So and so.' 'Ahh, you're kidding!' I didn't think we were evacuating, I couldn't see any reason in it. The fellows in the trenches were building them up with fresh sandbags. The Royal Engineers were putting up new wires behind our lines. I never dreamt of it. Anyhow we got orders to pack, 'Hey you're right chum.'[1] (Private George Ashurst)

At the same time, once the Intermediate Stage was under way, a number of other ruses were devised to preserve the usual appearance of both the front line and the areas behind it. Stacks of boxes were removed from the inside, leaving the pile unchanged from outside; tents were left in position, even though empty, and, at night, mules and limbers delivered non-existent rations in their usual way. Sergeant William Kirk of the Army Service Corps was given such a role:

> I was told to go to where the headquarters had been, find their dugouts and pick up all the paper, boxwood, old sacking, anything that would burn. I was to light fires where they'd usually done their cooking to send up smoke to make the Turks think they were still there. But they weren't – the headquarters had been evacuated.[2] (Sergeant William Kirk)

By day great care was taken to ensure that none of the extraordinary nighttime shipping remained in sight off the coast, but those men who remained were encouraged to be visible, playing games and moving around where before they had stayed carefully under cover.

It was a physical impossibility to evacuate all the accumulated stores in the depots and an effort was made to destroy as much as possible to deprive the Turks of anything of military value: 'Even the sandbags had to be slit with bayonets.'[3] It was a stupendous task.

> In early December I was to take a party to the advanced dump up the line and we had to destroy everything, make it uneatable. We made a pyre. Bags of sugar, cases of tea, tipped it all over mixed it all up, paraffin, lime, everything we'd got, even bacon was chucked on it. We pricked the cans of bully beef so that they went bad. . . . When it came to destroying the rum we didn't like the job and we saved a drop. The rest went on the heap. That's where I got let down as I was a bit soft hearted and when I saw some lads making for the boat I gave them a drop of rum in their water bottles. Some of them let me down and got on the boat drunk! One of my officers told me I'd got to make sure I destroy the rum next time.[4] (Sergeant William Kirk)

Some prepared slightly cruel practical jokes for the Turks. 'We were very naughty in our company. We got some rum in a rum jar and filled it up with paraffin so we hoped the Turks would take a swig.'[5]

The Intermediate Stage was blessed by good weather, the Turks were almost totally quiet throughout the whole period and everything proceeded according to schedule. The last twenty-four hours were extremely tense for the final garrison, most of whom were given some part to play as members of a 'stage army', and the success of these ruses in convincing the Turks that the positions were still held in strength was absolutely crucial.

> On the last night the Staff Captain said we were going off the peninsula. A lieutenant in the Army Service Corps, he got some mule carts filled with petrol tins that they used to carry the water in. 'Well,' he said, 'I want you to take them up as near to the Turkish front line as you can, Piccadilly Circus, and run them round, make as much noise as ever you can to let him think we were bringing stuff up.' And I did![6] (Private William Cowley)

The Turks caused a frisson of excitement at Suvla when their artillery opened up on Lala Baba, firing what was presumed to be some of the new ammunition supply from Germany since, instead of the usual proportion of duds, every shell exploded. The last of the British guns which had not yet been evacuated responded in kind and successfully fooled the Turks, who really do seem to have been unaware that the evacuation was actually under way during these last few hours. Colonel Hans Kannengiesser was commanding the Turkish forces in the Suvla Bay area:

> Opposite us there was peace with the exception of the usual fire from the enemy. About 11 o'clock in the morning our howitzer battery on Ismailtepe, with a field battery, had shelled Lala Baba, as a result of which Ismailtepe was immediately shelled by several enemy batteries. The usual picture. That evening Major Senftelben, commander of the heavy artillery of the Army Corps, visited me to report. I asked him whether he had noticed any diminution in the enemy artillery fire. He immediately produced his fire records and proved to me that the enemy land batteries had maintained their accustomed rate of fire on our positions throughout the 18th and 19th December. In addition the infantry fire from the trenches was as usual. The enemy, during the last few days, had worked hard to improve his position. . . . That appeared to indicate the intention of a stubborn resistance.[7] (Colonel Hans Kannengiesser)

Final preparations were made at all the divisional dumps to burn all the stores that remained.

Putting straw, anything that would burn amongst the boxes, even down to putting the petrol can at the side for my officer who was going to light it. My little section, about seven or eight of us, all volunteered to stay with the major if he wanted us. When I went off that night I went through the main depot to get to the ship and I've never been among so much oil and stuff in my life, it was running all over everywhere. So it would be a blaze when it was lit! There were notices everywhere, 'No Smoking', because of fire.[8] (Sergeant William Kirk)

All the arrangements worked perfectly. At Anzac on the night of 18 December, 9,900 men were taken off, leaving 10,040 for the last night. Although nine guns were eventually left behind, they were rendered useless and indeed were already worn out from ceaseless firing. On the next night the troops were divided into three groups: 4,000 in the 'A' party left as soon as darkness had fallen; the 'B' and 'C' parties then spread themselves to cover their absence and with the supplementary aid of automatic devices maintained the 'usual' amount of rifle fire and bombing. 'We rigged up a can of water which dripped into another can underneath and that was attached to the trigger of a gun. As it dripped down, the weight increased and it pulled the trigger. It sounded like continuous firing. You put more water in some than others so that it fired sooner.'[9] Then the 4,000 men of the 'B' party sneaked away at 21.00 and left the whole of the front line to 2,000 volunteeers of the 'C' party. These rearguards began to slip silently off beginning around 01.00 on the morning of 20 December, leaving only the automatic devices to man the front line. Their final departure time was sensibly varied to take account of the different circumstances and distances of the line from the beaches. Russell's Top was the last front-line post to be abandoned, at 03.14, and at 03.30, with the whole garrison clear, a mine was fired there. This provoked a mass of small-arms fire but no shelling of the beaches, and at 04.00 the last lighter left, followed ten minutes later by a final picket boat. Anzac was Turkish again.

Events went equally well at Suvla, where a variant on the same theme was practised owing to the greater distances which the troops had to cover on the way from the front line to the beaches.

The front-line trenches were all held until 01.30, with small garrisons also present in two reserve lines which had been dug to cover the two halves of Suvla Bay. The first wave of troops filed quietly back and embarked into the boats.

> We were loaded into small motorized barges and taken out to the bay where each group was allotted to a certain destroyer. Our one was called the *Partridge*. It was pitch dark and we had to cruise round with the naval bloke up the front yelling out: 'Partridge ahoy, Partridge ahoy.' We couldn't get any answer and some wag said: 'The bugger's flown!'[10] (Private Harold Boughton)

Once the artillery had fired their final programme, every gun was got away, a notable achievement by any standards. The inner defences were to be held until the front-line garrison had all passed through and been accounted for. At this point the gaps in their wire were closed and the inner-line garrisons would fall back. As at Anzac contact mines were laid to slow down any pursuit should the Turks catch wind of what was happening. Suvla Bay was effectively split in two by the flooded Salt Lake area. In the southern half under Major General Stanley Maude the final front-line party filed through the Salt Lake defence line at 02.30, the Lala Baba inner line at 03.15, and at 04.00 the last boat had departed. In the northern half under Major General Edward Fanshawe a similar timetable was followed, although the last boats were a little late in getting away just after 05.00. When the stores were set alight Kannengiesser and the Turks realized what was happening, but it was far too late. 'We crossed our front-line trenches and there we stood in "No Man's Land" between the opposing front lines. Mines continually detonated around us and still cost many unnecessary lives. I took with me five Arabs and sent them ahead to look for mines. My staff had never remained so respectfully behind me!'[11]

It had been a great triumph of military organization. Since the Cabinet's decision had been received, no less than 83,048 officers and men, 186 guns and 4,695 animals had been removed from Anzac and Suvla under the direct and, at some points, very close observation of the Turks. No casualties had been sustained, except 'one keen soul who had mopped up a good many tots of rum, and then fell over',[12] and Lord Curzon's vision of the 'nocturnal panic, the agony of the wounded, the hetacombs of the slain'[13] had not this time been realized. Instead it had been the first completely successful operation of the whole campaign. Kannengiesser grudgingly agreed: 'The retreat was entirely successful, even if considerably assisted by night and mist. . . . I had the impression that unuttered, the following opinion reigned: "Why unnecessary losses? The English are going away on their own."'[14]

The only disappointment was in the area of the stores. Despite the bonfires and parting shots from the navy, who bombarded the dumps throughout the day, an incredible amount of booty still remained for the Turks.

> The English had left everything as it was, because a removal under
> our eyes was simply not possible. Speaking roughly, the booty in
> my Corps area alone . . . consisted of 300km of telephone wire,
> 180km of barbed wire, millions of sandbags, three hundred
> splendid double-walled tents . . . guns, weapons, munitions,
> clothing, entrenching materials, food supplies, sanitary, tele-
> phone, light railway and shipbuilding material. . . . Stocks of
> tinned food, house high, had been drenched with petrol and fired.
> Stocks of flour had had hydrochloric acid poured over them. We
> succeeded in putting out the fires and saving a large quantity in
> spite of the English warships which patrolled up and down the
> coast like watchdogs and sought to hinder this work with their
> fire.[15] (Colonel Hans Kannengiesser)

Nevertheless one can only agree with the judgement of some Australian troops as they arrived at Mudros, on 20 December: 'I remember a voice shouting out: "Can we land?" then in a very low tone, "NO!" Then a cry of: "Can we evacuate?" and a tremendous cheer, "YES!"'[16]

The news of the evacuation of Anzac and Suvla was broken to the men at Helles on 20 December by their Corps Commander, Lieutenant General Sir Francis Davies, in a Special Order of the Day. Having first described the complete success of the operation, Davies then stated quite truthfully that a general evacuation was not about to proceed at Helles:

The position at Cape Helles will not be abandoned, and the Commander-in-Chief has entrusted to the Eighth Corps the duty of maintaining the honour of the British Empire against the Turks on the Peninsula and of continuing such action as shall prevent them, as far as possible, from massing their forces to meet our main operations elsewhere. . . . We must by strenuous labour make our positions impregnable, and while driving back every attack we must ever seek to make steady progress forward and maintain, both in spirit and action that offensive which, as every soldier knows, alone leads to success in war.[17] (Lieutenant General Sir Francis Davies)

However, three days after Davies published this order events in London threw his unequivocal tone into doubt.

On 23 December, Lieutenant General Sir William Robertson was appointed Chief of the Imperial General Staff. He, and many other senior commanders who thought like him, had never held much faith in the Gallipoli campaign and, like Monro, immediately appreciated the need to complete the evacuation at the earliest opportunity. On the day after his appointment Robertson told Monro to begin all the 'preparations necessary for the rapid evacuation of position at Cape Helles subject to condition that no steps are to be taken which will prejudice our power to remain there if decided'.[18] At Monro's headquarters on Lemnos, according to Captain Orlo Williams, who deciphered the cable, the arrival of the order passed round the General Staff like a wave of energy, as did the significance of the change of regime at the War Office. Now it was clear that Helles would be evacuated sooner rather than later and preparations could begin in earnest, so that once the final order was received the evacuation would be ready to get under way immediately. It had already been decided some weeks before to withdraw the French African troops from Helles, and the 29th Division had been sent down immediately after their evacuation from Suvla to replace them. Now, in order to overcome the difficulties of a joint command during the evacuation, the last few remaining French infantry were to be removed as well, their position on the extreme right of the line being taken over by the RND; but the French artillery was to remain under direct British command. The weakest British division at Helles, the 42nd Division, which had served there continuously since May, could also now be replaced and soon after Christmas their place along the Aegean coast was taken over by the 13th Division, to the utter dismay of the recently evacuated troops. 'I came off in the boat with Major Nathan, "We'll scrape the mud off your boots, Boughton, that's the last of the Dardanelles." We were back at Cape Helles within a week!'[19]

Careful steps were taken to prevent these changes, when they filtered through to the Turks via the mysterious spy network which operated across the Aegean islands, from being recognized as the preliminary steps of a general evacuation. To obscure their real purpose a routine general order was issued throughout the corps. Joe Murray stumbled across a copy of the order in an abandoned dugout in the support lines. It stated 'that "The VIII Army Corps will be relieved by the IX. Inform all concerned."'[20] But not all who read it were convinced. Thomas Macmillan believed that, despite what it said, 'To the discerning eye it was evident that a general evacuation was intended.'[21] In fact, at this stage this was not strictly true and Macmillan's divisional commander, Major General Paris, had received 'very definite orders . . . that we were to remain, the French only to clear out',[22] even declaring to the officers of the Hawke Battalion 'that the one reason for not evacuating Cape Helles that history could give would be that it was impossible'.[23] The effect of these declarations on his disbelieving men was to suggest that, like Davies, he was still keen to stay and see it through, which was not a sentiment they felt themselves.

> It was common talk that our Divisional Commander had reported to his superiors that the men of his Division were anxious to remain on the peninsula until the operations had been brought to a satisfactory conclusion. If our Divisional Commander was reported correctly, either he did not know the mind of his men, or it was a case of wishful thinking on his part. Our position appeared hopeless to any man with a spark of intelligence.[24] (Able Seaman Thomas Macmillan)

On 28 December this fact was recognized in a second cable from Robertson, who explained to Monro that 'The Government have decided that the Cape Helles position may now be evacuated. The withdrawal should be carried out as soon as practicable but at your complete discretion.'[25] Orlo Williams this time received the long-awaited order with foreboding. 'So this heads the final chapter of the Dardanelles tragedy, and may it not prove, as I fear it will, a bloody one.'[26] At the headquarters of the 29th Division the order to begin preparing for another evacuation was received with angry disbelief. 'So that is what we have been brought here for, to replace the French and 42nd East Lancashire Division, and clear out with the trenches 20 yards apart instead of 200 as at Suvla and the Turks on the look out for our going and with greatly increased artillery against us.'[27]

The effects of the first evacuation had already begun to make themselves all too apparent at Helles as the Turkish artillery started to concentrate exclusively on this one remaining front. Slowly, as the Turkish infantry followed suit and began to move south, the pressure on the British troops facing them started to increase. With the RND on the right, the centre of the British line was held by the 52nd Division and the left by the 13th Division. 2nd Lieutenant J. S. Millar, serving with the 1/5th KOSB, noticed a gradual increase in the level of Turkish aggression shortly after Christmas:

> The rifle and machine-gun fire from the Turkish positions appeared to increase and reconnaissance and fighting patrols became more active, probing into our positions with determination and vigour. These attempts were beaten off but occasional penetration was made into our lines. . . . The casualties were again steadily mounting. Now, it was becoming evident to us why this sudden increase of activity by the Turks. . . . Obviously the Turks were now bringing troops on to the Helles front and we were beginning to feel the effect.[28] (2nd Lieutenant J. S. Millar)

The resulting change of atmosphere was very clear and the now Lieutenant Colonel Norman Burge was immediately aware of it on his return from Egypt, where he had been recovering from wounds, to assume command of the Nelson Battalion. He also felt that the second evacuation would be more difficult than the first:

> At Anzac and Suvla the show was absolutely unexpected by the Turks – they got off all they could and left only the fighting men

till the last 2 nights. Well, we are doing that too – but with this difference – that up there the fire trenches are not, I believe, more than 1,500 yards from the beach. Here we are about 4 miles, and you have to stick to single file in communication trenches practically all the way – that delays things and wearies heavily laden men frightfully.[29] (Lieutenant Colonel Norman Burge)

As they had been at Anzac and Suvla, even before the final decision had been made, 'periods of silence' were introduced along the line to prepare the Turks for the empty trenches after the last men had gone. According to Millar, the troops were not allowed to make any noise or show any light:

No small arms, artillery, or machine-gun fire, no paratechnics (star shells, Verey lights, etc.). The Turks became suspicious and started again on their probing tactics only to find that our trenches were fully manned. They retired with bloody noses. Sometimes in the darkness it was quite uncanny. The Turks were obviously windy. Not risking a probing attack they would flood the sky with parachute and Verey lights only to find that 'no man's land' was vacant and that everything was as usual. The enemy was undoubtedly puzzled.[30] (2nd Lieutenant J. S. Millar)

To help increase the effectiveness of the silence the troops were ordered to wear sandbags on their feet. Murray remembered being stopped in the support lines on his way up to the front. 'We got held up by the Dublins before we entered the tunnel and we had to tie sandbags round our feet. So I said: "Well, this is bloody awkward!"'[31]

In another echo of Suvla and Anzac various automatic devices were established in the trenches. Catapults were made to hurl bombs and self-firing rifles set up to give the Turks an illusion of fully manned front lines. Although ingenious, most of these devices were quite straightforward variations on a theme. Sapper Leslie Matthews was given the task of setting them up in the front line:

We used to go up to the trenches and re-load the rifles. Each sapper was in charge of so many rifles. We stood them up on sandbags with tins tied on the trigger full of sand. They were tilted so that sand would gradually come out of one into the bottom one. When the weight of that one was full that used to pull the trigger. Every now and then you would get a rifle going off. We used to tremble in our blooming shoes when we went up there because we knew there was nobody in the front line at all.[32] (Sapper Leslie Matthews)

To deter a quick Turkish infantry follow-up, should the evacuation be discovered, all unused and empty trenches were filled in to prevent their use. Every possible obstacle was placed in position to impede the Turkish advance down to the beaches. On the right, in the old French lines, the RND were 'Leaving large numbers of contact mines behind us and various other little booby traps, which should throw a considerable amount of cold water (other-wise melinite) on any thrusting and inquisitive spirits'.[33] The Royal Engineers took a major role, and Major William Dixon-Nuttall was ordered to prepare mines behind the British lines at Fusilier Bluff, lay various trip and tread mines and bury stores of barbed wire and iron stakes in old dugouts or disused trenches, as well as preparing barbed-wire obstacles so that the evacuation routes could 'be closed effectively and expeditiously directly the last troops pass through'.[34] As each of these obstacles was completed, movement around the peninsula gradually became more difficult and frustrating.

> We'd been up and down these trenches hundreds of times and, bless my heart and soul, we came off today carrying our rations and "Oh! Trench blocked. What the hell's done that?" And you have to go, walk back, and find another way and find *that* one blocked. We got lost because *all* the trenches that we knew were blocked. Some at a convenient place had this concertina wire over on the side ready to be pulled in.[35] (Ordinary Seaman Joe Murray)

Others were less concerned about the Turkish infantry, who might easily be deterred by these obstacles, than by their artillery. 'If they get into our 1st line trenches and find we've gone pretty soon after we've left – as I said before we don't mind their infantry – but every gun here and on the Asiatic side will at once be brought to bear on our communication trenches and the beaches. So it's a gamble.'[36]

The final element of the military preparations was the establishment of beach defences in case the Turks should break through and follow the British as far as the sea. Two keeps were established at Gully Beach and W Beach for stragglers and in addition 'The far side of the crest of the semi-circular beach was fully entrenched and strengthened by a double apron barbed wire fence. Six hundred men, naturally called the Die-Hards, held these trenches to the last, ie until I gave them the order to retire as rapidly as possible to the beach.'[37] The staff of the 17th Stationary Hospital, positioned inland on the plateau above the tip of Cape Helles, were also to remain behind until the last to look after any wounded resulting from the evacuation's discovery. To protect them when taken prisoner each member of the staff was issued with a note in French and Turkish which, in translation, read: 'I am not a fighting soldier; my only work is in connection with the wounded and sick in hospital and in the field under the protection of the Geneva Convention.'[38]

The first plan for the evacuation of Helles was the same as that adopted at Anzac and Suvla. Dardanelles Army Order No. 2, issued on 1 January 1916, outlined an identical pattern of a long Intermediate Stage and a Final Stage of two nights, intended at that point to take place on the nights of 6 and 7 January. Troops were to be embarked at Gully, X, W and V Beaches with a naval patrol off De Tott's Battery and Y Beach on the flanks to pick up any stragglers. However, once the Intermediate Stage had got under way, Birdwood began to reconsider the wisdom of a prolonged Final Stage and, fearful of the ever more unpredictable weather, investigated the possibility of concentrating the two final nights into one. At first the maximum number of men who could be removed in one night was considered too small by Davies to be able to defend themselves in the event of a delay, but after improvements to the breakwaters and piers this number was raised to 17,000, which he considered sufficient. A new Army Order was therefore issued on 6 January to this effect, instituting a number of changes. X Beach was no longer to be used and only 400 men were to come away from Gully Beach. The remainder were all to proceed through W and V Beaches. The new, single Final Stage was to begin on the night of 8/9 January.

As each day of the Intermediate Stage passed, the number of

men remaining on the peninsula began to fall. By the end of December, with the French infantry gone and the 42nd Division replaced by only two brigades of the 13th Division, a strange air of emptiness had descended over Helles.

It was really frightening. We left Fusilier Bluff ... and came down at the Geogheghan's Bluff you see. That's alright, but there was nobody behind us. There was no troops to be seen anywhere. And we used to walk down to this dump through empty trenches, nobody there, and I thought to myself: 'Well, I don't know where the hell everybody's gone!'... We walked for hours, and did not meet a soul. When we got to the beach? Oh! tons of people on the beach. Some of them landing from boats ... coming inland. Bluff, because at night time they went away again. ... There were people carrying boxes from the lighters in the normal way. ... Everywhere on the beach seemed very, very lively and in the firing line ... but a proper vacuum in between. We had three miles there of nothing. Nobody at all.[39] (Ordinary Seaman Joe Murray)

At the base itself steps were taken wherever possible to obscure the extent of these changes. 'You could see great big guns being dragged across the beach below. They weren't big guns, they were tree trunks. There was ammunition piled up but it wasn't ammunition, it was empty boxes.'[40] The 17th Stationary Hospital itself was emptied, but in case they were needed later the tents were left in place with the added effect of presenting an outward appearance of continued use.

The Red Cross flags continued to flutter bravely and outwardly our Tented White City looked as busy as ever; there were stretcher-bearers supposedly bringing in patients from the Front, there were parades and work parties, and we even took the precaution of keeping lights ablaze at night, to lull the Turks into believing that our lives went on as usual.[41] (Lieutenant Lavell Leeson)

However, despite the reassurance of the hospital's unchanged appearance, even to Leeson, one of the remaining doctors, the changes seemed alarmingly clear.

There were sounds and signs of withdrawal all about us, in spite of the seemingly strong security that we were following. It was a sobering thought, watching the men slipping away down the cliff's edge to the beach, and becoming aware that their disappearance meant we were less protected every minute.[42] (Lieutenant Lavell Leeson)

The men who had not yet been ordered to leave became increasingly nervous, and reports and rumours began to circulate of Turkish foreknowledge of the evacuation.

On Christmas Day we catapulted over a tin of bully beef for a bit of fun. Three or four days later it came back to us. It was weighted with mud and stones. Inside there was a message written in good English: 'We are sorry you are leaving, we'll meet you again at Suez.' They knew that we were leaving.[43] (Trooper Edwin Pope)

News of incidents like this reached the Army Headquarters where Lieutenant Alec McGrigor, one of Birdwood's ADCs, noted that 'This morning a message thrown into our trenches contained the following rather feeble German joke: "When are you going? Will meet you again soon on the Canal. Our bully beef is better than yours." We presume the latter part referred to some tins that had been found at Anzac or Suvla.'[44]

The supply system began to break down and the quality of life rapidly began to deteriorate for the men still in the trenches. Private R. Loudon of the 1/4th Royal Scots found that 'From 2nd January onwards we lived on bully beef, hard biscuits and jam, while the men at the base and rest camp lived like lords, as far as food was concerned.'[45] Even Leeson suffered a strange diet at the hospital: 'Had anyone told us that we would be forced to exist for the last three days on Port wine and social tea biscuits we would have thought him daft! Yet that was our entire menu for the final agonizing days. Never again would I welcome either of those delicacies.'[46] The officers' mess of the Hawke Battalion found itself faced with a distressing crisis.

The situation seemed to us most serious of all when an order came to destroy all stores of alcoholic liquor, coupled with a request for a telegraphic report to the effect that the order had been carried out. Within the appointed time the Hawke Battalion orderly room reported that 'All *surplus* stores of alcoholic liquor have been destroyed,' but it appeared this qualitative interpretation of the intentions of the staff was incorrect, and thirty six hours later the mistake which had been made . . . was pointed out in terms which were commendably explicit.[47] (Lieutenant Douglas Jerrold)

The problem on the beaches was too much of everything, as troops, guns, pack animals, stores and munitions all competed for evacuation, while what remained was prepared for destruction. It required considerable organization to co-ordinate everything smoothly and avoid unnecessary delays. Brigadier General James O'Dowda was appointed military commander of W Beach on 1 January. It was not an easy task. 'I found a great deal of confusion and lack of organization reigning on the beach. This I proceeded to remedy as soon as I could, parcelling off areas of the shore to my various assistants and advising them how to create some order out of the confusion.'[48] He needed a sharp and enthusiastic staff to implement his decisions and one of those chosen was Lieutenant Patrick Campbell, whose regiment, the Ayrshire Yeomanry, had been evacuated on 30 December. It was a difficult and frustrating task.

> We are engaged, as you may judge, in infernally difficult work, and on two nights the weather has played the deuce with everything. I never had more difficulty in keeping my head in my life. Dealing at night with refractory piers, refractory boats, refractory Indians, and more refractory mules, and meanwhile shells at the rate sometimes of three to the minute, from two different directions and from as many as seven guns, is just about the limit.[49] (Lieutenant Patrick Campbell)

With large quantities of alcohol, as well as many other highly prized items, remaining in the abandoned canteens pending their destruction, looting was a potential problem. To prevent it O'Dowda instituted tight security over the stores he controlled at W Beach:

I noticed a good deal of looting going on. I had therefore to arrange for police and patrols to look after the dumps to stop this practice. Not that I minded the stores being taken, as I realized that thousands of tons would have to be destroyed, but it was very bad for the discipline of the area. . . . But on one occasion a very exalted General Officer and his Staff paid us a visit to see the progress we had made, and on their departure the General asked for some bales to be opened when he knew what the contents were, and in front of a considerable crowd of onlookers he and his staff proceeded to loot them properly.[50] (Brigadier General James O'Dowda)

In the face of such behaviour O'Dowda's response was both positive and sympathetic:

Well this rather took the wind out of my sails, so after the incident I allowed what I called organized looting, that is the men who arrived for embarkation were allowed to take what they wanted under the eyes of the police. Up to this time all comers had been supplied with new uniform and underclothes, and boots, but now they could take luxuries, such as mackintosh capes, gum and thigh boots, and even bicycles.[51] (Brigadier General James O'Dowda)

But even this new-found generosity did not extend to the stores of alcohol.

I decided that I must remove this source of temptation from those who were still to come. I therefore sent my police in charge of an officer and armed with crowbars to the Canteen, and they dealt very effectively with all that liquor. It was a very unusual sight, and one that brought tears to the eyes of some of the thirsty onlookers, to see a stream of mixed liquor making its way down to the beach, some of it fizzing merrily. Also the fumes were noticeable quite a long way off.[52] (Brigadier General James O'Dowda)

The most difficult problem was maintaining the embarkation facilities to allow the maximum number of men to leave the peninsula each night. Lieutenant Godfrey Taylor of the 3rd Engineering Field Company, RND, had been detached from his division and sent to W Beach to help restore the piers and breakwaters immediately after the great storm in November. His work, and that of everyone else on the beach, had been constantly disrupted throughout December both by the Turkish shelling and by the weather, which could change so rapidly that he had 'seen dead calm change to a gale in less than an hour several times'.[53] The shelling, which he remembered first beginning in earnest on 10 December, was carried out in a new and particularly irritating way. 'Ever since that day the beach has been shelled night and day not in spasms which allow one to take cover and come out again when it is over but 3 or 4 one minute then one 20 minutes later then perhaps none for an hour & so on. A most unpleasant method and merely a matter of luck who was hit.'[54]

Four piers had been constructed leading off W Beach, with two old hulks sunk to form a rough mole around the northern side. Taylor's job in December had been to build a breakwater of large stone blocks parallel to, but outside, No. 1 Pier. 'Our aim was to get out to two ships that had been sunk and close in the harbour.'[55] But, by the time the decision was taken to evacuate, the work had not been completed.

> Our breakwater was not finished and we had a gap of about 200 feet. No ship of any size could come alongside any of the piers so troops would have to get into barges & lighters & be taken out to the transports. If our breakwater had been completed we would have run out a light pier or bridge to the hulks and troops could have marched over to the outer hulk which was in deep water & could berth large ships. The navy produced an old Greek ship and said they would sink her and close the gap in the breakwater. They did it at night and to our horror in the morning we found ... it really did more harm than good as it diverted waves on to the line ... we wanted to bridge.[56] (Lieutenant Godfrey Taylor)

Some form of pontoon still had to be built to allow the troops to embark directly on to the larger ships moored to the hulks. 'I was given the job of building the floating bridge. It was in 6 sections 30 feet long and a sloping gangway up the side of the inner hulk ... alongside which came ships that would hold 2000 troops each.'[57] Eventually, by 7 January, it was ready.

However, on that day, the Turks unexpectedly launched a heavy bombardment on the front line in the Fusilier Bluff and Gully Ravine area.

At about eleven in the morning the Turks began an intensive bombardment of both sides of the Gully Ravine. It was soon obvious that this was the prelude to an attack. The question was – 'How long did we have to wait?' As the hours passed, thousands of shells crashed into the empty support trenches and those that fell in the front line took their toll. It was by far the most severe and prolonged shelling I have ever experienced.[58] (Ordinary Seaman Joe Murray)

Throughout the rest of the morning and into the afternoon the bombardment continued. The atmosphere was extremely tense as the retreating troops waited for the assault which could expose all their plans. At last it came.

The Turks charged over, shouting wildly. They had about a hundred yards to cover before reaching my particular part of the line though they had less ground to cover a little further to the left. After their four and a half hours' warning, we were ready for them. . . . They came in their hundreds, some carrying timber for use in bridging our trenches. Perhaps they thought that after these hours of shelling there would be no one to stop them, but they had not reckoned with the Staffordshires of the 13th Division and eight sappers who could handle rifles as well as the rest. We should be able to – we have had plenty of practice. We blazed away at the advancing Turks who did not now appear to be in such a hurry to get to the coast. Some were becoming hesitant when our warships helped them to make up their minds. I thought the Navy had deserted us long ago and it was very heartening to hear their salvoes. We certainly needed their help.[59] (Ordinary Seaman Joe Murray)

The attack was defeated. Despite the intensity of their preliminary bombardment, at some places in the line few Turkish soldiers could be exhorted to leave their trenches to attack the British line. Over near the coast, opposite Dixon-Nuttall, 'Only about 4 or 5 came over out of their trenches and were all killed. We must have hit a lot of them but most only showed their bayonets over the parapet & fired in the air and did no more.'[60] Nothing their officers could do would persuade the Turks to stand up and charge. Perhaps they too realized that the campaign would soon be over.

That night on the beaches the evacuation went smoothly. Taylor recalled that the weather 'was dead calm and at dusk we floated out our sections and the whole thing was most successful'.[61] However, most of the troops used the strong stone pier which ran out from V Beach, enabling troops to march right into the empty body of the *River Clyde* and embark directly on to the waiting trawlers.

'We are living in exciting times,'[62] wrote Major General Paris in his dugout on the morning of 8 January 1916. By this stage some 18,350 officers and men had been evacuated from Helles since the order to begin had been received on 28 December. Only 17,000 remained, awaiting the final night. 'Between now (11am) and 11.30pm is our dangerous time. If the Turks attack in real strength, they will no doubt lose heavily but we haven't sufficient men left to make it impossible for them to succeed.'[63] Yet, ironically, the strength of the British defence on the previous day, and in particular the vigour of the artillery counter-bombardment, had convinced the Turks that an evacuation was not imminent, and so for the remaining troops the day, which was fair and calm, was spent quietly in preparations for the end. In the morning Birdwood and his staff paid one final visit to the peninsula. In his diary McGrigor described what would otherwise have been considered perfectly normal: 'A beautiful day. . . . Not an unusual amount of shelling going on, though a few 9.2's were always whizzing about.'[64]

Despite the exhaustive efforts of the past few weeks, as at Suvla a great deal of material of potential value to the Turks had not yet been removed and a desperate attempt to destroy as much as possible was made during the final day. It was at the base camp and the divisional supply depots that the greatest efforts were made. Larger pieces of machinery had been prepared for destruction. 'When the service of the traction engine had been dispensed with and it was of no more use to us, the fire box was packed with a few sticks of gelignite, and as a booby trap when the door of the fire box was opened, the whole contraption would blow up.'[65] The men worked with a will. 'We spent the whole of the last day smashing everything, carts, bits of furniture, bicycles, harness and what was left of the food supplies. . . . I've never known a fatigue party work with such a will – they seemed to revel in destruction.'[66] Once this had been completed and the fatigue party sent off to the base in the late afternoon, one final, distressing task remained.

> There were about 15 horses and a few mules, and the three of us reluctantly decided that we must make a start. It was heartbreaking. The horses were so completely trusting. The first three or four we took a short way up the ravine and shot them – a vet had been around earlier in the day and told us how to do it; draw an imaginary line from each eye to the opposite ear, and shoot them where they crossed. After the first few the remainder seemed to sense what was happening and panicked. They were firmly tethered together so couldn't get away, but they were plunging and rearing and squealing. The Corporal said that he had been injured and couldn't carry on (I don't think he was) and disappeared to the first aid post and I never saw him again. The other man and I carried on and eventually the job was done. I hope we made a fairly clean job of it, but several had to have a second shot to make certain.[67] (Captain Wilfred d'A. Collings)

Not everyone was willing to co-operate in the slaughter of their animal friends.

> We went along to the dump and parked the ambulance, we let the horses free – the sergeant had said shoot them but we never had any guns and in any case it's not so easy to shoot a horse. We stripped them of the traces, saddles, bits, headpieces, dumped them and let the horses go.[68] (Gunner Harold Barrow)

Such acts of disobedience seem to have been quite common. 'I knew that the Turks wouldn't hurt a donkey so I left him there with plenty of hay so I knew he'd be alright, our moke. I didn't see why he should be shot.'[69]

Another vital task was to destroy all the remaining stocks of ammunition.

> A large cavern in one of the cliffs jutting out near to the beach . . . was crammed to its mouth with all the surplus guncotton, shell, SAA, grenades, limbers full of shell etc, etc all ready to be

blown up. There were about 25 dumps of stores, drenched with petrol and oil, ready to be set alight by means of fuses, and all these fuses were timed to last for half an hour.[70] (Brigadier General James O'Dowda)

The whole lot was intended to go up in a massive explosion once the last boats were well clear of the beach.

The Final Stage of the evacuation had been meticulously planned to take place in three waves. The first, of just over 7,000 men, was due to leave its original position immediately after dark and embark soon after 20.00; the second, slightly smaller wave was to follow three hours later, embarking between 22.30 and 23.30. All the men of these two waves were to embark at V and W Beaches, including those who had started at Gully Beach. But the third wave, approximately half the size of the first two, was to embark between 02.00 and 03.00 and included a small detachment of 400 men due to leave from Gully Beach in two lighters.

For the final night Burge had been detached from his battalion to help with the organization of these precise arrangements. He believed he had been selected for this because during the RND's earlier retreat from Antwerp he had acquired

a totally fictitious reputation for being able to 'see like a cat in the dark'. And talking of retreats, it strikes me the poor old Naval Division is becoming a thing of ill omen. As this is the 2nd occasion (Antwerp of course being the 1st), we've decided to call them 'advances to the coast' instead.[71] (Lieutenant Colonel Norman Burge)

His first job was the evacuation of the 2,000 troops living in the RND bivouacs, situated on either side of the Krithia Road where it crossed over Krithia Nullah:

The difficulty was that they *must* arrive on the beach in bodies of 100 exactly and as no unit was exactly that number, it meant adding a few of this battalion on to that and chucking in a few Royal Engineers or something of that sort as a make-weight. Still, not so difficult so far. *BUT* I'd only got one narrow road to form those troops up on – no one could move or show himself till 5.45pm and the whole body must start off at 6.15. So it meant falling in in the dark and detaching bodies to join other bodies, and in short doing most unmilitary things which, if I'd done in a promotion exam, would have ploughed me straight away. Well, they fell in at 5.45 – representatives of 11 units, ranging in varying numbers from 559 of my own battalion to 10 Medical Unit. At 6.10' they commenced to move off and at 6.20 the bivouacs were clear. I really do feel inclined to buck a little about that, because the text books lay down (I think) that 200 infantry in fours pass a given point in 1 minute – i.e. 1600 (which was the first bunch I sent) in 8 minutes. Well we only took 10 and that was in the dark.[72] (Lieutenant Colonel Norman Burge)

After despatching the remaining 400 men of the first wave Burge's next job was to run the RND rendezvous point. 'This delectable spot consisted of a small wooden bridge with flat desolate country populated with deserted and cold looking empty dugouts and a big spur which ended just behind me.'[73] Reaching it at 19.00, he was to remain there until the last RND man had passed through at 02.30. The plan was for the second wave, drawn mainly from the support lines, to pass 'through me soon after 9pm. They came all right – ahead of time of course because somehow there didn't seem to be any loitering on the way'.[74] Murray, although detached from his battalion, was still evacuated with the RND, leaving the support line a short while after dusk and starting to make his way down to the rendezvous.

All the gear that we had that jingled – water bottles, entrenching tools, even your bayonet scabbard – was taken away because it made a noise. We still had our sandbags on our feet and we were told: 'Empty the breech and you've got to make your way to Krithia Road.' We had a day's iron ration with us, a little bag with some small dog biscuits in to keep us going for a day and we had a bit of a bandage tied round our arm.[75] (Ordinary Seaman Joe Murray)

During the long march to the beach, Murray passed through the control points. 'There was somebody in a side trench checking us out ... one or two sometimes. I can't remember seeing more because I wasn't concerned. Every time the bloke in front of you stopped you stopped but you were asleep, walking in your sleep.'[76] Many of the men were upset at the prospect of leaving.

I thought to myself I don't like sneaking away like this after all this bloody trouble. I was really distressed in my own mind, I thought to myself we're stealing away. We stole away from Blandford, stole away from Egypt and now we're stealing away from Gallipoli. I remember when I came towards Backhouse Post, I thought to myself, Oh dear me! Poor old Yates and Parsons, all killed and buried here. When we first went to Backhouse Post on the 30th April I remember how happy and anxious we were to get stuck into the Turks. And here we were only a handful left.[77] (Ordinary Seaman Joe Murray)

Eventually Murray arrived at V Beach, where he waited, under the cliffs, for his turn to embark.

There was a bugler on top of Sedd el Bahr fort and he could see the flash of the gun or the flash of a gun – whether it was Asiatic Annie we don't know – but the moment he saw the flash he used to blow a low G, you know, and that meant to say: 'On its way.' Now, as soon as that went everybody dashed to the cliff. That was the instructions. We had 28 seconds, I think that was the time it took the shell to come over. That's not a lot of time to get back, and then all of a sudden, BANG![78] (Ordinary Seaman Joe Murray)

At about midnight, Murray left via the hulk of the *River Clyde*. Once inside the lighter it was a sordid and uncomfortable experience.

We were so packed we couldn't move our hands up at all. We couldn't! I remember the chap in front of me was as sick as a dog. Half of them were asleep and leaning. We were packed up like sardines in this blinking lighter. It was dark, of course. Apart from being dark, it was dark inside – no lights, no portholes. I remember a couple of fellows behind me pushing and shoving, and I thought to myself: 'Do as you bloody well like!' All of a sudden the damned thing started to rock, and it did rock! There must have been a shell – I couldn't hear it – there must have been a shell dropped pretty close, and you know we laughed at V

Beach shelling, we laughed, and there we were, no reason for laughing. There must have been hundreds in this blinking lighter, must have been, and every now and again it was rocking. All of a sudden it hit the pier. Those that were asleep were half awake and those that were sick were still being sick and, oh dear me, it was stifling hot, stifling hot! And then another one came along and I thought to myself: 'Why the hell don't we get out of it?' It may only have been a little while but to me it seemed hours and then all of a sudden we felt the gradual rock and I thought to myself: 'Well here we are; we are at sea now anyhow.' We left there like a lot of cattle, being dumped into a lighter and just pushed to sea, and nobody gave a tinker's cuss whether we lived or died.[79] (Ordinary Seaman Joe Murray)

For Burge, still at the RND rendezvous, the tension increased as the last of the second wave passed down the road towards Sedd el Bahr. 'Then came the anxious time. The firing line was left most dreadfully thin and if the Turks attacked or found out we were going – we – the last ditchers would of course have been done.'[80] Among the 'last ditchers' was Macmillan, who had been told he was to take position on the extreme left of the divisional front at a traverse called Stink Point and to bring up the rear. 'At 8.0pm I took position on the firing step, having my boots swathed in the blanket strips, while on my left forearm was fixed a piece of white bandage which was to serve as a mark of identification.'[81] The Turks were still unaware that anything extraordinary was happening.

That all seemed normal to the Turk was proved by his periodical rifle flashes from various fire positions; this is to show that his sentries were not sleeping. Little did he know that, at the moment, his rifle crackle and the rap-tap-tap of his machine-guns were to us the sweetest music under Heaven. Had he remained silent how ominous it all would have seemed to the anxious watchers of the skeleton garrisons.[82] (Able Seaman Thomas Macmillan)

At last, at 11.45, it was time to leave.

Rushing on I caught a glimpse of some of the boys who had lost their last chance of escaping and who waited in death the arrival of the enemy. Dr MacEwan and his faithful assistants had found old stretchers for them and with tender care had covered them over with blankets, leaving only their tackety boots to view. Running as fast as my legs would carry me I eventually got up with my party as they were leaving the communication trench for the open. There we halted and removed the blanket strips from our feet. When freed from our fetters, the gallop was resumed. . . . We found that the road had been broken up purposely by our engineers, and at frequent intervals we were precipitated, at times headlong, into holes of considerable depth. . . . On clearing the road, from which it was impossible to stray by reason of directing belts of wire, we were halted at the first blockhouse. The officer in charge and Pincher Martin satisfactorily accounted for our party to cool and calculating engineer non-commissioned officers, and on we passed to the next blockhouse.[83] (Able Seaman Thomas Macmillan)

At the RND rendezvous Burge was watching the withdrawal of these final parties as they moved quietly by, ensuring that every man in his division had been accounted for:

During this last period I had been naturally very busy, as I found the best way was to count every individual man who passed my bridge. Sketchley was in a dugout – Control Station – close near and knew, of course, exactly the numbers of each party due. So after the last feller-me-lad had passed according to my reckoning – I went and checked over the numbers with him. The Staff arrangements were perfect – and more than perfect – because they were fool-proof. There were small control stations dotted about everywhere that knew who and how many to expect (these were between my place and the firing line) and they 'phoned into Sketchley's place as each lot passed. So that if any small party had gone adrift, it would be known that it must be between two definite points. Well we checked our numbers – said 'Damyer ole man, it's all right' or some such nonsense to each other, the 4 signallers packed up their instruments and we made for the beach, feeling pretty happy.[84] (Lieutenant Colonel Norman Burge)

All of the RND, together with the 52nd Division, got away safely from V Beach.

At W Beach O'Dowda carefully controlled the embarkation of each wave of men from the moment they arrived there.

> The troops were met at the entrance of the defence works of the beach, which were on the top of the cliffs. From that point they were guided to forming-up places where they were sorted out and detailed for their respective troop carriers. Then they were marched to the beach by guides and either sent to the hulks by the floating pier or embarked in lighters alongside the jetties.[85]
> (Brigadier General James O'Dowda)

Working in close co-operation with his naval counterparts, O'Dowda had been obliged to embark each group in the exact number required by the capacity of their lighter. 'I had to produce the men, animals and stores at the right time, and at the right jetty, or at the floating pier leading to the hulk. The naval transport officers took over everything at what is termed "High Water Mark" and were responsible that the men, animals and stores were taken to their respective ships.'[86] But however strictly he and his staff controlled the embarkation, there was one problem they could not control: the weather.

Some hours before the arrival of the first wave, Taylor had begun to set up his floating bridge, which until that time had been concealed by No. 1 Pier. 'At 5.30 I floated out the raft & connected up & had it ready by 7 o'clock when there was quite a swell on. It was an odd looking thing formed of steel tanks, steel barrels & wooden barrels.'[87] It was on this rickety structure that the really smooth evacuation of W Beach depended, and the successful operation of the bridge was in turn dependent on fair weather. But gradually, as the hours passed, the weather worsened. 'At 7pm the breeze, which had been a gentle one, freshened. At 8 o'clock it had stiffened considerably, and by 9pm the wind had reached a velocity of 35 miles an hour and was increasing, and W was a very open beach.'[88] However, the first wave passed over the bridge success- fully. 'In spite of the motion we got 2,000 over the raft for the first flight and everything was well ahead of time.'[89] But then the wind began to disturb the bridge. For O'Dowda this created a new problem:

As the wind continued to gather force, the lighters became more and more unmanageable till finally one of them charged the floating pier and damaged it badly. However the Navy were able to repair it and again we went ahead. Then to make quite sure two lighters crashed into the pier simultaneously and carried it away altogether. This time it was beyond repair, and so we had to do without. The work from the jetties was very slow compared with the continuous stream of men marching along the floating pier to the hulks and then boarding destroyers or Thames steamers.[90] (Brigadier General James O'Dowda)

Working on W Beach that night was Coxswain P. Powell, in charge of one of the motorized lighters embarking men from No. 2 Pier, next along the beach from the floating bridge. As a result of the troubles there, Powell was forced to make more journeys to the waiting transports, including the old battleship HMS *Mars*:

By 11pm the wind had freshened blowing from the South; and a slight sea got up, and was causing much inconvenience on the beach. A floating bridge got carried away on W Beach necessitating us to make a trip to a destroyer with troops. The Turks seemed very quiet. I only noticed about six shells fired up to the present, but I found that one of these shells dropped on the last section that was coming aboard my lighter, one was killed, three injured.[91] (Coxswain P. Powell)

This seems to contradict the widely held view that there were no casualties at all suffered during the night of the actual evacuation. The lighters worked all night carrying the troops out to the waiting ships offshore.

11.15pm we were busy being loaded up as full as possible. Still, we made progress and by 11.45 I moved out after some difficulty for the wind and sea was blowing right on. I was ordered to the HMS *Mars* but it was a rather long trip, uncomfortable for us and certainly so for the soldiers, who had marched down five miles through trenches. We had great difficulty in getting alongside, and also remaining on. It was hard work for the troops to climb the ladders with 100lb pack and rifles, for the sea was very nasty.[92] (Coxswain P. Powell)

Above W Beach Leeson and the staff of the 17th Stationary Hospital had waited until the end of the second wave before they received the order to pack up and leave.

> We made a rather pathetic sight as we staggered to the cliff edge, laden down, weary, forlorn, our pockets filled with last minute items that we could not leave in the tents. Our orders had called for the lights to be left burning in the hospital area; how strange it was, walking away from our Tented White City, with lights blazing cheerfully, and not one person left behind.[93] (Lieutenant Lavell Leeson)

On reaching W Beach they had to set up temporary medical facilities which might be needed by the third wave. 'The dressing station was soon in working order; apart from a few minor injuries, such as sprains, cuts, and crushed fingers, we had little in the way of emergencies.'[94]

Despite the difficulties with the floating bridge, everything at W Beach had so far nearly happened according to plan. The second wave of the 13th Division from Gully Beach had arrived along the beach road on time and been successfully embarked. Behind them the road had been closed by a party of engineers, erecting the barbed-wire barricades and booby traps prepared over the preceding days; the final group of last-ditchers at Gully Beach was due to embark directly from the beach there. At 02.00 on 9 January these men embarked in their lighters; but by then the sea along the Aegean coast was so rough that one of the lighters had great difficulty clearing the shore and before it could head out to sea it was driven aground. In this lighter was Major General Maude and, together with around 160 of his men, he was forced to disembark again in an attempt to refloat it. They were successful, but the men were then left stranded on the beach as the sea prevented the lighter from approaching the shore to embark them a second time. There was no alternative for these men but to make as fast as possible for W Beach to join the third wave embarking there. It was a difficult journey.

We had all the kit of headquarters with us, for which we had provided two steamboats, but as the horses had been shot and the vehicles destroyed, it was somewhat of a problem to get it along. Luckily however the ADMS remembered that there were three or four vehicle stretchers lying handy, and these we got and loaded up. We could not go by the beach route as it was too heavy going, so we started up hill on to the plateau, and very hard work it was. We all puffed and blew like grampuses, especially as we were all warmly clad. I then sent Hildyard by the beach route to try and notify W Beach that we were going, and the ADMS and I and party pursued our weary way across the top.[95] (Major General Stanley Maude)

At W Beach O'Dowda, having received the original message, waited until he believed Maude and his party had arrived and then prepared to leave:

I packed up my dispatch case and, leaving my office, brought up the rear of the last party. Just at that moment a GSO, very disturbed, rushed up and told me that General Maude . . . had not yet arrived. . . . I asked what had happened and was informed that, after they had left Gully Beach General Maude discovered that his bedding roll had been left behind. He said that he was hanged if he was going to leave his bedding for the Turks, got two volunteers with a stretcher and went back for it. . . . The time was now 3.50am and there was no sign of the missing General. I therefore sent an Officer and a couple of men, who knew every inch of the beach, and gave them ten minutes to retrieve him. Fortunately they found him almost at once.[96] (Brigadier General James O'Dowda)

Leeson was one of the last to leave:

In the darkness, we heard the approach of General Maude, his fellow officer, and a wheeled stretcher carrying his suitcase. Having been in a state of near panic over the idea of leaving a general behind, the embarkation officer had composed a little verse:

Come into the lighter, Maude,
For the fuse has long been lit,

413

> Hop into the lighter, Maude,
> And never mind your kit.[97]
>
> (Lieutenant Lavell Leeson)

On the beach O'Dowda was clearing the final stragglers into the last three boats, aware that the fuses for the beach stores and ammunition packed into the cavern were inexorably burning. 'It was now nearing 4 am and the time for the cliff explosion ominously close. So after hustling the last two or three men and General Maude on board the last lighter, I too stepped, with what feelings of relief perhaps you can imagine, off the Gallipoli shore.'[98] By this time, the fierce pounding of the waves had begun to create conditions at W Beach similar to those which had driven the lighter ashore at Gully Beach, and these last, heavily laden craft were now also having serious problems clearing the piers and breakwaters which ran off the shore.

> We pushed off in some excitement, for the last men to leave the firing line had done so four hours before (12 midnight), and the Turks might be expected any time; the glare showed us up very clearly to Asia, and why they didn't shell us is a mystery still; then the magazine fuse had been lit and was due to blow up any minute. As we let loose the wind caught us, and for some moments we drifted back towards the shore and straight to where the magazine was, within 50 yards of the beach. For some seconds we thought all was up, but the skipper succeeded in getting the nose of the lighter into the wind again just in time, and we began to make way safely out to sea.[99] (Lieutenant Patrick Campbell)

From Powell's lighter, struggling to get away from the beach, 'The sight ashore now was becoming very fascinating but it also told us of our danger. Also a few large shells had come too close to be comfortable, so we now had to get clear of shore, as the only lighter in W Beach now was the hospital one about 300 yards down.'[100] Leeson was in the tense rush for that last boat:

> We scrambled to reach the hospital lighter tossing in the cruel waves, helping each other with supplies and kit bags. Were we in time? 'Leeson!' shouted Thomas. 'Get down.' I saw Thomas

crumpled on the deck, and the air was filled with mud, sand, clods of earth, pieces of shrapnel and the most incredible noise I had ever heard.[101] (Lieutenant Lavell Leeson)

The stores and ammunition had finally gone up. The explosion was shattering.

We had not gone 200 yards from the jetty when the expected terrific explosion nearly blew us out of the water. Thousands of tons of debris, rock, shell cases, bits of limber wheels, and other oddments hurtled over our heads. I could never understand how we escaped injury. The men had been battened down in the hold of the lighter and were safe, but the few of us who were on deck escaped I imagine because we were within the cone of the explosion ie the mass of stuff fell all round us like the outside of an open umbrella. At the same time the beach was lighted up as if for a Carnival, and would have delighted Mr Brock of fireworks fame. It truly was a magnificent sight.[102] (Brigadier General James O'Dowda)

Near by Powell was still trying to sail his lighter against the fierce tide:

Soon there was splashes in the water and the falling on deck of stone, earth and pieces of iron; marvellous not one of us on deck got hit. It's a mystery how we escaped. We soon found the reason of it, on looking ashore the whole point was covered in smoke of all shades . . . on the beach was flames of every colour, and now and again a column of smoke and flame would rise up illuminating the place like day. The sight ashore is difficult to describe, it was terrible, it was beautiful, one wanted to look at it, and one wanted to be away out of it, the whole place seemed full of revenge spreading its fury, and increasing as time went by, and the sea breaking up on the shore added to the awful sight.[103] (Coxswain P. Powell)

Further out, by this time on a destroyer whose captain was desperately trying to get clear, Taylor also witnessed the explosion:

I have never seen such a marvellous sight. The beach was in flames cliff high, from end to end, everything as light as day and then this terrific explosion. It shook the sea & the ship and one saw a huge red mushroom spurt up into the air with huge lumps of black rock in the red flame. I suppose we were further out than it seemed. I know I thought not one of us had a chance and that the decks would be piled up with earth & rock falling on us but we were only on the fringes of the shower. Six men were cut and none severely.[104] (Lieutenant Godfrey Taylor)

The evacuation was over. It had been successful in its aim of evacuating Helles with the minimum possible casualties. But it had been a more difficult and hazardous operation than its eventual success might suggest. Immediately, the fires on the beach and the massive explosion of the stores in the cliff face alerted the Turks, 'From the Asiatic shore, and from the whole Turkish line across the peninsula, hundreds of red rockets began to stab the darkness, and in immediate answer to this warning signal a violent bombardment was opened on the empty beaches and piers.'[105] It had been a close-run thing.

The evacuation was, and has been since, rightly hailed as a brilliant operation and the epitome of successful military planning; but the satisfaction with the evacuation's success could not over-come the magnitude of the campaign's failure – Gallipoli was a great victory for the Turks.

The mixed emotions of failure and betrayal, relief and gladness, pervaded the rest camps on the islands of Imbros and Lemnos during the following weeks while the men rested and re-equipped. Lieutenant C. S. Black of the 1/6th HLI felt an initial gladness following the evacuation, but this feeling soon changed:

Cape Helles had no happy memories for us; no one wanted to see the place again. But what of the men we were to leave behind us there? The good comrades, who had come so gaily with us to the wars, who had fought so gallantly by our side, and who would now lie for ever among the barren rocks where they had died. . . . No man was sorry to leave Gallipoli; but few were really glad.[106] (Lieutenant C. S. Black)

They would soon be in action again. The 29th Division, the Anzacs and the Royal Naval Division, the Gallipoli originals, would all arrive in France in time for the Battle of the Somme. The 42nd and the 11th Divisions, after periods in Egypt, would eventually join them. The 13th Division went instead to Mesopotamia. The other divisions stayed in Egypt and fought their way up through Palestine towards Syria. That nothing had changed was made immediately clear to the Hood Battalion.

> General Paris was justly proud of his division, and whether it was his intention to visit all battalions in turn in order to express his appreciation, I know not. Suffice it to say that the 'Hoods' were paraded for the General's inspection; and after saying some nice things, he announced his intention of giving the officers leave to England and the men, if they cared, leave to Malta. His speech was listened to in silence, but when the acting commander called for three cheers for the General the gallant 'Hoods' gave him the 'raspberry'. The General went pink and, in a fit of choler, cancelled all leave for the battalion and confined all ranks to camp for seven days.[107] (Able Seaman Thomas Macmillan)

Some grievances were growing that linger even today, exacerbated every year on 25 April with the celebration of what has become known as Anzac Day.

> Anniversary of landing – much annoyed at prominence that is given to Australians who are the most boastful of men in the old & new worlds & nothing at all said of 29th Division who did all the dirty work & had much the worst time of it & did most magnificently. No it's all Australia & makes one quite sick. It's always the poor old regular army who gets no credit for anything & the way so much is made of Terriers and New Army is rotten. . . . Why is it the Regulars' job to fight for his country more than anyone else? It's every man's job – the only thing about it is the regular realized it much sooner by ever becoming a soldier whereas the rest only realized it afterwards & wanted several weeks' training to prepare for it. Nobody outside the service ever recognizes that fact.[108] (Captain Humphrey Gell)

This view is as firmly based in reality as the populist Australian view and, hopefully, now that the dust has finally settled on the graves of most of the participants, there is no longer any necessity to take sides in such a fashion. All the troops engaged at Gallipoli, whether British, Australian, New Zealander, French, Indian, North African or Turkish, went through a terrible experience during which most conducted themselves as well as can be expected.

Conclusion

Gallipoli has aroused much controversy and in the years since the final evacuation of Helles many of the major protagonists of the campaign have sought to demonstrate the worthiness of the Gallipoli project by explaining how close the campaign came to a magnificent success. As Gallipoli was a comprehensive strategic failure, this has been an impossible task, and attention has therefore centred on a few 'key' moments in the campaign which have been portrayed as 'lost opportunities' where the British would have swept to a crushing success and achieved all their strategic aims but for a crucial mistake or a piece of cruel misfortune which thwarted them. Unfortunately these golden tactical opportunities depended for the most part on the assumption of an almost total absence of any further resistance from the Turks. In a sense these incidents symbolize the reasons why the campaign failed and the futility of attempting to justify a strategic concept by the chimera of tactical fluctuations on the battlefield.

It is tempting to see Gallipoli as a gambler's unlucky hand, a fair risk that failed, but the odds were never fair. The procrastination of the British and French governments and their failure to commit themselves unreservedly to an attack on Turkey meant that the cards were stacked high against success before they were dealt out to the hapless Sir Ian Hamilton. A worthwhile strategic concept is not negated by tactical failure on the battlefield, but tactical failure can be made almost inevitable if the strategy is faulty: and the British strategy was fundamentally flawed. Gallipoli was seen as the easy option to avoid fighting the war to a finish on the Western Front, but Lord Kitchener consistently balked at assigning enough troops and resources to give it any real chance of achieving success. After each failure troops were grudgingly made available who could have ensured success if only they had been present for the previous battle. By the time they arrived they merely restored the status quo by making up losses from battle and disease. The Turks always managed to concentrate more troops at the crucial points for the simple reason that they had more troops readily available for use on the Gallipoli Peninsula. When Hamilton managed to achieve short-term tactical surprise, as during the initial landings or in August, the Turks merely moved up their 'strategic' reserves to negate any tactical advantage he had temporarily gained.

In the face of these unfavourable odds the ordinary British soldiers and their allies drove themselves more than once to a point where victory did seem fleetingly possible. Yet, whenever they managed to attain some vital position which significantly threatened the Turkish line, it was only after being reduced in numbers to an almost helpless rump incapable of retaining that position – so the indomitable Turks threw them back. The British lost the Gallipoli campaign not on the beaches or in the gullies of the peninsula but in London. As Malcolm Hancock, a distinguished veteran later to hold the position of President of the Gallipoli Association, remarked: 'There are two kinds of muddles. One known as O.M.C.U. which was "Ordinary Military Cock Up". The other was rather more serious and that was known as I.B.U. and that is an "Inextricable Balls Up". A bit of a joke, but really very serious.'[1] His observation offers a fine epitaph for the campaign at Gallipoli.

Appendix

Thursby's claim that the landing at Gaba Tepe actually took place close to where he intended has been interpreted to mean that he changed its location after the issue of his orders. Yet there is no basis for this. The landing is usually examined from a military perspective, and most calculations of the location of the intended landing place are made using a statute mile of 1,760 yards. But Thursby's orders were couched in naval terminology, spacing each of the three battleships four cables apart. Assuming a consistency of terminology, although not specified as such, the mile given in his orders would have been a nautical mile of 2,025 yards, considerably longer than a statute mile. If this distance north of Gaba Tepe is used to plot the southern flank of the landing based on the position of the *Queen*, the difference between the intended and actual landing is reduced to less than 500 yards. Bean, *Story of Anzac*, I, Map 10, shows the *Queen* as approximately 2,700 yards north of Gaba Tepe. Given the fact that No. 2 Tow was theoretically to take up a station around 75 yards to her starboard and No. 1 Tow was then to be a further 150 yards to starboard of No. 2, the southern flank of the line of tows on this map would have been 2,500 yards north of Gaba Tepe, compared to a nautical mile of 2,025 yards.

The claim was also made in relation to the landing of the whole covering force. The destroyers which followed close behind the battleships were ordered forward soon after first light at 04.10. Metcalf's movement was by then taking effect, but it had no effect on the destroyers, which proceeded to land their troops as originally intended in line with the stations taken up by the battleships. On the southern flank of the destroyers' line HMS *Beagle* ended up roughly in the position which would have been adopted by No. 1

Tow had it moved directly east. In this context Thursby's sanguine claim does not appear so unreasonable.

It should also be remembered that the battleships finally anchored a considerable time after they had stopped their engines at 03.20. During the intervening period they remained under way, moving eastward without power. Although the normal current off the coast was insufficient to account for the movement of the tows, it might well have been strong enough to move the heavier, drifting battleships a few hundred yards to the north and thus explain the difference between their eventual and intended stations without challenging Thursby's statements. But this would have had no effect on the positions from which the tows began their approach.

Source References

1. A Bad Start

1. IWM DOCS, Lieutenant Colonel J. D. Wyatt MC, ms diary, entry dated 9 December 1914.
2. Brigadier General C. F. Aspinall-Oglander, *History of the Great War Based on Official Documents: Military Operations–Gallipoli*, I (London: William Heinemann, 1929), p. 27.
3. Aspinall-Oglander, *Military Operations: Gallipoli*, I, p. 29.
4. Aspinall-Oglander, *Military Operations: Gallipoli*, I, p. 53.
5. Aspinall-Oglander, *Military Operations: Gallipoli*, I, p. 55.
6. Aspinall-Oglander, *Military Operations: Gallipoli*, I, p. 55.
7. Winston Churchill quoted in Trevor Wilson, *The Myriad Faces of War* (Cambridge: Polity Press, paperback edition 1988), p. 113.
8. IWM DOCS, Commander H. F. Minchin RN, ms letters, letter dated 28 February 1915.
9. Aspinall-Oglander, *Military Operations: Gallipoli*, I, p. 82.
10. IWM DOCS, P. Rooke, ms diary, entry dated 11 March 1915.
11. IWM DOCS, Rear Admiral H. Miller, papers relating to his service as Naval Secretary to Rear Admiral Rosslyn Wemyss, Box 73/11/2, ms signal from First Lord of the Admiralty to Admiral Carden, 13 March 1915.
12. Quoted in Alan Moorehead, *Gallipoli* (London: Hamish Hamilton, 1956), p. 84.
13. IWM DOCS, Rear Admiral I. W. Gibson, MVO, ms diary, entry dated 13 March 1915.
14. IWM DOCS, Captain D. J. Claris RN, ms diary, entry dated 18 March 1915.
15. Gibson, diary, 18 March 1915.
16. Claris, diary, 18 March 1915. Aspinall-Oglander, *Military Operations: Gallipoli*, I, p. 97, gives the number of the *Bouvet*'s survivors as forty-eight.
17. IWM SR 4141, William Jones.
18. Quoted in Captain E. W. Bush, RN, *Gallipoli* (London: George Allen & Unwin, 1975), p. 56.
19. Gibson, diary, 18 March 1915.

20. Admiral of the Fleet Sir Roger Keyes, *The Fight for Gallipoli* (London: Eyre & Spottiswood, 1941), p. 69.
21. Gibson, diary, 18 March 1915.

2. The Dawn of a Perfect Day

1. General Sir Ian Hamilton, *Gallipoli Diary* (London: Edward Arnold, 1920), I, p. 37.
2. Aspinall-Oglander, *Military Operations: Gallipoli*, I, p. 99, and Hamilton, *Gallipoli Diary*, I, p. 39.
3. Admiral of the Fleet Lord Wester-Wemyss, *The Navy in the Dardanelles Campaign* (London: Hodder & Stoughton, 1924), p. 41.
4. IWM DOCS, Special Miscellaneous X4: Instructions for General Officer Commanding Mediterranean Expeditionary Force, paragraph 7.
5. Aspinall-Oglander, *Military Operations: Gallipoli*, I, p. 124.
6. IWM DOCS, Captain H. E. Politzer, ts copy of a letter written by 'George' (?F. G. C. Morris), 10 September [1914].
7. IWM SR 7498, George Horridge.
8. IWM SR 11965, Robert Spencer.
9. Spencer, SR 11965.
10. IWM SR 10648, George Peake.
11. IWM SR 8274, Rupert Westmacott.
12. IWM SR 8721, Thomas Henry (Harry) Baker.
13. Sir Alan Herbert CH, *A.P.H.: His Life and Times* (London: William Heinemann, 1970), p. 40.
14. IWM SR 8201, Joseph Murray.
15. Murray, SR 8201.
16. Murray, SR 8201.
17. Hamilton, *Gallipoli Diary*, I, p. 83.
18. Hamilton, *Gallipoli Diary*, I, p. 4.
19. Hamilton, *Gallipoli Diary*, I, p. 46.
20. IWM DOCS, Major General A. E. Williams CBE DSO MC, ts memoir, p. 27.
21. IWM DOCS, Captain A. D. Talbot, ms letters, letter to Captain T. Slingsby, dated 3 February 1915.
22. Reverend O. Creighton CF, *With the Twenty-Ninth Division in Gallipoli* (London: Longmans, Green, 1916), pp. 6–7.
23. IWM SR 10656, Robert Bird.
24. A. E. Williams, p. 29, reporting the comments of the SWB's Transport Officer, 2nd Lieutenant W. Rawle.
25. Bird, SR 10656.
26. Bird, SR 10656.

27. IWM DOCS, Dr Orlo C. Williams, ms diary, entry dated 18 April 1915, referring to the report given to GHQ after the *Manitou*'s safe arrival at Mudros.

28. PRO WO95/4263, GHQ General Staff War Diary, February–April 1915,
entry dated 19 April 1915.

29. Creighton, *With the Twenty-Ninth Division*, p. 42.

30. IWM DOCS, Major General Sir Steuart Hare, ts diary, entry dated 18 April
1915.

31. Hare, diary, 19 April 1915.

32. Hare, diary, 20 April 1915.

33. IWM DOCS, Colonel G. W. Geddes DSO, ts account of the landing from
the *River Clyde* by a Company Commander, p. 1.

34. Creighton, *With the Twenty-Ninth Division*, p. 44.

35. Surgeon Rear Admiral T. T. Jeans CMG, *Reminiscences of a Naval Surgeon*
(London: Sampson Low, Marston, 1927), p. 249.

36. IWM DOCS, Brigadier T. S. Louch MC, ts memoir, p. 14.

37. IWM DOCS, Captain D. Hearder, ts account, p. 10.

38. IWM SR 4026, Henry Blaskett.

39. IWM DOCS, Miscellaneous 262, ts account by an anonymous soldier of the
11th Battalion, AIF, p. 1. The original copy of the account is very badly
typed and all quotations from it have been edited to remove these errors.

40. IWM SR 4240, Walter Stagles.

41. Major R. R. Willis VC, 'The Landing in Gallipoli', in the *Gallipoli Gazette*,
July 1934, p. 72.

42. Willis, *Gallipoli Gazette*, p. 72.

43. Geddes, ts account, p. 2.

44. Geddes, photocopy of ms diary, 25 April 1915.

3.   The Landing

1. Aspinall-Oglander, *Military Operations: Gallipoli*, I, Maps and Appendices,
p. 44.

2. *Memorandum A/32: Naval Orders for Second Squadron*, 19 April 1915,
Appendix IV, para. 6, copy used in IWM DOCS, General Sir William
Godfrey, file 'G'. An epitome of the orders is also given in Aspinall-Oglander,
Military Operations: Gallipoli, I, Maps and Appendices, p. 32. A cable is a
nautical measurement of about 203 yards.

3. *Naval Orders for Second Squadron*, Appendix III, para. 10.

4. IWM DOCS, Captain J. S. Metcalf DSC RD RNR, ts account of the landing
attached to a chart showing the course which he believed was followed by
the tows. The chart, however, is misleading. While the course for the
southern tows does appear to be correct, that of the northern tows contradicts

the evidence of those in these boats that they continued at the beach with little change in course.

5. Aspinall-Oglander, *Military Operations: Gallipoli*, I, p. 174; Sir Julian Corbett, *History of the Great War: Naval Operations*, II (London: Longmans, Green, 1921), p. 321, and C. E. W. Bean, *Official History of Australia in the War of 1914–1918: The Story of Anzac* (University of Queensland Press: St Lucia, Queensland, 1981), a reprint of the 3rd edition printed in 1942, I, Preface p. xlv.

6. See Bush, *Gallipoli*, p. 111.

7. In Bush, *Gallipoli*, pp. 111–14. Bush was the Midshipman in command of No. 8 Tow.

8. Metcalf, ts account.

9. See Bush, *Gallipoli*, p. 114.

10. *Naval Orders for Second Squadron*, Appendix III, para. 10. See IWM DOCS Captain E. W. Bush RN, personal papers and research notes Box 75/65/1, photocopy of ms 'Orders' p. 2, and IWM DOCS, Commander C. D. H. H. Dixon RN, 'Copy of Orders for Landing Troops', following Midshipman's Journal entry dated 21 April 1915.

11. IWM DOCS, Vice Admiral E. W. Longley Cook, ts 'Extracts from Diary of Lieut. Commander J. B. Waterlow R. N.' sent to H. V. Howe by Waterlow's nephew and forwarded by Howe to Longley Cook with a letter dated 16 April 1970. An almost identical extract is quoted in Bush, *Gallipoli*, p. 113. Waterlow was killed at Jutland while serving in HMS *Black Prince*.

12. See Bean, *Story of Anzac*, I, Map no. 10, p. 251, which shows the position of the ships off Ari Burnu at 04.30 on 25 April 1915 including the line of battleships from which the tows made their approach.

13. See H. V. Howe, 'The Anzac Landing – a Belated Query', in *Stand-To: Journal of the Australian Capital Territory Branch Returned Sailors, Soldiers and Airmen's Imperial League of Australia*, vol. 7 no. 5 (September–October 1962), pp. 1–3, which raised this question in print. Following Howe's lead Robert Rhodes James later examined the possibility further in *Gallipoli* (London: Pan Books, paperback edition, 1974) pp. 105–6. Yet neither Howe nor James was able to produce independent evidence of a move to the north. After seven years of research into the landing and correspondence with many of the living participants, Howe finally accepted the explanation produced by Bush and discounted his own earlier belief of a deliberate change (see Bush, papers Box 75/65/2, file 'H. V. Howe', letter from Howe [*c*. 20 December 1969]).

14. Bean, *Story of Anzac*, I, Preface, pp. xli–xlii. In his preface Bean immediately appeared to call into question the reliability of the source he had just mentioned by adding, 'the strength of this evidence is not known' (*Story of Anzac*, I, p. xlii).

15. National Maritime Museum MS86/012, papers of Admiral Sir Cecil Thursby KCB, Box 2 Item 3, ms account of his command of the 2nd Squadron at

Gaba Tepe [27pp, unnumbered]; an edited version of the central section of the account is included in Wester-Wemyss, *Navy in the Dardanelles*, pp. 89–102. For further details on this point, see Appendix above.

16. 'A New Gallipoli diary' in the *Journal of the Australian War Memorial*, no. 16 (April 1990), p. 67.

17. IWM SR 7094, E. W. Longley Cook. This interview is a copy of one held in the Liddle Collection, Edward Boyle Library, University of Leeds.

18. Bean, *Story of Anzac*, I, Preface, p. xlvi.

19. Metcalf, ts account.

20. *Journal of the AWM*, no. 16, p. 67.

21. IWM DOCS, Captain R. W. Wilkinson OBE RN, ms and ts letters, ts copy of letter dated 3 April–8 June 1915.

22. Bush, papers Box 75/65/2, file 'Anzac Day', letter from Brigadier T. S. Louch MC dated 15 December 1969.

23. IWM SR 4155, Andrew K. Kirk.

24. Louch, memoir, pp. 14–15.

25. *Journal of the AWM*, no. 16, p. 68.

26. Hearder, p. 13.

27. IWM DOCS, Atatürk, ts memoir, p. 5.

28. IWM SR 4037, Frank Brent.

29. Brent, SR 4037.

30. Brent, SR 4037.

31. Atatürk, pp. 8–9.

32. Blaskett, SR 4026.

33. Brent, SR 4037.

34. IWM SR 4146, Frank Kennedy.

35. Aspinall-Oglander, *Military Operations: Gallipoli*, I, p. 296.

36. Captain Stair Gillon, *The Story of the 29th Division* (London: Thomas Nelson, 1925), p. 27.

37. Longley Cook, SR 7094.

38. Printed in Aspinall-Oglander, *Military Operations: Gallipoli*, I, Maps and Appendices, pp. 34–6.

39. Thursby papers, Box 2 Item 2, *A/33 Memorandum Re-embarkation*, 24 April 1915.

40. Liddell Hart Centre for Military Archives, King's College London, papers of General Sir Ian Hamilton, file 05/10, ms signal from Birdwood to Hamilton, 25 April 1915.

41. Thursby papers, ms account.

42. Hamilton papers, file 05/10, ms signal from Hamilton to Birdwood, 25 April 1915.

43. Quoted in Aspinall-Oglander, *Military Operations: Gallipoli*, I, pp. 164–5.

44. IWM DOCS, Lieutenant Colonel G. B. Stoney DSO, ts copy of a report by Lieutenant Colonel H. E. Tizard on the landing at V Beach, p. 5.

45. Minchin, letter dated 27 April 1915.

46. PRO WO95/4311, War Diary of the 2nd SWB.

47. IWM DPB, ts report by Colonel Mahmut, commander of the 3rd Battalion of the 26th Regiment, on the landings, translated from the Turkish, p. 3.

48. For full details of how this was done see Captain H. C. Lockyer CB RN, *The Tragedy of the 'Battle of the Beaches'* (London: privately published, revised edition 1936).

49. IWM DOCS, Captain H. C. Lockyer RN, correspondence concerning *The Tragedy of the 'Battle of the Beaches'*, letter to Lockyer from Commander S. E. Norfolk RN dated 3 September 1936.

50. Mahmut, p. 4.

51. IWM DOCS, Commander A. M. Williams DSC RN, ts account, p. 7.

52. Talbot, letter to Slingsby, 2 May 1915.

53. Willis, *Gallipoli Gazette*, p. 72.

54. Talbot, letter to Slingsby, 2 May 1915.

55. Talbot, letter to Miss Dorothy Turle, 2 May 1915.

56. Willis, *Gallipoli Gazette*, p. 73.

57. Willis, *Gallipoli Gazette*, p. 73.

58. Hare, diary, 25 April 1915.

59. IWM DOCS Admiral J. H. Godfrey CB, ts naval memoirs, II, p. 5.

60. Hare, diary, 25 April 1915.

61. Hare, photocopy of an ms letter to Hare from Major Mynors Farmar, 22 May 1915.

62. Major General J. C. Latter CBE MC, *The History of the Lancashire Fusiliers 1914–1918* (Aldershot: Gale & Polden, 1949), I, p. 51.

63. Geddes, ts account, p. 2.

64. National Army Museum (NAM) 6405–86, Captain D. French, ms letter, p. 9.

65. IWM DOCS, J. C. Wedgwood, 1st Baron of Barlaston, ts copy of a letter to Winston Churchill, 24–26 April 1915.

66. French, p. 10.

67. Geddes, ts account, p. 3.

68. Geddes, photocopy of a ts extract from a letter dated 30 April 1915.

69. IWM SR 4103, W. Flynn.

70. IWM DOCS, Lieutenant G. L. Drewry VC RNR, ms letters, letter dated 12 May 1915, pp. 6–6A.

71. Mahmut, p. 3.

72. Geddes, ms diary, 25 April 1915.

73. Geddes, ms diary, 25 April 1915.

74. Flynn, SR 4103.

75. Geddes, letter, 30 April 1915.

76. Geddes, ts account, p. 4.

77. Stoney, ts report by Tizard, p. 10.

78. Stoney, ts report by Tizard, p. 8.

79. Geddes, ms diary, 25 April 1915.

80. Captain Richard Willis, Sergeant Alfred Richards and Private William Keneally, gazetted on 24 August 1915, and Major Cuthbert Bromley, Sergeant Frank Stubbs and Corporal John Grimshaw, gazetted on 17 March 1917.

81. Commander Edward Unwin RN, Midshipman George Drewry RNR, Midshipman Wilfred Malleson RN, Seaman George Samson and Able Seaman William Williams, all gazetted on 16 August 1915.

82. IWM DOCS, Major General G. P. Dawnay, ms letters, letter dated 3 May 1915.

83. Quoted in Gillon, *The Story of the 29th Division*, p. 21.

84. PRO WO95/4304, War Diary 29th Division General Staff. See also Aspinall-Oglander, *Military Operations: Gallipoli*, I, p. 238.

85. WO95/4304.

86. WO95/4263, War Diary, General Staff GHQ, February–April 1915.

87. Dawnay, letter dated 29 April 1915.

88. Stoney, ts report by Tizard, p. 13.

89. IWM DOCS, Major G. W. Nightingale MC, ts transcription of letters, letter dated 1 May 1915.

90. Nightingale, letter dated 4 May 1915.

91. Hare, ms signal from Brigade Major 86th I. B. to GHQ, 2.30 pm, 25 April 1915.

92. IWM SR 7377, R. B. Gillett. A transcript of the recording, together with a copy of his diary, is also held in DOCS.

93. Gillett, SR 7377.

94. Gillett, SR 7377.

95. Nightingale, letter dated 4 May 1915.

96. IWM SR 7497, Cecil Tomkinson.

97. Hamilton papers, file 17/7/33, ms transcript of a letter written by Captain R. D. Whigham, 25 April–10 May 1915, pp. 5–6.

98. Hamilton papers, file 17/7/33, Whigham letter, pp. 7–8.

99. Aspinall-Oglander, *Military Operations: Gallipoli*, I, p. 212.

100. Hamilton papers, file 17/7/33, Whigham letter, p. 10.

101. Aspinall-Oglander, *Military Operations: Gallipoli*, I, p. 215. (One and a half Turkish battalions were equal to six companies at the given strength of 266 men per company.)

102. Stoney, ts report by Tizard, p. 16.

103. IWM DOCS, Mrs L. O. Doughty Wylie, ms copy of a letter from Lieutenant Colonel W. de L. Williams to Captain I. Pollen, ADC to Sir Ian Hamilton, 22 May 1915.

104. Nightingale, letter dated 4 May 1915. Nightingale played a conspicuous part in the clearance of Sedd el Bahr on 26 April and for his actions was specifically named by Aspinall-Oglander, *Military Operations: Gallipoli*, I, p. 277. Among his own papers a ts memorandum signed by Geddes, then his CO, on 1 November 1915 states that 'from what Colonel Doughty-Wylie

said before his death, I am of [the] opinion that Captain Nightingale would have been strongly recommended for the V.C.'. Instead, he was Mentioned in Despatches.

105. Stoney, ms letters, letter dated 10 May 1915.
106. Stoney, ts report by Tizard, p. 18.
107. *Cork Examiner*, 24 August 1915, 'Cosgrove: The Aghada V. C.'
108. Gibson, diary, 26 April 1915.
109. Stoney, letter dated 10 May 1915.
110. Flynn, SR 4103.
111. In addition to those mentioned in this chapter, the VC was awarded to Sub-Lieutenant Arthur St Clair Tisdall RNVR of the Anson Battalion, RND for his efforts to rescue the wounded on V Beach during 25 April.
112. Hare, ms signal from 29th Div. to Colonel Wolley Dod, 2.32 on 26 April 1915. Also quoted in Aspinall-Oglander, *Military Operations: Gallipoli*, I, p. 277.
113. Stoney, ts report by Tizard, p. 18.
114. Nightingale, letter dated 4 May 1915.
115. Mahmut, p. 12.

4.   The End of the Battle of the Beaches

1. Aspinall-Oglander, *Military Operations: Gallipoli*, I, p. 278.
2. IWM DOCS, 2nd Lieutenant D. A. J. Buxton RAF, ts transcript of diary, entry dated 26 April 1915.
3. Aspinall-Oglander, *Military Operations: Gallipoli*, I, p. 279.
4. A. E. Williams, p. 31.
5. Quoted in Creighton, *With the Twenty-Ninth Division*, p. 184.
6. Quoted in Creighton, *With the Twenty-Ninth Division*, p. 184.
7. A. E. Williams, p. 32.
8. Farmar quoted in Creighton, *With the Twenty-Ninth Division*, p. 184.
9. Quoted in Creighton, *With the Twenty-Ninth Division*, pp. 186–7.
10. Quoted in Creighton, *With the Twenty-Ninth Division*, pp. 187–8.
11. Dawnay, letter dated 3 May 1915.
12. NAM 5603–50, ts transcription of a letter by Lieutenant H. D. O'Hara.
13. Hamilton, *Gallipoli Diary*, I, p. 164.
14. Aspinall-Oglander, *Military Operations: Gallipoli*, I, p. 315.
15. Quoted in Creighton, *With the Twenty-Ninth Division*, p. 189.
16. IWM DOCS, Major K. M. Gresson, ms diary with ts transcription, entry dated 26 April 1915.
17. Aspinall-Oglander, *Military Operations: Gallipoli*, I, p. 296.
18. Hearder, pp. 14–15.
19. IWM DOCS, Major General A. R. Chater, photocopy of ts memoir p. 5.

20. Baker, SR 8721.
21. Hearder, pp. 15–16.
22. For detailed casualty figures see Bean, *Story of Anzac*, I, pp. 536–7.
23. Atatürk, p. 13.
24. Baker, SR 8721.
25. Parker's decoration was not gazetted until 22 June 1917.
26. IWM SR 11268, Joseph Clements.
27. Gresson, 2 May 1915.
28. Chater, p. 6.
29. Baker, SR 8721.

5.   Deadlock

1. Hamilton, *Gallipoli Diary*, I, p. 183.
2. Hamilton, *Gallipoli Diary*, I, pp. 186–7.
3. Aspinall-Oglander, *Military Operations: Gallipoli*, I, p. 303.
4. Figures given in Hamilton, *Gallipoli Diary*, I, p. 204.
5. Hamilton, *Gallipoli Diary*, I, p. 204.
6. Nightingale, letter dated 4 May 1915.
7. A. E. Williams, p. 34.
8. Aspinall-Oglander, *Military Operations: Gallipoli*, I, p. 321, and Hamilton, *Gallipoli Diary*, I, p. 199.
9. Gresson, diary, 6 May 1915, ts transcription.
10. Murray, SR 8201. Although referring to real people and actual events, when he wrote his book *Gallipoli – As I Saw It* (London: William Kimber, 1965), Joe Murray changed the names of his friends so as not to distress the families with details of their deaths. From that time on, he used the altered names whenever describing the same incidents and he declined to tell Peter Hart what the real names were, although he did confirm what he had done.
11. Horridge, SR 7498.
12. Peake, SR 10648.
13. Horridge, SR 7498.
14. Aspinall-Oglander, *Military Operations: Gallipoli*, I, Maps and Appendices, p. 72.
15. Hamilton, *Gallipoli Diary*, I, p. 211.
16. Brent, SR 4037.
17. Gresson, diary, 8 May 1915, ts transcription.
18. Gresson, diary, 8 May 1915, ts transcription.
19. Brent, SR 4037.
20. Aspinall-Oglander, *Military Operations: Gallipoli*, I, p. 346.
21. Dawnay, letter dated 11 May 1915.
22. Aspinall-Oglander, *Military Operations: Gallipoli*, I, p. 347.

23. O. C. Williams, diary, 9 May 1915.

24. Hamilton, *Gallipoli Diary*, I, p. 205.

25. O. C. Williams, diary, 9 May 1915.

26. Aspinall-Oglander, *Military Operations: Gallipoli*, I, pp. 349–50.

27. Aspinall-Oglander, *Military Operations: Gallipoli*, II (London: William Heinemann, 1932), p. 7.

28. Aspinall-Oglander, *Military Operations: Gallipoli*, II, p. 8.

29. Dawnay, letter dated 3 May 1915.

30. IWM DOCS, Rear Admiral H. T. England, ts recollections, p. 3.

31. Westmacott, SR 8274.

32. Wilkinson, letter dated 3 April–8 June 1915.

33. Aspinall-Oglander, *Military Operations: Gallipoli*, II, p. 13.

34. Stagles, SR 4240.

35. Aspinall-Oglander, *Military Operations: Gallipoli*, II, p. 19.

36. IWM SR 4008, Henry Barnes.

37. Stagles, SR 4240.

38. Barnes, SR 4008.

39. Westmacott, SR 8274.

40. *Journal of the AWM*, no. 16. p. 70.

41. Lieutenant Colonel J. H. Patterson, *With the Zionists in Gallipoli* (London: Hutchinson, 1916), pp. 163–4.

42. Ellis Ashmead Bartlett, *Despatches from the Dardanelles* (London: George Newnes, 1915), p. 110.

43. Buxton, diary, 2–5 May 1915.

44. IWM DOCS, T. Rowatt MM, photocopy of an unpaginated ms memoir, vol. I.

45. Rowatt, vol. I.

46. Talbot, letter to Slingsby, 30 May 1915.

47. Nightingale, letter dated 13 June 1915.

48. Talbot, letter to Dorothy, 24 May 1915.

49. Murray, SR 8201.

50. IWM DOCS, Lieutenant Commander W. B. C. Weld-Forester RN, papers, ms letter dated 15 May 1915.

51. IWM SR 4187, W. G. Northcott.

52. Rowatt, vol. I.

6.   Trench Warfare at Helles

1. Lieutenant General Sir William Marshall, *Memories of Four Fronts* (London: Ernest Benn, 1929), p. 79.

2. IWM DOCS, Lieutenant Colonel N. O. Burge, ms letters, letter dated 6 June 1915.

3. IWM DOCS, R. Sheldon, ts memoir, pp. 46–7.

4. IWM SR 8278, Arthur Watts.

5. Murray, SR 8201.

6. Murray, SR 8201.

7. Marshall, *Memories of Four Fronts*, pp. 80–1.

8. IWM DOCS, Captain R. M. E. Reeves, ms diary, entry dated 4 June 1915.

9. IWM DOCS, G. V. Sharkey, ms diary, entry dated 4 June 1915.

10. Murray, SR 8201.

11. Watts, SR 8278.

12. Murray, SR 8201.

13. IWM DOCS, T. Macmillan, ts memoir, p. 43.

14. Macmillan, pp. 43–4.

15. Peake, SR 10648.

16. Reeves, diary, 4 June 1915.

17. IWM DOCS, Captain L. R. Grant, ts memoirs, pp. 40–1.

18. Marshall, *Memories of Four Fronts*, p. 71.

19. Marshall, *Memories of Four Fronts*, pp. 75–6.

20. IWM DOCS, F. W. Johnston, ms diary, entry dated 28 June 1915.

21. Johnston, diary, 28 June 1915.

22. IWM DOCS, S. W. Evans, ts memoir, pp. 9–10.

23. Johnston, diary 28 June 1915.

24. Hamilton, *Gallipoli Diary*, I, p. 345.

25. Grant, pp. 56–8.

26. Quoted in Aspinall-Oglander, *Military Operations: Gallipoli*, II, p. 92n.

27. Hamilton, *Gallipoli Diary*, I, p. 346.

28. Geddes, ms diary, 5 July 1915.

29. Captain R. Blair, quoted in Lieutenant Colonel R. R. Thompson, *The Fifty Second (Lowland) Division 1914–1918* (Glasgow: Maclehouse, Jackson, 1923), p. 77.

30. Major D. Yuille, 4th RSF, quoted in Thompson, *The Fifty Second Lowland Division, 1914–1918*, p. 90.

31. G. F. Scott Elliot, *War History of the 5th Battalion King's Own Scottish Borderers* (Dumfries: Robert Dinwiddie, 1928), p. 33.

32. Chater, p. 11.

33. Johnston, diary, 13 July 1915.

34. Johnston, diary, 13 July 1915.

35. Johnston, diary, 13 July 1915.

36. Johnston, diary, 13 July 1915.

37. Thompson, *The 52nd Lowland Division, 1914–1918*, pp. 121–2.

38. IWM SR 8342, Alexander Burnett.

7. New Hope at Anzac

1. Aspinall-Oglander, *Military Operations: Gallipoli*, II, p. 63.
2. Aspinall-Oglander, *Military Operations: Gallipoli*, II, p. 65.
3. Aspinall-Oglander, *Military Operations: Gallipoli*, II, p. 132.
4. Hamilton papers, file 03/19, ms letter from Lieutenant General Sir Aylmer Hunter Weston to Sir Ian Hamilton, 11 August 1915.
5. Hamilton, *Gallipoli Diary*, I, p. 285.
6. Aspinall-Oglander, *Military Operations: Gallipoli*, II, Maps and Appendices, p. 16.
7. Aspinall-Oglander, *Military Operations: Gallipoli*, II, p. 149.
8. Aspinall-Oglander, *Military Operations: Gallipoli*, II, pp. 149–150.
9. Aspinall-Oglander, *Military Operations: Gallipoli*, II, Maps and Appendices, p. 19.
10. Aspinall-Oglander, *Military Operations: Gallipoli*, II, Maps and Appendices, p. 31.
11. Aspinall-Oglander, *Military Operations: Gallipoli*, II, Maps and Appendices, p. 34.
12. IWM SR 7499, Joseph Napier.
13. IWM SR 10475, Tressilian Nicholas.
14. Aspinall-Oglander, *Military Operations: Gallipoli*, II, pp. 173–4.
15. IWM DOCS, Lieutenant General Sir Carl Jess, ts transcription of diary, 6 August 1915.
16. Napier, SR 7499.
17. Hans Kannengiesser Pasha, *The Campaign in Gallipoli* (London: Hutchinson, [1927]), p. 207.
18. Quoted in Harry Davies, *Allanson of the 6th* (Worcester: Square One Publications, 1990), pp. 45–6.
19. IWM DOCS, Lieutenant General Sir Frederick Shaw, ts diary, entry dated 8 August 1915.
20. Davies, *Allanson of the 6th*, p. 50.
21. Davies, *Allanson of the 6th*, p. 60.
22. IWM DOCS, Colonel E. S. Phipson, typed article 'Thoughts on a Royal Inspection', p. 2.
23. IWM DOCS, Captain T. P. Watson, ms letters, letter dated 15 August 1915.
24. Phipson, 'Thoughts on a Royal Inspection', pp. 2–3.
25. Phipson, 'Thoughts on a Royal Inspection', p. 4.
26. IWM DOCS, A. G. Scott, ms letter dated 1 December 1915.
27. Phipson, 'Thoughts on a Royal Inspection', pp. 4–5.

8. The Landing at Suvla

1. Bush, *Gallipoli*, p. 243.
2. H. M. Denham, *Dardanelles: A Midshipman's Diary, 1915–16* (London: John Murray, 1981), p. 141.
3. Denham, *Midshipman's Diary*, p. 142.
4. IWM DOCS, Captain F. M. M. Carlisle, ms letters, letter dated 8 August 1915. The letters were published as *My Own Darling: Letters from Montie to Kittie Carlisle* (London: Carlisle Books, 1989).
5. Carlisle, letter dated 8 August 1915.
6. IWM DOCS, G. E. Dale, ts diary, dated 6/7 August 1915.
7. Dale, diary, 6/7 August 1915.
8. IWM DOCS, Sir Ivone Kirkpatrick, ts memoir, p. 16.
9. Kirkpatrick, p. 17.
10. IWM DOCS, G. A. Handford, ms memoir, pp. 17–18.
11. Dale, diary, 6/7 August 1915.
12. IWM SR 9178, William Kirk.
13. Aspinall-Oglander, *Military Operations: Gallipoli*, II, pp. 246–7.
14. Aspinall-Oglander, *Military Operations: Gallipoli*, II, p. 264.
15. Aspinall-Oglander, *Military Operations: Gallipoli*, II, p. 264.
16. Aspinall-Oglander, *Military Operations: Gallipoli*, II, p. 273.
17. IWM SR 8185, Terence Verschoyle.
18. Aspinall-Oglander, *Military Operations: Gallipoli*, II, p. 276.
19. Aspinall-Oglander, *Military Operations: Gallipoli*, II, p. 277n.
20. Aspinall-Oglander, *Military Operations: Gallipoli*, II, p. 276.
21. Aspinall-Oglander, *Military Operations: Gallipoli*, II, p. 277.
22. Coleridge, quoted in Major C. H. Dudley Ward, *History of the 53rd (Welsh) Division (TF), 1914–1918* (Cardiff: Western Mail, 1927), p. 24.
23. Aspinall-Oglander, *Military Operations: Gallipoli*, II, p. 279.
24. John Still, *A Prisoner in Turkey* (London: The Bodley Head, 1920), pp. 27–8.
25. Dale, diary, 9 August 1915.
26. IWM SR 10401, Ernest Haire.
27. IWM SR 9927, Arthur Hemsley.
28. Lieutenant Colonel A. Drage quoted in Ward, *History of the 53rd (Welsh) Division*, pp. 32–3.
29. Drage quoted in Ward, *History of the 53rd (Welsh) Division*, p. 33.
30. IWM DOCS, E. Lye, ts memoir, p. 12.
31. Hamilton, *Gallipoli Diary*, II, pp. 72–3.
32. Haire, SR 10401.
33. Haire, SR 10401.
34. Captain Kenneth Taylor quoted in Ward, *History of the 53rd (Welsh) Division*, p. 39.
35. IWM SR 8736, Field Marshal Lord Harding.

36. Hamilton, *Gallipoli Dairy*, II, p. 91.
37. Hemsley, SR 9927.
38. IWM SR 8867, Claude Dawson.
39. IWM SR 9317, Tom Williamson.
40. IWM SR 9172, Reginald Johnson.
41. Williamson, SR 9317.
42. Verschoyle, SR 8185.
43. Kirkpatrick, pp. 29–30.
44. IWM DOCS, Lieutenant W. E. Hertslet, ts transcription of letters, letter dated 14 August 1915.
45. IWM SR 9756, Horace Manton.
46. Harding, SR 8736.
47. IWM DOCS, Reverend H. A. Thomas, ts memoir, p. 27.
48. Aspinall-Oglander, *Military Operations: Gallipoli*, II, p. 325.
49. Aspinall-Oglander, *Military Operations: Gallipoli*, II, p. 325.
50. Aspinall-Oglander, *Military Operations: Gallipoli*, II, p. 326.
51. Hamilton, *Gallipoli Diary*, II, p. 105.
52. Hamilton, *Gallipoli Diary*, II, p. 105.
53. Hamilton, *Gallipoli Diary*, II, pp. 117–18.
54. Nightingale, letter dated 25 August 1915.
55. Lye, p. 19.
56. Nightingale, letter dated 25 August 1915.
57. Geddes, ts diary, 20 August 1915.
58. Nightingale, letter dated 25 August 1915.
59. Hamilton, *Gallipoli Diary*, II, p. 129.
60. IWM DOCS, C. C. M. Millis, ms diary, entry dated 21 August 1915.
61. IWM SR 10410, Arthur Bull.
62. Millis, diary, 21 August 1915.
63. Millis, diary, 21 August 1915.
64. Nightingale, letter dated 25 August 1915.
65. IWM DOCS, E. Miles, ts transcription of diary, entry dated 21 August 1915.
66. Lye, pp. 19–20.
67. Miles, diary, 21 August 1915.
68. Major Bryan Cooper, *The Tenth (Irish) Division in Gallipoli* (London: Herbert Jenkins, 1918), p. 191.
69. Cooper, *The Tenth (Irish) Division*, pp. 192–3.
70. Cooper, *The Tenth (Irish) Division*, pp. 200–1.
71. Cooper, *The Tenth (Irish) Division*, pp. 203–4.
72. Lye, p. 20.

9. Conditions at Gallipoli

1. IWM SR 8667, Harold Boughton.
2. Napier, SR 7499.
3. Murray, SR 8201.
4. Murray, SR 8201.
5. IWM DOCS, Brigadier F. D. Howitt, ms diary, entry dated 1 October 1915.
    6. Hemsley, SR 9927.
7. IWM SR 7496, Harold Pilling.
8. Verschoyle, SR 8185.
9. IWM SR 9100, John Pearson.
10. Hemsley, SR 9227.
11. Murray, SR 8201.
12. IWM SR 8174, Donald Penrose.
13. Boughton, SR 8667.
14. Thomas, p. 44.
15. Captain F. W. Walker quoted in *The History of the Old 2/4th (City of London) Battalion The London Regiment Royal Fusiliers* (London: Westminster Press, 1919), p. 54.
16. Verschoyle, SR 8185.
17. Watson, letter dated 2 December 1915.
18. Thomas, p. 50.
19. Thomas, p. 50.
20. Thomas, p. 51.
21. Thomas, p. 50.
22. Thomas, p. 51.
23. IWM SR 11219, Richard Yorston.
24. Rowatt, vol. I.
25. Macmillan, p. 57.
26. IWM SR 8326, Cecil Meager.
27. IWM SR 8257, Steve Moyle.
28. Burge, letter dated 6 June 1915.
29. Moyle, SR 8257.
30. IWM SR 8323, Arthur George Beeton.
31. IWM SR 8232, Leslie Matthews.
32. Patterson, *With the Zionists in Gallipoli*, pp. 46–7.
33. Grant, p. 44.
34. IWM SR 11114, John Chitty.
35. Watson, letter dated 7/10 July 1915.
36. Watson, letter dated 26 July 1915.
37. Peake, SR 10648.
38. IWM DOCS, Lieutenant Colonel H. V. Gell, ms diary, entry dated 9 June 1915.
39. Peake, SR 10648.

40. Murray, SR 8201.
41. IWM SR 8327, Harold Barrow.
42. Boughton, SR 8667.
43. IWM DOCS, Colonel F. Hardman, unpublished ts 'History of 10th Battalion, Manchester Regiment' by Captain A. G. Wynne, p. 33, in Box 76/27/2.
44. IWM SR 8834, T. V. Northcote.
45. Buxton, diary, 17 June 1915.
46. Macmillan, p. 54.
47. Murray, SR 8201.
48. Buxton, diary, 9 June 1915.
49. IWM DOCS, Lieutenant Colonel C. E. Foster, ts transcription of letters, letter dated 13 July 1915.
50. Boughton, SR 8667.
51. Foster, 13 July 1915.
52. Burge, letter dated 22 June 1915.
53. Hemsley, SR 9927.
54. Macmillan, pp. 59–60.
55. Macmillan, p. 54.
56. Harold Pilling, SR 7496.
57. Baker, SR 8721.
58. Murray, SR 8201.
59. Kirkpatrick, p. 21.
60. Hemsley, SR 9927.
61. Bird, SR 10656.
62. A.P. Herbert, quoted in Douglas Jerrold, *Georgian Adventure* (London: William Collins, 1937), p. 143.
63. IWM SR 8272, Edwin Pope.
64. Baker, SR 8721.
65. Sir Arthur Hurst, *Medical Diseases of War* (London: Edward Arnold, 1940), p. 195.
66. Murray, SR 8201.
67. IWM SR 8866, William Cowley.
68. IWM SR 8226, Arthur Bonney.
69. Burnett, SR 8342.
70. Murray, SR 8201.
71. Bonney, SR 8226.
72. Pilling, SR 7496.
73. Barrow, SR 8327.
74. IWM SR 8320, William Davies.
75. Davies, SR 8320.
76. Murray, SR 8201.
77. Foster, letter dated 17 November 1915.
78. Foster, letter dated 10 November 1915.
79. Bonney, SR 8226.

80. Hemsley, SR 9927.
81. Nightingale, letter dated 18 May 1915.
82. Nightingale, letter dated 22 May 1915.
83. Pope, SR 8272.
84. IWM SR 4052, R. J. Carless.
85. Murray, SR 8201.
86. IWM DOCS, Lieutenant G. R. Hughes, ts memoir, p. 14.
87. Hughes, p. 17.
88. Hughes, p. 21.
89. Hemsley, SR 9927.
90. Peake, SR 10648.
91. Burnett, SR 8342.
92. Pilling, SR 7496.
93. Horridge, SR 7498.
94. Moyle, SR 8257.
95. Murray, SR 8201.
96. Peake, SR 10648.
97. IWM DOCS, A. W. Skipper, p. 31.
98. Baker, SR 8721.
99. Burge, letter dated 10 October 1915.
100. Chitty, SR 11114.
101. Hughes, p. 15.
102. Miles, diary, 3 November 1915.
103. Hughes, pp. 15 and 21.
104. IWM SR 8230, Reginald Rathbone.
105. Burge, letter dated 6 June 1915.
106. Murray, SR 8201.
107. Rowatt, vol. I.
108. Macmillan, p. 87.
109. Burge, letter dated 16 September 1915.
110. Macmillan, pp. 90–1.
111. IWM DOCS, Sir Patrick Duff, ts transcription of letters, letter dated 5 October 1915.
112. Boughton, SR 8667.
113. Gell, diary, 19 June 1915.
114. IWM DOCS, Surgeon Lieutenant D. A. J. Williamson RNVR, ms diary, entry dated 18 August 1915.
115. Williamson, diary, 20 August 1915.
116. Gell, diary, 23 June 1915.
117. Foster, letter dated 7 September 1915.
118. IWM DOCS, B. J. Fielder, ms letters, letter dated 21 July 1915.
119. Talbot, letter to Dorothy, 18/19 May 1915.
120. IWM DOCS, Reverend C. I. O. Hood, ts transcription of diary, entry dated 4th November 1915.

121. Hood, diary, 25 November 1915.
122. Hardman, ms letters, letter to parents dated 9 July 1915, in Box 76/27/2.
123. Hughes, p. 35.
124. Thomas, pp. 36–7.
125. Thomas, pp. 48–9.
126. Barrow, SR 8327.
127. Pope, SR 8272.
128. Moyle, SR 8257.
129. Haire, SR 10401.
130. Burge, letter dated 16 September 1915.
131. Baker, SR 8721.
132. Verschoyle, SR 8185.
133. Barrow, SR 8237.
134. Rathbone, SR 8230.
135. Grant, p. 50.
136. IWM DOCS, Major General Sir Henry Hodgson, ms letters, letter dated 3 November 1915.
137. Baker, SR 8721.
138. Watson, letter dated 30 July 1915.
139. Burge, letter dated 22 June 1915.
140. Burge, letter dated 22 June 1915.
141. Burge, letter dated 22 June 1915.
142. IWM SR 9755, Harold Medcalf.
143. Murray, SR 8201.
144. Clements, SR 11268.
145. Chitty, SR 11114.
146. Boughton, SR 8667.
147. Pilling, SR 7496.
148. Grant, p. 42.
149. Baker, SR 8721.
150. Baker, SR 8721.
151. Moyle, SR 8257.
152. IWM SR 7396, Malcolm Hancock.
153. Napier, SR 7499.
154. IWM SR 8273, Frederic Sanders.
155. Clements, SR 11268.
156. Clements, SR 11268.
157. Hancock, SR 7396.
158. Murray, SR 8201.
159. Hancock, SR 7396.
160. Watson, letter dated 11 July 1915.
161. Hancock, SR 7396.
162. Penrose, SR 8174.
163. Hancock, SR 7396.

164. IWM SR 9090, Eric Wolton.
165. Murray, SR 8201.
166. Murray, SR 8201.
167. Murray, SR 8201.
168. Murray, SR 8201.
169. IWM SR 4194, N. W. Prophet.
170. Prophet, SR 4194.
171. Murray, SR 8201.
172. Murray, SR 8201.
173. Prophet, SR 4194.
174. Burge, letter dated 22 June 1915.
175. Howitt, diary, 18 August 1915.
176. IWM SR 10733, Edward Robinson.
177. IWM SR 7397, Robert Cook.
178. Beeton, SR 8323.
179. Beeton, SR 8323.
180. Captain S. W. Roskill (ed.), *Documents Relating to the Naval Air Service*, I (London: The Navy Records Society, 1969), p. 257.
181. Roskill, *Documents Relating to the Naval Air Service*, I, p. 222.
182. Beeton, SR 8323.
183. Hancock, SR 7396.
184. Beeton, SR 8323.
185. IWM SR 11461, Harry Robinson.
186. Yorston, SR 11219.
187. Yorston, SR 11219.
188. Sheldon, p. 63.
189. Wolton, SR 9090.
190. Haire, SR 10401.
191. Haire, SR 10401.
192. Barrow, SR 8327.
193. Watts, SR 8278.
194. IWM SR 8287, Frederick Coakes.
195. Hood, diary, 23 October 1915.
196. Thomas, p. 58.
197. IWM SR 7375, Stanley Parker Bird.
198. Baker, SR 8721.
199. Murray, SR 8201.
200. IWM DOCS, Lieutenant J. W. Parr, ms letter from A. P. Herbert, 18 July 1915.
201. Beeton, SR 8323.
202. Grant, p. 53.
203. Murray, SR 8201.
204. Wolton, SR 9090.
205. Hancock, SR 7396.

441

206. Macmillan, p. 67.
207. Penrose, SR 8174.
208. Peake, SR 10648.
209. Penrose, SR 8174.
210. Burge, letter dated 22 June 1915.
211. Horridge, SR 7498.
212. Foster, letter dated 30 July 1915.
213. Hardman, ms letter to his wife dated 21 May 1915 in Box 76/27/1.
214. Westmacott, SR 8274.
215. Grant, pp. 40–1.
216. Burge, letter dated 22 June 1915.
217. Nightingale, letter dated 9 June 1915.
218. Napier, SR 7499.
219. Nightingale, letter dated 4 June 1915.
220. Nightingale, letter dated 13 June 1915.
221. Nightingale, letter dated 4 June 1915.
222. Burnett, SR 8342.
223. Boughton, SR 8667.
224. Wharton, SR 8322.
225. Skipper, p. 31.
226. Murray, SR 8201.
227. Tomkinson, SR 7497.
228. Pilling, SR 7496.
229. Williamson, diary, 15 July 1915.
230. Murray, SR 8201.
231. IWM SR 8227, Basil Rackham.

10.   Admission of Defeat

1. Aspinall-Oglander, *Military Operations: Gallipoli*, II, p. 370.
2. Hamilton, *Gallipoli Diary*, II, pp. 132–3.
3. Hamilton, *Gallipoli Diary*, II, p. 141.
4. Hamilton, *Gallipoli Diary*, II, p. 163.
5. Hamilton, *Gallipoli Diary*, II, pp. 163–4.
6. Hamilton, *Gallipoli Diary*, II, p. 180.
7. Hamilton, *Gallipoli Diary*, II, p. 185.
8. Hamilton, *Gallipoli Diary*, II, p. 210.
9. Hamilton, *Gallipoli Diary*, II, p. 215.
10. Aspinall-Oglander, *Military Operations: Gallipoli*, II, p. 376.
11. Keyes, *The Fight for Gallipoli*, pp. 239–40.
12. Keyes, *The Fight for Gallipoli*, p. 241.
13. Aspinall-Oglander, *Military Operations: Gallipoli*, II, p. 366.

14. Aspinall-Oglander, *Military Operations: Gallipoli*, II, p. 392.
15. Hamilton, *Gallipoli Diary*, II, p. 248.
16. Hamilton, *Gallipoli Diary*, II, p. 249.
17. Hamilton, *Gallipoli Diary*, II, p. 253.
18. Aspinall-Oglander, *Military Operations: Gallipoli*, II, p. 384.
19. Aspinall-Oglander, *Military Operations: Gallipoli*, II, p. 384.
20. Hamilton, *Gallipoli Diary*, II, p. 272.
21. Hamilton, *Gallipoli Diary*, II, p. 273.
22. Hamilton, *Gallipoli Diary*, II, p. 276.
23. Keyes, *The Fight for Gallipoli*, p. 255.
24. Aspinall-Oglander, *Military Operations: Gallipoli*, II, p. 403.
25. Winston S. Churchill, *The World Crisis, 1911–1918*, II, (London: Odhams Press, 1938), p. 908.
26. Aspinall-Oglander, *Military Operations: Gallipoli*, II, p. 430.
27. IWM SR 4119, Frederick Griffiths.
28. Watson, letter dated 2 December 1915.
29. Murray, SR 8201.
30. Griffiths, SR 4119.
31. Murray, SR 8201.
32. Clements, SR 11268.
33. Watson, letter dated 2 December 1915.
34. Thomas, p. 70.
35. Thomas, p. 71.
36. Boughton, SR 8667.
37. Lye, pp. 31–2.
38. Griffiths, SR 4119.
39. Thomas, p. 72.
40. Murray, SR 8201.
41. IWM SR 9100, John Pearson.

11.   Stealing Away

1. IWM SR 9875, George Ashurst.
2. Kirk, SR 9178.
3. Rathbone, SR 8230.
4. Kirk, SR 9178.
5. Rathbone, SR 8230.
6. Cowley, SR 8866.
7. Kannengiesser, *The Campaign in Gallipoli*, pp. 245–6.
8. Kirk, SR 9178.
9. IWM SR 10655, Ernest Tysall.
10. Boughton, SR 8667.

11. Kannengiesser, *The Campaign in Gallipoli*, p. 249.
12. C. R. Samson, *Fights and Flights* (London: Ernest Benn, 1930), p. 286.
13. Curzon, quoted in Aspinall-Oglander, *Military Operations: Gallipoli*, II, p. 430.
14. Kannengiesser, *The Campaign in Gallipoli*, pp. 250–1.
15. Kannengiesser, *The Campaign in Gallipoli*, p. 253.
16. IWM SR 8871, Henry Denham.
17. Lieutenant General Sir Francis Davies, Special Order of the Day, 20 December 1915, quoted in Macmillan, p. 109.
18. O. C. Williams, diary, 24 December 1915 with attached original ms signal.
19. Boughton, SR 8667.
20. Murray, SR 8201.
21. Macmillan, p. 110.
22. IWM DOCS, Major General Sir Archibald Paris, microfilm of ms letters, letter dated 8/10 January 1916.
23. Paris quoted in Jerrold, *Georgian Adventure*, p. 154.
24. Macmillan, pp. 109–10.
25. Aspinall-Oglander, *Military Operations: Gallipoli*, II, p. 467.
26. O. C. Williams, diary, 28 December 1915.
27. IWM DOCS, Brigadier General L. H. Abbott, ms diary, entry dated 29 December 1915.
28. IWM DOCS, Lieutenant Colonel J. S. Millar, ts memoir, p. 35.
29. Burge, letter dated 4/10 January 1916.
30. Millar, pp. 35–6.
31. Murray, SR 8201.
32. Matthews, SR 8232.
33. Burge, letter dated 4/10 January 1916.
34. IWM DOCS, Major W. F. Dixon-Nuttall, order dated 3/4 January 1916.
35. Murray, SR 8201.
36. Burge, letter dated 4/10 January 1916.
37. IWM DPB, Lieutenant P. M. Campbell, *Letters from Gallipoli* (Edinburgh: privately printed, 1916), with accompanying unsigned ts lecture notes which internal evidence shows to have been written by Brigadier General J. W. O'Dowda, p. 13.
38. IWM DOCS, Lieutenant Colonel L. H. Leeson, ts memoir, p. 115.
39. Murray, SR 8201.
40. Ashurst, SR 9875.
41. Leeson, pp. 126–7.
42. Leeson, p. 126.
43. Pope, SR 8272.
44. IWM DOCS, Captain A. M. McGrigor, ms diary, entry dated 30 December 1915.
45. IWM DOCS, R. Loudon, ts memoir, p. 30.
46. Leeson, p. 130.

47. Jerrold, *The Hawke Battalion: Some Personal Recollections of Four Years* (London: Ernest Benn, 1925), pp. 108–9.
48. Campbell, *Letters from Gallipoli*, O'Dowda, lecture notes p. 4.
49. Campbell, *Letters from Gallipoli*, p. 91.
50. Campbell, *Letters from Gallipoli*, O'Dowda, lecture notes p. 7.
51. Campbell, *Letters from Gallipoli*, O'Dowda, lecture notes pp. 7–8.
52. Campbell, *Letters from Gallipoli*, O'Dowda, lecture notes p. 9.
53. IWM DOCS, Captain G. M. C. Taylor, ts transcription of letter dated 12 January 1916.
54. Taylor, letter dated 12 January 1916.
55. Taylor, letter dated 12 January 1916.
56. Taylor, letter dated 12 January 1916.
57. Taylor, letter dated 12 January 1916.
58. Murray, *Gallipoli – As I Saw It*, p. 218.
59. Murray, *Gallipoli – As I Saw It*, p. 218.
60. Dixon-Nuttall, ms letter dated 20 January 1916.
61. Taylor, letter dated 12 January 1916.
62. Paris, letter dated 8/10 January 1916.
63. Paris, letter dated 8/10 January 1916.
64. McGrigor, diary, 8 January 1916.
65. Miller, p. 36.
66. IWM DOCS Major General W. d'A. Collings, ts memoir, p. 29.
67. Collings, pp. 29–30.
68. Barrow, SR 8327.
69. Bird, SR 10656.
70. Campbell, *Letters from Gallipoli*, O'Dowda, lecture notes p. 14.
71. Burge, letter dated 4/10 January 1916.
72. Burge, letter dated 4/10 January 1916.
73. Burge, letter dated 4/10 January 1916.
74. Burge, letter dated 4/10 January 1916.
75. Murray, SR 8201.
76. Murray, SR 8201.
77. Murray, SR 8201.
78. Murray, SR 8201.
79. Murray, SR 8201.
80. Burge, letter dated 4/10 January 1916.
81. Macmillan, p. 119.
82. Macmillan, p. 121.
83. Macmillan, p. 122.
84. Burge, letter dated 4/10 January 1916.
85. Campbell, *Letters from Gallipoli*, O'Dowda, lecture notes p. 10.
86. Campbell, *Letters from Gallipoli*, O'Dowda, lecture notes pp. 9–10.
87. Taylor, letter dated 12 January 1916.
88. Campbell, *Letters from Gallipoli*, O'Dowda, lecture notes p. 11.

445

89. Taylor, letter dated 12 January 1916.
90. Campbell, *Letters from Gallipoli*, O'Dowda, lecture notes p. 12.
91. IWM DOCS, P. Powell, ms diary, entry dated 8 January 1916.
92. Powell, diary, 8 January 1916.
93. Leeson, pp. 146–7.
94. Leeson, p. 147.
95. Quoted in Sir C. E. Callwell, *Life of Sir Stanley Maude* (London: Constable, 1920), p. 184.
96. Campbell, *Letters from Gallipoli*, O'Dowda, lecture notes pp. 14–15.
97. Leeson, pp. 150–1.
98. Campbell, *Letters from Gallipoli*, O'Dowda, lecture notes pp. 15–16.
99. Campbell, *Letters from Gallipoli*, pp. 96–7.
100. Powell, diary, 8 January 1916.
101. Leeson, pp. 151–2.
102. Campbell, *Letters from Gallipoli*, O'Dowda, lecture notes p. 16.
103. Powell, diary, 8 January 1916.
104. Taylor, letter dated 12 January 1916.
105. Aspinall-Oglander, *Military Operations: Gallipoli*, II, p. 478.
106. Quoted in Thompson, *The Fifty-Second (Lowland) Division, 1914–1918*, p. 240.
107. Macmillan, p. 128.
108. Gell, diary, 25 April 1916.

Conclusion

1. Lieutenant Colonel Malcolm Hancock MC, recording of a talk given in Oxford, 17 November 1987, made by Nigel Steel. Copy held in IWM SR.

Bibliography

For reasons of space only sources from which quotations have been taken or to which reference is made in the endnotes are detailed in the following lists. The authors would like to thank all of those who have given permission for these sources to be used. In particular they would like to acknowledge those individuals who hold the copyright of the collections of unpublished papers held in the Imperial War Museum. Every effort has been made to obtain permission from the relevant copyright holders. But this has not always been possible and the authors would be pleased to hear at the Museum from anyone with whom contact has not been established.

Published sources

1. BOOKS

Aspinall-Oglander, Brigadier General C. F., *History of the Great War Based on Official Documents: Military Operations–Gallipoli*, 2 vols (London: William Heinemann, 1929 and 1932)

Bartlett, Ellis Ashmead, *Despatches from the Dardanelles* (London: George Newnes, 1915)

Bean, C. E. W., *Official History of Australia in the War of 1914–1918: The Story of Anzac*, 2 vols (St Lucia, Queensland: University of Queensland Press, 1981; a reprint of the 3rd edition originally printed in 1942)

Bush, Captain E. W., RN, *Gallipoli* (London: George Allen & Unwin, 1975)

Callwell, Sir C. E., *Life of Sir Stanley Maude* (London: Constable, 1920)

Campbell, Lieutenant P. M., *Letters from Gallipoli* (Edinburgh: privately printed, 1916)

Carlisle, Captain F. M. M., *My Own Darling: Letters from Montie to Kittie Carlisle* (London: Carlisle Books, 1989) (see also ms letters)

Churchill, Winston S., *The World Crisis, 1911–1918*, II (London: Odhams Press, 1938)

Cooper, Major Bryan, *The Tenth (Irish) Division in Gallipoli* (London: Herbert Jenkins, 1918)

Corbett, Sir Julian S., *History of the Great War Based on Official Documents: Naval Operations*, II (London: Longmans, Green, 1921)

Creighton, the Reverend O., *With the 29th Division in Gallipoli* (London: Longmans, Green, 1916)

Davies, Harry, *Allanson of the 6th* (Worcester: Square One Publications, 1990)

Denham, H. M., *Dardanelles: A Midshipman's Diary, 1915–16* (London: John Murray, 1981)

Elliot, G. F. Scott, *War History of the 5th Battalion King's Own Scottish Borderers* (Dumfries: Robert Dinwiddie, 1928)

Gillon, Captain Stair, *The Story of the 29th Division: A Record of Gallant Deeds* (London: Thomas Nelson, 1925)

Hamilton, General Sir Ian, *Gallipoli Diary*, 2 vols (London: Edward Arnold, 1920)

Herbert, Sir Alan, *A. P. H. His Life and Times* (London: William Heinemann, 1970)

The History of the Old 2/4th (City of London) Battalion The London Regiment Royal Fusiliers (London: The Westminster Press, 1919)

Hurst, Sir Arthur, *Medical Diseases of War* (London: Edward Arnold, 1940)

James, Robert Rhodes, *Gallipoli* (London: Pan Books, paperback edition 1974, reprinted 1984)

Jeans, Surgeon Rear Admiral T. T., *Reminiscences of a Naval Surgeon* (London: Sampson Low, Marston, 1927)

Jerrold, Douglas, *The Hawke Battalion: Some Personal Recollections of Four Years* (London: Ernest Benn, 1925)

——, *Georgian Adventure* (London: William Collins, 1937)

Kannengiesser Pasha, Hans, *The Campaign in Gallipoli* (London: Hutchinson, [1927])

Keyes, Admiral of the Fleet Sir Roger, *The Fight for Gallipoli* (London: Eyre & Spottiswood, 1941)

Latter, Major General J. C., *The History of the Lancashire Fusiliers 1914–1918*, 2 vols (Aldershot: Gale & Polden, 1949)

Lockyer, Captain H. C., RN, *The Tragedy of the 'Battle of the Beaches'* (London: privately published, revised edition 1936)

Marshall, Lieutenant General Sir William, *Memories of Four Fronts* (London: Ernest Benn, 1929)

Moorehead, Alan, *Gallipoli* (London: Hamish Hamilton, 1956)

Murray, Joseph, *Gallipoli – As I Saw It* (London: William Kimber, 1965)

Patterson, Lieutenant Colonel J. H., *With the Zionists in Gallipoli* (London: Hutchinson, 1916)

Roskill, Captain S. W., RN (ed.), *Documents Relating to the Naval Air Service*, I, (London: The Navy Records Society, 1969)

Samson, C. R., *Fights and Flights* (London: Ernest Benn, 1930)

Snelling, Stephen, *Gallipoli VCs* (Norwich: Gliddon Books, 1994)

Still, John, *A Prisoner in Turkey* (London: The Bodley Head, 1920)

Thompson, Lieutenant Colonel R. R., *The Fifty Second (Lowland) Division, 1914–1918* (Glasgow: Maclehouse, Jackson, 1923)

Ward, Major C. H. Dudley, *History of the 53rd (Welsh) Division (TF), 1914–1918* (Cardiff: Western Mail, 1927)

Wemyss, Admiral of the Fleed Lord Wester-, *The Navy in the Dardanelles Campaign* (London: Hodder & Stoughton, 1924)

Wilson, Trevor, *The Myriad Faces of War* (Cambridge: Polity Press, paperback edition 1988)

2. PERIODICALS

Cork Examiner, 24 August 1915, 'Cosgrove: the Aghada V.C.'

Stand-To: Journal of the Australian Capital Territory Branch Returned Sailors, Soldiers and Airmen's Imperial League of Australia, vol. 7, no. 5 (September–October 1962), H. V. Howe, 'The Anzac Landing – A Belated Query'

Journal Of The Australian War Memorial no. 16 (April 1990), F. Loud, 'A New Gallipoli Diary'

Gallipoli Gazette (July 1934), Major R. R. Willis VC, 'The Landing in Gallipoli'

Unpublished Manuscript Sources

1. IMPERIAL WAR MUSEUM, DEPARTMENT OF DOCUMENTS (IWM DOCS)

Abbott, Brigadier General L. H.
Atatürk
Burge, Lieutenant Colonel N. O.
Bush, Captain, E. W., RN
Buxton, 2nd Lieutenant D. A. J.
Carlisle, Captain F. M. M.
Chater, Major General A. R.
Claris, Captain D. J., RN
Collings, Major General W. d'A.
Dale, G. E.
Dawnay, Major General G. P.
Dixon, Commander C. D. H. H., RN
Dixon-Nuttall, Major W. F.
Doughty Wylie, Mrs L. O.
Drewry, Lieutenant G. L., VC RNR
Duff, Sir Patrick

England, Rear Admiral H. T.

Evans, S. W.

Fielder, B. J.

Foster, Lieutenant Colonel C. E.

Geddes, Colonel G. W.

Gell, Lieutenant Colonel H. V.

Gibson, Rear Admiral I. W.

Godfrey, Admiral J. H.

Godfrey, General Sir William

Grant, Captain L. R.

Gresson, Major K. M.

Handford, G. A.

Hardman, Colonel F.

Hare, Major General Sir Steuart

Hearder, Captain D.

Herbert, A. P., *see* Lieutenant J. W. Parr

Hertslet, Lieutenant W. E.

Hodgson, Major General Sir Henry

Hood, Reverend C. I. O.

Howitt, Brigadier F. D.

Hughes, Lieutenant G. R.

Jess, Lieutenant General Sir Carl

Johnston, F. W.

Kirkpatrick, Sir Ivone

Leeson, Lieutenant Colonel L. H.

Lockyer, Captain H. C., RN

Longley-Cook, Vice Admiral E. W., including extracts from the diary of Lieutenant Commander J. B. Waterlow RN

Louch, Brigadier T. S.

Loudon, R.

Lye, E.

McGrigor, Captain A. M.

Macmillan, T.

Metcalf, Captain J. S., RNR

Miles, E.

Millar, Lieutenant Colonel J. S.

Miller, Rear Admiral H.

Millis, C. C. M.

Minchin, Commander H. F., RN

Nightingale, Major G. W.

Norfolk, Commander S. E., RN, *see* Captain H. C. Lockyer RN

Paris, Major General Sir Archibald

Parr, Lieutenant J. W.

Phipson, Colonel E. S.

450

Politzer, Captain H. E.
Powell, P.
Reeves, Captain R. M. E.
Rooke, P.
Rowatt, T.
Scott, A. G.
Sharkey, G. V.
Shaw, Lieutenant General Sir Frederick
Sheldon, R.
Skipper, A. W.
Stoney, Lieutenant Colonel G. B., including a ts report by Lieutenant Colonel H. E. Tizard
Talbot, Captain A. D.
Taylor, Captain G. M. C.
Thomas, Reverend H. A.
Tizard, Lieutenant Colonel H. E., *see* Lieutenant Colonel G. B. Stoney
Waterlow, Lieutenant Commander J. B., RN, *see* Vice Admiral E. W. Longley-Cook
Watson, Captain T. P.
Wedgwood, J. C., 1st Baron of Barlaston
Weld-Forester, Lieutenant Commander W. B. C., RN
Wilkinson, Captain R. W., RN
Williams, Major General A. E.
Williams, Commander A. M., RN
Williams, Dr O. C.
Williamson, Surgeon Lieutenant D. J., RNVR
Wyatt, Lieutenant Colonel J. D.

Miscellaneous 262: ts account by anonymous soldier of 11th Battalion AIF
Special Miscellaneous X4: Instructions for General Officer Commanding Mediterranean Expeditionary Force

2. IMPERIAL WAR MUSEUM, DEPARTMENT OF PRINTED BOOKS (IWM DPB)

Mahmut, Colonel, commander of the 3rd Battalion of the 26th Regiment, ts report on the landings translated from the Turkish, 116.17 K34980
Unsigned ts lecture notes about the evacuation of Cape Helles which internal evidence shows to have been written by Brigadier General J. W. (later Lieutenant General Sir James) O'Dowda held with Lieutenant P. M. Campbell, *Letters from Gallipoli* (see above)

3. LIDDELL HART CENTRE FOR MILITARY ARCHIVES, KING'S COLLEGE LONDON

Papers of General Sir Ian Hamilton:
File 05/10, ms signals from Lieutenant General Sir William Birdwood to Hamilton and from Hamilton to Birdwood, night of 25–26 April 1915
File 17/7/33, ms transcript of a letter written by Captain R. D. Whigham, 25 April–10 May 1915
File 03/19, ms letter from Lieutenant General Sir Aylmer Hunter Weston to Hamilton, 11 August 1915

4. NATIONAL ARMY MUSEUM, DEPARTMENT OF ARCHIVES, PHOTOGRAPHS, FILM AND SOUND (NAM)

5603–50, Lieutenant H. D. O'Hara, ts letters
6405–86, Captain D. French, ms letter

5. NATIONAL MARITIME MUSEUM

MS86/012, Admiral Sir Cecil Thursby, papers including an ms account of his command of the 2nd Squadron at Gaba Tepe

6. PUBLIC RECORD OFFICE

WO95/4263, War Diary, General Staff GHQ, February–April 1915
WO95/4304, War Diary, 29th Division General Staff
WO95/4311, War Diaries, 87th Brigade

Unpublished Oral Sources

IMPERIAL WAR MUSEUM, DEPARTMENT OF SOUND RECORDS (IWM SR)

Ashurst, George, Interview 9875
Baker, Thomas Henry (Harry), Interview 8721
Barnes, Henry, Interview 4008
Barrow, Harold, Interview 8327
Beeton, Arthur, Interview 8323
Bird, Robert, Interview 10656

Blaskett, Henry, Interview 4026
Bonney, Arthur, Interview 8226
Boughton, Harold, Interview 8667
Brent, Frank, Interview 4037
Bull, Arthur, Interview 10410
Burnett, Alexander, Interview 8342
Carless, R. J., Interview 4052
Chitty, John, Interview 11114
Clements, Joseph, Interview 11268
Coakes, Frederick, Interview 8287
Cook, Robert, Interview 7397
Cowley, William, Interview 8866
Davies, William, Interview 8320
Dawson, Claude, Interview 8867
Denham, Henry, Interview 8871
Flynn, W., Interview 4103
Gillett, R. B., Interview 7377
Griffiths, Frederick, Interview 4119
Haire, Ernest, Interview 10401
Hancock, Malcolm, Interview 7396
Harding, Field Marshal Lord, Interview 8736
Hemsley, Arthur, Interview 9927
Horridge, George, Interview 7498
Johnson, Reginald, Interview 9172
Jones, William, Interview 4141
Kennedy, Frank, Interview, 4146
Kirk, Andrew K., Interview 4155
Kirk, William, Interview 9178
Longley-Cook, E. W., Interview 7094
Manton, Horace, Interview 9756
Matthews, Leslie, Interview 8232
Meager, Cecil, Interview 8326
Medcalf, Harold, Intervidw 9755
Moyle, Steve, Interview 8257
Murray, Joseph, Interview 8201
Napier, Joseph, Interview 7499
Nicholas, Tressilian, Interview 10475
Northcote, T. V., Interview 8834
Northcott, W. G., Interview 4187
Parker Bird, Stanley, Interview 7375
Peake, George, Interview 10648
Pearson, John, Interview 9100
Penrose, Donald, Interview 8174
Pilling, Harold, Interview 7496

453

Pope, Edwin, Interview 8272
Prophet, N. W., Interview 4194
Rackham, Basil, Interview 8227
Rathbone, Reginald, Interview 8230
Robinson, Edward, Interview 10733
Robinson, Harry, Interview 11461
Sanders, Frederic, Interview 8273
Spencer, Robert, Interview 11965
Stagles, Walter, Interview 4240
Tomkinson, Cecil, Interview 7497
Tysall, Ernest, Interview 10655
Verschoyle, Terence, Interview 8185
Watts, Arthur, Interview 8278
Westmacott, Rupert, Interview 8274
Wharton, Harry, Interview 8322
Williamson, Tom, Interview 9317
Wolton, Eric, Interview 9090
Yorston, Richard, Interview 11219

INDEX OF PEOPLE

Only names mentioned in the text have been indexed: we gratefully acknowledge the help of all those whose contributions can be found in the Source References.

455

461

INDEX OF FORCES

All ships are to be found in the General Index.

GENERAL INDEX

Landing beaches A, B, C, will be found under Suvla; S, V, W, X, Y, under Helles; Z under Gaba Tepe.

471

472

443P